Across the Mediterranean Frontiers

International Medieval Research

Selected Proceedings of the International Medieval Congress

University of Leeds

International Medieval Research

Across the Mediterranean Frontiers
Trade, Politics and Religion, 650-1450

Selected Proceedings of the
International Medieval Congress
University of Leeds,
10-13 July 1995, 8-11 July 1996

edited by
Dionisius A. Agius
and
Ian Richard Netton

Turnhout, Brepols
1997

Articles appearing in this volume are indexed in
"International Medieval Bibliography"

Printed in Belgium
D/1997/0095/36
ISBN 2-503-50600-3

Contents

I ISLAMIC SPAIN AND SICILY

II ECONOMIC AND CULTURAL EXCHANGES

III ISLAMIC AND WESTERN POLITICS RELIGIOUS THOUGHT

IV WORK AND WARFARE IN THE MEDITERRANEAN: ACROSS THE FRONTIERS

V ISLAMIC SOURCES AND TRANSMISSION

Acknowledgement

Gratitude is due to Mr Alec McAllister for his design of some of the fonts used in the production of this book. His ever-willing advice has been greatly appreciated.

Notes about the Contributors

David Abulafia is Reader in Mediterranean History at the University of Cambridge. He is a Fellow of Gonville and Caius College, and author of several books on the Norman kingdom of Sicily, the Italian city-republics and the trade of the medieval Mediterranean.

Marvin H. Mills is architect and Adjunct Associate Professor at the School of Architecture and Community Design, University of South Florida. His main interests are the history of Islamic art and architecture in Spain, and its Phoenician, Roman and Jewish influences.

Jorge López Quiroga is Master in Medieval Studies at the Université de Paris, Sorbonne, and Master in History at the École des Hautes Études en Sciences Sociales, Paris. He is author of several articles on late antiquity and early medieval history and archaeology of the northwest of the Iberian peninsula.

Mónica Rodríguez Lovelle is Master in Medieval Studies at the Université de Paris, Sorbonne, and Master in History at the École des Hautes Études en Sciences Sociales, Paris. Her publications include articles on late antiquity and early medieval history and archaeology of the northwest of the Iberian peninsula.

Marta vanLandingham is a doctoral candidate at the University of California, Los Angeles. Her thesis focuses on the administration and household of Pere the Great of the Crown of Aragon. She has published articles on death and burial practices in canon law, and on the social history of the Mudejar community in Valencia.

Nikolas Jaspert is Assistant Lecturer at the Freie Universität Berlin, author of *Stift und Stadt. Das Heiliggrabpriorat von Santa Anna und das Regularkanonikerstift Santa Eulàlia del Camp im mittelalterlichen Barcelona, 1145-1423* (Berlin, 1996) as well as several articles on the medieval history of Spain and the Crusader States. His current research project is on the kingdom of Naples in the fourteenth century.

Silvia Orvietani Busch received her PhD in History from the University of California, Los Angeles. Her areas of specialisation focus on Medieval Mediterranean commerce, archaeology, port and coastal development, travel and navigation. She is currently working at the Getty Research Institute in Santa Monica, California, on a multi-volume editorial project.

Eleanor A. Congdon has recently received her doctorate at Gonville and Caius College in the University of Cambridge. Her dissertation deals with the Venetian mercantile presence in the western Mediterranean (1398-1405) based on research done in archives in Prato and Venice.

John E. Dotson is Professor of History at Southern Illinois at Carbondale. He is author and editor of a book and several articles on medieval maritime history in the Mediterranean.

Oliver Leaman is Professor of Philosophy at Liverpool John Moores University. He is author of several publications on Islamic and Jewish philosophy.

Xénia Celnarová is Senior Scholar at the Institute of Asian and African Studies, Slovak Academy of Sciences in Bratislava, Slovakia. She is at the moment studying the influence of Hellenistic philosophy on the theosophy of Sufism and the interaction between European culture and the culture of the Islamic world.

Gabriella Airaldi is Professore Ordinario in Medieval History at the Università di Genova. She is author of several articles on medieval Mediterranean history, with particular interest in Genoese history and the European expansion as well as political and economic thought in the medieval Mediterranean.

Juan Manuel Bello León is a graduate of Universidad de la Laguna. His thesis is on foreign trade and Atlantic navigation in the late middle ages and the kingdom of Seville. Since then, he has focused his research on the study of Castilian overseas trade as well as foreign presence and influences in Spain in the Late Middle Ages.

Dolores Serrano-Niza is Profesor Asociado at the Universidad de la Laguna. She is author of several articles with particular focus on Andalusī Arabic dress terminology.

María Arcas Campoy is Profesora Titular at the Universidad de la Laguna. She has published several articles on Islamic Law (mālikī) in the history of al-Andalus.

Esther M. Martínez is at the William Paterson College of New Jersey. Her main interests and many publications are in Muslim-Christian-Jewish literary interaction in Medieval Spain, Mudejar literature and theory of literary translation in medieval and early Renaissance Spain.

Myriam Salama-Carr is Lecturer at the University of Salford. She has published a book and several articles on the subject of medieval Arabic translation.

Stoyanka Kenderova is Senior Research Associate at the Oriental Department of SS Cyril and Methodius National Library in Sofia, where she has been involved in the cataloguing of Oriental manuscripts and publicity of catalogues. Her interests lie in the life of the Muslim Balkans through Oriental sources.

Editors' Introduction

The vision of a Mediterranean as a sum of individual histories is Fernand Braudel's echo of the forties; two major truths he claimed here remained unchallenged, the first being the unity and coherence of the Mediterranean region and the second being the greatness of the Mediterranean. Both realities are well-presented in this volume with David Abulafia's key article on the economic interactions between law and war in the medieval Mediterranean.

The volume falls logically into five major sections: the first dealing with Islamic Spain and Sicily surveys such diverse topics as heresy and holiness, the Hohenstaufen heritage, the Arab invasion of Spain as well as a provocative attempt to discover the Phoenician origins of the mosque of Cordoba. In the second section we move to economic and cultural considerations. It is almost certainly a truism that the Mediterranean basin was "created" for both. We range in this section from an analysis of commercial centres such as Pisa, Venice and Catalunia to a vivid analysis of fourteenth-century Italian merchants' manuals.

Of course, the Mediterranean was not just a basis for the carrying of trade and culture but the arena across which much philosophy and theology was transmitted. The third section does consider two of the great figures of Islamic thought, Al-Ghazālī and Ibn Rushd as well as lesser figures like the Arabic Pseudo-Empedocles. Of course, every religion needs its sacred space and in an entertaining article on the paradise and the city some preliminary remarks are offered on Muslim sacral geography. The section concludes with an interesting analysis of Turkish Ṣūfī poetry.

One of the ironies of medieval Mediterranean history is that while great wars were fought between Mediterranean states, trade often continued unabated between merchants from those opposing states. In the fourth section, we consider the twin themes of work and warfare ranging from Italy and Spain and conclude with a study of ships which carried both warriors and workers.

In many but not of course all the diverse studies of the medieval Mediterranean, the religion of Islam provides a kind of glue. The concluding section of this volume deals with a variety of aspects of Islam under the general heading of Islamic sources and transmission. Here we examine an aspect of that most complex but delightful literary genre the *Aljamiado* genre; we look at the Moroccan traveller, Ibn Baṭṭūṭa through juridical spectacles; and in a third article we stress the importance of translation for the whole area, as undertaken by Al-Jāḥiẓ and Ḥunayn Ibn Ishaq. The concluding two articles provide an illuminating vocabulary of Islamic Andalusian dress and remind us of the great literary treasures of former Communist states like Bulgaria. This is a rich and entertaining volume which should find an honoured place on the shelves of both students and scholars alike

The Impact of the Orient: Economic Interactions between East and West in the Medieval Mediterranean

David Abulafia
University of Cambridge

I. SOME PROBLEMS OF DEFINITION

At first sight it seems a straightforward enough task at least to enumerate the manifold products that reached the medieval west from the Orient in the middle ages, and perhaps even to weigh their significance against one another.[1] More demanding, certainly, is the question of the economic changes that contact with markets in and beyond the Islamic world engendered in western Europe, though here a long historiographical tradition, culminating in the works of Roberto Lopez and Eliyahu Ashtor, has provided tempting, if not

[1] This paper started life as a *relazione* on "I prodotti industriali: Medioevo", at the XXIX Settimana di Studio of the Datini Institute in Prato, devoted to *Prodotti e techniche d'Oltremare nelle Economie Europee, secc. XIII-XVIII*, and an earlier pre-print version under that title was distributed to participants in the colloquium. I am very grateful to Richard Goldthwaite, Michael Mallett, Michel Balard and others for their helpful comments during the discussion on 4 April 1997.

always conclusive, answers for the end of the middle ages.[2] But on looking closer at the literature, one finds that the emphasis lies not on the products of the east, but on the way the trade routes were managed by western merchants: going back to the classic work of Heyd, a tradition has been established of studying the institutional and legal framework within which trade could take place, notably the granting of privileges and the acquisition of warehouses and other vital facilities; and some attention has also been given to the volume of trade, as far as it can be recovered from extremely partial figures.[3] The role of particular commodities (industrial and otherwise) has been studied less, and much has been taken for granted, though some important tentative conclusions about the movement of bullion have been offered by Lopez, Day and others.[4] In particular, the insights of art historians and archaeologists have been ignored by economic historians, even when some of the most valuable evidence for the arrival of eastern products in western lands is to be found in such collections as the Museo di San Martino at Pisa.[5]

[2] R. S. Lopez, "The trade of Europe: the South", in *Cambridge Economic History of Europe*, vol. 2 (Cambridge, 1987; second edition); also my own article in the same volume, "Asia, Africa and the trade of medieval Europe"; E. Ashtor, *Levant Trade in the Later Middle Ages* (Princeton, NJ, 1983), and the various collections of Ashtor's articles, notably *Studies on the Levantine Trade in the Middle Ages* (London, 1978), and *East-West Trade in the Medieval Mediterranean*, ed. B. Z. Kedar (London, 1986).

[3] W. Heyd, *Histoire du commerce du Levant au Moyen Age*, trans. F. Raynaud, 2 vols. (Leipzig, 1885-86); this is to be preferred to the German original (Stuttgart, 1879), in view of the author's further additions.

[4] J. Day, *The Medieval Market Economy* (Oxford, 1987); R. S. Lopez, "Il problema del bilancio dei pagamenti nel commercio di Levante", in *Venezia e il Levante fino al secolo XV*, 2 vols. (Venice, 1973), 1:431-52.

[5] David Abulafia, "The Pisan *bacini* and the medieval Mediterranean economy: a historian's viewpoint", in *Papers in Italian Archaeology* 4, *The*

A particular difficulty in approaching this topic is the application of the word "industrial" to the products arriving from the east and from Africa in medieval Europe. Clearly, it is necessary to adopt the widest possible definition, embracing processed and semi-processed goods such as drugs and dyestuffs, as well as the products of workshops in the Islamic world: leather goods, ceramics, metalwork, textiles; silk has been much studied, however, and will largely be left to one side here.[6] Particular emphasis will be placed here on the role of industrial crops, including cotton, flax and indigo; but in order to understand their relative significance in international trade, it will be necessary to refer quite often to the most prominent food flavourings as well, notably pepper and ginger (itself often processed and packed in wooden cassettes). Wax is an important African product which deserves consideration under the heading of semi-processed goods. Imports of alum, used *inter alia* in the textile industry, are also a constant theme that needs to be borne in mind.

To make sense of the subject it is also important to consider briefly the role of frontier societies within what is commonly defined as Europe (notably those of Sicily and of both reconquered Valencia and unconquered Granada) in the trade networks bringing eastern products, or at any rate products characteristic of the eastern markets, to western consumers; the "agricultural revolution" following the rise of Islam transplanted some distinctive eastern

Cambridge conference, part 4, ed. C. Malone and S. Stoddart (Oxford, 1985), pp. 287-302.

[6] See in particular: *La seta in Europa, sec. XIII-XX. Atti della XXIV Settimana di Studi, 4-9 maggio 1992*, ed. S. Cavaciocchi, Istituto internazionale di storia economica "F. Datini", Prato (Florence, 1993).

products to Mediterranean lands.[7] Not just eastern plants such as the banana, rice and citrus fruits, but methods for making certain processed goods travelled westwards. Paper is the prime example of such a commodity, with an ancestry that can, as is well known, be traced back to China; imported from Alexandria in the middle of the twelfth century, it was readily available in Mediterranean Spain from local, Valencian, mills by the late thirteenth, and by the fifteenth century the paper of Fabbriano had acquired a significant place in the cargoes of Anconitan merchants bound for the Levant.[8] Glazed pottery, for which the technology did not really exist north of Sicily, or perhaps Rome, in the twelfth century, was being produced in central Italy during the thirteenth century, and had ceased being a curiosity imported from Muslim Spain, Morocco, Tunisia and the Levant.[9] Glass offers an excellent example of an item exported from the east which was followed by the borrowing of the appropriate technology, to the point where western glass easily surpassed eastern in quality; however, the best glass of Murano and its rivals continued to rely on ingredients imported from the Levant. In the case of silk, we can see a transplantation of technology that led, by the fifteenth century, to the creation of successful silk workshops in Genoa, Florence, Lucca and elsewhere; but at the same time rulers such as the Sforzas of Milan and the Gonzagas of Mantua gave the fullest encouragement to the planting of mulberry trees and the nurturing of silkworms, so that even dependence on outside supplies of raw materials, whether from

[7] A. Watson, *Agricultural Innovation in the Early Islamic World* (Cambridge, 1983).

[8] E. Ashtor, "Il commercio levantino di Ancona nel basso medioevo", *Rivista storica italiana* 88 (1976), 215, 241; repr. in his *Studies on the Levantine trade*.

[9] Abulafia, "The Pisan *bacini*".

Sicily and Calabria or Spain or Byzantium or the east was significantly reduced.

It was the Muslim world which was the major source of luxury items; but it would be wrong to ignore the other frontiers of Christendom, nor to forget that the Byzantine territories were often capable of furnishing the west with comparable goods to those found in the Levant. From the Baltic and eastern Europe there did, of course, arrive in the medieval west a number of highly prized products, notably furs and (though in limited quantities) amber; but the major characteristic of trade with the Baltic and the further reaches of the Atlantic was that finished goods were sent outwards - armaments to the Teutonic Knights in Livonia and Estonia, in exchange for grain, for instance - while imports were dominated by basic foodstuffs, in particular rye and fish, whether herrings from the Baltic Sound or stockfish from Iceland and Greenland.[10] The major luxury item from Greenland was a much prized species of falcon. By the late fifteenth century some dyes were being obtained in the Canary islands, where they occupied a significant place in the local economy; and Madeira was to become an important sugar producer.[11] But the rise of Madeira itself reflected the decline in dependence on eastern markets, which were now increasingly under threat from the Turks.

In dealing with these issues, historians have often been content to rely on the rich but problematic information contained in Pegolotti's *Pratica della Mercatura* of the early fourteenth century

[10] Ph. Dollinger, *The German Hanse*, trans. S. H. Steinberg (London, 1970).

[11] F. Fernandez-Armesto, *The Canary Islands after the Conquest. The Making of a Colonial Society in the Early Sixteenth Century* (Oxford, 1982), pp. 69-74; Rui Carita, *Historia da Madeira (1420-1566). Povoamento e produção açucareira* (Funchal, 1989), pp. 187-213.

(though in part reflecting conditions half a century earlier) in assessing what items were available to western merchants in what eastern ports.[12] One problem is that Pegolotti is not by any means unique as a source of such information; many other *pratiche* have been neglected, and their own usefulness is occasionally compromised by the fact that they often seem to have borrowed uncritically from one another: one thinks of Antonio da Uzzano here, whose own *Pratica* dates to 1442 but (in Evans' words) "offers much the same kinds of information as are to be found in the early parts of Pegolotti's book".[13] Expressed differently, the *pratiche* cannot be seen simply as "objective" statements of what was available and accessible in eastern markets, but as an idealised view of what merchants might seek in the east, based as much on out-of-date reports as upon exact knowledge of contemporary conditions.[14] Similar problems arise with Marco Polo's (d. 1323) account of the east, recently once again under attack for its veracity; but for readers in the late medieval west it remained an important account of the place of origin and physical nature of the dyes and spices they received in desiccated or powdered form from a mysterious Orient.[15] Thus the question becomes not simply "What did western merchants acquire from the east?" but "What did they think they could acquire from the east?" Similar problems arise concerning north-west Africa, where the magnificent portolan charts and atlases produced in medieval Majorca and Italy convey a sense

[12] Francesco Balducci Pegolotti, *La pratica della mercatura*, ed. A. Evans (Cambridge, Mass., 1936).

[13] Pegolotti, p. xxxix.

[14] Particular value may, however, attach to several fifteenth-century merchant guides, such as that of Benedetto Cotrugli, *Della mercatura et del mercante perfetto* (Brescia, 1602).

[15] F. Wood, *Did Marco Polo go to China?* (London, 1995).

of awed awareness of the potential of the southern Sahara as a source of gold (in particular); but once again myth and history easily became intertwined, so that information about rulers of the gold lands, such as the fourteenth-century distributor of largesse Mansa Musa, information by now long out of date, was still being replicated in the mid-fifteenth century.[16]

Our ability to describe the commodities reaching western markets is limited by the simple fact that contracts for maritime trade do not as a general rule specify the items being carried out from the west, nor those that the travelling merchants are expected to purchase. Partly this reflects the fact that trade was conducted in stages, and the further a merchant went, the more likely it was that he was selling, buying and reselling as he travelled. At best, something can be said about which goods were traded, from the references that do exist in these documents; but any attempt at quantification soon founders, beyond generalities to the effect that pepper was the number one spice and ginger stood at number two; it was food flavourings rather than industrial goods such as eastern cloths that stood at the apex of the distribution system. Documents similar to bills of lading are rare, though some fragmentary documentation of this sort can be found in Marseilles. More revealing perhaps, though not sure evidence in themselves of what actually arrived, are the tariff lists of which several survive from the Catalan ports such as Tortosa and Collioure.[17] These can be compared with tariff lists from the Islamic world, most importantly the twelfth-century *Minhāj* of al-Makhzūmī, to which the late

[16] E.g. in the great Catalan map in the Este library at Modena, dating from the mid-fifteenth century.

[17] M. Gual Camarena, *Vocabulario del comercio medieval* (Tarragona, 1968; Barcelona, 1976).

Claude Cahen devoted his attention.[18] What is missing is a secure price series for the major imports, although some scholars such as Ashtor have bravely attempted to collate information about prices. This aspect of the imports from the east will have to be left to one side here.

In pursuing this topic a decision has to be made where to draw the line between east and west in describing the late medieval economy. Clearly, the boundaries of Europe as now conceived were not coterminous either with those of Christendom or with those of what might loosely be termed a "western economy", based until about 1250 on exchanges in silver and dominated by the production of basic foodstuffs, generally, too, lacking the vast metropolises characteristic of the Near and Far East. Fundamental to the discussion that follows is the belief that the Islamic city fulfilled a much wider range of economic functions than most western cities, as a highly diversified centre of trade and industry which evolved in what was often a hostile environment, or at least one which was incapable, or barely capable, of meeting its essential needs. Specialisation and the creation of a vast labour force producing finished goods for a wide variety of markets was thus the key to survival; and this was reflected at every level of economic activity, from the greater diversity of the diet of even lowly city dwellers, to

[18] For this important source, see: C. Cahen, "Un traité financier inédit d'époque Fatimide-Ayyubide", *Journal of the Social and Economic History of the Orient* 5 (1962), 139-59; idem, "Contribution à l'étude des impôts dans l'Égypte médiévale", *Journal of the Social and Economic History of the Orient* 5 (1962), 244-78; and in particular idem, "Douanes et commerce dans les ports méditerranéens de l'Égypte médiévale d'après le *Minhadj* d'al-Makhzumi", *Journal of the Social and Economic History of the Orient* 7 (1964), 217-314; also, H. Rabie, *The Financial System of Egypt A.H. 564-741/A.D. 1169-1341* (London, 1972), pp. 11-12.

the role of the city as a redistribution centre for exotic goods imported from as far away as the Indies.[19] The Islamic city produced a vast variety of quality goods, and what is perhaps most surprising is the concentration of interest among western merchants on a narrow band of commodities, particularly pepper, though, as will be seen, cotton and indigo acquired an increasingly important position too. Differently expressed, what attracted western merchants to the Islamic world was not simply its own products, but also (at times primarily) the produce that was trans-shipped through Muslim lands from much further to the east.

The different character and needs of the Islamic city generated a different relationship with the surrounding countryside to that generally found in the west; such centres had developed in western Europe in the early middle ages, but primarily in areas under Muslim rule: Córdoba, Seville, Palermo are the three giants that fall into this category; and what is noticeable about them is that Christian conquest steered the economy in a new direction, back to the production and distribution of basic bread grains, and away from the more diverse range of foodstuffs and textile fibres (most significantly, cotton) earlier characteristic of these cities and their surrounding regions.[20] Nonetheless, vestiges of the old order can be identified in Christian centres seized from Islam such as Valencia and its *horta* (*huerta*) or Majorca, still a major source of dried fruits some time after their conquest. Although there appears to have been a serious contraction of cotton production in Sicily after about 1200, cotton remained a significant export in the thirteenth century,

[19] On Islamic cities, see I. Lapidus, *Muslim Cities in the Later Middle Ages* (Cambridge, 1984; second edition).

[20] T. Glick, *From Muslim Fortress to Christian Castle* (Manchester, 1996).

carried aboard Catalan ships towards Barcelona, for processing in Catalan workshops. Techniques as well as raw materials moved westwards: it is now considered likely that the art of knitting travelled along such routes from Old Cairo to Muslim and Christian Spain; by the fifteenth century knitters' guilds existed in Barcelona itself.[21]

The imitation by western producers of eastern products lessened dependence on eastern markets for high quality cloths and other goods. Western merchants could even sell their imitations in the east to those who had once produced similar items. Whereas before 1200 western merchants had expressed interest in luxury cloths produced in Egypt and Syria, by 1300 their interest was more heavily concentrated on the dyestuffs available in the east; they were selling to Levantine consumers cloths they themselves had produced using the dyes, and in some cases the raw fibres, they had bought in eastern markets. It is not necessary to accept every aspect of Ashtor's fervently held belief in the industrial decline of the Middle East in the late middle ages to acknowledge how profound the process of substitution was: at one end of the spectrum, as has been seen, the silks of Tuscan, Lombard and Ligurian workshops came to supplant those of the Muslim East and China (though the process was a slow one, with the Sforza dukes of Milan massively extending Lombard mulberry plantations in the late fifteenth century); at the other end of the spectrum, humdrum fustians took their name from the virtual capital of the Islamic world, Cairo (in its form of Fusṭāṭ, the name given to Old Cairo); and elsewhere on the spectrum of quality there were the western *baldacchini*, named after Baghdad, and other good quality textiles now produced in Italy, Flanders or Germany. The spread of imitative silks began early,

[21] Information I owe to Montse Stanley of Anglia Polytechnic University.

while Islam still dominated the Mediterranean, and resulted in al-Andalus in the bizarre habit of manufacturing local silks carrying standardised Islamic designs (themselves of Persian and Coptic ancestry) and the blatantly erroneous label "made in Baghdad". In the case of textiles produced in Christian lands, however, the success of the cloth exports towards the Levant, "dumped" on eastern markets, Ashtor insisted, was sufficient to alleviate significantly the outflow of silver bullion, since the west had few other products to offer eastern consumers apart from humble items such as wood and base metals (banned under papal edicts which sought to limit the eastward flow of armaments). Indeed, it was these humble items, plus slaves, that had dominated the primitive Levant trade of the Amalfitans around 1000.

II. THE ROLE OF COTTON

Trans-Mediterranean traffic in the centuries before the rise of the Italian republics is recorded in the letters of, and may well have been dominated by, the so-called Geniza merchants of Fusṭāṭ, analysed by Goitein.[22] Goitein's primary interest lay in the India trade, bringing spices and luxury cloths up the Red Sea for redistribution towards Tunisia, Muslim Sicily and al-Andalus. Incidentally, he revealed a strong interest in flax, cotton and silk, the latter of which constituted a standard form of investment around 1050; flax and cotton were seen by the twelfth-century writer al-

[22] S. D. Goitein, *A Mediterranean Society. The Jewish Communities of the Arab World as Portrayed in the Documents of the Cairo Genizah*, vol. 1, *Economic Foundations* (Berkeley; Los Angeles, 1967).

Makhzūmī as prime exports of Egypt.[23] The major change that occurred after 1100 was a double transformation in the management of the trade routes, so that the Indian Ocean and Red Sea routes came increasingly under the control of the Egyptian Muslim *karimi* merchants, while the Mediterranean sea routes were conquered by the fleets of Genoa, Pisa and Venice; at the same time, rising wool production in the west necessitated more and more intensive searches for the most suitable fixative, alum.[24] This was to be found in the twelfth century, as the *Minhāj* of al-Makhzūmī shows, in Egypt itself, though attention shifted to the mines of Phocæa in Turkey by the late thirteenth century; it was only in the mid-fifteenth century that large, high quality alum mines were identified in the west, at Tolfa. Similarly, potash was in demand among western textile producers, while alkaline ashes for soap production (again linked to the textile industry) were an interest of Anconitan merchants in the Levant during the late middle ages; the Anconitans form a group of particular interest, since by 1300 cotton and ancillary items needed for the textile industry were their main import from the Levant, rather than the spices favoured by most other Italian merchants.[25]

In addition to dyestuffs, the west became increasingly dependent on eastern sources for certain textile fibres, especially

[23] Cahen, "Douanes et commerce".

[24] C. Cahen, "L'alun avant Phocée. Un chapitre d'histoire économique islamo-chrétienne au temps des croisades", *Revue d'histoire économique et sociale* 41 (1963), 433-47; Rabie, pp. 82-5.

[25] Ashtor, "Commercio levantino di Ancona"; David Abulafia, "The Anconitan privileges in the Latin Kingdom of Jerusalem and the Levant trade of Ancona", in *I comuni italiani nel regno crociato di Gerusalemme*, ed. G. Airaldi and B. Z. Kedar (Genoa, 1986), pp. 525-70.

cotton.[26] In the twelfth century, the Genoese were still able to export very significant amounts of cotton from Sicily, and it is possible that at this stage it was cotton rather than grain that drew them so enthusiastically into treaty relations with the Norman kings of Sicily from 1156 onwards, though it is generally agreed that the quality of Sicilian cotton remained relatively low.[27] Equally, the island's capacity to supply cotton contracted as traditional Arab agricultural practices were supplanted by a feudal régime which laid emphasis on the extraction of rent from staple crops; as wheat production expanded, cotton plantations, and the necessary skills, went into decline. There were still Catalan merchants in mid-thirteenth-century Sicily who went there to buy cotton, while Genoa, Milan and Pavia were still bringing in Sicilian cotton in the late fourteenth and fifteenth centuries.[28] The small Sicilian dependency of Malta appears to have continued to produce cotton of better quality throughout the middle ages (increasing its production significantly in the fifteenth century); but it was Egypt, Syria and ultimately India that became the major sources for raw cotton (in wool form or spun into fibre) used in western industries.[29] Indeed, it was the Arabs who first made cotton the everyday wear of inhabitants of the Middle East. It was they who encouraged the planting of cotton during springtime, alternating it with winter wheat or barley, and developing sophisticated irrigation networks so that normally dry soils could be used to good effect. Areas that played a notable role

[26] M. F. Mazzaoui, *The Italian Cotton Industry in the Later Middle Ages, 1100-1600* (Cambridge, 1981).

[27] David Abulafia, *The Two Italies. Economic Relations between the Norman Kingdom of Sicily and the Northern Communes* (Cambridge, 1977).

[28] Mazzaoui, p. 32; David Abulafia, "Catalan merchants and the western Mediterranean, 1236-1300", *Viator* 16 (1985), 209-42.

[29] Mazzaoui, pp. 14-27.

in cotton production in the early Islamic world included the coastline of Syria and the outskirts of Damascus and Acre.[30] Mazzaoui has noted that in some parts of Syria a monoculture developed by the thirteenth century, based around the production of cotton for export; certain of these areas lay within the political control of the Latins themselves, as rulers of the Kingdom of Jerusalem.[31] Egypt, on the other hand, was famed more for the quality than the quantity of its cotton, and flax remained the major industrial crop exported from the region, in twenty-two identifiable varieties. In fact, much of the cotton cloth worn in Egypt seems to have been made from imported raw materials. Similarly, the coast of North Africa contained both cotton plantations and workshops transforming the fibres into finished cloth, notably at Tunis (where a mixed cotton-linen weave was common) and at Sijilmasa, terminal of the gold caravans arriving from the southern Sahara. What we are thus observing is the widespread use of cotton to satisfy the elementary clothing needs of the population of the Islamic lands.

The fashion for cotton was not, however, confined solely to the *dār al-Islām*. By the mid-twelfth century signs exist of a north Italian cotton industry that was processing the imported raw cotton of Sicily, Africa and the east. A Genoese tariff list indicates that Alexandria, Antioch and Sicily were sources of cotton around 1140. There are enough references to cotton in the earliest notarial contracts to survive in Genoa (Giovanni Scriba, 1154-64) to make the significance of this product in the Levant trade abundantly clear. In fact, Mazzaoui says: "references to both raw cotton and Italian cotton cloth in Genoese notarial contracts of the second half of the twelfth century and the opening decades of the thirteenth occur with

[30] Watson, *Agricultural Innovation.*

[31] Mazzaoui, pp. 35-38.

a frequency that suggests a phenomenal growth rate in the early stages of the industry". Notarial acts from Cyprus, dating to around 1300, reveal the intense interest of the merchants of Ancona, acting in conjunction with Christian Syrian merchants, in the supply of Levantine cotton to cloth producers in central Italy.[32] In Genoa, as in Marseilles and Barcelona, one aim of the cotton importers may have been to supply the shipping industry, in need of heavy canvas-type cotton cloths (apparently producing much later on the English words *jeans*, from "Gênes", and *denim*, "de Nîmes"). Nor was the use of cotton confined to clothing and naval equipment. Wax candles were produced with cotton wicks, in the Arab fashion; there is also a possibility, though opinions differ, that cotton (*bombax*) was an important ingredient of early forms of paper (*carta bombacynis*), even though other textile fibres, especially linen, seem to have become more important from an early stage.

A second stage in the development of the European cotton industry began in the late fourteenth century, with the emergence of a south German cloth industry, based especially around Ulm, which became a major importer of raw cotton via Venice, seat of the *fondaco dei Tedeschi*.[33] Where appropriate, mixed linen and cotton fustians incorporating local or foreign flax were also produced; all this was to the detriment of the north Italian cotton industry. What is impressive is that the means now existed to transport considerable quantities of eastern cotton across the Alps; the late fourteenth and fifteenth centuries were not, as far as this industry was concerned, a period of recession, at least in Germany. Some reflection of changing circumstances can be seen in Ashtor's classic study, "Observations on Venetian trade in the XIVth century", where he

[32] Abulafia, "Anconitan privileges", pp. 551-58.

[33] Mazzaoui, pp. 139-46.

was able to show that around 1380 there was a significant increase in the volume of Venetian trade in cotton out of Greece, Crete, Syria and Egypt. A whole new line of cogs had to be established in consequence.[34] Even so, Ashtor considered that this was only the beginning of what was to grow prodigiously in the fifteenth century into a major department of Venetian trade.

In sum, the emergence of the cotton industry in the west was a chapter in a longer process which saw western producers supplant those of the east, drawing from the Levant the raw or semi-processed materials they needed, but creating their own textile industries which transformed the fibres into cloth. Still, this was not possible without dependence on the east for fixatives, notably alum, and colourings, notably indigo. Such products were long to play a major role, alongside the leading condiments, in the "spice trade" with the Levant.

III. INDIGO AND THE LEVANT TRADE

The significance of dyestuffs in the Levant trade can be observed further if we examine the important place of indigo in east-west traffic, with the help of a new study by Jenny Balfour-Paul.[35] Indigo was much in demand both in east and west. Large quantities were produced in India, from which its name derived: it was the Indian product *par excellence*; but such was the pressure of demand that by the twelfth century it was readily available from new sources in Syria, Egypt and Yemen. It is recorded as a local product in the

[34] E. Ashtor, "Observations on Venetian Trade in the Levant in the XIVth century", *Journal of European Economic History* 5 (1976), 533-86.

[35] J. Balfour-Paul, *Indigo in the Arab World* (Richmond, 1997).

Palestinian city of Jericho in the tenth century. Al-Khaṭīb Baghdādī (d. 463/1070-1) in the years around 1200 was much impressed by the sheer quantity of indigo produced in Egypt, but he was less impressed by the quality, which was inferior to that of India. *Color indicus in Aegypto conficitur*, Frederick Barbarossa of Germany was informed by an emissary to the Ayyūbid court.[36] The diffusion of indigo should thus be seen as part of the wider dissemination of eastern crops that followed the Islamic conquest of the southern shores of the Mediterranean. But Spain itself was always dependent on imports of this dyestuff; under Muslim rule, the Jewish merchants of Almería were particularly active in the indigo trade, as they were in the silk trade and associated areas of business. In 1252 the dyers of Valencia, steeped in Islamic tradition, still preferred "Baghdad indigo", which a Catalan buyer in 1385 said was "the best of all", though the Catalans also handled Persian and Egyptian varieties. What this seems to mean is that Baghdad retained its special place as the emporium through which top quality indigos from further east were redistributed westwards. At times Baghdad indigo was taxed in Italian ports at twice the rate charged on less perfect strains.[37]

Institutional factors also helped the spread of indigo: in the eighth century and after, the ᶜAbbāsid choice of black as the colour of the régime meant that they had settled on a colour which could only effectively be produced from an indigo base. Good quality black remained something of a luxury in east and west for several centuries. Indigo was also a key component in many of the rich colours being produced in the west, such as purples and vivid greens, which were used to dye the prestige woollen cloths of

[36] Ibid., pp. 20, 22-24.
[37] Ibid., pp. 23, 28-29.

Flanders and northern Italy, in conjunction with madder and other high grade ingredients. It was preferable to woad (to which it is closely related botanically); and the disappearance of the purple *murex* shellfish made it the most valuable colouring agent after saffron. There were, it is true, several false indigos derived from mulberries and blueberries, but it was oriental indigo that was always especially prized for its vivid hues. Since it arrived in the form of small cakes, it was difficult for purchasers to understand that they were handling a plant product, and for many centuries it was assumed to be of mineral origin. Nor should its role in the arts be ignored here: indigo had an important place in the paintings of the Italian schools in the fourteenth century, as can be seen clearly in the work of Simone Martini. It was used in art as in life as a signifier of luxury. So too was ultramarine of special importance in art, though not practical for use in cloth dyeing. It derived from semi-precious *lapis lazuli*, mostly of Persian origin; a method for making this colour is described in a thirteenth-century work attributed to Frederick II's (1198-1250) astrologer Michael Scott (d. c. 1234) and now preserved in Cambridge in the library of Gonville and Caius College; alchemical treatises are a neglected source for information about eastern products such as alum and gemstones.[38]

Colouring agents from the Islamic world and beyond were of capital importance to the western medieval artist.[39] In this sense many a spectacular "Madonna and Child" reveals a heritage from the Levant trade. In the eleventh century al-Andalus, Muslim Spain, was a prime source of fine colours, especially saffron and *kermes* (*qirmiz*), even though indigo, brazilwood and lac were not locally

[38] Gonville and Caius College, Cambridge, MS 81/214.

[39] D. Thompson, *The Materials and Techniques of Medieval Painting*, (New York, 1956), contains invaluable information on colouring agents.

available, and were imported by the Geniza merchants and their colleagues, arriving in Almería in the early twelfth century; the Andalusī merchants appear to have been notorious for their demand for brazilwood around 1060, a period in which the luxurious *taifa* courts were flourishing all over Spain. *Kermes* and *grana*, two very similar insect based dyes, were imported from Spain, as was the best cinnabar, a native red sulphide of mercury. The name *kermes* itself gave rise to the term "crimson", while the identification of *grana* with tiny insects or worms is the source of the word *vermiculum* or "vermilion". Red could also be derived from brazilwood and lac, items which constantly appear in the baggage of the medieval spice merchant. Brazilwood in combination with lye potash or alum produced quite different shades of red, and the use of alum guaranteed a warmer colour. Daniel Thompson, in his fundamental study of *The Materials and Techniques of Medieval Painting* observed that "the amount of brazil wood colour used in the middle ages both for painting and dyeing was colossal", vastly exceeding even the much handled insect dyes. For example, it was employed in the reddish purple ink favoured by some Italian humanists.[40]

IV. THE EVIDENCE OF THE TARIFF LISTS

Indigo and cotton, then, help define the nature of the problem. Raw or semi-processed materials for the cloth industry occupied a prime role in the traffic from the Levant towards western Europe after about 1150. Taking a stance around 1300, several sources identified

[40] As well as Thompson, *Materials and Techniques*, see on dyes obtained in Spain O. R. Constable, *Trade and Traders in Muslim Spain* (Cambridge, 1994; Spanish ed., Barcelona, 1996).

so far allow us to examine the movement of goods at different stages in the journey from east to west. Marco Polo identifies centres of production in the Indies for the most exotic and furthest travelled goods; Pegolotti indicates the transfer of oriental goods from eastern Mediterranean ports to Italy, Catalonia and southern France, and the tariff lists from Catalonia document the arrival of these products in western Europe. It thus makes sense to begin at the westernmost extremity, with these tariff lists, and to move the focus gradually eastwards until reaching the point of production. It is therefore necessary to emphasise that the Catalan documents record, explicitly or implicitly, a particular intense contact with North Africa, rather than with the Levant. Christian merchants of course faced similar problems in North Africa to those they experienced in the Middle East: their confinement in close quarters; the periodic confiscation of goods (often a good source of information about what was in their warehouses); interruptions as the result of embargoes and crusades. However, trade with the Maghrib was less obviously dominated by high value goods such as spices. In some cases, western merchants found themselves able actually to supply Maghribī consumers with spices acquired in the Levant, particularly as the domination of Mediterranean waters by Catalan and Italian navies became more complete.

An early example of a tariff list comes from Valencia in 1243, shortly after the Catalan conquest.[41] It may thus reflect the commercial needs of a large Islamic city as much as it does those of a new settler population (the Muslims were removed from Valencia proper, but they rapidly established a *morería* outside the walls). It is also very difficult to be sure which way certain products were flowing, since the region had an established reputation as a source

[41] Gual Camarena, doc. 3, pp. 69-74.

of specialised crops. However, the reference to a tax on paper must reflect the movement of paper from Xàtiva (Játiva) out of the Kingdom of Valencia, while it is clear that pepper and some of the cloths mentioned (from Lleidà, Narbonne and elsewhere) were imports from further to the north. Mastic, gum and wax could originate from several sources, but wax was certainly imported in very significant quantities from the Maghrib towards Majorca and the south of France in this period. Among dyestuffs, the famous *grana* was, as has been seen, a characteristic product of late medieval Spain, while saffron had a special role, here and in Italy, as the major spice and dyestuff produced in the west for export to the east. A further tariff list from Valencia of about 1271 indicates that alum of Aleppo in Syria, as well as Castilian alum, was taxed at 8d per load (*carga*); this item of course had special importance in the cloth finishing industry, and demand for alum rose as the textile industry of Barcelona and its neighbours expanded. Cotton was also arriving in the city, though its origin can only be the subject of speculation: as has been seen, some Sicilian cotton was being handled at this period by Catalan merchants trading to Barcelona, but Muslim Spain and the markets of Alexandria (which themselves drew on sources as far east as India) cannot be excluded either.

The series of *lezde* or *leude* from Collioure, the outport of Perpignan, starting around 1249, are perhaps a better guide to the arrival of goods in Europe from the Islamic lands, since at this end of the Catalan world Islamic agricultural techniques had not struck any roots, and it is therefore easier to be sure of the foreign origins of the goods mentioned in the tariff lists.[42] Major items imported

[42] Ibid., doc. 4, pp. 75-80. On Collioure, see David Abulafia, *A Mediterranean Emporium. The Catalan Kingdom of Majorca* (Cambridge,

appear to have been pepper, wax, alum, ginger, cinnamon, cloves, lac, brazilwood, indigo, vermilion, coral, sugar, saffron, mastic and of course silk: largely a familiar mixture of dyestuffs and food flavourings. But there were also many humbler local products such as eels and hake that attracted the same tax rate of 2s 2d per *carga* in 1249 (the rate for the leading products fell to 2s 0d in 1252 and 1297/8).[43] This was the top tax rate and may plausibly be taken as an indication of which items were seen as the most valuable ones by the Crown (which maintained a substantial castle in the port, still in place). In the 1297/8 *lezda*, alum of both Aleppo and Vulcano (in the Aeolian islands) appear, the former taxed at twice the rate of the latter, not surprisingly in view of its superior quality. The picture presented by the *lezda* documents from Collioure, which include several further tariff lists from about 1365 and later, is remarkably consistent, and this in itself serves as a warning: it was easier to insert items into the list than it was to delete them from it, since it was often difficult to know whether an item that had not been seen for some years would eventually reappear.

When looking at finished products passing through Collioure, and also taxed at 2s 2d, it seems that the great majority were textiles originating in southern France or Flanders, but high quality "Cordovan" leather was also traded through the port, and, as Gual Camarena pointed out, at this period much of it was brought not from Andalucia but from North African ports such as Bougie (Bijāya).[44] The *lezda* of Collioure in fact establishes a hierarchy of goods, with localised products such as linseed oil, pastel, salted fish

1994; Spanish ed., Barcelona, 1996), pp. 126-27, 142-43, 153-55, 166-67, 259-61.

[43] Gual Camarena, docs. 9 and 24, pp. 102-07, 161-69.

[44] Ibid., pp. 281-82.

(still a speciality of the region), tartar of Urgell in the Catalan interior, butter (*manteca*), cheese, figs of Alacant, Tarragona, Majorca, Málaga (then still under Muslim rule) and elsewhere, lentils, peas and beans, all attracting lower rates of taxation than the prestige goods brought from the Maghrib and the Levant. Of course, it remains uncertain whether the goods described actually arrived in the port in significant quantities. However, the strategic position of Collioure at the point where Catalonia and France converged gave it privileged access to goods crossing the Mediterranean and to those, such as northern cloths, that were being exported across the Mediterranean. It is not surprising that the contemporary *lezda* of neighbouring Perpignan, or that of 1284 from the same city (now administrative capital of the new Majorcan kingdom) lays far more emphasis on the arrival of northern cloths, often finished in the city, and less on the network of maritime exchanges that linked Collioure to the Islamic world.[45] The 1284 *lezda* classifies as *totz auers de Leuant* pepper, ginger (*gingibre gros o menut*), incense (*ensens*), wax, cotton and sugar, though it cannot really be assumed that in all cases these items were brought from the east. In other sections of the same document there figure cloths from Alexandria, which Gual Camarena thought might well have been produced in other centres, merely imitating Egyptian models;[46] several types of cloth (*bagadels*, *boquerans*, *camelotz*) identified as *d'Outramar*, probably not just the crusader states *Outremer* but the Levant as a whole, but rather few references to alum, which twice appears in the form of *alum de Bolcan*, that is, the alum of the Lipari islands, rather than that of Egypt or Turkey.[47]

[45] Ibid., doc. 16, pp. 142-47.

[46] Ibid., p. 196.

[47] Ibid., pp. 200-02.

By contrast, in the *lezda* of Tortosa, of 1252, there is quite a strong emphasis on the import of spices, as well as *alum de pluma*, alum from North Africa (that of Phocæa does not figure in the Catalan tariff lists): pepper, cumin, aniseed (*batafalua*), cedar wood (*citoal*), wax, ginger, cinnamon, cloves, lac, brazilwood, nutmeg (*nous noscades*), as well as colouring agents such as indigo, vermilion, *grana*, resins such as mastic and gum arabic, prepared flavourings of rose and violet. Once again more local products including cheap alums, and middle range foodstuffs such as cheeses, wines and dried grapes (*azebib*), tended to attract markedly lower tax rates.[48] It should be borne in mind that in the mid-thirteenth century the Catalans were not market leaders in the Levant trade, and the presence of many of these goods in the Catalan ports is not proof that all were brought directly from the Levant; still, there was some contact with the east, and there were significant intermediary trading stations at Palermo and Tunis, where such goods were readily available. It is therefore striking that the tariff lists do not simply survive from the major ports of the Catalan world (Barcelona, Tarragona, Collioure), but also from small trading centres such as Cambrils, from which a *lezda* list survives dating to 1258.[49]

It is hazardous to assume that, simply because an item appears at the top of the list of taxes chargeable, it must have been the most important. Ordinances for trade through Barcelona of 1271 do start their list of taxable imports with pepper and ginger, but several dyes are also very prominently placed:

> Primerament carga de pebre, e de gingebre, e de lacha, d'encens, de breyl, de nous d'exarch, de

[48] Ibid., doc. 8, pp. 94-102.
[49] Ibid., doc. 11, pp. 110-13.

> cubebes saluatges, de citoual, de succre: prenen los corredors per corredures per cascuna carga VIII diners del comprador e altres VIII diners del uenedor, e per cascuna carga d'aquests auers XVI diners de reua.[50]

The tariff list then mentions indigo *de Bagadel* and *de Golf*, which indicates the prestigious "Baghdad indigo" and indigo from the Persian Gulf.[51] As the textile industry of Barcelona took off from about 1300 onwards, demand for high quality dyes also began to soar. Tariff lists from Saragossa indicate that indigo also penetrated to the inland capital of the Aragonese kingdom.[52]

A further perspective on these commodity movements is provided by an invaluable document from Marseilles, dating to 1296, in which a law suit is initiated against a galley master named Guillem Franc; he insisted on obtaining written texts of the bills of lading for two sea journeys made in 1289 from Marseilles and Aigues-Mortes to Majorca by a group of Provençal and Italian merchants, from Marseilles, Piacenza and Genoa.[53] The Piacenzans had loaded on board pepper, lac and *porcellanas*, while Provençal merchants had contributed wine, lac, incense, cinnamon and *porcellanas*; a Pisạn had added cloves and aspic as well. On the second voyage a more varied cargo included ginger, coral and textiles. Altogether this is the sort of cargo one would expect to find on a galley of this period: small quantities of high value goods which could be carried by a ship ill-suited to bulkier products. It is striking that these goods were being taken out of western Europe

[50] Ibid., doc. 14, p. 127.

[51] Ibid., p. 337.

[52] Ibid., docs. 10 and 19, pp. 107-10, 152-56.

[53] Discussed in Abulafia, *Mediterranean Emporium*, pp. 116-17.

through Majorca, itself a major springboard for penetration into the markets of North Africa; the document thus illustrates the increasingly important intermediary role acquired by western merchants in trade between the Middle East and the Far West of Islam (Granada, Morocco, Algeria). However, Guillem Franc did not apparently cover that leg of the journey himself, preferring to load goods in Majorca for import into continental Europe: cloves, already taken out to Majorca, were also part of his cargo on his return, indicating the complexity of the routes by which eastern spices reached and were distributed in the western Mediterranean; other products were more characteristic of the western Mediterranean as a whole, such as fine treated leathers, probably from the Maghrib, semi-treated cowhides, cheeses, dates and wax; cumin was available both from Levantine and local markets (such as the Maltese archipelago). Particularly interesting are the *porcellane* or cowrie shells (apparently named after their shape, similar to that of a baby piglet); these were exported towards Majorca and the Maghrib, and they originated in the Indian Ocean, but were in demand in West Africa where they functioned as a means of exchange.[54] For the Latin merchants, the sale for specie of humble cowrie shells in North Africa was literally a golden opportunity. Similar evidence that western merchants acted as intermediaries carrying industrial produce of the eastern lands to other Islamic destinations is provided by the references in the notarial cartulary of Amalric, of 1248, preserved in Marseilles, to the export from Marseilles of cotton bound for Ceuta in north-west Africa. But it is clear that the emphasis lay on the carriage of semi-processed or

[54] Abulafia, *Mediterranean Emporium*, p. 117; cf. J. Hogendorn and M. Johnson, *The Shell Money of the Slave Trade* (Cambridge, 1986).

unprocessed goods, rather than on finished items made in Africa and Asia.

V. PEGOLOTTI'S MEDITERRANEAN

The function of the Mediterranean ports such as Aigues-Mortes, Palermo, Barcelona and Ciutat de Mallorca was not simply the redistribution of eastern goods towards the European continent, and of European goods (notably textiles) towards the Islamic world; in addition they functioned as bridges linking the central Islamic lands with the Maghrib and what remained of al-Andalus. The conquest of the Mediterranean by the Italian and Catalan navies catapulted the merchants of Genoa, Barcelona and the Tuscan cities into mastery over the distribution of eastern spices in north-west Africa, Islamic Spain and also those parts of the former Byzantine Empire where they operated trading stations. Equally, loss of mastery over the routes leading to the Levantine ports engendered new decisions about where to turn for the eastern produce on which western consumers had become increasingly dependent. An image of the trans-Mediterranean links at a critical moment in the struggle for mastery over the Levant is supplied by Pegolotti's *Pratica*.

Pegolotti provides not merely a summary of the taxes payable across the Mediterranean, but also a summation of material that already existed in written form. His debt to a Pisan brokers' tariff of 1323, and apparently also to documentation available to him from Flanders, has been noted by his editor, Evans.[55] In addition, the references to Acre as an active port make it abundantly clear that he based part of his account of Syrian trade upon manuals in use before

[55] Pegolotti, pp. xxvi-xxxvii.

the fall of the Latin Kingdom of Jerusalem in 1291, and the subsequent abandonment of Acre as a transit port for the Levant trade.[56] His image of Acre is one of a centre for the export of pepper (cited, as usual, in first place), ginger, wild brazilwood (*verzino*), indigo and cotton, whether in the form of thread or "wool" (*cotone filato*, *cotone mapputo*); mercury (*argento vivo* or quicksilver) also passed through both Acre and Alexandria.[57] The list of spices and dyes is very similar to that found in the Catalan tariff lists: lac, zedoary, mastic, mace, nutmeg, cinnamon all appear. Although he refers also to salted meats and both cattle and buffalo leather, it cannot be presumed that these were travelling westwards from Acre, which was also a major centre for the redistribution of western imports to Alexandria and Syria; Sicilian ham and bacon appears to have been in demand among the Christian inhabitants of the Latin East.[58] One spice, saffron, which Pegolotti mentions under the heading of Acre, was clearly imported from San Gimignano and other centres in central Italy, while sugar exports to the west were balanced by honey imports from the west (notably from Ancona, and, to judge from other evidence, Narbonne as well).[59] He indicates a supply line carrying spices and also pearls to Barletta in southern

[56] Ibid., pp. 63-69.

[57] Ibid., pp. 63-64.

[58] Ibid., p. 64.

[59] Ibid., p. 64; for San Gimignano saffron, see David Abulafia, "Crocuses and crusaders: San Gimignano, Pisa and the Kingdom of Jerusalem", in *Outremer. Studies in the History of the Crusading Kingdom of Jerusalem*, ed. B. Z. Kedar, H. E. Mayer and R. C. Smail (Jerusalem, 1982), pp. 227-43; for Narbonne honey see David Abulafia, "Narbonne, the lands of the Crown of Aragon and the Levant trade 1187-1400", in "Montpellier, la Couronne d'Aragon et les pays de Langue d'Oc (1204-1349)", Actes du XIIe Congrès d'Histoire de la Couronne d'Aragon (Montpellier, 1985), *Mémoires de la Société archéologique de Montpellier* 15 (1987), 189-207.

Italy, later on a major Venetian base.[60] In describing Alexandria, Pegolotti mentions some additional eastern goods, notably cassia bark, "dragon's blood" (another dyestuff) and tamarind, from India.[61] Hidden among the great catalogue of spices available in Egypt we also find soap, rice, raisins, sal nitric and other products which were counted as *spezie* by medieval merchants. His list reads as a veritable pharmacopoeia of the medieval Mediterranean. It is interesting to observe that western merchants in Alexandria also appear to have handled Maghribī products such as *scorza di Buggiea*, a type of cinnamon substitute from Bougie, acting presumably as intermediaries between north-west Africa and Egypt, rather as they have already been observed acting as intermediaries in the trade in *porcellane* between the Levant and the Maghrib.[62] It is important to recall that Egypt drew commodities from further east for resale to Italian and other western merchants, and also produced its own versions of several of those commodities. The *Minhāj* of al-Makhzūmī from the late twelfth century makes plain the active export of locally produced spices such as cumin; Egypt was also a source of emeralds at certain periods. Most ghoulish of all its products was what Pegolotti called *mummia*, desiccated mummy powder, which was used as a medicine throughout the Mediterranean region, and was regarded even by rabbis as a permissible drug, since the human bodies from which it was derived now counted as no more than the dust of the earth.[63] Gum arabic derived, at least in its purest forms, from either East or West Africa,

[60] Pegolotti, *Pratica*, p. 66.
[61] Ibid., p. 70.
[62] Ibid.
[63] Ibid.

and its presence in the markets of Alexandria is thus testimony to links down the Red Sea to the Zanzibar Coast.

A not dissimilar picture emerges from Pegolotti's treatment of Famagusta, which in the early fourteenth century took over from Acre as the major way station for western merchants attempting to trade with the Levant, and which could be used either as a base for penetration into Cilician Armenia, Syria and Egypt, or, during periods of strictly enforced emabargo against the Mamlūk ports, as a collection point for goods illicitly crossing the lines; Pegolotti's image of a vibrant centre of exchanges, to which he devotes an especially large amount of space in his book, hardly fits the modest needs of Famagusta itself, or the requirements of the down-at-heel Lusignan rulers of the kingdom.[64] At the very start of the fourteenth century a particularly active group of Syrian Christian merchants regularly carried cotton there for resale in Ancona and other Italian ports, and various types of cotton (in addition, as it happens, to local Cypriot wool) are mentioned by Pegolotti. The author had spent upwards of five years on the island, and it is this part of his survey of the Mediterranean that perhaps inspires most confidence in its accuracy. He even observes what sort of bottles are to be used for Cyprus syrups, and in what sort of cases they are to be packed.[65] The presence of these syrups is evidence that at a mid-point in the long journey from east to west some of the spices were being processed into concoctions, made without any doubt using the sugar of Cyprus to which Pegolotti also devoted much attention. For it seems clear enough that the major Levantine centres trading with the west exploited their position by developing local industries for the production of drugs, sweetmeats and syrups or jams: the

[64] Ibid., pp. 77-102.
[65] Ibid., pp. 317-18.

zenzeverata da mangiare attributed to Alexandria appears to fulfil this role, though some arrived from India already packed in little wooden cassettes (Pegolotti was worried that confusion might result concerning the weight of ginger packed with and without covers).[66]

Further to the west, in the Maghrib, Pegolotti's picture lays far less emphasis on spices; Tunis attracts his attention as a centre of exchange for cotton, linen, wool, canvas and such modest foodstuffs as carobs, nuts, oil (often imported from Italy) and chestnuts; he says little about Tunis as a source of wax.[67] From the Tunisian island of Jerba, a Sicilian possession for much of this period, oil alone seems to have been sent across the sea to Palermo and Messina.[68] Some characteristic products of this region, such as leather, wool and pottery, hardly aroused his interest. He is uninformative about trade through Ceuta, Bougie and other major ports of the Maghrib, though he does note the sale of *magaluffa*, wild goat hides (an unfamiliar term to his contemporaries, for he takes the trouble to explain it), in Safi, a port on the Atlantic coast of Morocco, which was also a source of grain; and he indicates that merchants penetrate into the interior as far as Meknes, Fez and Rabat.[69] He also discusses the trade of *Niffa*, that is, Anfa or the modern Casablanca (Dar el-Beida), which had, to judge from Dufourcq's studies of Catalan merchants, become a significant port for trade with the west by this period.[70] "Morocco" leathers completely dominate the picture: cowhides, whether from grown cattle or young calves; camelskins; goat and lambskins; but wax, wool, almonds and grain were also available. At Arzila there was

[66] Ibid., p. 70.
[67] Ibid., pp. 130-36.
[68] Ibid., p. 137.
[69] Ibid., pp. 273-74.
[70] Ibid., p. 275.

apparently some trade in indigo, alum and ivory, and a local bark appears to have been exported to the western Mediterranean as a cinnamon substitute (*erba d'uscian*).[71] Ivory, often under the title *denti di Liofante*, appears several times in Pegolotti's work, as far east as Acre, but evidently Africa was a significant source, and surviving artefacts from Sicily and Spain reveal that this traffic had antecedents in the tenth, eleventh and twelfth centuries.[72] It is not surprising to find "elephants' teeth" among the goods attributed to the markets of Majorca by Pegolotti.[73] Overall, though, North Africa presents a very different picture to that available either for the Levantine ports or for southern Spain (whether reconquered Seville or unconquered Granada and Málaga). Seville appears in Pegolotti as a redistribution centre for spices such as pepper and ginger, hardly surprisingly, given its access to the Mediterranean trade routes via the Straits of Gibraltar, and its entrepreneurial role between the Mediterranean and the Atlantic trade routes; and very striking is the role of that "Mediterranean Emporium", Majorca, which, true to its function as a centre of exchange for any type of goods entering the western Mediterranean, from the Levant, the Atlantic or from the European and African land masses, could supply almost anything that originated in the Islamic world and beyond:

> Pepe tondo, mandorle sanza guscio, cera, cotone mapputo, giengiovo, lacca e gherbellasi, allume, verzino scorzuto, cannella, grana d'ogni ragione, zucchero in pani, e polvere di zucchero d'ogni ragione, cassia fistola, tartero cioè gromma,

[71] Ibid., p. 276.

[72] Ibid., pp. 63, 69, 78, 123, 141, 294.

[73] Ibid., p. 123.

> incenzo d'ogni ragione, galla d'ogni ragione, comino, gomerabica, vernice.
> A cantara della terra vi si vendono: Argento vivo, e vermiglione cioè cinabro, e mele d'ape, e lino, e sapone in pezze, e stoppe, e carne, e saime insalate, e fichi secchi dell'isola, e gli altri a sporta che dè essere cantaro 1 della terra; indaco d'ogni ragione salvo del golfo, e mondiglia di verzino, e avorio d'ogni ragione, e denti di liofante, e mastico, turbitti, zettoara, zucchero candi, chitirra cioè draganti, orpimento, galbano, zolfo, tamerindi, mirra, sene, timiame <cioè> incenso di greci, zafflore, erba da vermini, landano, lisciadro cioè salarmoniaco, polvere d'oriallo, tuzia, biacca, verderame, guado, agnellina di Maiolica, agnellina di San Matteo, lana e agnellina d'Inghilterra, agnellina di Maiorica.[74]

The impression is of a vast mingling of goods, which barely merit any form of classification into categories; but dyestuffs certainly have a prominent place in the list, and their marriage with English, Spanish or Balearic wools brought prestige to the Catalan textile industry. Later Pegolotti points to the arrival also of Barbary leathers, *zibibbo* or raisins (mentioned also in Pisan tariff lists of this period as an import into Majorca), and North African wool (*lana di Garbo*). Drugs and dyes include myrobalan, "dragon's blood", sandalwood, rhubarb and mummy powder.[75]

Cotton, of course, figures prominently in Pegolotti's work; raw cotton, he says, was being sold at Tana in the Crimea, an

[74] Ibid.
[75] Ibid., p. 124.

important Venetian base; Mazzaoui notes that this picture is confirmed by a trade agreement between Ancona and Dubrovnik of 1372, setting a tariff of 6d per *centenario* for cotton imported from *Gazaria* (i.e. the former land of the Khazars) and Tartary. Pegolotti actually provides a rank order of cotton producers in Syria, ranging from Hama in Syria, and its close rival Aleppo, down to Cyprus and Lattakiah (Laodicea). Mazzaoui's view is that western purchasers were unable to penetrate far into the interior to obtain cotton from such sources as Persia and Turkestan, and that Syrian cotton was thus the Middle Eastern cotton with which they were most familiar. Transport costs for such a bulky commodity meant that merchants who penetrated as far as Tabriz were not likely to buy cotton there. Certainly, the Venetian colony established in Aleppo after 1207/8 seems to have seen pearls, gemstones and cotton as its main targets. However, sea routes that penetrated deep into cotton producing areas could be exploited to bring the commodity from very far afield: the Ragusan and Anconitan interest in Crimean cotton has already been mentioned, and they also made contact with sources in the Caucasus. After 1300 Anatolia became an important source of inferior quality cotton. In addition, it seems logical to argue that much of the cotton purchased in Egypt around 1300 was in fact obtained from India, and carried along the sea routes up the Red Sea. In that case significant quantities of Indian cotton may periodically have been available in the west.

For information about the Indies there was no more popular source of information after 1300 than Marco Polo's description of his return journey to the west, in which he offered descriptions of large numbers of products the origins of which could only previously be the subject of guesswork. Thus he describes the high quality of Ceylon's brazilwood, and refers to the excellent buckram cloths available from the Malabar coast:

> In this kingdom there is great abundance of pepper and also of ginger, besides cinnamon in plenty and other spices, turbit and coconuts. Buckrams are made here of the loveliest and most delicate texture in the world. Many other articles of merchandise are exported. In return, when merchants come here from overseas they load their ships with brass, which they use as ballast, cloth of gold and silk, sendal, gold, silver, cloves, spikenard and other such spices that are not produced here. You must know that ships come here from very many parts, notably from the great province of Manzi, and goods are exported to many parts. Those that go to Aden are carried thence to Alexandria.[76]

Gujarat is praised for its indigo, cotton and leather, both goat and buffalo hides, as well as unicorn skins! Embossed leather mats are a local speciality; indeed, "in this kingdom are produced leather goods of more consummate workmanship than anywhere in the world, and of higher value". Cambay is another important export centre for buckram cloth, cotton and indigo, and Marco Polo cannot even be bothered to name the other products traded there, the list is so vast.

[76] Marco Polo, *Travels*, ed. and trans. R. Latham (Harmondsworth, 1958), p. 290.

VI. HARDWARE FROM THE EAST

Further evidence of commercial, or at any rate diplomatic, contact with the east is provided by the survival in the west of metalwork, ceramics and glass of eastern origins. Some scholars who favour a diffusionist approach have argued that the development of Limoges enamels betrays eastern influence, and that the aquamanile, a common form of cast bronze animal sculpture, is copied from Islamic models; certainly some aquamanili, such as a famous example that long stood high on the roof of Pisa Cathedral, were acquired in the middle ages from Muslim courts, whether in Spain, North Africa or Egypt, along with metal basins and bowls that still occasionally survive. Similarly the evidence of the ceramic *bacini* incorporated in the towers and façades of the churches of Pisa and several other Italian cities seems to reveal regular contact with the ports of the Islamic Mediterranean, though some (such as those at the church of San Sisto) were most likely acquired by piracy, notably the Pisan-Genoese raid on al-Mahdiyya in 1087. Tin glazed wares of such high quality finish were not produced north of Lazio; on the other hand, it is hard to press the claim that these were all especially costly items. Some may have arrived as ballast in the bottom of Pisan trading vessels. By about 1200 *bacini* were arriving from Egypt, Tunisia, Morocco, Spain and Sicily; and western technology only began to catch up in the thirteenth century, when comparable glazing methods were developed in Tuscany. At that point the Pisan churches turned more and more to local products in order to decorate the exterior.[77] Meanwhile some Islamic jars were certainly reaching the west, as archaeological evidence shows, perhaps as containers for higher value goods. By the late middle

[77] Abulafia, "Pisan *bacini*", pp. 287-96.

ages, Muslim Spain and Valencia had become significant sources of high grade glazed pottery, so that "hispano-moresque" tableware was found in Medicean Florence, in Bruges and in England; the techniques of production were, however, imitated first by Spanish Christians and then in central Italy. The history of glass making reveals that, as with ceramics, the west was able to learn its skills from the east, in this case developing them to a new peak: by the late fourteenth century the west was exporting glass to the Mamlūk realms, while the alkali used in glass production at Murano were themselves derived from the Levant. Ashtor saw this as another example of the failure of the Levant to sustain the technological lead it clearly possessed in the early middle ages.

Of course, there were other finished goods produced in the east which were of a quality that could not be mimicked in the west. Celadon wares of great delicacy were filtering through the Islamic world to decorate the tables of the kings of Sicily in the thirteenth century, to judge from archaeological evidence at Lucera in Puglia. A century ago, the National Museum in Dublin acquired an early fourteenth-century Chinese porcelain vase, the "Fonthill Vase", which was probably brought to Europe by a diplomatic mission around 1338. Since then it has peregrinated through Hungary, Naples (possibly) and France.[78] Its high relief decoration suggests that it was itself a great rarity in China, not to mention the west. In other words, it was a curio, even for the Chinese; it serves as a reminder that the surviving artefacts cannot be assumed to be typical

[78] Jan Chapman, "The Fonthill Vase", *The Irish-Chinese Cultural Society Newsletter* 3 (December 1981), 1-2; I am grateful to Professor Seymour Phillips of University College, Dublin, for his kindness in providing a copy of this little known study of the vase.

of the products of the east reaching Europe, most of which ended up in the dyer's vat or as food flavourings.

VII. CONCLUSION

By the beginning of the thirteenth century a shift in the economic relationship between east and west was already becoming visible. Demand for eastern cloths was beginning to decline, while demand for raw materials, notably cotton, grew, in order to satisfy the needs of an Italian cotton industry which would, by 1400, become well established north of the Alps as well. In addition, western producers were beginning to find a good market for their own woollen cloths, from as far away as Flanders and England, as well as Italy and Catalonia, in North Africa and the Levant. Some of the Mediterranean wool producers were, indeed, making use of raw wool from the Maghrib. As western cloth production grew, to satisfy demand both in the Christian West and in the Islamic lands, so too demand for high quality dyestuffs to colour the best European cloths grew. This demand could only in part be met locally; apart from saffron, the best colouring agents had to be acquired through trade with the Levant, though most of them, especially indigo, hailed from far to the east. In addition, the fixatives and mordants used in the processing of cloth, especially alum, could be found in the east. Thus the history of the European textile industry reveals a complex interdependence between workshops producing the best woollens, fit for a king (or sultan), and merchants bringing westwards materials that were essential to the industry's success. Less prestigious, but equally dependent on supply lines from the east, was the developing cotton industry in western Europe.

The resale in the east of goods partially manufactured using raw materials from the east marked, in Ashtor's eyes, the great triumph of western technology and commercial expertise over that of the Islamic world. It also alleviated the outflow of silver bullion, even though few have challenged the orthodoxy that the balance of payments broadly continued to favour the Levant throughout the middle ages. Yet another approach might be to see the relationship between east and west as one of a growing mutual interdependence. In saying this, it is important to beware of using such terms as "underdevelopment" in describing the relationships under examination here; the eastern lands continued to be major centres of production, meeting local demand, while it was the west that experienced rapid growth that reduced significantly dependence on the Levant for finished goods, but certainly not for many raw materials.[79] Some of these raw materials, it is true, were used to process items that were then sold to consumers in the Levant. It is thus the sense that the Mediterranean world functioned in some respects as a single economy that stands out most forcibly. East and west were not simply hostile worlds whose contact was sharply constrained by religious differences and military confrontation. Ashtor's analysis thus needs to be modified: the Levant lost what mastery it had possessed over western markets, but it would be an exaggeration to say that it fell under western economic hegemony.

Janet Abu-Lughod has argued that in the period 1250 to 1350 a global economy was coming into being, only to be disrupted by

[79] The importance of local demand and of economic integration at a regional level is brought out by S. R. Epstein, *An Island for Itself. Economic Development and Social Change in Late Medieval Sicily* (Cambridge, 1992; Italian ed., Turin, 1996), which might serve as a useful model for the description of other regions bordering the Mediterranean, Christian and Islamic, as well.

the shock of the Black Death.[80] Her argument partly depends on the traditional emphasis placed on the trans-Asia trade routes created as a result of the Mongol conquests in Asia; another view might be that the great spice trade through the Indian Ocean to Alexandria was never seriously replaced by the new Asiatic routes carrying silk and slaves. But that is not to deny signs of a global economy coming into existence, bringing together in a common enterprise the Christian and Islamic shores of the Mediterranean. That common enterprise was the textile industry, both luxury woollens and humbler cotton cloths. The evidence presented here suggests that in some sectors of the western European economy the presence of items imported from the east was of critical importance to further expansion. The political, cultural and religious barriers across the Mediterranean proved permeable; cotton, indigo and alum were the agents binding together east and west.

[80] J. Abu-Lughod, *Before European Hegemony. The World System, AD 1250-1350* (New York, 1989).

I ISLAMIC SPAIN AND SICILY

Phoenician Origins of the Mosque of Cordoba, Madina Azahara and the Alhambra

Marvin H. Mills
University of South Florida

Evidence for the origins of three great monuments of Islamic Spain, the Mosque of Cordoba, Madina Azahara and the Alhambra, suggests attributions that preceded Islam. If the basic structural and construction aspects of these complexes were in place prior to Islam, considering the key importance to architectural history of these three monuments, then a paradigm shift may be needed to explain the origins and development of ancient and medieval Spanish architecture.[1]

The Phoenician presence in Andalusia spanned 500 years until it was replaced by the Carthaginians in the sixth century BC. Its presence is substantiated by remains of their many settlements, trading posts and artefacts. It is believed that they founded Cadiz as

[1] M. Mills, "The pre-Islamic provenance of the Mosque of Cordoba", *Al-Masaq. Studia Arabo-Islamica Mediterranea* 4 (1991), 1-16. In this earlier article, the author explored the possibility of a pre-Islamic origin of the Mosque of Cordoba. The present article seeks to expand the inquiry to include all three major Islamic monuments in Spain.

early as the eleventh century BC, and that they engaged in extensive commerce throughout the Mediterranean and beyond. The lure of metals including silver, copper, lead and tin brought them into contact with the Tartessians of Andalusia and perhaps the people in Cornwall in south-west England with its rich tin deposits. Their ability to handle technology, science and building construction as well as their artistic sophistication is well established.[2] The acknowledged remains of Phoenician construction are rare - but we may be overlooking monuments that incorporate the foundations and structures of three of their best architectural achievements which managed to survive, though altered in the course of centuries. An appreciation of their commercial, military and cultural value may have overridden the opportunity to destroy them by their successive new owners: the Carthaginians, Romans, Visigoths, Arabs/Berbers, and Franks.

My assumption that the building that became known as the Mosque of Cordoba existed prior to the reign of the Umayyads from the second/eighth to the fifth/eleventh century is based partly on serious doubts concerning the efficacy of its design as a mosque. What then could the Mosque of Cordoba originally have been designed to be? Apparently, not to be a mosque. A basic requirement for a mosque is that it face Makka. This building orients 48 degrees away from the direction of Makka. Instead of 12 degrees south of east, the direction of Makka from Cordoba, it orients 60 degrees south of east. It does not face due south - an alternate sacred possibility considering that Makka is south of Madina, the two holiest cities in Arabia. For reasons not yet clarified, or perhaps by coincidence, the main longitudinal axis of

[2] S. Moscati, *The Phoenicians* (New York, 1988). This comprehensive work confirms the versatility, sophistication and high artistic and technical ability of the Phoenicians.

the mosque seems approximately parallel to the south-west wall of the Kaᶜba in Makka.[3] Could its orientation have been just a local tradition honoured by the *ᶜulamāʾ* in Cordoba? Possibly, but not likely.[4] The mandate of Muḥammad in the Qur'ān is that the faithful face Makka in prayer.

The mosque's first stage is said to have been built in 170/786 by ᶜAbd al-Raḥmān I (138-172/756-788), and finally completed by the chief minister, Ibn Abī ᶜĀmir, called al-Manṣūr (bi-llāh) (d. 393/1002) in 377/987. The shape of the building after its alleged south-east expansion of eleven naves and eight aisles by al-Ḥakam II (350-366/961-976) in 351/962 would have given it an attenuated form from minaret to *miḥrāb* which is atypical of mosques. That form could not respond functionally to the need for the congregation to be grouped around the prayer leader in front of the *miḥrāb*. Almost invariably, when an oblong prayer hall space is designed, it is the short dimension that is perpendicular to the *qibla* wall - the wall facing Makka - as is evident in the Mosque of Damascus which was built in 71/690, and has been regarded as a source of inspiration for the Mosque of Cordoba. This anomaly suggests that there was no staged development up to 351/962 as is invariably claimed. It is more reasonable to assume that the original construction up to this time was built at one time, at an earlier period, for another purpose

[3] Gerald S. Hawkins and David A. King, "On the orientation of the Kaᶜba", *Journal for the History of Astronomy* 13, ii (1982), 106. Based on their data, the southwest side of the Kaᶜba orients to 58$^1/_2$ degrees south of east.

[4] D. A. King, "Faces of the Kaᶜba", *The Sciences* 22, v (May/June, 1982), 16-20. This article provides valuable insights into the possible alternate variations to orienting the medieval mosque to the Kaᶜba. But King informs us that "... all mosques are supposed to face that direction. But hundreds of medieval mosques, scattered from Andalusia to Central Asia are not properly aligned toward Makka", p. 17. He does not explore the possibility that they may have had other origins.

and by a different people. Its configuration may have been as depicted in Figure One.

There are many more unexplained features of what must later have become a mosque. Why does it have basement areas, whose original extent is not yet documented?[5] Mosques do not have basements. Was this the basement of an earlier church or was it even earlier a Phoenician storage space for products?

Why the 73-metre high minaret? No call by a human voice to prayer could have been heard from its high balcony. Perhaps it was a signal tower and observatory. Its current Renaissance jacket built between 1593 and 1653, when it was converted to a bell-tower, conceals its elegant original design. At that great height, one could have observed and signalled ships on the Guadalquivir River, studied stars in the heavens or provided forewarning of approaching armies.

Why the formidable defence design of the exterior wall including massive rectangular buttresses and crenellated parapets? From whom was there fear of invasion of a mosque? But a Phoenician warehouse containing valuable metals would have been a temptation requiring a fortified exterior wall.

Why is its location at the edge of the city on its waterfront prime commercial area? Why not in the centre of the city where it would have been more accessible as the city's congregational mosque? Phoenician temples were located apart from the city and close to the water where they also served as commercial centres. In an earlier study, I explored the possibility of its being an ancient

[5] I have examined two basement spaces in October 1990, that were accessible. At the time, it was not possible to determine the original extent of these areas or whether they constituted one continuous space unless considerable excavation were undertaken.

Roman warehouse, but subsequently I rejected that hypothesis.[6] It has little stylistic resemblance to extant Roman remains in Cordoba and elsewhere in Spain. Wherever Rome built throughout its empire, the buildings were designed to resemble the architecture in Rome with purposeful disregard for the culture of the occupied territories. While it has been pointed out that the double arcades of the sanctuary resemble the double arcades of the Roman bridge that crossed the Guadalquivir, the Romans rarely or perhaps never used the horseshoe arch so prevalent in the Mosque of Cordoba. Nor in the records of Roman construction in Cordoba is there any mention of this building's construction. But it is likely that the Romans, having come into possession of such a useful property, would have adapted it to serve as a warehouse.

If we hypothesise a Phoenician attribution, a more plausible scenario falls into place. The future mosque could have originally served as a temple, commercial centre, warehouse and observatory. It could have been the main Phoenician commercial centre in the heart of the Tartessian hinterland. There were Tartessian products to be exchanged, metals to be stored in the basement, grain on the first floor. The basement would have provided air circulation and cooling to prevent rotting of the grain above. After loading exports on boats at the river front, the boats could have been floated down to Cadiz at the mouth of the river, then reloaded on larger vessels for the return trip to Phoenicia, or to Assyria for tribute. The future minaret in character and appearance is not unlike the still extant Roman lighthouse at Coruña in north-west Spain on the Atlantic. It was too early in the history of Islamic minarets for one of the

[6] M. Mills, "Scenario for a Roman provenance for the Mosque of Cordoba", in *The Medieval Mediterranean: Cross-Cultural Contacts* (Medieval Studies at Minnesota, 3), ed. M. J. Chiat and K. L. Reyerson (St. Cloud, Minnesota, 1988), pp. 42-50.

greatest minarets in the world to have been built then and in Spain.[7] Where were the precedents one would expect?

The *miḥrāb* was perhaps originally the focal point of the temple area at the south end of the Phoenician warehouse and meeting hall. It was the locus of Melqarth, the god of commerce. *Miḥrābs* have traditionally not been rooms as this is, but were invariably niches. In each new Phoenician settlement, the first building to be put up would have had its focus devoted to Melqarth.

In my imaginative reconstruction of the mosque as it could have been in the seventh century BC (Figure One), its south-east wall points to the setting summer solstice sun on 21 June just about $1^1/_2$ diameters above the flat horizon.[8] Since Melqarth was a sun

[7] Jonathan M. Bloom, "Five minarets in Upper Egypt", *Journal of the Society of Architectural Historians* 43 (May, 1984), 162-167:

> Generally antagonistic to the pretensions of the ᶜAbbasid caliphs of Baghdad, the Umayyads of Spain appear to have accepted the mosque tower by the middle of the ninth century, a period of strong ᶜAbbasid influence on all aspects of Andalusian culture and society .... (p. 165).

Bloom explains why the Fāṭimids of Egypt rejected the minaret up to 391/1000 since they had their own caliph and were antagonistic to Baghdad. He offers no explanation as to why in 347/958 ᶜAbd al-Raḥmān III (300-350/912-961), who had assumed the role of caliph in 317/929, should have built a magnificent minaret, the hated symbol of the ᶜAbbāsids.

[8] M. Mills, p. 16. In a letter of 14 November 1990, from Gerald S. Hawkins, who successfully applied the computer to uncovering astronomical relationships at Stonehenge as described in his book, *Stonehenge Decoded* (Doubleday, 1965), concerning the southeast wall of the Mosque of Cordoba:

> Assuming the wall is at Azimuth 60 degrees, and the skyline is flat, then the declination is 22.9 degrees. The sun would, today, stand approximately on that line at the summer solstice, being about one diameter above the skyline ... in 3,000 BC, the solstice sun would be about 2 diameters above the flat horizon. You can interpolate for dates in between.

god, and given the astronomical concerns of the Phoenicians as great navigators, it would have reinforced the central importance of the temple to relate astronomically to the sun. We can conjecture that the location of Cordoba was placed at that latitude along the Guadalquivir River where its 60-degree orientation would produce a solar solstice reading. There is the possibility that the meridian of longitude chosen for the location of Cordoba was calculated to be at exact degrees of longitude from the west boundary of ancient Egypt,[9] their main commercial centre in the heart of the Tartessian countryside.

One of the samples from a wood ceiling beam in the sanctuary roof that I had Carbon-14 dated showed it to be of the seventh century BC. This wood piece plus four other samples provided a range of dates extending from the seventh century BC to the fourteenth century AD.[10] Apparently, the mosque had a long history of repair, rework and change of function.

In this revised historical perspective, the Cadiz-Cordoba axis that controlled the Guadalquivir River guaranteed that the main hinterland area of Tartessos was secure for trade. Cadiz secured the commercial relations with the Tartessian Rio Tinto silver mine area around Huelva; Cordoba and its palatine military encampment,

[9] Peter Tompkins, *Secrets of the Great Pyramid* (New York, 1971). Tompkins, citing Stecchini, says the Egyptians set their western boundary at 29 degrees 50 minutes east. The coordinates of Cordoba, according to the *Oxford Atlas of the World* (New York, 1995), p. 37, are four degrees 50' W, 37 degrees 50' N. Thus Cordoba would be exactly 33 degrees west of Egypt's west boundary. According to Tompkins, many ancient cities were set in relation to Egypt, including Makka. He tells us that ancient Makka's coordinates were 39 degrees east of the western boundary of Egypt and 10 degrees south of Behdet, Egypt's pre-dynastic capital. Cordoba, whose latitude was apparently set by its location on the bank of the Guadalquivir River, obviously could not at the same time respond to Egypt's latitude.

[10] M. Mills, p. 14.

Madina Azahara, controlled the river valley and its agricultural products. What then was the role of the Alhambra? Originally it may have been a Phoenician governmental centre fortified to control the hinterland inland from the Mediterranean coast where the Phoenician settlements of Toscanos, Chorreras and Almunecar were located.

Like many other Phoenician settlements, the Alhambra was located on a height for protection with the help of an encircling stone wall. There are certain problems with the current explanation of the Alhambra as an Islamic palace-city of the thirteenth-fourteenth centuries, supposedly basically a product of the Naṣrid Dynasty which ruled Granada from 635/1237 to 898/1492. If Granada was the last gasp of power of Islam in Spain, would they have built such an expensive and ambitious project at that time?

Nor is it known why the rooms were arranged the way they were and how they functioned. Names attributed to the rooms like the Hall of the Sisters are only fanciful later Spanish titles based on legend. Oleg Grabar, a leading Islamic art historian, in confronting this problem concludes that they must have been designed in a random non-functional fashion.[11] But, to my knowledge, there are few precedents in the history of architecture that demonstrate random design in key buildings. Architecture typically responds in some purposeful manner to clients' needs.

In what has been referred to as the "Bargebuhr hypothesis", there is strong evidence of an earlier origin. Frederick P. Bargebuhr,

[11] O. Grabar, *The Alhambra* (Cambridge, 1978), p. 54. In speaking of the uses to which the various rooms were put, he says: "It would seem altogether preferable to accept that the function of all these very different architectural fragments are simply unknown except for the two small oratories"; and p. 140: "At this stage in our search for the meanings and uses of the Alhambra, we may simply conclude that there was none, other than sensuous satisfaction".

a German scholar who died in 1965, points out that in a famous poem, Ibn Gabirol (d. 444/1052), the Spanish Jewish poet, describes a palace court so vividly that it could only have been the Alhambra's Court of the Lions.[12] Reference to an earlier Jewish construction in the fifth/eleventh-century Zīrid dynasty is noted in the "Memoirs" of ᶜAbdallāh b. Buluggīn (465-483/1064-1090), the last Zīrid king of Granada.[13] Palace construction was promoted by the powerful Jewish vizier Samuel Nagrallah and his son Yūsuf. On the south-west slope of the Alhambra hill was the Jewish quarter connected to the fortress by the Vermilion towers and gate. The

[12] F. P. Bargebuhr, "The Alhambra palace of the eleventh century", *Journal of the Warburg and Courtauld Institutes* 19, iii-iv (July-December, 1956), 192-258:

> we do not doubt that the rest of the castle, including the Fount of the Lions, as described by Ibn Gabirol, existed during his time. Such a doubt could spring only from unfamiliarity with this type of panegyric poetry with its accepted documentary value, or from a prejudice which has its origin in political fears and interests, and which will imperil true historical investigations, even after 900 years. (p. 232).

[13] E. Lévi-Provençal, "Les mémoires de ᶜAbd Allah, dernier roi ziride de Grenade", *Al-Andalus* 3, ii (1935), 232-344 and *Al-Andalus* 4, i (1936), 29-145; and "Deux nouveaux fragments des mémoires du roi ziride ᶜAbd Allah de Grenade", 6, i (1941), 1-63:

> Cependant, le fossé creusé entre le juif et la population allait s'élargissant et les troubles augmentaient. Le juif, par crainte de la populace, déménagea de sa maison pour aller résider dans l'Alcazaba, jusqu'au moment où ses espoirs seraient réalisés. Çela lui valut la désapprobation des habitants, de même que la construction par ses soins de la forteresse de l'Alhambra, où il comptait se retransporter avec sa famille lorsque Ibn Sumādih pénétrerait dans Grenade, jusqu'au moment où la situation se rétablirait .... (Lévi-Provençal, 3, ii (1935), pp. 299-300).

fifth-/eleventh-century Alhambra was probably built to protect the Jews of Granada who were numerous and influential.

But Dario Cabanelas Rodríguez does not rule out the possibility of an even earlier castle existing in Roman times, though he agrees that there is abundant evidence for a Jewish castle erected in the eleventh century.[14] Could there have been an even earlier Phoenician fortified palace whose foundations and wall still survive? We know so little of the Phoenician history in Andalusia that, admittedly, we can only conjecture. But the absence of affirmative evidence of their presence in Granada should not rule out their having been there in strength. The question is: Which of the three possible castles do we see today? Could it be that the existing elegant finishes and Qur'ānic inscriptions are only repairs and cosmetic refinements of Castle 3 to Castles 1 and 2?

As in the Mosque of Cordoba, the two small Alhambra chapel "mosques" do not face Makka, nor do they face in similar directions. The supposed use of the Cuarto Dorado's south wall as the location for a throne for the king to receive visitors is almost too ridiculous to comment on. It is obviously too cramped a space and beset by pedestrian traffic. The lack of information about the location of a mosque ample enough to serve a large congregation in the vicinity of the palace, and the absence of a mosque in the fortified Alcazaba, should create doubt concerning the supposed Islamic design of the layout.

My reconstruction drawing (Figure Two) shows how the Alhambra may have been organised as a Phoenician administrative and military centre comparable to Madina Azahara. A characteristic

[14] D. Cabanelas Rodríguez, "The Alhambra: an introduction", in *Al-Andalus - the Art of Islamic Spain*, ed. J. D. Dodds (New York, 1992), pp. 127-133. "It is not possible to say whether buildings existed on the site of the present Alhambra during the time of the Romans and Visigoths", p. 133, n. 1.

feature of eastern Mediterranean cities from the time of the Bronze Age is the provision for ceremonies that traverse the area by means of a "processional way". This is true of the Ishtar Gate in Babylon of the sixth century BC and the route from Athens to its Acropolis in the fifth century BC. From Granada on the slopes and plain below, a processional group could have made its way up to the encircling wall, through the Vermilion Towers, ascended the walk up to the Gate of the Law, through the Wine Gate, to a plaza where later was built the Renaissance Palace of the sixteenth century, through the Court of the Myrtles and on to the Hall of the Ambassadors, perhaps originally a Phoenician temple with nine surrounding chapels, each devoted to a separate deity.

The Court of the Lions and its surrounding buildings and rooms could have housed the royal family and administrators. The famous Lion's Fountain, focal point of the Court of the Lions, was probably Phoenician, which would explain this perplexing anomaly of naturalistic sculpture in an Islamic building. Its style is more appropriate to Phoenician art than to Islamic art. Bargebuhr has pointed out that the twelve lions supporting the overflowing basin is an interpretation of the "brazen sea", the bronze fountain in front of Solomon's temple in Jerusalem, which similarly had an overflowing basin, but which was supported by twelve oxen rather than lions. That the Court of the Myrtles and the Court of the Lions were built as a unified whole was demonstrated with generating lines and geometric relationships by Henri and Anne Stierlin.[15] The main palace was conceived as a unit and did not grow essentially by accretion. A possible grand reception hall on the east side of the plaza could have been used to accommodate large meetings (Figure Two).

[15] H. and A. Stierlin, *Alhambra* (Paris, 1991).

Like the Alhambra, the specific functional interrelationships of Madina Azahara are not known. Madina Azahara may have been the main Phoenician palatine city for Andalusia - their Versailles. It is not likely that it was built by the Romans, though they probably made good use of it. Its north-south axis is approximately 24 degrees east of north - an orientation of settlements not characteristic of the Romans who preferred the cardinal directions (Figure Three). The rich and beautiful forms and décor owe no allegiance to Rome or Islam. They are basically eastern and unique. The sculpted arabesque wall plaques have symmetrical, self-contained design patterns rather than infinitely expanding patterns as is typical of Islamic design. Above the entrance gate at the south wall enclosure is said to have existed a statue of Venus which the local people identified with a favourite of the caliph. It is not likely that the Muslims would have introduced a three-dimensional realistic sculpture in such a prominent location. It is more likely that it was a Phoenician statue of Astarte who later became identified with Venus, the goddess of love.

However, the mosque in Madina Azahara may be an original mosque. Its peripheral location east of the South Terrace and at a lower level, remote from the palace and the mass of the people of the city, suggests that it was the last best site available. The Palace living quarters to the north-east are some 300 metres away from the mosque and about 38 metres higher up on the slope, a location which would have been very inconvenient for the royalty in relation to the mosque (Figure Three). Instead of being the first building to be built in Azahara in 330/941, it may have been the last. It faces Makka because it was probably built by the Muslims to fill their need for a mosque, in which case it resembles the Mosque of Cordoba because it was patterned after the existing building. On the other hand, the mosque may have been a pre-existing Phoenician temple, reworked and used as a mosque. This would account for the confusion concerning the date it was built and how long it took to build. Inscriptions on the mosque say that it took four years to build, but the historian al-Maqqarī (d. 1041/1631-2) says it took 48 days.[16]

Whereas the mosque at Azahara was described by al-Maqqarī as having been built with amazing speed, the whole palace city, he says, took forty years to build. Why the desperate pace for the mosque and the relaxed pace for the city as a whole? After all, the somewhat apocryphal Azahira city-palace built by al-Manṣūr is said to have taken only two years to build. Based on his historian of choice, Ibn Ḥayyān (d. 469/1076-7), he catalogued how, beginning in 325-326/936-937, Azahara made use of 400 columns, 15,000 door leafs, 10,000 workmen and slaves. Yet, the detailed account does not include an account of the excavation. The explanation may be that he is describing rework, not original construction.[17]

It is interesting to note that the water supply to Azahara was said to be new construction which continued on to supply Cordoba and its Great Mosque. If this were true, why haven't scholars raised

[16] Aḥmad b. Muḥammad al-Maqqarī, *The History of the Mohammedan Dynasties in Spain,* trans. Pascual de Gayangos, 2 vols. (London, 1834), 1:237-238:

> The mosque of Az-zahrá did not fall short of the rest of the building. Although matchless in design and faultless in preparation, the whole structure was raised and its interior arrangements completed in the space of forty-eight days, for An-nássir kept continually employed on it one thousand skillful workmen ....

[17] ibid., 234-235. He quotes Ibn Ḥayyān

> An-nássir began the construction of the palace and the city of Az-zahrá in the year 325 of the Hijra (A.D. 936-7) and the building was continued for forty consecutive years; that is to say, 25 years of the life of An-nássir and 15 of that of his son and successor, Al-hakem ....

the question: what did Cordoba and the Great Mosque do for water before Azahara was built? It is more likely that the port of Cordoba, its temple and its palace-city were all built at the same time by the Phoenicians, along with its water supply, including the four-part upper pools and gardens on the South Terrace, which have the same theme as the gardens of the Court of the Lions in the Alhambra, and are part of the varied and intricate water supply system. The design derives from earlier Persian and Indian garden design.

Both the Alhambra and Azahara have basic features in common which suggests a common origin. Both are supplied with water courses, fountains and cisterns; they both have rooms surrounding interior courts; they are both encircled by walled fortifications; they are both on a height commanding a valley; and, while their exterior walls are plain and formidable, their interiors are both light and delightful.

On ceremonial occasions, from Azahara to the Mosque of Cordoba (then the Temple of Melqarth), there may have been a processional movement from the palace area of Azahara, through Azahara's magnificent archways, proceeding east three and a half miles to what was then the port city of Cordoba, turning south down the main avenue to the entry alongside the observation tower that later was converted to a minaret, across the court, down the wide central nave to the sacred area, later to become the *maqṣūra*. Azahara in ancient times was known as "Old Cordoba". The later Roman expansion of "Old Cordoba's" port city is indicated by the shift to a north-south orientation of the city's northern expansion.

Phoenician art and architecture appeared in the Mediterranean even before 1200 BC. It had five hundred years to mature in Andalusia by the seventh century BC when the Phoenician presence was at its height before being replaced by Carthaginian power. The light and graceful aura of Phoenician aesthetics suggests a society that was humanistic, joyous and comfortable - perhaps like the earlier Minoan civilisation. The best evidence of the architecture of the Phoenicians is depicted on the Nineveh palace wall slabs during the reign of Sennacherib (705-681 BC) and the Balawat bronze doors during the reign of Shalmaneser III (858-824 BC) which show Phoenician cities like Tyre being conquered or subservient to the Assyrians. This elegance and lightness does not seem to be true of their inheritors, the Carthaginians, with their imperialist ambitions and more sombre art forms.

This unified theory of the origins of the three monumental complexes overcomes many of the problems raised by the standard explanations which assume their Islamic origins. It accounts for the alleged sudden or mature appearance of bold Islamic forms such as the horseshoe arch, the double arch, the monumental minaret and the chambered *miḥrāb* in the Mosque of Cordoba. It offers an explanation for the unclear function of spaces within the complexes, and it suggests an alternative role for the buildings as part of Phoenician history. The next step should be to date these buildings scientifically by means of Carbon-14 and thermoluminescence analysis with multiple samplings to determine at least which centuries we are talking about. Stylistic considerations are useful but could be misleading. Epigraphic evidence is the least dependable because building inscriptions can easily be appended at a later date to wipe out the memory of a past history. I am confident that additional, comprehensive, scientific dating will corroborate this hypothesis.

Figure One
Reconstruction of pre-Islamic Mosque of Cordoba
with astronomical orientation

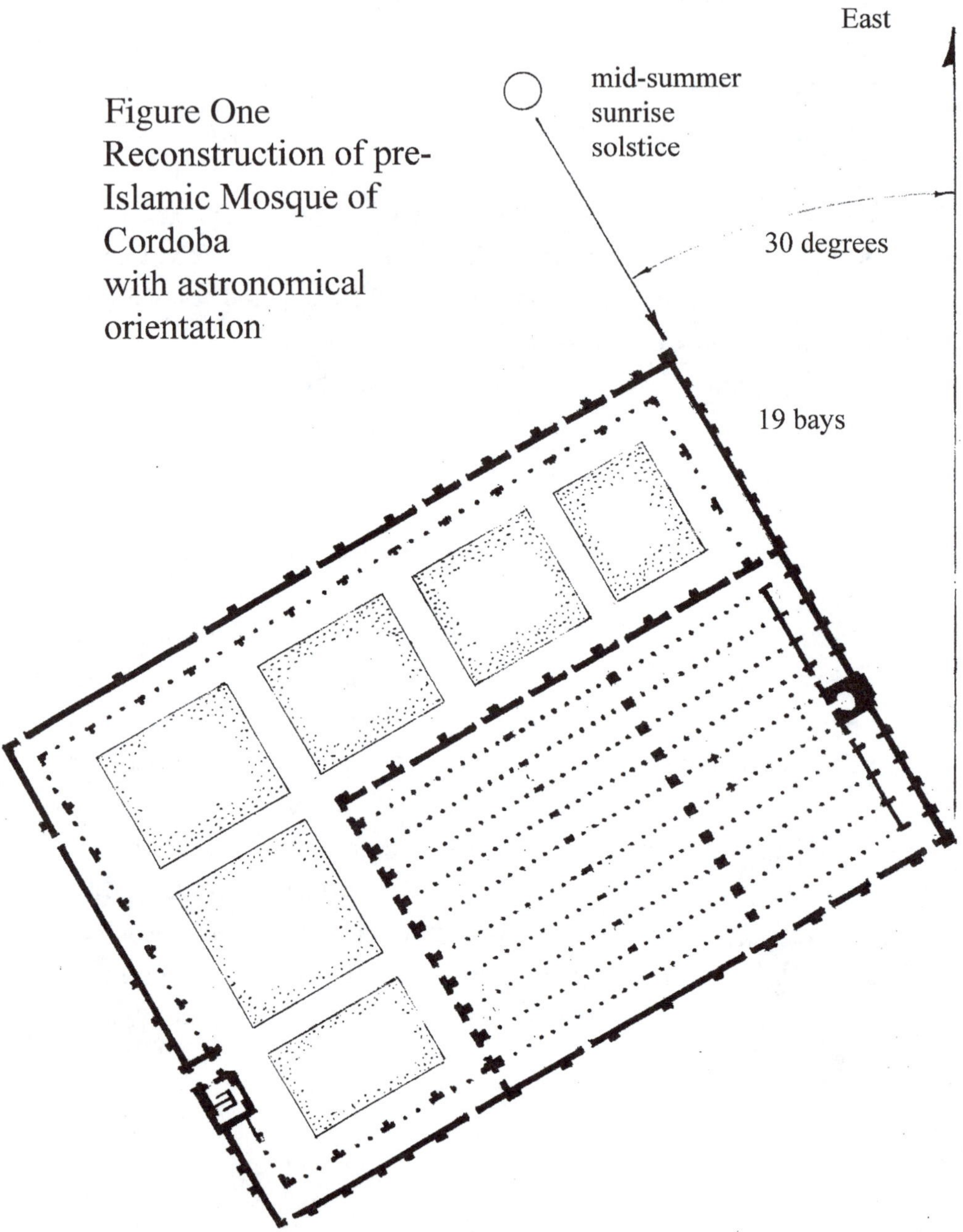

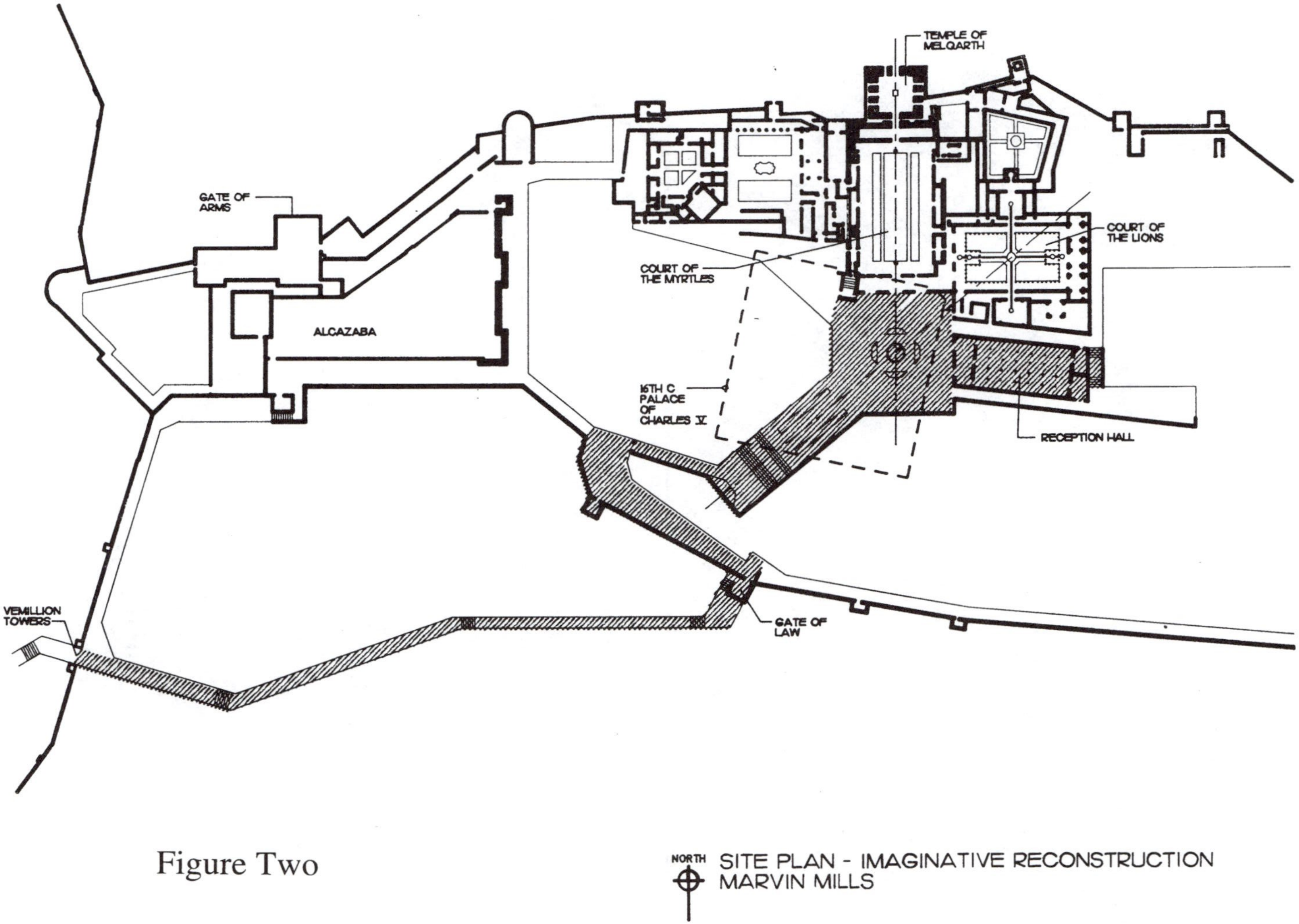

Figure Two

SITE PLAN - IMAGINATIVE RECONSTRUCTION
MARVIN MILLS

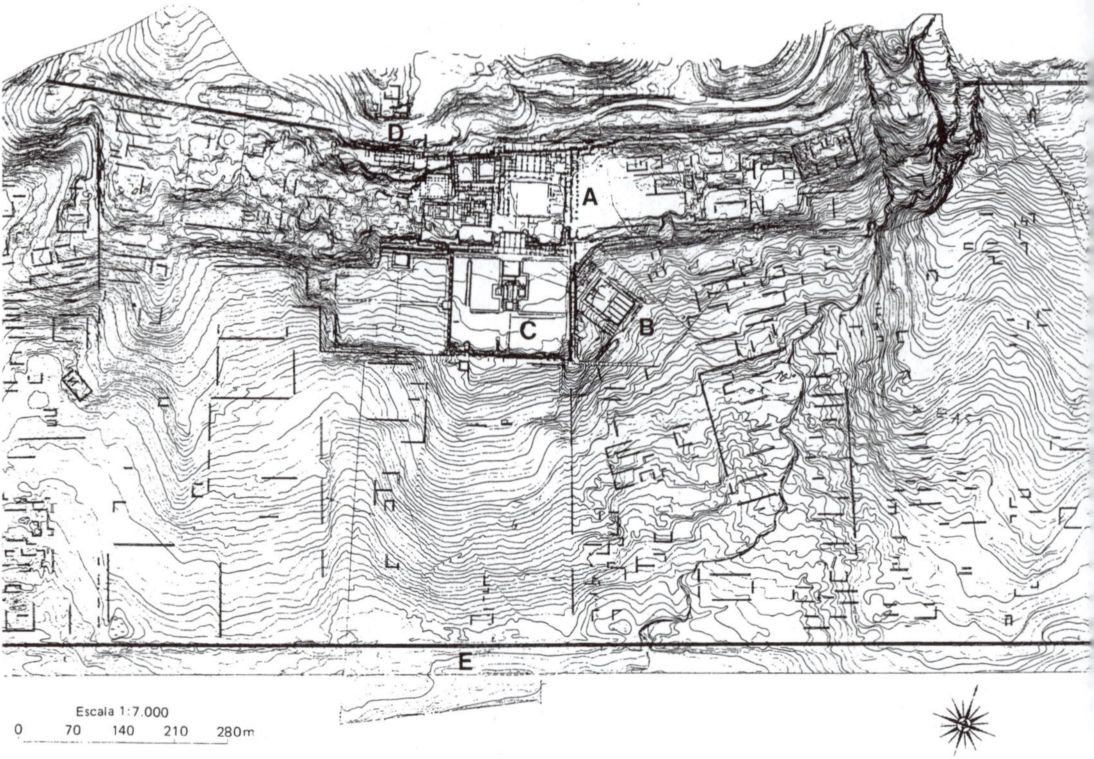

PALACE-CITY OF MEDINA-AZAHARA

A= ROW OF ARCHES

B= MOSQUE

C= SOUTH TERRACE

D= PALACE LIVING QUARTERS

E= SOUTH BOUNDARY WALL

Figure Three

La Invasión Árabe y el Inicio de la "Reconquista" en el Noroeste de la Península Ibérica (93-251/711-865)

Jorge L. Quiroga and Mónica R. Lovelle
Universidad de Santiago de Compostela

La historiografía sobre el tema objeto de estudio es extraordinariamente abundante. Por ello, un repaso de la misma nos llevaría a salirnos de los objetivos y del espacio disponibles para la elaboración de este trabajo. Nuestra intención es hacer algunas reflexiones, nuevas lecturas e interpretaciones a través de las fuentes escritas y arqueológicas sobre los acontemientos sucedidos entre el 93/711 y el 251/865 (marco cronológico de este estudio). En cuanto al ámbito espacial centraremos nuestro análisis sobre el espacio comprendido entre los rios Miño y Duero (que abarca tierras del Norte de Portugal y del Sur de la región de Galicia en España). Dicho espacio ha sido un escenario tradicional, según Sánchez Albornoz y otros investigadores, afrectado por la "invasión" árabe y sus consecuencias: la "despoblación", la "Reconquista" y la "Repoblación". La limitación de nuestro ámbito espacial a una parte del valle del Duero, no significa que los análisis e interpretaciones que hagamos se circunscriban estrictamente a dicho espacio. Muy al contrario, todo el espacio comprendido entre el mar Cantábrico y el rio Duero puede ser sometido al mismo análisis; aunque, las interpretaciones deban de tener en cuenta matizaciones regionales que impiden una vision únivoca y globalizadora a la que nos tiene tan acostumbrados la historiografía tradicional.

Abordaremos en este trabajo tres aspectos que han sido fuertemente mitificados tanto por las fuentes de la época como por la historiografía nacionalista posterior: la presencia de los musulmanes en las tierras al Norte del Duero; las campañas de Alfonso I (739-757) entre el 124/741 y el 137/754 a lo largo del valle del Duero; y las consecuencias de ambos hechos sobre la organización política, adnistrativa y religiosa en dicho espacio, entre el 137/754 y el 251/865.

1. LOS ÁRABES Y BEREBERES EN EL VALLE DEL DUERO (96-123/714-740)

Es un lugar común que, en el año 93/711 los árabes han invadido España - como lo ha señalado Pierre Guichard en un artículo publicado ya hace 20 años en la revista *Annales*.[1] La llegada de los árabes a la Península Ibérica ha sido estudiada también por García Moreno en un artículo bastante reciente,[2] en respuesta a otro polémico artículo de Joaquín Vallvé.[3] En este artículo, Vallvé hace una nueva interpretación sobre el lugar de llegada de los árabes a

[1] Pierre Guichard, "Les arabes ont bien envahi l'Espagne. Les structures sociales de l' Espagne musulmane", *Annales* 6 (1974), 1483-1513.

[2] L. A. García Moreno, "Los últimos tiempos del reino visigodo", *Boletín de la Real Academia de la Historia* 189, Cuaderno III (Sept. Dic., 1992), 425-429.

[3] J. Vallvé, "Nuevas ideas sobre la conquista árabe de España. Toponimia y Onomástica", *Alqantara* 10 (1988), 51-149.

través de una relectura de las fuentes. No vamos a entrar en dicha polémica. Nos interesa destacar, sin embargo, el punto de vista de García Moreno respecto a las fuentes. Para él, la *Continuatio Hispana* o *Crónica mozárabe* del 137/754 es la fuente que mejor relata los acontecimientos del año 93/711. Por otra parte, este investigador hace una relectura de la crónica en lo que concierne a los últimos años del reino de Toledo. Ello le permite precisar mejor la cronología de los acontecimientos y, sobre todo, el problema del paso del reino de Witiza (702-710) al de Ruderico (710-711). Otro aspecto abordado por García Moreno, es el de las expediciones árabes enviadas por Mūsā ibn Nuṣayr (m. 98/716-7) en la Península antes de atravesar él mismo el estrecho de Gibraltar. Así, para este historiador, una mejor puntuación en una frase de la crónica - *id est Tariq Abuzara et ceteros* - permite interpretar la existencia de dos expediciones antes de la llegada de Mūsā ibn Nuṣayr en el año 94/712. Finalmente, para García Moreno, será Algeciras el lugar de llegada de Mūsā ibn Nuṣayr y de su ejército de árabes y bereberes y de su lucha con Rodrigo sobre el Guadalete.

1.1. LA CAMPAÑA DE MOUSA EN "GALICIA" EN EL 714

Después del desembarco de Mūsā ibn Nuṣayr en Algeciras en el 94/712, éste va atacar Medinasidonia, Carmona y Sevilla.[4] En 95/713 la ciudad de Mérida cae y Mousa parte hacia Toledo para pasar el invierno en la antigua capital de los visigodos. En la primavera del 96/714 Mūsā ibn Nuṣayr va decidir conquistar las zonas que todavía permanecían libres de la presencia musulmana: la

[4] C. Sánchez Albornoz, "Itinerario de la Conquista de España por los musulamanes", *Cuadernos de Historia de España* 7 (1947), 21-57.

parte oriental de España (Aragón y Cataluña) y la parte occidental ("Galicia": las actuales León, Asturias, Galicia y Norte de Portugal).

No debemos olvidar que la campaña de Mūsā ibn Nuṣayr en "Galicia" es precedida de la de Ṭāriq ibn Ziyād (m. después 98/716-7) en el 93/711 y 94/712. En esta campaña Ṭāriq ibn Ziyād, según las fuentes árabes estudiadas por Sánchez Albornoz,[5] habría llegado hasta Astorga y allí dado media vuelta hacia Toledo. El insigne medievalista a mostrado claramente como los árabes han seguido las vias romanas en sus desplazamientos por el interior de la Península Ibérica. Lo que nos interesa, respecto al valle del Duero y al territorio entre ese río y el Miño, es saber si las tropas de Mūsā ibn Nuṣayr han atravesado dicho espacio en su ruta hacia Lugo o en su vuelta a Damasco en respuesta a la llamada del Califa, al-Walīd I (86-96/705-715). El primer hecho a destacar es la casi ausencia de noticias en las fuentes árabes en lo que se refiere a las operaciones militares en el Noroeste de la Península Ibérica, como bien ha señalado Barrau-Dihigo a principios de este siglo.[6] Veamos cual ha sido el itinerario de Mūsā ibn Nuṣayr.

A partir de Toledo (dónde se instaló en el invierno del 45/713), Mūsā ibn Nuṣayr y Ṭāriq ibn Ziyād se dirigieron hacia Zaragoza. Como señala Sánchez Albornoz, todas las fuentes árabes excepto Ibn al-Qūṭiyya (m. 366/977) coinciden con el relato de la crónica mozárabe del 137/754 sobre el ataque de Mūsā ibn Nuṣayr a Zaragoza desde Toledo.[7] El problema que se plantea es el de saber

[5] C. Sánchez Albornoz, *Fuentes de la historia hispano-musulmana del siglo VIII. En torno a los Orígenes del Feudalismo* 2 (Mendoza, 1942).

[6] L. Barrau-Dihigo, *Recherches sur l'histoire politique du royaume asturien (718-910)* (Tours, 1921).

[7] *Sicque non solum ulteriorem Spaniam, sed etiam et citeriorem usque ultra Caesaraugusta antiquissiman ac florentissiman civitatem dudum Dei patenter apertam gladio fame et captivitate depopulat, civitates decoras igne*

cuales han sido las rutas seguidas por los dos jefes militares después de la conquista de Zaragoza. Según las fuentes árabes, Mūsā ibn Nuṣayr habría atravesado los Pirineos; pero, para Sánchez Albornoz, los historiadores árabes confunden la tierra de los francos (al Norte de los Pirineos) con Cataluña[8] y además, según este historiador, sería Ṭāriq ibn Ziyād y no Mūsā ibn Nuṣayr el que ataca Cataluña. Mūsā ibn Nuṣayr, en persona, se dirigiría a la conquista del Noroeste (lo que los árabes denominaban "Galicia"). Barrau-Dihigo, subraya como el *Akhbār Majmū'a* no habla de esta campaña ni de ninguna otra actividad de los árabes en el Noroeste.[9] Las fuentes que hacen referencia a esta campaña son: el relato de Ibn al-Qūṭiyya; el Pseudo Ibn Qutayba (m.276/889-90); y la más tardía la de Ibn al-Athīr (m. 630/1232-3).[10] Barrau-Dihigo, lógicamente, somete a una fuerte crítica todos estos textos que relatan las campañas de los árabes en el Noroeste. Para él, las interpretaciones hechas por Saavedra[11] son contradictorias, legendarias y critica a ese historiador su lectura demasiado literal de las fuentes árabes. Para el historiador francés, Mūsā ibn Nuṣayr no ha estado nunca ni en Viseo ni en Portugal y, sobre todo, la identificación de *Lucus Asturum* con una población en Asturias y no con *Lucus Augusti* en

concremando precipitat seniores et potentes seculi cruci adiudicat, iubenes atque lactantes pugionibus trucidat

(Anónimo, *Crónica mozárabe de 754*, ed. J. E. López Pereira (Zaragoza, 1980), p. 35).

[8] Sánchez Albornoz, "Itinerario", 57-60.

[9] Barrau-Dihigo, p. 294.

[10] Estas son las fuentes referidas por Barrau-Dihigo, pp. 294-297. Sánchez Albornoz además de éstas refiere otras fuentes: Sánchez Albornoz, "Itinerario", 63-64.

[11] M. Saavedra, *Estudio sobre la invasión de los árabes en España* (Madrid, 1892).

Galicia, no sería correcta.[12] Para Sánchez Albornoz, mucho menos crítico con las fuentes, la campaña de Mūsā ibn Nuṣayr en el Noroeste ha existido verdaderamente. Gracias al conocimiento de este historiador de la red viaria romana, le ha sido posible trazar el itinerario de los árabes en la Península y, por supuesto, el seguido por en la campaña encuestión. Después de hacer referencia a las dos vias que van de Zaragoza a Astorga (*Asturica Augusta*), considera que la via que va de Briviesca (Burgos) a Astorga es la tomada por Mousa en su ataque a "Galicia".[13] Además, añade que Mūsā ibn Nuṣayr ha llegado hasta Lugo (*Lucus Augusti*) siguiendo la via romana que atravesando el puerto del Cebrero va de Astorga a Lugo. Ello debido a la importancia política, militar y religiosa de Lugo. Desde allí, Mūsā ibn Nuṣayr recibirá la llamada del califa y volverá a Damasco.[14] Tanto la crónica mozárabe del 754 como las otras fuentes árabes no nos informan sobre campañas en el Noroeste y sólo refieren la vuelta de Mūsā ibn Nuṣayr a Damasco y de como éste deja a su hijo ᶜAbd al-ᶜAzīz (m. 98/716) a cargo de los territorios sometidos.[15]

De la lectura de las fuentes, el relato de los hechos y las interpretaciones señaladas podemos deducir con cierta seguridad, aunque con prudencia, que la región entre el Miño y el Duero no ha sido ni atravesada ni saqueada en la campaña de Mūsā ibn Nuṣayr del 96/714. Este, habría atravesado la parte oriental de la actual Galicia y probablemente atacado Lugo, pero el territorio al Sur de los ríos Miño y Sil ha quedado en ese momento libre de la presencia

[12] Barrau-Dihigo, p. 299.
[13] Sánchez Albornoz, "Itinerario", 68.
[14] ibid.
[15] "*Nam in era DCCL anno imperii eius sexto, Arabum LXLIII Muze expletis XV mensibus a principum iussu premonitus Abdelaziz filium linquens in locum*", Anónimo, p. 72.

musulmana. Este interpretación iría al encuentro de lo sostenido hasta ahora por la historiografía tradicional, que hace de todo el valle del Duero una zona "arrasada", desde los primeros momentos de la conquista, por los árabes.

1.2. LA INSTALACIÓN DE LOS ÁRABES Y LOS BEREBERES EN EL NOROESTE Y SUS CONSECUENCIAS (96-123/714-740)

Las fuentes árabes no nos mencionan otras campañas en el Noroeste, sin embargo, sabemos por las fuentes cristianas que ha habido contingentes de árabes y bereberes que se han instalado sobre la línea del Duero. Concretamente las crónicas asturianas del finales del s.III/IX nos informan de estos hechos. Hay también otro tipo de documentos como las cartas y diplómas. Es precisamente, una de estas cartas, considerada como completamente falsa por Barrau-Dihigo, la que nos refiere una campaña de ᶜAbd al-ᶜAzīz en el 716 en la cual habría atacado las ciudades de Oporto, Braga, Tuy y Orense (todas al Sur o sobre la línea del Miño).[16] Incluso si el documento en cuestión es completamente falso, es cierto que ha habido una instalación de guarniciones árabo-bereberes con el objetivo de recoger el tributo. La crónica mozárabe de 137/754 nos dice como ᶜAbd al-ᶜAzīz, el hijo de Mūsā ibn Nuṣayr, impone la paz en toda la Península Ibérica durante tres años a través del pago del

[16] *Era DCCLIII Abdelaziz cepit Olixbonan pacifice, diripuit Colimbriam et totam regionem, quam tradidit Mahameth Alhamar Ibentarif; deinde portucale, Bracham, Tudim, Luccum, Auriam vero depopulavit usque ad solum,*
(citado por Barrau-Dihigo, p. 110 y nota 2).

tributo.[17] Alaor, el sucesor de ᶜAbd al-ᶜAzīz, según la misma crónica, cambia radicalmente la política de paz e inicia una serie de campañas y luego de pactos, organizando la Península a través de la sumisión al tributo.[18] Vemos, por lo tanto, que por las mismas fechas de la información dada por el falso documento, la crónica mozárabe del 137/754 nos habla de campañas militares. No sería sorprendente entonces, ver ahí el reflejo de un verdadero hecho histórico, confirmado por la crónica y considerar el año 96/716 como el de la instalación de guarniciones árabo-bereberes en el territorio entre el Miño y el Duero, sobre las principales ciudades que bordean la via romana de Lisboa a Lugo: Oporto, Braga, Tuy y Orense. Según Barbero y Vigil, los árabes y bereberes se habrían instalado en los mismos lugares ocupa dos por los romanos y los visigodos para controlar los "insumisos" pueblos de la franja cantábrica;[19] y serían esos mismos lugares los tomados por Alfonso I en sus campañas de mediados del s.II/VIII a través de las cuales desmantelería el *limes* del Duero.[20] El tema del *limes* sale del ámbito de este estudio; pero, debemos señalar nuestro absoluto rechazo a

[17] "*Per idem tempus in era DCCLIII, anno imperii eius VIIII, Arabum LXLVII, Abdellazis omnem Spaniam per annos tres sub censuario iugo pacificans*", Anónimo, p. 76.

[18]
> *Huius tempore Alaor per Spaniam lacertos iudicum mittit, atque debellando et pacificando pene per tres annos Galliam Narbonensem petit et paulatim Spaniam ulteriorem vectigalia censiendo componens ad iberiam citeriorem se subrigit, regnans annos supra scriptos,*

(Anónimo, pp. 78-80).

[19] A. Barbero y M. Vigil, "Sobre los orígenes sociales de la Reconquista: cántabros y vascones desde fines del Imperio romano hasta la invasión musulmana", en *Sobre los orígenes sociales de la Reconquista* (Barcelona, 1974), pp. 77-89.

[20] Barbero y Vigil, pp. 77-89.

una tal teoría inaplicable en la Península Ibérica.[21] En todo caso, el hecho a destacar es la presencia a partir del 98/716 de guarniciones árabo-bereberes en el territorio entre el Miño y el Duero con el objeto de recaudar el tributo. El límite norte de estas guarniciones es también un problema complejo y sometido a mitificaciones por parte de la historiografía tradicional. En este contexto se situa el problema de la presencia de un gobernador en Gijón (Asturias). Concretamente las crónicas cristianas nos hablan de la presencia de un tal Munnuza en *Legione*,[22] pero la interpretación del nombre de ese lugar plantea problemas que han sido solventados de manera subjetiva por la historiografía. Así, frente a la duda de leer Gijón o León, Sánchez Albornoz se inclina por la primera hipótesis y defiende la teoría de la presencia musulmana en Asturias y la de un gobernandor en Gijón.[23] Esta interpretación conviene perfectamente a la idea de "Reconquista" defendida por Sánchez Albornoz y a la de la "aplastante victoria" de Pelayo sobre los musulmanes en el año 100/718 en la mítica batalla de Covadonga. Ciertamente esta teoría - como otras que veremos - no escatima en imaginación e incluso el mismo Sánchez Albornoz tiene numerosas dudas sobre su propia

[21] Ello a pesar de que haya medievalistas de gran prestigio que sostienen la teoria de Barbero y Vigil: J. A. García de Cortazar, "Del Cantábrico al Duero", en *Organización social del espacio en la España medieval. La Corona de Castilla en los siglos VIII al XV* (Barcelona, 1985), pp. 43-83; J. M. Minguez, *La Reconquista* (Madrid, 1989).

[22] Sólo la versión erudita de la crónica de Alfonso III utiliza la nomenclatura *Gegione*: "*Per idem tempus in hac regione Asturiensium in civitate Gegione praepositus Chaldeorum erat nomine Munnuza*", *Chroniques Asturiennes*, ed. Y. Bonnaz (Paris, 1987), p. 44. Las otras versiones de la crónica utilizan el término *Legione*: "*Praefatus vero Munnuza, dum factum comperit, ex civitate legione*"; "*Per idem tempus in hac regione Asturiensium in civitate Legione*", *Chroniques Asturiennes*, p. 44.

[23] C. Sánchez Albornoz, *Orígenes de la nación española. El reino de Asturias,* 3 vols. (Oviedo, 1974), 2:171 ff.

interpretación y no puede dar argumentos que la sostengan.[24] En efecto, la presencia musulmana en Asturias y al Norte de la línea formada por Lugo-Astorga-León-Amaya-la Bureba y Alava es muy cuestionable. Para García de Cortazar, ese sería el límite de la presencia musulmana en el Norte de la Península.[25] En nuestra opinión, la lectura atenta de las fuentes permite en efecto establecer ahí el límite de la presencia musulmana. Pero, no en razón del mantenimiento del *limes* como defienden García de Cortazar, Minguez y Barbero y Vigil; sino, por la falta de interés de los árabes hacia unas regiones que no pueden aportarles nada y en la que se encuentran en un medio completamente hostil y totalmente diferente al que estan acostumbrados. En este sentido la "Batalla de Covadonga" y los comienzos de la "Reconquista" han de ser interpretadas como una de las muchas escaramuzas entre los pueblos habitantes de esas zonas montañosas y las guarniciones árabo-bereberes encargadas de recaudar el tributo. De esta forma, la tan mitificada idea de "Reconquista" no es sino el resultado de las tendencias expansivas desde época romana generadas en el interior de las sociedades situadas en la franja montañosa del Norte de la Península.[26] La minoría dirigente romano-goda (los "huidos" de Toledo) utilizaría y aglutinaría en torno a ella esas tendencias expansivas para crear una dinastía y unos móviles políticos en que basar su avance hacia el Sur. Como subraya J. Mattoso, hoy ya no es necesario hacer referencia a la "revuelta de Pelayo" y a la "Batalla de Covadonga" para trazar la historia de este período.[27] Este gran medievalista portugués subraya con gran acierto los aspectos

[24] Sánchez Albornoz, *Orígenes*, p. 173.

[25] García de Cortazar, 48-50.

[26] Minguez, p. 22 ff.

[27] J. Mattoso, "Portugal no Reino Asturiano-Leonés", *Historia de Portugal (dir. J. Mattoso)*, 8 vols. (Lisboa, 1993), 1:441.

ideológicos y subjetivos de las teorías de Sánchez Albornoz y la atracción que estas ideas ejercen en el gran público. De ahí la dificultad para los historiadores actuales de construir una teoría más objetiva y menos mítica que la sostenida por Sánchez Albornoz.

La presencia musulmana en el Noroeste no va a cambiar nada desde el punto de vista de las unidades administrativas existentes ni en el sistema de propiedad territorial, como era norma habitual de los musulmanes en sus conquistas.[28] Así, en el caso concreto del territorio entre el Miño y el Duero las antiguas divisiones administrativas romanas en *conventus* y diócesis van a ser utilizadas por los árabes para establecer los distritos o *Kuwar*, pudiendo situarse probablemente sus capitales en Braga y Chaves. Pequeñas guarniciones han podido ser instaladas en ciudades de importancia estratégica como Oporto y Orense, aunque - insistimos - la presencia musulmana al norte del Duero es muy débil y la arqueología nada nos dice en nuestro estado actual de conocimientos. El único cambio que la invasión árabo-bereber produce al norte del Duero es el del ejercicio del poder, pero el resto del sistema organizativo queda en su lugar.

1.3. LA REVUELTA DE LOS BEREBERES Y DE LOS "GALLEGOS" FRENTE A LOS ÁRABES (123-133/740-750)

Esta débil presencia musulmana al norte del Duero y concretamente en las tierras del Noroeste de la Península va a finalizar como consecuencia de la revuelta de los bereberes en Africa en el 123/740. La crónica mozárabe del 137/754 nos informa del estado

[28] J. Vallvé, *La División territorial de la España musulmana* (Madrid, 1986), pp. 227-251.

de guerra civil en el Norte de Africa a causa de la rebelión de los bereberes que quieren liberarse de la opresión de los árabes. La noticia de esta rebelión en Africa va a provocar la de los bereberes instalados en el Norte de la Península que van a obligar a los árabes a retroceder hacia el Sur del Sistema Central.[29] En efecto, los bereberes españoles van intentar ayudar a los bereberes de Africa y van a dirigir tres ejércitos: uno contra Toledo, otro contra Córdoba y otro contra Ceuta.[30] Pero los bereberes españoles van a ser aplastados en el 124/741 y los bereberes africanos lo serán a su vez en el 125/742 por Abdelmelic. El *Akhbār Majmūʿa*, crónica anónima datada por Sánchez Albornoz del s.II/VIII nos informa sobre la revuelta de los bereberes españoles y de cómo éstos han asesinado a los árabes de "Galicia", de Astorga y de otras ciudades.[31] Este hecho tuvo como consecuencia el vaciamiento de toda esa región de la mayoría de su población musulmana y pone fin a su presencia al Norte del Duero, provocando una verdadera guerra civil entre los musulmanes que quedaron y la población local. Precisamente, en el 128/745 el *Akhbār Majmūʿa* nos informa de la revuelta de los "gallegos" frente a los musulmanes y del avance del reino de

[29] *Eo tempore ... Abdelmelic Spanias preerat. Cumque prefatam tertiam partem intelligit pervenire ad portum, naves retemtsndo eis denegat transitum. Sed uni Spaniae Mauri hoc ita cognoveriunt factum, in prelio congregati cupiunt Abdelmelic prostrare sibi et regnum eius adsumtum transmarinis soldalibus prebere transiti navigerium,*

(Anónimo, pp. 109-110).

[30] *Adque in tres turmas divisi unam ad Toletum prevalidum civitatis murum destinant feriendum, aliam Abdelmelic Cordoba in sede dirigunt iugulandum, tertiam ad Septitanum portum porrigunt ob proventum supra fatorum, qui de prelio Maurorum evaserat, vigilandum,*

(Anónimo, p. 110).

[31] Referido en Barrau-Dihigo, p. 137 y nota 2.

Asturias.[32] En efecto, como consecuencia del abandono de las tierras al Norte del Miño por parte de los bereberes en el 741 el rey Alfonso I (739-757) puede avanzar por el norte de la actual Galicia. Esto es interpretado por las crónicas cristianas como grandes victorias, tratándose en realidad de simples escaramuzas. En el año 750 los árabes son expulsados de Galicia.[33] De esta forma, los árabes habrían permanecido 30 años escasos en el Noroeste peninsular. Es necesario subrayar, además, que no es la capacidad militar o la iniciativa de Alfonso I lo que permite el avance cristiano sino la debilidad de los árabes y la desaparición de sus guarniciones en "Galicia".

2. LAS CAMPAÑAS DE ALFONSO I: UN MITO HISTORIOGRÁFICO

Con el relato de las campañas de Alfonso I por las crónicas de finales del s.III/IX, nos enfrentamos a uno de los problemas más apasionantes de la historia medieval europea. Las crónicas, en sus diferentes versiones, nos señalan como Alfonso I va atacar una serie de ciudades poseidas antes por los árabes y cómo transforma en desierto la zona que se denominaba "Campos Góticos" hasta el Duero, y cómo haciendo esto engrandecía el reino asturiano.[34] La

[32] ibid., pp. 138-139 y nota 2.

[33] ibid., p. 139 y nota 1.

[34] El relato más extenso es el de la crónica de Alfonso III:
Inimicorum ab eo semper fuit audacia compressa, qui cum frate Froilane saepius exercitus movens, multas civitates bellando cepit, id est: Lucum, Tudem, Portugalem, Anegiam, Bracaram Metropolitanam, Viseo, Flavias, Letesman, Salamantican, Numantiam quae nunc vocitatur Zamora, Abelam, Astoricam, Legionem, Septimancas,

consecuencia lógica de estas campañas, según la historiografía tradicional, es la "despoblación" y la "repoblación". Así, según la misma crónica, Alfonso I va a "repoblar" Asturias, Primorias, la Liébana, la Transmiera, Sopuerta, Carranza, Bardulia y la parte maritima de Galicia.[35] Como señala García de Cortazar, se trata de una franja de 300 km de largo entre los rios Navia y Nervión - de Oeste a Este - y entre el mar y las montañas cantábricas - de Norte a Sur.[36] Como se ha indicado, el pasaje correspondiente a las campañas de Alfonso I es el orígen de la teoría de Sánchez Albornoz (que retoma los argumentos del historiador portugués Herculano) sobre el "desierto estratégico del valle del Duero" con el objetivo de situar entre el reino asturiano y el Islam un territorio "vacio". Para ello, Alfonso I, habría llevado con él a la población del valle del Duero.[37] Tanto Menéndez Pidal como Pierre David han expresado sus reticencias a la teoría de Sánchez Albornoz.[38] Con ellos otros historiadores y geográfos portugueses han sostenido y sostienen la imposibilidad del "despoblamiento" total del valle del

> *Saldaniam, Amaiam, Secobiam, Oxoman, Septempublicam, Argantiam, cluniam, Mave, Aucam, Mirandam, Revendecam, Carbonaricam, Abeicam, Cinisariam et Alesanco, seu castra cum villis et viculis suis omnes quoque Arabes gladio interfeciens, Christianos autem secum ad patriam ducens,*

(*Chroniques Asturiennes*, p. 45).

[35] "*Eo tempore populatur Asturias, Primorias, Libana, Transmera, Subporta, Carrantia, Bardulies qui nunc vocitatur Castella et pars maritima Gallaeciae*", *Chroniques Asturiennes*, p. 46.

[36] García de Cortazar, 51.

[37] C. Sánchez Albornoz, *Despoblación y Repoblación en el Valle del Duero,* (Buenos Aires, 1947).

[38] R. Menéndez Pidal, "Repoblación y tradición en la cuenca del Duero", *Enciclopedia Linguística Hispánica*, vol. 1 (Madrid, 1960); Pierre David, *Etudes historiques sur la Galice et le Portugal du vie au XII siècles* (París/Lisboa, 1947).

Duero y, sobre todo, del espacio comprendido entre el Miño y el Duero.[39] En lo que respecta a los historiadores españoles, las tésis de Sánchez Albornoz también han sido puestas en cuestión aunque de una forma menos radical que la de los historiadores portugueses.[40] Las teorías de Sánchez Albornoz, han encontrado también defensores tanto entre los historiadores portugueses como

[39] A. Sampaio, "As 'villas' do Norte de Portugal", *Portugalia*, 1, ii, 1899-1903, 97-128; 281-324; 549-584 y 757-806; A. Jesús da Costa, *O Bispo D. Pedro e a organizaçao da diócese de Braga* 2 vols. (Coimbra, 1959); ibid., "Povoamento e colonizaçao do territorio Vimaranense nos séculos IX a XI", en *Actas do Congresso Histórico de Guimaraes a sua Colegiada,* 2 vols. (Guimaraes, 1981), pp. 135-196; ibid., "A comarca eclesiástica de Valença do Minho (Antecedentes da diócese de Viana do Castelo), en *I Coloquio Galaico-Minhoto* (Ponte de Lima, 1981), pp. 69-240; ibid., "O Bispo D. Pedro e a organizaçao da diócese de Braga", *IX Centenário da dedicaçao da diócese de Braga*, 2 vols. (Braga, 1990), 1:379-434; O. Ribeiro, *A formaçao de Portugal* (Lisboa, 1987); ibid., H. Lautensach, S. Daveau, *Geografía de Portugal*, vol. 3 (Lisboa, 1989); J. Mattoso, "Portugal no reino astur-leonés", pp. 441-565.

[40] A. Barbero y M. Vigil, *La formación del feudalismo en la Península Ibérica* (Barcelona, 1978); J. A. García de Cortazar, *La sociedad rural en la España medieval* (Madrid, 1988); ibid., "Del Cantábrico al Duero", pp. 43-83; ibid., "Organización social del espacio: Propuestas de reflexión y análisis histórico de sus unidades en la España medieval", *Studia Historica* 6 (1988), 195-236; ibid., "Sánchez Albornoz y la Repoblación del Valle del Duero", *Sanchez Albornoz a Debate. Homenaje de la Universidad de Valladolid con motivo de su centenario* (Valladolid, 1993); J. M. Minguez, *La Reconquista* (Madrid, 1989); A. Barrios García, "Repoblación de la cuenca meridional del Duero. Fases de ocupación, procedencia y distribución espacial de los grupos repobladores", *Studia Historica* 3 (1985), 38-82; M. C. Pallares y E. Portela, *Galicia na época medieval* (La Coruña, 1991); M. C. Pallares, "El poblamiento rural gallego en la Edad Media", *Revista Obradorio* 2 (1978), 3-14; ibid., "Organización social del territorio", en *Historia de Galicia*, (La Coruña, 1991) 1:213-232; C. Baliñas, "Gallaecia y la invasión musulmana", en *Historia de Galicia*, (La Coruña, 1991), 1:197-212; ibid., *Do Mito à realidade; A definición social territorial de Galicia na Alta Idade Media (séculos VIII e IX)* (Santiago, 1992).

españoles, aunque su número es muy escaso.[41] En efecto, la casi totalidad de los investigadores que han abordado el problema están contra los argumentos del insigne medievalista español. Frente a las tésis de Sánchez Albornoz sobre los efectos de las campañas de Alfonso I, hay una doble reacción algo contradictoria: por una parte, la forma radical de expresar sus argumentos provoca una necesidad de moderación e incluso de re chazo por parte de los historiadores que han abordado el tema; por otra parte, la enorme erudición, el extraordinario conocimiento de las fuentes y el volúmen de los argumentos de Sánchez Albornoz, provoca una gran admiración y nadie ha osado contradecir uno por uno los argumentos que sostienen la tésis de la "despoblación del valle del Duero". Ha habido, como hemos señalado, tentativas sobre aspectos parciales y hoy en día es unánimemente aceptada la imposibilidad de la "despoblación total" del valle del Duero. Los medievalistas españoles y portugueses a través de los mismos documentos utilizados por Sánchez Albornoz sostienen lo contrario de éste. El resultado es un desarrollo clásico sobre la evolución del poblamiento entre los s.II/VIII y IV/X: el nacimiento de la aldea, la progresiva estructuración (la "organización social del espacio"), la ordenación de los campos a través de la progresiva diferenciación del *ager* y del *saltus* (con la continua reducción de éste), las modalidades de organización espacial (de tamaño, de composición, etc.) de las comunidades aldenas, etc. Todos estos temas, muy interesantes, han perdido todo interés desde el momento en el que un modelo fijado no hace sino repetirse para cada espacio o región

[41] T. Sousa Soares, "O repovoamento do norte de Portugal no século X", *Biblos* 18, i (1942), 5-26; ibid., "Reflexoes sobre a origem e a formaçao de Portugal", *Revista Portuguesa de história* 7 (1957), 193-342; ibid., *A presuria de Portugale (Porto) em 868, seu significado nacional* (Porto, 1967); S. de Moxó, *Repoblación y sociedad en la España cristiana medieval* (Madrid, 1979).

estudiada, con matizaciones de orden cronólogico y tipológico. Ello sin plantearse las cuestiones claves y admitiendo, consciente o insconcientemente, la ruptura sostenida por Sánchez Albornoz a mediados del s.II/VIII. Es decir, que se hace necesario establecer la unión entre la evolución del poblamiento antes y después de mediados del s.II/VIII. Si no ha habido un despoblamiento radical: ¿dónde se ha instalado la población que ha quedado tras las campañas de Alfonso I? ¿Es que es suficiente decir que la geografía montañosa del Norte de Portugal a permitido el refugio de un pequeño número de personas? ¿Es que es suficiente decir que los "castros" han servido de refugio gracias a las murallas que han quedado intactas desde época romana? ¿A falta de pruebas materiales sobre la continuidad de la población (que nadie es capaz de dar), porque es necesario sostener que las palabras *depopulare* y *populare* son simples ficciones jurídicas para apropiarse del derecho de propiedad sobre tierras "sin señor", si poseemos centenas y centenas de documentos que nos dicen lo contrario? En nuestra opinión, no es suficiente con creer. Es necesario presentar pruebas materiales de la permanencia de la población en el valle del Duero después de las campañas de Alfonso I entre el 124/741 y el 137/754. La constatación sobre más de 200 lugares situados entre el Miño y el Duero - por lo tanto, en plena zona tradicionalmente considerada como de "despoblación" - de la permanencia de la población antes y después de las campañas de Alfonso I pone en cuestión las tésis de Sánchez Albornoz. En efecto, sobre esos lugares se sitúan necrópolis datables en el s.II/VIII y que están en relación inmediata con los acontecimientos de ese siglo. La repartición de estas necrópolis en relación a la red de vias romanas y a la lista de ciudades tomadas por Alfonso I (Tuy, Oporto, Anegia, Braga y Chaves), nos muestra como este tipo de inhumaciones (excavadas directamente en la roca) se situan a proximidad pero al mismo tiempo suficientemente alejadas de la red viaria romana (continuamente utilizada a lo largo de la alta Edad Media) y en relación también con la ciudades tomadas y "despobladas" por Alfonso I. Topográficamente, estas necrópolis se situan sobre lugares elevados (bien sean "castros", pequeñas colinas o grandes sistemas montañosos). Es decir, que las consecuencias de las campañas de Alfonso I sobre el habitat se situan sobre un doble plano: por una parte, una desorganización del poblamiento existente, lo que provoca el abandono de los habitats establecidos desde época romana y la desaparición de una organización económica que tiene también su orígen en esa época; por otra parte, una desorganización de las estructuras políticas, administrativas y religiosas (con la huida de las clases dirigentes: obispos y miembros de la aristocracia romano-goda). El primero de los fenómenos ha tenido por consecuencia la instalación de un hábitat inestable basado en una economía de tipo pastoril hasta la llegada de los *pressores*[42] y la reordenación del hábitat, que es lo que la historiografía tradicional ha venido denominando como "Repoblación".

[42] J. A. García de Cortazar, "Del Cantábrico al Duero"; J. Mattoso, "Portugal no reino astur-leonés".

3. LA DESORGANIZACIÓN POLÍTICA, ADMINISTRATIVA Y RELIGIOSA (137-251/754-865).

Es esta la segunda consecuencia de las campañas de Alfonso I entre los años 124/741 y 137/754. En efecto, este vasto territorio sometido a una permanente situación de inseguridad, debe ser considerado como una verdadera zona de frontera entre la cristiandad y el Islam durante el período comprendido entre las campañas de Alfonso I y las de Ordoño I (850-866). Este será el ámbito cronológico escogido para el último apartado de nuestro estudio. Con la llegada a la línea del Miño en el 251/865, se iniciará el vasto proceso de reordenación territorial y de implantación de un poder y unas estructuras políticas estables sobre los territorios limítrofes con el Duero. Pero antes, ese espacio al Sur del Miño será según la historiografía tradicional un *no man's land.*

A partir de las campañas de Alfonso I, el reino asturiano ha proseguido su expansión - "Reconquista", según algunos historiadores - hacia las partes oriental (el norte de la actual Galicia) y occidental (las regiones de Liébana, Transmera, Sopuerta, Carranza y Bardulia) del pequeño reino asturiano. Esta expansión, no ha sido tan fácil como una cierta historiografía nacionalista ha pretendido demostrar.[43] En efecto, la romanización y la integración de esta parte de la Península Ibérica en el organigrama político imperial de Roma ha sido peculiar, como recientes investigaciones ponen de manifiesto.[44] Las estructuras existentes en época pre-romana han sido adaptadas y tenidas en cuenta porla nueva entidad política, pero no han sido suprimidas.[45] Durante la época visigoda,

[43] C. Sánchez Albornoz, *Orígenes de la nación española.*

[44] G. Pereira Menaut, "La formación histórica de los pueblos del Norte de Hispania. El caso de *Gallaecia* como paradigma", *Veleia* 5 (1984), 271-287.

[45] ibid.

esta parte del Norte de la Península nunca llegó a estar totalmente integrada en el reino de Toledo y fueron necesarias diversas campañas militarespara "integrar" dichos territorios en el conjunto peninsular.[46] Tras las campañas de Alfonso I y con la desaparición de los cuadros dirigintes (civiles y eclesiásticos) y la ausencia de un poder político "in situ", las particularidades regionales y los diferentes pueblos asentados en ese territorio van a volver a manifestarse con fuerza. La crónicas asturianas nos hablan más de los esfuerzos del pequeño reino astur por conquistar y someter los territorios que los rodean por el Este y el Oeste, que de la "Reconquista" a base de una sucesión de campañas militares victoriosas. A parte de los enfrentamientos con los musulmanes,[47]

[46] A. Besga Marroquín, *La situación política de los pueblos del Norte de España en la época visigoda* (Deusto, 1983); la crónica de Juan de Biclaro nos informa de las diversas campañas llevadas a cabo por Leovigildo entre el 573 y el 585, para integrar las tierras del Noroeste (el antiguo reino suevo) en el organigrama político-administrativo de Toledo. En el 573, Leovigildo lleva a cabo una campaña en la región de *Sabariam* (zona situada al oeste del rio Sabor, desde Braganza a Torre de Moncorvo) contra el pueblo de los *Sappos*: "*Liuvigildus rex Sabariam ingressus Sappos vastat et provinciam ipsam in suam redigit dicionem duosque filios suos ex amissa coniuge Hermenegildum et Reccaredum consortes Regni facit*", Juan de Biclaro, *Crónica*, ed. J. Campos (Madrid, 1960), p. 83. En el 575, Leovigildo va a integrar la región de los montes *Aregenseds* (identificada con la parte oriental y montañosa de la actual provincia de Orense) frente al noble local *Aspidium*: "*Liuvigildus rex Aregenses montes ingreditur, Aspidium loci seniorem cum uxore et filiis captivos ducit opesque eius et loca in suam redigit potestatem*", de Biclaro, p. 85. En el 576, el obispo de Gerona, nos informa de otra campaña de Leovigildo muy cerca de la base territorial del reino suevo, es decir, al Este del rio Sabor (la región entre la Sierra de Larouco al norte y la Sierra do Marao al Sur): "*Liuvigildus rex in Gallaecia Suevorum fines conturbat*", de Biclaro, p. 86.

[47] Como el enfrentamiento con los musulmanes en Puentedeume (La Coruña), durante el reinado de Fruela (757-768): *Chroniques Asturiennnes*, p. 180. En el 794, en el tercer año del reinado de Alfonso II (791-842), los musulmanes lanzarán una expedición contra Oviedo, que va a destruir la capital,

los monarcas asturianos deberán hacer frente a esa rechazo a ser integrados en la estructura política del reino asturiano. Es lo que las crónicas denominan "revueltas internas". Así, Fruela I (757-768) encontrará la oposición de los "vascones"[48] y la de los gallegos.[49] Estas dos campañas servirán como conquista en el caso de los vascones y de afirmación de poder frente a los gallegos (puesto que

y sólo serán vencidos en el también mítico lugar de *Lutos* (lugar identificado por Sánchez Albornoz cerca del monasterio de Belmonte y de la aldea de Lodos, a proximidad de una via romana) de regreso a sus bases:

> *Huis regni anno tertio Arabum exercitus ingressus est Asturias cum quodam duce nomine Moketi, qui, in loco qui vocatur Lutos, a rege Adefonso praeoccupati, simul cum supradicto duce, septuaginta fere milia ferro atque coeno sunt interfecti,*

(*Chroniques Asturiennes*, p. 50). En el 816, una doble expedición musulmana va atacar de nuevo Galicia, siguiendo la característica estrategia en "tenazas": una expedición desembarcará en el fondo de la ria de Vigo para llegar a Anceo (cerca de Puente Caldelas, Pontevedra); la otra, seguirá probablemente la via romana desde Astorga y entrar en Galicia por el Puerto del Cebrero y llegar a Narón (cerca de Chantada, Lugo). Este doble ataque será rechazado por el ejèrcito de Alfonso II:

> *Huis regni anno tricesimo geminus Chaldaeoprum exercituum Gallaeciam petiit, quorum unos ducum eorum vocabatur Alhabbaz et alius Melik, utrique Alkorescis. Igitur audacter ingressi sunt, audacius et deleti sunt, uno namque tempore unus loco qui vocatur Anceo, alter in fluvio Naron perierunt,*

(*Chroniques Asturiennes*, p. 51). En el 823 las crónicas árabes nos informan de un nuevo ataque sobre la región de Alava; Barrau-Dihigo, *Recherches*, pp. 164-165.

[48] "*Vascones rebellantes superavit atque edomuit. Muniam quandam aduscentulam ex Vasconum praeda sibi seruari praecipiens, postea eam in regali coiugio copulauit, ex qua filium Adefonsum suscepit*", *Chroniques Asturiennes*, p. 47.

[49] "*Gallaeciae populos contra se rebellantes simul cum patria deuastauit*", *Chroniques Asturiennes*, pp. 47-48.

la parte costera de la actual Galicia había sido conquistada unos años antes por Alfonso I). Una vez conquistados militarmente estos territorios Fruela I procederá a su integración política, administrativa, religiosa (apoyándose en el Monasterio de Samos, restaurado por él, y convirtiéndolo en un eje de colonización y estructuración del poblamiento)[50] y de reordenación territorial (apoyándose en monasterios y obispados a través, fundamentalmente, de la nobleza eclesiástica). Durante le reinado de Aurelio (768-774) no habrá "revueltas", pero bajo el de Silo (774-783), nuevamente los "gallegos" manifestarán de nuevo su oposición a la integración política en el reino astur, en el monte *Cupeiro* (en el límite entre las provincias de Lugo y de Asturias, sobre el emplazamiento de un antiguo "castro").[51] En el reinado de Ramiro I (842-850), tendrá lugar la conocida "revuelta" del conde Nepociano, que será sofocada por Ramiro I con un ejército reunido en Lugo y encerrando a Nepotiano en un monasterio hasta su muerte.[52] Esta

[50] "*idem locus (Samanos) de ratione eccelsie sancte fuit, iuxta quod dive memorie dominus Froila ad eandem baselicam perpetim iure perenni afirmavit*", M. Lucas Alvarez, *El Tumbo de San Julián de Samos, s.VIII-XII* (Santiago, 1986).

[51] "*Populos Gallaeciae contra se rebellantes, in monte Cupeiro bello superauit et suo imperio subiugauit*", *Chroniques Asturiennes*, p. 49.

[52]

> *Propter huius absentiam accidit ut Nepotianus, palati comes, regnum sibi tyranice usurpasset .... Itaque Ranimirus ut didicit consobrinum suum Adefonsum a saeculo migrasse et Nepotianum regnum inuasisse, Lucensem ciuitatem Gallaeciae ingressus est, sibique exercitum totius prouinciae adgregauit. Post pacum uero temporis in Asturias irruptionem fecit, cui Nepotianus ocurrit ad pontem fluvii Narceiae, adgregata manu Asturiensium et Vasconum. Nec mora a suis destitutus in fugam est versus captusque a duobus comitibus, Scipione uidelicet et Sonnane, in territoire Premoriense, sic digna factis recipiens, euulsis oculis, monasterio deputatus est ...,*

"revuelta" debe ser interpretada como la oposición entre facciones en el interior del reino asturiano y no como la expresión de rivalidades nacionales entre la parte del reino - Galicia - agrupada entorno a Ramiro I y la que lo está entorno a Nepociano - los astures y vascones. En todo caso es completamente rechazable la idea de ver en estos acontecimientos una expresión de sentimiento nacional.[53] Bien al contrario, estos acontecimientos muestran claramente la oposión que la monarquía astur encontró en los momentos iniciales de su expansión. Esto ha sido denominado por la historiografía tradicional como "Reconquista" y ha sido magnificado y mitificado por las crónicas y toda la documentación posterior para justificar la incorporación de los territorios al Sur del reino astur. Durante el largo período que se extiende entre las campañas de Alfonso I (entre el 124/741 y el 137/754) y la integración de los territorios al norte del Miño, culminada en el reinado de Ordoño I (850-866), el territorio entre el Miño y el Duero (como el resto del espacio próximo a este rio) ha estado sometido a un triple proceso de desorganización: *política*, con la ausencia de un poder político directo sobre ese espacio; *administrativa*, consecuencia del anterior, va a desaparecer el organigrama administrativo regional y local, que será restaurado a finales del s.III/IX a través de una nueva organización administrativa (los *comitatus*, los *comissa*, las *mandationes* y las *terras*) y *religiosa*, con la huida de los obispos hacia las sedes situadas al Norte del Miño, pero con el mantenimiento como señala Pierre David del

(*Chroniques Asturiennes*, p. 53).

[53] Idea sostenida ya en el s.XIX por López Ferreiro y retomada en la actualidad por C. Baliñas, *Do Mito a Realidade. A Definición Social e Territorial de Galicia na Alta Idade Media (Séculos VIII-IX)* (Santiago de Compostela, 1992).

cuadro diocesano y parroquial.[54] La interrupción de las listas episcopales no significa, como sostiene Sánchez Albornoz, la ruptura poblacional. La Arqueología nos muestra hoy todo lo contrario, a través de vestigios materiales de la continuidad de la población y de los edificios de culto.[55]

CONCLUSIÓN

Hemos visto a través de estos tres epígrafes, de una forma breve, como la presencia musulmana en las tierras al Norte del Duero, al menos en el espacio comprendido entre los rios Miño y Duero, no ha tenido lugar desde los primeros momentos de la invasión en el año 93/711. No ha sido hasta a partir del año 98/716, que el espacio en cuestión ha visto la instalación de guarniciones árabo-bereberes. Los conflictos surgidos en las tierras del Noroeste como consecuencia de la rebelión de los bereberes en Africa, prueban esta presencia musulmana. Pero, tan sólo durante 30 años; lo que, evidentemente, no ha provocado el vacimiento demográfico que la historiografía tradicional sostiene. Tan sólo un cambio en la estructura del poder, sustituyendo el organigrama administrativo de la época romano-visigoda por el característico del mundo islámico. El único objetivo: la recaudación del tributo, de lo cual se encargaban las guarniciones instaladas en el valle del Duero. Pero, sin superar la "media luna montañosa" que separa las cumbres del valle.

[54] David, *Etudes historiques*.

[55] Jorge L. Quiroga y Mónica R. Lovelle, "El mundo urbano en la 'Gallaecia' (Conventus Lucense-Conventus Bracaraugustano) entre la Antiguedad tardía y la alta Edad Media (s.IV-X)", en *Actas del IV Congreso Nacional de Arqueología Medieval Española* (Alicante, 1993), pp. 47-57.

Otro aspecto polémico que ha sido abordado, son las campañas de Alfonso I entre el 124/741 y el 137/754 a lo largo del valle del Duero. El objetivo de este monarca no ha sido el desmantelamiento del *limes* romano-visigodo, sino que aprovechando el enfrentamiento entre árabes y bereberes y su desplazamiento al Sur del Sistema Central, conquistará una serie de lugares fortificados de gran importancia estratégica. Estas campañas, tampoco han tenido las consecuencias demográficas señaladas por Sánchez Albornoz. Tanto la atenta relectura de la cumentación, como la geografía y las cada vez más abundantes y concluyentes pruebas materiales aportadas por la Arqueología, indican todo lo contrario. Aunque, no se puedan establecer explicaciones unívocas y globales para todo el valle del Duero y haya que tener muy en cuenta las matizaciones regionales que los estudios en curso están poniendo de manifiesto.

Otro aspecto analizado, es el de la expansión del pequeño reino asturiano, definido tradicionalmente como "Reconquista", y la situación de desorganización política, administrativa y religiosa, entendida como "despoblación" y "repoblación", que se encontró a lo largo de las tierras próximas al valle del Duero. Para ello, hemos partido del estudio de la situación en el Noroeste de la Península (la actual Galicia y el norte de Portugal) entre el final de las campañas de Alfonso I y la conquista de las tierras al norte del Miño, finalizada hacia el 251/865 (puesto que entre este año y el 267/880 - toma de Oporto por el conde Vimara Petri - se procederá a la integtración de las tierras entre ese rio y el Duero). A través de una utilización crítica de las fuentes hemos visto como la "Reconquista" aparece más como un proceso de conquista perfectamente organizado y que ha encontrado una gran oposición en sus inicios (tanto en tierras de la actual Galicia como del Pais Vasco).

En definitiva, sería necesario, bajo nuestro punto de vista, comenzar a eliminar del discurso historiográfico términos como "Reconquista", "despoblación" y "Repoblación", y sustituirlos por otros que reflejen mejor los hechos acontecidos. La lectura crítica de las fuentes nos muestra como una "dinastia de oportunistas", según la expresión de Roger Collins,[56] buscando una justificación religiosa de enfrentamiento con el Islam y conjugando su interés personal con el proceso expansivo de una sociedad en continuo movimiento desde época pre-romana, aprovecha el momento histórico clave del año 93/711 para proceder a un vasto proceso de conquista (por la fuerza de las armas, unas veces, frente a lo que las crónicas llaman "rebeliones internas" y frente al enemigo árabe; por la de los argumentos jurídicos, a través de la *pressura*, en otras ocasiones) perfectamente planificado y estructurado desde la corte de Oviedo.

Esperamos haber contribuido con este trabajo a poner de relieve como la investigación actual puede y debe de superar la herencia del mito recibido a través de una visión idílica de la Historia de España, por el de una realidad mucho más compleja y, precisamente por ello, mucho mas instructiva y enriquecedora.

[56] Roger Collins, *The Arab Conquest of Spain 710-797* (Southampton, 1989), pp. 141-167.

The Hohenstaufen Heritage of Costanza of Sicily and the Mediterranean Expansion of the Crown of Aragon in the later Thirteenth Century

Marta VanLandingham
University of California, Los Angeles

The ability of the medieval queen to affect the policies and government of her realms varied considerably. During the earlier middle ages, when governance was more personal than legally circumscribed, a queen could easily become involved in the course of public decision-making. By the thirteenth century, however, the informal structures of power surrounding kings had begun to develop into well-defined, efficient, and inflexible systems of administration, which many modern historians argue left little room for the influence of family members with no ordained roles in the system.[1] According to the idealised dictates of the Castilian king

[1] For this point of view see for example Marion F. Facinger, "A study of medieval queenship: Capetian France, 987-1237", *Studies in Medieval and Renaissance History* 5 (1968), 3-48, as well as the articles by Lois L. Huneycutt and John Carmi Parsons in *Power of the Weak: Studies on Medieval Women*, ed. Jennifer Carpenter and Sally-Beth MacLean (Urbana, 1995). Miriam Shadis, however, in her unpublished dissertation entitled "Motherhood, lineage, and

Alfonso X's (1226-1284) law code, the *Siete Partidas*, a thirteenth-century queen was expected to be a good wife and mother, to bring honour to her king, her children, and her country, and if possible to increase the wealth of them all.[2] The queens who remained bounded within the limited scope of these duties offer little material for the study of applied queenly power, though their stories may provide insight into many other aspects of the female experience. But what if a powerful royal administration of the thirteenth century, through a fateful confluence of circumstance and ambition, was restructured solely in order to enforce the foreign rights of the queen, to pursue goals to which she was the key? Such was the case of Costanza of Hohenstaufen (d. 1302) deposed heiress to the kingdom of Sicily and wife of the determined and ambitious king Pere the Great (1276-1285) of the realms of Aragon. This paper will examine the sources, the extent, and the limitations of the power she wielded, both through her influence over the king and through her direct public authority, in the course of the expansion of the Crown of Aragon into the Mediterranean.

Costanza was the granddaughter of the Hohenstaufen emperor Frederick II (1198-1250), who held the throne of Sicily as well as the imperial crown. Frederick had been declared deposed and stripped of his titles in 1245 by Innocent IV (1243-1254), as part of the papacy's long struggle to destroy the hated Hohenstaufen "race

royal power in medieval Castile and France: Berenguela de León and Blanche de Castille" (Duke University, 1994), argues convincingly that the many exceptions to this rule of centralisation weakening the power of women, including the examples of Blanche of Castile, Berenguela of Castile and León, Maria of Portugal and Leonor de Guzman, tend to undermine the rule in its entirety. The analysis I provide herein of queen Costanza's political role also serves as evidence against this long-prevailing assertion.

[2] *Las Siete Partidas*, trans. Samuel Parsons Scott (Chicago, 1931), part 2, title 6, laws 1, 2.

of vipers".[3] While Frederick continued to rule at war with the papacy, the holders of the see of St. Peter set about the difficult task of finding a foreign prince willing to fight to take over the Sicilian throne. After Frederick's death, however, his son Manfred (1250-1266) donned the crown of Sicily and ruled with popular support, regardless of the lack of recognition of his status by the pope and his allies. But Manfred also needed allies in the wider world. His only child Costanza was reaching the age when she could be offered to form a marriage alliance. Manfred turned to the Arago-Catalan realms, whose ruling dynasty was quickly growing in international status due to the conquests of king Jaume I (1213-1276), and whose coastal towns played an increasingly important role in Mediterranean trade. The Aragonese king and his favourite son Pere could not help but be drawn to the prospect of union with the storied and well-situated kingdom of Sicily, despite the excoriation of the pope and other powerful crowned heads of Europe. The marriage of Costanza to prince Pere took place in 1262.[4]

From that moment on, the direction Pere's reign was to take was settled. The overriding policy guiding all of his actions and those of his court, from his marriage to his death in 1285, was the expansion of his holdings into the Mediterranean via the implementation of the hereditary rights of his wife to the rulership of the lands of Sicily. This enforcement required a momentous struggle because in June of 1263 pope Urban IV (1261-1264) handed over the rights to the crown of Sicily to Charles of Anjou

[3] David Abulafia, *Frederick II: A Medieval Emperor* (New York, 1992), p. 373.

[4] Daniel Girona, "Mullerament del Infant En Pere de Cathalunya ab Madona Constança de Sicilia", in *Congrés d'Història de la Corona d'Aragó dedicat al rey en Jaume I y a la seua época* (Barcelona, 1909), part 1, pp. 238-241.

(1226-1285), the French king, Louis IX's (1215-1270) youngest brother, offering him every aid in taking the kingdom by force of arms. Charles' forces defeated the Sicilians and killed Manfred at the battle of Benevento in 1266.[5] Charles had successfully usurped the crown of Sicily - in order to retrieve it, Pere would have to face vastly superior numbers under an able leader backed by the greatest powers of Europe. Just before Pere's marriage, king Jaume, under extreme pressure from the pope and from the kings of France and Castile, had made a solemn agreement never to interfere on behalf of Manfred in his struggle to hold his throne, and to ensure his son's neutrality. While Jaume lived, Pere obeyed the king by not becoming openly and actively involved in the battle against Charles of Anjou. But the court of Pere and Costanza soon became a centre for Ghibelline dissatisfaction and for dreams of revenge against the Angevin usurpers. The prince began to plot and to establish a network of conspirators in preparation for the day when his father's constraints would be gone and he could act freely.[6] Once Pere ascended to the throne, still proceeding under a shroud of secrecy, he prepared to act against the Angevins by working to fulfil the conditions which the chronicler Ramon Muntaner reports he considered necessary prior to engagement[7] - security for his lands through the establishment of internal stability and the neutralisation of foreign enemies, and external financing for his ventures, gained

[5] The only other possible claimant to the Hohenstaufen inheritance, Frederick's young grandson Conradin, was executed in 1268 after the battle of Tagliacozzo.

[6] See Helene Wieruszowski, "Der Anteil Johanns von Procida an der Verschwörung gegen Karl von Anjou", in *Politics and Culture in Medieval Spain and Italy* (Roma, 1971), pp. 173-183, and "La corte di Pietro d'Aragona e i precedenti dell'impresa siciliana", ibid., pp. 185-222.

[7] Ramon Muntaner, *Crònica*, in *Les quatre grans chroniques*, ed. Ferran Soldevila (Barcelona, 1983), ch. 37.

through negotiations with the eastern emperor Michael VIII Paleologus (1258-1282). Once the conditions had been met, and as a result of Pere's covert operations combined with Angevin misrule, the people of Sicily rose up in March of 1282 to massacre the French garrison and destroy its fleet in an event known as the Sicilian Vespers. Pere sailed with his fleet to Tunis soon afterwards, ostensibly on a crusade against the infidel. When the people of Sicily realised they could not stand alone against Charles of Anjou and his allies, they turned to Pere, the husband of the kingdom's rightful heir, who was close at hand with a large military force, and offered him the crown. Pere accepted, and spent the rest of his short reign involved in the successful struggle to hold the title against overwhelming odds.[8]

Now the question arises of the extent of Costanza's influence in directing her husband's actions. Did she push him to avenge her family and help her reclaim her rightful heritage, or was Pere impelled by the prospect of expanding into the Mediterranean, to the benefit of his close allies, the merchants, and to the everlasting glory of his own name? In addition to the quasi-legal standards of behaviour presented in the *Siete Partidas*, queens of the thirteenth century were also compared in their comportment to the biblical queen Esther and to the virgin Mary. The images of both these women provided powerful models of feminine intercession with masculine rulers on behalf of their subjects.[9] The ideological leaders of the day therefore held it acceptable if not praiseworthy for queens

[8] The best-known narratives for the Aragonese incursion into Sicily are Michele Amari, *La guerra del Vespro siciliano*, 9th ed. (Milan, 1886), with a new edition by Francesco Giunta, 2 vols. (Palermo, 1969); and Steven Runciman, *The Sicilian Vespers: A History of the Mediterranean World in the Later Thirteenth Century* (Cambridge, 1958).

[9] See articles by Huneycutt and Parsons cited in n. 1.

to exercise their influence in worthy causes. Contemporary chroniclers portray Costanza as wielding her emotions to influence her husband on behalf of her family and her people; for example, Muntaner wrote

> Anyone can imagine the grief with which my lady the Queen, his wife, lived when she knew that her father and her uncles had been killed. And the lord King En Pere loved my lady the Queen more than anything on earth .... And when the lord King heard the queen's lament, it pierced his heart, wherefore he considered all the dangers and decided that revenge should be taken by him.[10]

The Sicilian chronicler Bartolomeo Neocastro portrays a more active campaign, with Costanza incessantly reminding her husband of the torture and murder of her family members, and attributing to cowardice all that delayed the hour of vengeance.[11] Regardless of the reliability of detail in these accounts of her intercessionary efforts, it is clear that her contemporaries considered Costanza a driving force behind her husband's actions, with her earnest anxiety on behalf of those she had left behind greatly magnifying her husband's own desire to intervene.

Moreover, Costanza's physical presence helped create an atmosphere which reminded Pere continuously of his duty and his opportunity. Costanza's coming transformed her husband's court to a much greater degree than most young queens, nearly alone and far from home, could hope to approach. The Neapolitan court in which she had been raised was legendary for its sumptuousness and brilliance. According to the chronicler Ramon Muntaner, "King

[10] Muntaner, ch. 37.

[11] Bartolomeo da Neocastro, *Historia Sicula* (Bologna, 1922), ch. 16.

Manfred lived more magnificently than any other lord in the world".[12] Costanza was able to exert her influence to raise the general standard of luxury at Pere's court: the foods served at the table became much richer in variety, expenses on clothes and other sumptuary items increased for everyone at court, and even bathing began to appear regularly in the household account records.[13] Pere's court developed along lines more fitting for a ruler with imperial ambitions. More importantly, Costanza brought from her homeland many noble companions, such as her nurse's son Ruggero Loria and her close relatives Corrado and Manfredi Lancia, who were all later to prove indispensable in the struggle to reclaim Costanza's inheritance. The three boys began as pages in Costanza's court; by 1283 her foster-brother Loria had been named grand admiral of Catalonia, Manfredi Lancia was captain of Malta and Gozo, and Corrado Lancia was *maestre racional*, a sort of accountant general for the realms.[14] Also, the battle of Benevento and the subsequent conquest of the island brought many Sicilian exiles and refugees to the Arago-Catalan court, further inflaming the atmosphere of fervent passion for revenge and restitution. Among these exiles was Giovanni da Procida, an important courtier to Frederick II and Manfred as well as to Pere, who was instrumental in furthering the

[12] Muntaner, ch. 11.

[13] See primarily Ferran Soldevila, *Pere el Gran. Primera part: L'Infant* (Barcelona, 1950), pp. 161-169. My own research into Costanza's influence on the Arago-Catalan royal court will be presented as part of my dissertation, "The court and the state in the middle ages: the administration and household of Pere the Great of the Crown of Aragon, 1276-1285", UCLA, in progress. János M. Bak also discusses foreign queens bringing "civilising" influences to their new homes in "Roles and functions of queens in Árpádian and Angevin Hungary (1000-1386 A.D.)", in *Medieval Queenship*, ed. John Carmi Parsons (New York, 1993), pp. 13-24.

[14] Wieruszowski, "La corte di Pietro d'Aragona", pp. 192-194.

conspiracy to overthrow the Angevins and who from 1284 served as Pere's chancellor in Sicily.[15] Costanza's intercession on behalf of her people, therefore, was accomplished by more than just her entreaties and the effect of her anguish upon her husband. She also was able to bring to bear the influence of various men who filled important positions in the king's retinue and effected policy from within his administration. If Pere had been of a temperament to see absolutely no use in taking on half the known world in pursuit of a small kingdom in the Mediterranean, all Costanza's urgings might have been for naught. But Pere was determined, methodical, and most of all ambitious; his opportunities for conquest on the mainland had been terminated by his father's treaties, but the Mediterranean still provided opportunities for the bold ruler. With his wife by his side to keep his goals alive and to provide the rationale for conquest, he was willing and able to proceed.

In addition to opportunities for general influence provided by proximity to the king, a medieval queen was also able at times to rule directly. Such opportunities most often arose during regencies, while serving for a husband or son who was away on campaign or during a minority. Very rarely, such as in the case of queen Urraca of Castile-León (1109-1126) and queen Petronila of Aragon (1137-1164), did a queen maintain personal sovereignty over her lands even within the state of marriage.[16] Such a position represented the

[15] ibid. For Procida as chancellor and C. Lancia as *maestre racional*, see Josep Trenchs, *Casa, corte y cancillería de Pedro el Grande (1276-1285)* (Rome, 1991), p. 25 and p. 61.

[16] See Joseph F. O'Callaghan, *A History of Medieval Spain* (NewYork, 1975), p. 258. For more on the reign of Queen Urraca, see Bernard F. Reilly, *The Kingdom of León-Castilla under Queen Urraca, 1109-1126* (Princeton, 1982).

highest degree of political power and public authority to which a medieval woman could aspire.

Costanza herself did serve various times as Pere's regent, most notably within her homeland of Sicily. But why did she have to serve as regent there, when the crown by right of inheritance belonged to her directly, and after her to her sons? Why was Pere crowned king of Sicily, and not prince-consort? Contemporary chroniclers, even when purporting to record Pere's own words, exhibit a clear understanding of the fact that the natural rights to the throne of Sicily belonged to Costanza rather than to Pere. Bernat Desclot portrays Pere as telling the Sicilian ambassadors come to offer him the throne; "You know full well that the kingdom of Sicily is the realm of my lady the Queen and of my sons and that this King Charles gained the land by great injustice".[17] And upon Costanza's arrival in Sicily to rule in her husband's absence, "the people received her as their rightful sovereign with much honor, she being the granddaughter of the Emperor Frederick", according to Desclot.[18] Muntaner writes of the Sicilian ambassadors telling Pere that one of the reasons he should come to the islanders' aid is that

> the island of Sicily and all the kingdom should belong to my lady the Queen, your wife, and after her to the Princes, your sons, because they are of the sacred lineage of the virtuous Emperor Frederick and of the virtuous King Manfred, who were our legitimate lords; and so it follows that my lady Queen Costanza, your wife, should be our

[17] Bernat Desclot, *Llibre del rei en Pere*, in *Les quatres grans chroniques*, ch. 88.

[18] Desclot, ch. 103.

> ruler, and after her your sons and hers should be
> our kings and lords.[19]

The registers of royal documents also show evidence of awareness that the Sicilian crown was by right Costanza's private inheritance. Costanza laid claim to the title of *regina* in her household documents sporadically starting from mid-1265, and after 1268 she was always referred to as the queen, even if solely for propaganda purposes within the ambience of the court. This was done with Pere's full approval, even though he was still only a prince.[20] So why did she later accept the status of queen-consort rather than queen-regnant in her father's kingdom?[21] The only historian, medieval or modern, whom I know to have raised this question answers that Costanza renounced her throne because of an excess of love for her consort and her sons, which argument is not only unconvincing but also fails to lead to a useful line of inquiry.[22] The fuller answer is that the circumstances of time and place left Costanza with little or no choice in this matter.

While the claims of female heirs were strongly discouraged in favour of male primogeniture in the Crown of Aragon, the majority of the precedent for Pere's accession to the throne, through the

[19] Muntaner, ch. 54.

[20] Wieruszowski, pp. 188-89; also Soldevila, pp. 212-213.

[21] For a discussion of the circumstances under which queens reigned in their own right, see Armin Wolf, "Reigning queens in medieval Europe: when, where, and why", in *Medieval Queenship*, ed. John Carmi Parsons (New York, 1993), pp. 169-188. See also Lois L. Huneycutt, "Female succession and the language of power in the writings of twelfth-century churchmen", in *Power of the Weak: Studies on Medieval Women*, ed. Jennifer Carpenter and Sally-Beth MacLean (Urbana, 1995), pp. 189-201.

[22] Lia Pierotti Cei, *Madonna Costanza: Regina di Sicilia e d'Aragona* (Milan, 1995), p. 248. This work in general is a highly romanticised biography of Costanza, written for a popular audience.

inheritance rights of his wife and sons, lies in the Sicilian context. The most immediate example of a queen who lost the right of sovereignty to her inherited kingdom can be found in the case of Costanza's great-grandmother Costanza of Sicily, the posthumous child and eventual heiress of the great Norman king Roger II of Sicily, who delivered her rights over her kingdom to the Holy Roman Emperor Henry VI (1190-1197) upon their marriage. This vast joint inheritance, dangerously encircling the papal territories, came to their son Frederick II and began the long hard-fought battle between the Hohenstaufens and the papacy.[23]

But much more important than this precedent is the fact that in Sicily, unlike in most other parts of Europe, election to the throne by a "parliament" of barons was still at least as important in the constitution of a king as was inheritance. This practice had developed in direct opposition to the claims of the papacy to overlordship of the island. At various times when a pope had attempted to choose the island's ruler in conflict with the wishes of the inhabitants, a congregation of barons and leading townsmen had met to bypass the papal proclamation and crown their own candidate.[24] A king chosen in this way was assured of the immediate and active support of his subjects in defence of his claims. In 1282, therefore, when the Sicilian ambassadors approached Pere to be their king, Costanza's ancestry played only a partial role in their request. The decisive factors were Pere's immediate availability

[23] Abulafia, especially pp. 79-82.

[24] Abulafia, p. 412. In 1130, Roger II was granted a royal crown (having previously only held the title of count) in spite of the wishes of the pope. In 1190, Tancred of Lecce, bastard son of Roger II's oldest son, was given the crown in opposition to the emperor Henry VI's foreign claims. In 1264 Manfred was offered the crown that more legitimately belonged to Conradin, a minor in far-away Germany.

across the way at Tunis with a large fleet at his command, his own renown as a warrior and just king, and the fact that Pere was more than willing to fight their Angevin enemy to the death. The Sicilian parliament proclaimed Pere king because of his availability and military capacity. Costanza, naturally, could not offer these advantages, and would have to be content to serve as queen-consort and sometime-regent in her father's land.

There is no evidence, however, that Costanza was in any way unhappy with her status as queen-consort. It would be naive and anachronistic to speculate that she was, in view of her moderate personality, her strong family feeling, and the medieval expectations of queenship. She was after all undeniably female, and there is no reason to believe that her ideas about the limitations of her gender would have differed remarkably from those which prevailed in her day. But when she did have the opportunity to reign when serving as regent in Sicily, or rather as co-regent with her son Jaume, what sort of ruler was she? How much power could she wield, and did she do so ably? While Costanza also served at various times as co-regent in Pere's home territories, her regency in Sicily provides a better forum for a study of the extent and limitations of Costanza's public authority, as it was of longer duration and highlighted her rule among her own natural subjects. But contemporary accounts of her regency vary quite dramatically.

The background narrative to the events of Costanza's regency begins with the arrival of Pere and his fleet in Sicily at the end of August 1282, to great acclamation and the endowment of a crown. Charles of Anjou withdrew his fleet to the mainland, surrendering the island and allowing Pere to pursue the battle onto the Calabrian coast. In a shrewd attempt to slow and possibly reverse Pere's offensive, Charles appealed to Pere's chivalry and his fiscal concerns and challenged him to a tournament to decide the difficult conflict at one stroke. Pere accepted. The terms were laid out in December for a combat to be held in Bordeaux in June 1283. Pere had to close his operations in Italy and call on his wife and son to come take his place. Costanza arrived in Sicily in mid-April 1283, with Jaume, her second son and heir to Sicily, her younger son Frederic, and her daughter Violant. Pere left for Catalonia soon thereafter. The controlled combat never took place, allegedly due to French treachery, but Pere remained on the mainland thereafter, seriously occupied in fighting off the largest crusade ever mounted against a Christian prince. He defeated the invading forces in 1285, but died soon afterwards, never again having returned to Sicily. Jaume was then crowned king, ending Costanza's official co-regency.

The chroniclers agree that within this co-regency, Pere's basic intent was to leave Costanza in charge, with the experienced Giovanni da Procida at her side to provide counsel and Ruggero Loria to command the continued operations of her fleet. Her son Jaume was fifteen at that time,[25] and was to gain experience as co-regent for when he would inherit the kingdom. Within this initial structure, however, accounts diverge widely regarding how much power Costanza actually exercised, with the two most detailed reports, written by the Catalan chroniclers, representing the poles of the debate.[26] Ramon Muntaner's portrayal of Costanza echoes

[25] Soldevila, pp. 169-75, calculates that Jaume was born on 10 August 1267.

[26] Too small a sample of royal documents survives to be useful in an analysis of Costanza's regency. The chancery registers of the *Archivio di Stato di Palermo*, which would have held the majority of documents authored by Costanza, have largely been destroyed - see that archives' publication, *R. Cancelleria di Sicilia: Inventario sommario, sec. XIII-XIX* (Rome, 1950). What few documents remain are included in Giuseppe La Mantia, *Codice diplomatico dei re aragonesi di Sicilia (1282-1355)* (Palermo, 1918). Records of Pere's

closely the contemporary expectations for queenly behaviour, such as those expressed in the *Siete Partidas*. Muntaner's Costanza is basically powerless, deferring in every decision to her son and to her military and civil advisors. For example, after her arrival in Palermo, Costanza immediately holds council with Procida, Corrado Lancia, the princes, and others who came with her, "and asked them to advise her what to do". They tell her to convene a parliament, where she has Pere's instructional letter read, informing them that Pere

> sent them Queen Costanza, his wife and their natural sovereign; and that he commanded and told them to accept her for their ruler and their queen and obey her in everything she commanded.

After the queen and himself, they were to look to Jaume as their lord. Costanza, however, quickly has Procida speak out for her, commanding instead that

> henceforth, you look upon the Prince En Jaume as your lord, in the place of the lord King his father, and in hers; because, as it is not given to her to go about the territories, he will have to visit all the places as lord, and he will have to go to the wars and to all affairs, as well as to feats of arms and to other problems.[27]

transactions regarding Sicily, including very rarely instruction letters to his wife and son, have been gathered by Isidoro Carini in *De rebus regni Siciliae* (Palermo, 1882), and in *Gli archivi e le biblioteche di Spagna in rapporto alla storia d'Italia in generale e di Sicilia in particolare*, 2 vols. (Palermo, 1884). These few surviving royal documents which involve Costanza touch only upon very minor matters, necessitating that we investigate her regency through the analysis of contemporary narrative chronicles.

[27] Muntaner, ch. 99.

After that announcement, Costanza almost disappears from the deeds of the chronicle, except as an intercessor on behalf of a group of her natural subjects taken prisoner fighting for the Angevins. Costanza pleads eloquently and successfully with her son for their lives, causing the "fame and great renown of my lady the queen's sanctity to go through all the land and afterwards throughout all the world".[28] Muntaner's Costanza embodies the Marian ideal of holy and gentle intercession so perfectly, with so little individual humanity shining through, that one may question whether Muntaner was interested in the queen at all other than as an ideal.

In stark contrast to Muntaner's most merciful and ladylike queen, Bernat Desclot paints a picture of Costanza as a strong, bold, respected military as well as civil leader. All of the many successful actions of the fleet are commanded by her - Loria and the others act upon her strategies and quick decisions. One example can be found in the story of the operation mounted to take the island of Malta. While her men are laying siege to the castle there, Costanza learns that Charles of Anjou is sending a fleet from Marseilles to relieve the island. Desclot writes,

> when my lady the Queen learned of this affair, she had a light swift ship of forty oars made ready and sent it to Malta to the soldiers that she had sent there earlier, commanding them to abandon the siege and to establish themselves within the city of Malta and to keep good watch, since the galleys of king Charles were on their way .... Then my lady the Queen caused twenty-two galleys to be manned with the Catalans and the Almogàvers who had been left at Messina .... When these

[28] Muntaner, ch. 105.

> galleys were armed and in readiness, my lady the Queen summoned into her presence the admiral and the captains of the ships and commanded them to sail along the shores of Sicily and to search out the galleys of the Provençals and, if they did not find them there, to chase them on to Malta.[29]

Because of Costanza's quick actions, Loria succeeds in defeating the Provençal fleet and completing the conquest of Malta. Desclot's recounting of the deeds occurring on the Sicilian front during Pere's absence is filled with such tales of the effectiveness of the queen regent.[30] Desclot, in contrast to Muntaner, never reverts to the standard *topoi* of queenship when writing about Costanza.

Of the two contemporary Catalan chroniclers, other evidence shows that Desclot is likely to provide a much more accurate representation of Costanza's range of power and ability. While both Desclot and Muntaner were contemporaries of our monarchs and were familiar with the events of the reign through their positions at court, Desclot was the elder of the two. His chronicle was recorded shortly after Pere's death, while Muntaner's was not begun until forty years later. For this and other reasons, Desclot's chronicle is known to be more consistently reliable, although both are valuable primary sources. Muntaner's accuracy specifically for the events of Sicily is highly questionable, and in many instances his anecdotes can be proven by recourse to the royal registers to have been entirely invented, while Desclot is often considered the authority for these episodes. For example, Muntaner wrote that Pere had already returned to Barcelona before sending out his wife and children to Sicily, while in fact Pere and Costanza overlapped on the island for

[29] Desclot, ch. 110.

[30] See, for example, Desclot, ch. 114, 119, 120, 129.

at least several days.[31] Also, Desclot's version is supported in several instances by Italian chroniclers of the time, in particular by Bartolomeo Neocastro, Saba Malaspina, and Brunetto Latini.[32] Finally, logic dictates that a queen in the prime of her life, raised and educated at the sophisticated court of her father and experienced in regency in the Aragonese realms, held in esteem by her husband and revered by her Sicilian people as their natural sovereign, would be a much more likely ruler for a kingdom at war than her inexperienced son. Accepting in overview, if not necessarily in detail, Desclot's view of Costanza as an active monarch, it is quite clear that she wielded her power effectively, efficiently, and well, gaining the respect of most who came in contact with her.

The history of medieval queenship includes too vast a number of variations and exceptions to be easily condensed into a coherent narrative. Women's lives, their rights, duties and obligations, the powers they could exercise, all these factors were dependent upon combinations of circumstances - including region, era, class, and individual personality - nearly as numerous as there were human experiences. In this short study I have attempted to analyse the extent of the power of a woman whose queenship had a much greater affect on the policies and fate of her kingdom than that of

[31] Ferran Soldevila, in his notes to Muntaner's chronicle which he edits in *Les quatre grans chroniques*, refers various times to Muntaner's power of invention as exhibited regarding various details of the Sicilian adventure; see for example ch. 98, n. 1.

[32] Bartolomeo Neocastro, *Historia Sicula*; Saba Malaspina, *Rerum Sicularum Historia*; Brunetto Latini, *Il tesoro*. An example of agreement with Desclot regarding Constanza's active rule can be found in the latter, in chapter 157, where he writes, "When Queen Costanza ... discovered [the Angevin fleet had sailed from Marseilles], she immediately ordered that 40 galleys be armed in Messina and sent to the gulf of Naples, in order to encounter King Charles and his men as soon as they arrived".

many other medieval queens, due to her ancestry and upbringing, her innate ability to lead, and the respect she engendered in her family and her Sicilian people. Because of who she was, the crown of Aragon dramatically expanded its holdings across the Mediterranean. That is not to say, of course, that her husband's capabilities, strengths, and ambitions were less decisive in this enterprise, but still Costanza's contribution is highly significant. The interesting, eventful, and troubled life of Dante's "good Costanza",[33] "mother of the pride of Sicily and Aragon",[34] is worthy of much further study in order to enlighten our understanding of the range of medieval queenship.

[33] Dante Alighieri, *La divina commedia: Purgatorio*, ed. and trans. John D. Sinclair (New York, 1961), canto 3, line 143.

[34] *Purgatorio*, canto 3, lines 115-116.

Heresy and Holiness in a Mediterranean Dynasty: the House of Barcelona in the Thirteenth and Fourteenth Centuries

Nikolas Jaspert
Freie Universität Berlin

Towards the end of his life, around the year 1340, Don Juan Manuel (1282-1348), the son of prince Manuel of Castile (d. 1284), wrote the *Libro de armas*.[1] The book is one of the lesser known works by the author of *El conde Lucanor*, owing to its autobiographical character and polemic slant, but literary fame will hardly have been the main reason the nobleman had for writing it. In fact, its object was to underline the royal descent of the Manuelines and their right to a realm of their own, which, according to the author, had

[1] Don Juan Manuel, *Obras completas*, 2 vols., Biblioteca Románica Hispánica IV, textos 15, ed. José Manuel Blecua (Madrid, 1981-1983), pp. 117-141; Andrés Giménez Soler, *Don Juan Manuel. Biografía y estudio crítico* (Zaragoza, 1932); Germán Orduna, "El libro de las armas: clave de la justicia de Don Juan Manuel", *Cuadernos de Historia de España* 67-68 (1982), 259-268; Daniel Devoto, *Introducción al estudio de Don Juan Manuel, y en particular de El Conde Lucanor. Una bibliografía* (Madrid, 1972), pp. 247-251; María Cecilia Ruiz, *Literatura y política: el Libro de los estados y el Libro de las armas de Juan Manuel*, Scripta Humanistica 57 (Potomac, 1987), pp. 58-131.

wrongfully been withheld from them by Alfonso X, *el Sabio* (1252-1284).[2] Don Juan Manuel proves his point in three *razones*: in the first he describes the illustrious weapons he inherited from his father, in the second he expounds why the Manuelines are allowed to arm knights - a right reserved for kings alone - and in the third he recounts a conversation he had with king Sancho IV (1284-1295) at the latter's death-bed. Though only remotely connected, the *razones* combine to show the lineage of the Manuelines as morally superior to the royal family, in whose stead they are consequently better fit to reign. Secondary sources and the author's memories are intricately interwoven to form the picture of a family deliberately defrauded of its rightful claims. Methodically speaking, in certain aspects the *Libro de armas* is nothing less than an early example of oral history in the middle ages: Don Juan Manuel frequently retells stories, giving references as to where and by whom they were originally related.[3] The tales touch a wide spectrum of topics, and most of them recount events which occurred between the birth of the author's father in 1234 and death of his uncle, king Sancho IV of Castile, in 1295. One of them tells the touching tale of a virtually unknown thirteenth-century Catalan princess, Sancia.[4]

[2] On Juan Manuel's importance as a feudal lord see Aurelio Pretel Martín, *Don Juan Manuel, señor de la llanura. Repoblación y gobierno de la Mancha albacetense en la primera mitad del siglo XIV* (Albacete, 1982); Reinaldo Ayerbe Chaux, "Don Juan Manuel y la Corona de Aragón. La realidad política y el ideal de los tratados", in *Don Juan Manuel, VII centenario* (Murcia, 1982), pp. 17-26; Gregorio Sánchez Doncel, "Un gran señor medieval: Don Juan Manuel", *Anales de la Universidad de Alicante. Historia Medieval* 1 (1982), 87-116.

[3] Alan Deyermond, "Cuentos orales y estructura formal en el Libro de las Tres Razones", in *Don Juan Manuel: VII Centenario* (Murcia, 1982), pp. 75-88; Béatrice Leroy, "Le prince écrivain politique: l'infant Don Juan Manuel de Castile", in *Les princes et le pouvoir au moyen âge* (Paris, 1993), pp. 91-105.

[4] Don Juan Manuel, pp. 127-128.

A daughter of king James I (1213-1276), *el Conqueridor*, Sancia appears to have refused to marry and become part of the wide-spread web of matrimonial ties which connected the House of Barcelona with the principal dynasties of Christendom.[5] Instead, she retired to Acre, the last bastion of the crusader states, where she lived and worked in a hospice caring for pilgrims, without however betraying her identity: "Et ovo ... la infanta Sancha, que nunca caso. Et oy dezir que muriera en el ospital de Acre o estava desconocidamente serviendo a los romeros".[6] The inhabitants of Acre were miraculously told of her death by the bells of the town, which began to chime of their own accord. Upon arriving at the hospital, they found the corpse with a letter firmly clenched in its fist. Only when the patriarch or bishop - the author is not quite sure - ordered Sancia to open her hand did the corpse release the letter which informed the bystanders of the true identity of the deceased:

> ... quando esta infanta fino en Acre en el ospital que se movieron todas las campanas de la villa a tanner por su cabo, commo las tannen quando ay algun cuerpo finado, et las gentes ... fallaron que [the corpse] tenia una carta en la mano; et quando

[5] See Odilo Engels, "König Jakob I. von Aragón und die internationale Politik im 13. Jahrhundert", in *X Congreso de Historia de la Corona de Aragón. Jaime I y su época. Ponencias* (Zaragoza, 1979), pp. 213-240. On female refusal to play a part in matrimonial politics see Marie Thérèse Caron, "Mariage et mesalliance: la difficulté d'être femme dans la société nobiliaire à la fin du moyen âge", in *La femme au moyen-âge*, eds. Michel Rouche and Jean Heuclin (Maubeuge, 1990), pp. 315-326; Claudia Opitz, *Evatöchter und Bräute Christi. Weiblicher Lebenszusammenhang und Frauenkultur im Mittelalter* (Weinheim, 1990), pp. 15-30. Milagros M. Rivera, "Parentesco y espiritualidad femenina en Europa. Una aportación a la historia de la subjetividad", in *Santes, monges i fetilleres. Espiritualitat femenina medieval*, Revista d'Historia medieval 2 (Valencia, 1991), pp. 29-51.

[6] Don Juan Manuel, p. 127.

> la quisieron tomar para leer non gela pudieron sacar de la mano fasta que vino un gran perlado, non me acuerdo si oy dezir si fuera patriarca o obispo. Mas bien me acuerdo oy dezir que fuera perlado et desque vio que la carta non gela podian sacar de la mano, mando en virtud de sancta obediencia que diese la carta. Et ella ... abrio la mano et tomo el perlado la carta et leola a todo el pueblo et fallo que dezia la carta commo era la infanta donna Sancha, fija del Rey don Jaymes de Aragon y la Reyna donna Violante[7] ...

The modern historian may be prone to dismiss this story as an apologetic legend, invented to foster the importance of a specific lineage. Indeed, the political stance of the *Libro de las armas* in favour of the Manuelines is absolutely indisputable and the influence of literary models, such as the life of Saint Alexios, well known at the time through the *Legenda aurea*[8] or even contemporary *gestae*, is clearly evident in the story.[9] The few surviving hagiographic sources of the Crusader states do not

[7] Don Juan Manuel, pp. 127-128.

[8] Geneviève Brunel, "Les saints franciscains dans les versions en Langue d'Oc et Catalan de la *Legenda Aurea*", in *Legenda Aurea: sept siècles de diffusion*, Actes du colloque international, Québec, 11-12 mai 1983 (Montreal, 1986), pp. 103-112; Stefano Maria Cingolani, "La vida de Sant Alexi catalana: noves rimades didattico-religiose fra Catalogna e Occitania", *Romania Vulgaria Quaderni* 12 (1988), 79-112; Dominique de Courcelles, *Les histoires de saints, la prière et la mort en Catalogne* (Paris, 1990), pp. 4-7, 21.

[9] *Acta Sanctorum, Iulii* (Venice, 1748), 4:238-270; Martí de Riquer, "La leyenda de la infanta Doña Sancha hija de Don Jaime el Conquistador", in *Homenaje a Millás Vallicrosa*, 2 vols. (Madrid, 1954-56), 2:229-41. De Riquer's main interest lies in defining the literary models for the story of Princess Sancia, which he sees in works such as *quatre fils Aymon* (Renaut de Montauban) or *Li coronemenz* and of course in the legend of Saint Alexios.

mention the princess;[10] neither does modern research concerning the Hospitallers' *donatae, conversae et sorores*, even though the documentary sources for their history are relatively abundant in Catalonia.[11] However, there could well be more to Sancia's life as reported by Don Juan than a mere dynastic legend. For one, praise of one's ancestors cannot have been the reason for simply inventing

[10] Jean Richard, "L'Orient latin et le monde des missions", in *Hagiographies. Histoire internationale de la littérature hagiographique latine et vernaculaire en Occident des origines à 1550, I*, ed. Guy Philippart (Turnhout, 1994), pp. 189-199.

[11] "La Spagna offre il materiale documentario più cospicuo per una trattazione sulle *Donate*" (Lorenzo Tacchella, *Le "Donate" nella storia del Sovrano Militare Ordine di Malta* (Verona, 1987), p. 10). On the four female houses of the order in Catalonia and Aragon (Sigena, Cervera, Alguaire and Siscar) see (with further references) ibid., 10-30; Tommasi, *Uomini e donne*, 199-201; Jesus Alturo i Perucho, "Marquesa de la Guàrdia, fundadora, comanadora i benefactora del monestir femení de la Mare de Deu d'Alguaire de l'orde de Sant Joan de Jerusalem", *Ilerda* 50 (1992-93), 51-54. On general questions concerning the female branches of the military orders, particularly the Hospitallers, see Alan Forey, "Women and the military orders in the twelfth and thirteenth centuries", *Studia Monastica* 27 (1987), 63-92; Francesco Tommasi, "Il monastero femminile di San Bevignate dell'ordine di San Giovanni Gerosolimitano (secoli XIV-XVI)", in *Templari e Ospitalieri in Italia. La Chiesa di San Bevignate a Perugia*, eds. Mario Roncetti, Pietro Scarpellini and Francesco Tommasi (Milano, 1987), pp. 53-78; Lorenzo Tacchella, *Le 'Donate' nella storia del Sovrano Militare Ordine di Malta* (Verona, 1987); Francesco Tommasi, "Uomini e donne negli ordini militari di Terrasanta. Per il problema delle case doppie e miste negli ordini giovannita e teutonico (sec. XII-XIV)", in *Doppelklöster und andere Formen der Symbiose weiblicher und männlicher Religiosen im Mittelalter*, Berliner Historische Studien 18, Ordensstudien 8, eds. Kaspar Elm and Michel Parisse (Berlin, 1992), pp. 177-202; Kaspar Elm, "Die Spiritualität der geistlichen Ritterorden des Mittelalters. Forschungsstand und Forschungsprobleme", in *"Militia Christi" e crociata nei secoli XI-XII*, Atti della undecima settimana internazionale di studio, Mendola, 28.8.-1.9.1989, Miscellanea del Centro di Studi Medioevali 13 (Milan, 1992), pp. 477-518, pp. 499-501.

the tale, as the author was not an offspring of the House of Barcelona: although his father had been betrothed to one of James I's daughters in his first marriage, Juan Manuel was a son of prince Manuel's second wife and consequently no direct relative to Sancia. Also, other members of the Catalano-Aragonese royal family are held in rather low esteem in the *Libro de las armas*, like James' second daughter, who married Alfonso X, the ultimately negative figure of the book. And finally, the use of literary topoi was in no way uncommon among medieval hagiographers and therefore does not contradict Sancia's life of humble charity.[12]

Don Juan Manuel himself does word his narrative rather cautiously and even seems to question the absolute truth of the story in all its literary embellishment: "Todo esto non lo digo yo afirmando que en toda guisa fue todo asi, mas digo que me paresce que lo oy en esta manera".[13] However, he never doubts it outright,

[12] André Vauchez, "L'influence des modèles hagiographiques sur les représentations de la sainteté dans les procès de canonisations (XIIIe-XVe siècles)", in *Hagiographie, cultures et sociétés, IVe-XIIe siècles*, Actes du colloque organisé à Nanterre et à Paris, 2-5 mai 1979 (Paris, 1981), pp. 585-596; Michael Goodich, *Vita Perfecta: The Ideal of Sainthood in the Thirteenth Century*, Monographien zur Geschichte des Mittelalters 25 (Stuttgart, 1982), pp. 7, 59-68; Thomas J. Hefferman, *Sacred Biography. Saints and their Biographers in the Middle Ages* (New York and Oxford, 1988), pp. 28-31; Friedrich Prinz, "Der Heilige und seine Lebenswelt. Überlegungen zum gesellschafts- und kulturgeschichtlichen Aussagewert von Viten und Wundererzählungen", in *Santi e demoni nell'Alto Medioevo (secoli V-XI)*, 36 Settimana del Centro Internazionale (Spoleto, 1989), pp. 285-318. Gábor Klaniczay, "Legends as life-strategies for aspirant saints in the later middle ages", in idem, *The Uses of Supernatural Power. The Transformation of Popular Religion in Medieval and Early-Modern Europe*, (Oxford, 1990), pp. 95-110.

[13] Don Juan Manuel, p. 128.

and he goes to great length to name his sources.[14] Who, then, was princess Sancia? Did she exist at all? Works on the life and family of James I have hitherto referred exclusively to the *Libro de las armas* to prove that she did,[15] and the king himself does not mention her in his autobiography, the *llibre dels feits*.[16] Don Juan Manuel, however, has no doubts in this respect,[17] and indeed, contemporary documents prove that James I did have a daughter of that name. She is first mentioned in 1248 while still a child and also figures in her

[14] "... et paresceme oy ... o a la infanta donna Ysabel, fija de Rey de Mallorcas [and consequently Sancia's niece], que fue la primera muger con que yo casé, o duennas de su casa ..." (Don Juan Manuel, p. 128). The historiographic worth of the *Libro de las armas* is not beyond dispute. But though the work contains considerable faults on some points, it is trustworthy on others. In favour of the *Libro* as a historical source, see Orduna, p. 260, Ruiz, pp. 73-76.

[15] Geronimo Zurita, *Anales de la Corona de Aragón*, eds. Antonio Ubieto Arteta and Laureano Ballesteros Ballesteros, 3 vols. (Valencia, 1968; published originally in Zaragoza, 1669), 3:174; Próspero Bofarull i Mascaró, *Los Condes de Barcelona vindicados y cronología y genealogía de los reyes de España, considerados como soberanos independientes*, 2 vols. (Barcelona, 1836), 2:236; Ferran Soldevila, *Vida de Jaume I el Conqueridor*, 2nd ed. (Barcelona, 1969), pp. 25, 263, 309.

[16] Jaume I, *Crònica o llibre dels feits*, Les quatre grans cròniques, Biblioteca Perenne 26, ed. Ferràn Soldevila, 2nd ed. (Barcelona, 1982), pp. 1-402. However, he frequently referred to members of his family, especially to Sancia's mother, Violant (see Robert I. Burns, "The spiritual life of James the Conqueror, king of Arago-Catalonia, 1208-1276. Portrait and self-portrait", *Catholic Historical Review* 62 (1976), 1-35. On the family life of the king, see also Cynthia L. Chamberlin, "The 'Sainted Queen' and the 'Sin of Berenguela': Teresa Gil de Vidaure and Berenguela Alfonso in documents of the crown of Aragon, 1255-1272", in *Iberia and the Mediterranean World in the Middle Ages: Studies in Honor of Robert I. Burns S. J.*, The Medieval Mediterranean 4, ed. Larry Simon (Leiden, 1995), pp. 303-321.

[17] "... et ovo fijas la infanta donna Violante ... et la infanta Constança ... et la infanta donna Sancha ..." (Don Juan Manuel, p. 127).

mother's will in 1251,[18] in which she inherited part of the queen's jewellery. By that time, she was obviously regarded as fit for matrimony: on 30 May 1251, her father obtained permission from pope Innocent IV to marry off Sancia and her brother Peter, the condition being that the blood ties to the respective spouses not be too close.[19] Two years later she figured as a prospective wife to Theobald of Navarre in a peace treaty signed between the latter and James I.[20] Ultimately however, Sancia seems to have chosen not to form part of the royal marriage-market. By 1275, Sancia had died, for in that year her remains were transferred together with those of her mother to the Cistercian monastery of Vallbona, where her sarcophagus can be seen to this day.[21] Thus, if Sancia existed and if there are no compelling grounds for not taking the core of Don Juan Manuel's account at its face value, then one should further ask where the roots for the behaviour of the Catalan princess lay. On leaving the court and caring for the sick, on renouncing worldly possessions and seeking a life of poverty and humbleness, did she follow an established or even archetypal model of royal piety? Is hers an unusual or even unheard-of case?

[18] Ferran Soldevila, *Pere el Gran, primera part: l'infant* (Barcelona, 1950), p. 26; Ambrosio Huici Miranda, Colección diplomática de Jaime I (Valencia 1916); *Documentos de Jaime I de Aragón*, eds. Ambrosio Huici Miranda and Maria Desamparados Cabanes Pecourt, 3 vols. (Valencia, 1976-1978), nr. 585: "Item demito joyas meas, quas habeo in Cardenio et ubicumque alibi et lapides preciosos filiabus meis Constancie, Sancie, Marie, Helisabet, dividendas inter eas ad arbitrium domini regis"; Riquer, p. 230.

[19] *Les registres d'Innocent IV*, Bibliothèque des Écoles Françaises d'Athènes et de Rome, Sér. 2, 4, ed. Élie Berger, 4 vols. (Paris, 1884-1897), 2:218, nr. 5230.

[20] *Documentos de Jaime I de Aragón*, nr. 624.

[21] Josep J. Piquer i Jover, *Abaciologi de Vallbona. Història del monestir, 1153-1990* (Vallbona de les Monges, 2nd ed. 1990), p. 96.

It is well known that the middle ages saw a considerable number of kings and queens, princes and princesses who turned their backs on secular life to enter monastic institutes or embrace other forms of religious life. In fact, founding a monastery and joining it late in life to lead it as abbess or prioress can be described as a specific form of piety demonstrated by many noblewomen, not necessarily all of royal standing. Needless to say, other aspects, such as ensuring a socially accepted life in old age as well as political considerations, may also have led to, or eased, taking this step. Economic interests will, if at all, have only played a secondary role. One need not look beyond the Pyrenees to find examples of such forms of royal patronage and monastic life: Sancia's great-grandmother, queen Sancia of Castile, wife to Alfonso II, *el Casto* (1162-1196), founded the monastery of Sigena in eastern Aragon in 1188 and assigned it to the order of Saint John of Jerusalem. After binding herself to her foundation through the tie of *confraternitas*, she was termed *soror* of the house in August 1196, four months after her husband's death. Although she did not remain in Sigena for any length of time, queen Sancia did exercise the role of superior to the community: she represented it in its contacts with the pope, the Order of Saint John, and with the king, she patronised it extensively and controlled its financial affairs.[22]

But cases like those of queen Sancia differed substantially from princess Sancia's in that the latter is said to have chosen a life of poverty and self-humiliation. Traditional forms of royal piety evidently were no model for her. The ideal she was reported to have

[22] M. de Pano, *La santa reina doña Sancha, hermana hospitalaria fundadora del monasterio de Sijena* (Zaragoza, 1943); Antonio Ubieto Arteta, "La documentación de Sigena (1188-1300)", *Saitabi* 15 (1965), 21-36; Antonio Ubieto Arteta, *El real monasterio de Sigena, 1188-1300* (Valencia, 1966), pp. 15-65.

followed was one of her own time and day, one of a new spirituality which was changing the face of the church, a form of spirituality closely connected to early Franciscanism. Personal poverty, asceticism, and charity were the fundamental ideals of this new form of religious life. If one wants to find cases of similarly radical abnegation, one has to turn to the *sancti moderni*[23] like Saint Claire (d. 1253)[24] or Saint Ubaldesca (d. 1206)[25] - both of them women who gave up all personal belongings in order to lead a life of poverty and, particularly in the case of the Pisan saint, of charity.

But Claire and Ubaldesca were neither princesses nor queens; were there no members of royal families on whom Sancia could

[23] On this change in spirituality and sanctity see Ortrud Reber, *Die Gestaltung des Kultes weiblicher Heiliger im Spätmittelalter. Die Verehrung der Heiligen Elisabeth, Klara, Hedwig und Brigitta* (Hersbruck, 1963); André Vauchez, *La sainteté en occident aux derniers siècles du moyen age d'après les procès de canonisation et les documents hagiographiques*, Bibliothèque des Écoles Françaises d'Athènes et de Rome, Sér. 1, 241 (Rome, 1981), pp. 206-208, 234-236, 450-455; František Graus, "Mittelalterliche Heiligenverehrung als sozialgeschichtliches Phänomen", in *Heiligenverehrung in Geschichte und Gegenwart*, eds. Peter Dinzelbacher and Dieter R. Bauer (Ostfildern, 1990), pp. 86-102; Anna Benvenuti Papi, *"In Castro Poenitentiae". Santità e società femminile nell'Italia medievale*, Italia Sacra 45 (Rome, 1990); Giulia Barone, "I Santi poveri", in *La conversione alla povertà nell'Italia dei secoli XII-XIV*, Atti del 27 convegno storico internazionale, Todi, 14-17 ottobre 1990 (Spoleto, 1991), pp. 355-368; Gábor Klaniczay, "I modelli di santità femminile tra i secoli XIII e XIV in Europa centrale e in Italia", in *Spiritualità e lettere nella cultura italiana e ungherese del basso medioevo*, eds. Sante Graciotti and Cesare Vasoli (Florence, 1995), pp. 75-109.

[24] Rosalind B. Brooke and Christopher N. L. Brooke, "St. Clare", in *Medieval Women*, Studies in Church History, Subsidia 1, ed. Derek Baker (Oxford, 1978), pp. 275-288; Marco Bartoli, *Chiara d'Assisi*, Bibliotheca Seraphico-Capuccina 37 (Rome, 1989); *Chiara di Assisi*, Atti del 20 convegno internazionale della Società Internazionale di Studi Francescani (Spoleto, 1993).

[25] *Acta Sanctorum, Maii* (Venice, 1739), 6:199-202; I. Felici, *Vita di Santa Ubaldesca Taccini* (Pisa, 1956).

have modelled herself? Indeed, one princess and saint stands out among the *saintes reines du moyen âge*[26] as the paradigm of charitable service and self-humiliation: Saint Elisabeth of Hungary (d. 1231).[27] The daughter of Andrew II of Hungary (1175-1234) and wife to Louis IV (1286-1347), Landgrave of Thuringia, not only founded a hospital at Marburg, but also joined it as a *soror in saeculo*, humbling herself in a hitherto unknown fashion while she cared for the sick and poor. A princess from central Europe who spent her life in Hungary and Thuringia may seem a distant model for a person living on the western shores of the Mediterranean, but the relationship between the two was closer than it might seem at first glance. The two charitable princesses were not only kindred

[26] Goodich, pp. 186-191; Robert Folz, *Les saintes reines du moyen âge (VIe-XIIIe siècles)*, Subsidia Hagiographica 76 (Bruxelles, 1992); Patrick Corbet, *Les saints ottoniens. Sainteté dynastique, sainteté royale et sainteté féminine autour l'an Mil*, Beihefte der Francia 15 (Sigmaringen, 1986); Klaus Schreiner, "Hildegard, Adelheid, Kunigunde. Leben und Verehrung heiliger Herrscherinnen im Spiegel ihrer deutschsprachigen Lebensbeschreibungen aus der Zeit des späten Mittelalters", in *Spannungen und Widersprüche. Gedenkschrift für Frantisek Graus*, eds. Susanna Burghartz, Hans-Jörg Gilomen and Guy P. Marchal e. a. (Sigmaringen, 1992), pp. 37-50; Elisabeth Kovács, "Die Heiligen und heiligen Könige der frühen Habsburger (1273-1519)", in *Laienfrömmigkeit im späten Mittelalter. Formen, Funktionen, politisch-soziale Zusammenhänge*, Schriften des Historischen Kollegs, Kolloquien 20, ed. Klaus Schreiner (Munich, 1992), pp. 93-126.

[27] *Sankt Elisabeth. Fürstin, Dienerin, Heilige* (Marburg, 1981); Kaspar Elm, *Elisabeth von Thüringen. Persönlichkeit, Werk und Wirkung*, Marburger Universitätsreden 3 (Marburg, 1982); Folz, *Les saintes*, pp. 105-125; *Herzöge und Heilige. Das Geschlecht der Andechs-Meranier im europäischen Hochmittelalter*, eds. Josef Kirmeier and Evamaria Brockhoff (Munich, 1993); Ortrud Reber, *Die Heilige Elisabeth. Leben und Legende* (St. Ottilien, 1984); Matthias Werner, "Mater Hassiae - Flos Ungariae - Gloria Teutoniae. Politik und Heiligenverehrung im Nachleben der hl. Elisabeth von Thüringen", in *Politik und Heiligenverehrung im Hochmittelalter*, Vorträge und Forschungen 42, ed. Jürgen Petersohn (Sigmaringen, 1994), pp. 449-540.

spirits, but actually related: Sancia was Elisabeth's niece. For Sancia's mother was princess Violant of Hungary (d. 1251), Elisabeth's half-sister. Violant was married to James I, in 1235, four years after her sister's death and just a year after her speedy canonisation.[28] Sancia will undoubtedly have grown up with full knowledge of her illustrious aunt, the first princess or queen of the twelfth or thirteenth century to have been raised to the honour of the altars.[29] The influence Elisabeth's example had on various of the subsequently canonised and beatified members of European dynasties, especially among the Arpads of Hungary, is well known: Anna (d. 1265) and Saint Hedwig of Silesia (d. 1243), Agnes of Bohemia (d. 1252) and both Saint Margaret (d. 1270) and princess Cunegond of Hungary (d. 1292) declared the *Landgräfin* to be their model.[30] Other, less zealous queens and princesses in Poland, Bohemia, Hungary and France showed a deep devotion to their holy relative.[31] Sancia's life could well be a further indication of Elisabeth's hitherto unknown influence in Catalonia-Aragon and of the geographical extent of her veneration.

A number of facts corroborate this assumption. As Sancia is said to have done, Elisabeth also showed a deep admiration for the

[28] F. Oliver Brachfeld, *Doña Violante de Hungria, reina de Aragón* (Madrid, 1942).

[29] Saint Margaret of Scotland and Saint Cunigond, though canonised in 1249 and 1200, respectively, were eleventh-century queens. On the practice of canonisation in the thirteenth and fourteenth centuries, cf. Goodich, pp. 21-47 and Vauchez, *L'influence des modèles*.

[30] J. Manikowska, "Zwischen *Askesis* und *Modestia*: Buß- und Armutsideale in polnischen, böhmischen und ungarischen Hofkreisen im 13. Jahrhundert", *Acta Poloniae Historica* 47 (1983), 33-53; Klaniczay, "Legends as life strategies"; idem, "I modelli", passim.

[31] Werner, pp. 481-83, 519-527; Klaniczay, "Legends as life-strategies", pp. 99-108. With references to the state of research, see Klaniczay, "I modelli", pp. 81-94.

Order of Saint John. Only after her death did Konrad von Marburg (d. 1233) and her brother-in-laws, Heinrich Raspe and Konrad, succeed in tying her veneration to the Teutonic Order.[32] In her relationship to the Hospitallers, the Hungarian princess continued a family tradition reaching back to Geza II and Bela III.[33] Her father, Andrew II, had also copiously patronised the order, explicitly referring to his personal perception of its charitable work while doing so.[34] Therefore, in binding herself to the Order of Saint John, Sancia may well have followed a heritage not only of the Catalo-

[32] Wilhelm Maurer, "Zum Verständnis der heiligen Elisabeth von Thüringen", in *Wilhelm Maurer, Kirche und Geschichte. Gesammelte Aufsätze*, eds. Ernst-Wilhelm Kohls and Gerhard Müller, 2 vols. (Göttingen, 1970), 2:231-282, 271, 280; Werner, pp. 462-70; Werner Moritz, "Das Hospital der Heiligen Elisabeth", in *Sankt Elisabeth. Fürstin, Dienerin, Heilige* (Marburg, 1981), pp. 101-117, 112.

[33] *Cartulaire de l'Ordre des Hospitalliers de S. Jean de Jérusalem*, ed. Jean Delaville Le Roulx, 4 vols. (Paris, 1894-1906), 1:203-207; René Grousset, "La Hongrie et la Syrie chrétienne au XIIIe siècle", *Nouvelle Revue de Hongrie* 66 (1937), 232-237; cf. the general outline on the dynasty by Gyula Kristó, *Die Arpadendynastie. Die Geschichte Ungarns von 895 bis 1301* (Szekszárd, 1993).

[34] Verum quia sacratissimam domum Hospitalis sancti Johannis Baptiste de Jerusalem, prout antea dediceramus auditu, cum ad Sancte Terre subsidium accessimus, diversis virtutum operibus in totius christianitas proficuum et honorem resplendescere cognovimus .... (*Cartulaire*, p. 231, nr. 1590). The importance of the hospital at Acre for the medical care of the town before its fall in 1291 is beyond dispute (Z. Goldmann, *Akko at the Time of the Crusades. The Convent of the Order of Saint John* (Acre, 1982); Marie-Luise Windemuth, *Das Hospital als Träger der öffentlichen Armenfürsorge im Mittelalter*, Sudhoffs Archiv, Beihefte 36 (Stuttgart, 1995), pp. 70-72; Karl Borchardt, "Spendenaufrufe der Johanniter aus dem 13. Jahrhundert", *Zeitschrift für bayerische Landesgeschichte* 56 (1993), 1-61, 36-47). On legends concerning the Order of Saint John and its houses in the Holy Land see ibid., pp. 19-35.

Aragonese crown, best symbolised by her great-grandmother and namesake, but also that of her Hungarian forefathers.[35]

Queen Sancia was the first, but by no means the only female member of the Barcelonese dynasty to enter a Hospitaller monastery: her daughter Dolça and later princesses are also known to have joined and headed the house of Sigena, which had all the characteristics of a royal foundation,[36] and several members of the Provençal branch of the family contemporaries to princess Sancia had spiritual ties to the order and were buried in its houses.[37] This leads us to a further indication of the influence Elisabeth of Hungary had in Catalonia. It is a well known fact that the choice of royal names was no random affair in the middle ages, but rather had a definitely programmatic character.[38] In this context, it is of some

[35] Her father, James I, also patronised the order, including the nunnery of Sigena, which at one time he had even chosen as his place of burial: *Documentos de Jaime I de Aragón*, nr. 22, 26, 32, 76, 78, 89, 93, 94, 97, 101, 106, 107, 130, 131, 173, 182, 211, 214, 223, 226, 260, 291, 313, 446, 548, 645. (See also Alan Forey, *The Military Orders from the Twelfth to the Early Fourteenth Centuries* (Toronto, 1992), p. 104; Maria Bonet Donato, *La Orden del Hospital en la Corona de Aragón. Poder y gobierno en la Castellanía de Amposta (ss. XII-XV)*, Biblioteca de Historia 22 (Madrid, 1994), pp. 45-50). In fact, not long before Sancia is reported to have travelled to the Holy Land, an aristocratic compatriot of hers, Estefania de Guàrdia, on joining the order explicitly mentioned the option of living as a *soror* in the Hospitallers' house in Palestine (Tacchella, p. 31).

[36] Regina Sáinz de la Maza Lasoli, *El monasterio de Sijena. Catálogo de documentos del Archivo de la Corona de Aragón I (1208-1348)* (Barcelona, 1994), pp. XIX-XX. "Sigena est, sans conteste, l'école des infantes" (Martin Aurell, "Nécropole de donats: les comtes de la maison de Barcelone et l'Hôpital, XIIe-XIIIe siècles" in *Les maisons de l'ordre de l'hôpital de Saint Jean de Jérusalem dépendant du grand prieuré de Saint Gilles du XIIe au XVIe siècle*, Provence Historique 45 (Marseille, 1995), pp. 7-25, 18).

[37] Aurell, "Nécropole", pp. 12-17.

[38] Gertrud Thoma, *Namensänderungen in Herrscherfamilien des mittelalterlichen Europa* (Kallmünz, 1985), pp. 27-169; Michael Mitterauer, "Zur

importance that *Elisabeth* becomes a fairly common name in the Barcelonese dynasty from the middle of the thirteenth century onward. Princess Sancia's sister - also a niece of the Hungarian saint - was the first of the family to be thus christened. One generation later, her niece, a daughter of Peter the Great and wife of Dionis of Portugal, bore the name, just as a daughter and grand-daughter of James II did. Finally one must mention princess Elisabeth of Majorca, Sancia's great-niece, the last of the royal dynasty of Majorca. Contemporary documents prove that the Catalano-Aragonese kings and queens knew full well that a renowned saint was among their forefathers. Sancia's parents, James the Conqueror and queen Violant, even endowed a chapel in Tarragona and founded a Clariss monastery in Valencia dedicated to her name,[39]

Nach-benennung nach Lebenden und Toten in Fürstenhäusern des Frühmittelalters", in *Gesellschaftsgeschichte. Festschrift für Karl Bosl zum 80. Geburtstag*, 2 vols. (Munich, 1988), 1:386-399; David A. Postles, "The baptismal name in XIIIth-century England. Processes and patterns", *Medieval Prosopography* 13 (1992), 1-52; Michael Mitterauer, *Ahnen und Heilige. Namensgebung in der europäischen Geschichte* (Munich, 1993).

[39] Barcelona Arxiu de la Corona d'Aragó, Cancelleria, Reg. 194, fol. 289r; Andrés Ivars Cardona, "Año de fundación y diferentes advocaciones que ha tenido el monasterio de la Puridad de la ciudad de Valencia", *Archivo Ibero-Americano* 19 (1932), 435-464; Robert I. Burns, *The Crusader Kingdom of Valencia. Reconstruction of a Thirteenth-Century Frontier*, 2 vols. (Cambridge/MA, 1967), 1:231, 2:506; J. Cortés-Vicent Pons, "Geografia dels monestirs femenins valencians en la baixa Edat Mitjana", in *Santes, monges i fetilleres. Espiritualitat femenina medieval*, Revista d'Historia Medieval 2 (Valencia, 1991), pp. 77-91. M. Andrés Antón, *El monasterio de la Puridad: primera fundación de Clarisas en Valencia y su reino, siglos XIII-XV* (Valencia, 1991); Ernest Morera Llauradó, *'Tarragona christiana'. Historia del arzobispado de Tarragona y del territorio de su provincia*, 2 vols. (Tarragona, 1889-1899, repr. Tarragona, 1981-1982), 2:72. It is interesting to note that Hungarians living in Catalonia endowed the convent with donations (Felipe Mateu i Llopis, "El 'Rex Hungariae' y el 'Rex Valenciae'. Sincronismos monetarios y sigilográficos (en torno a Doña Violante de Hungría)", in *Jaime I y su época*, X Congreso de la

and a second house, that of Lleida, showed the same patronage as early as 1240.[40] Queen Sancia of Naples, a Catalan princess from the Majorcan branch of the family, showed great devotion to Elisabeth and repeatedly referred to her as a shining example among her relatives.[41] Even French and Castilian chroniclers of the thirteenth century mention that the daughters of James I were related to the Hungarian Saint.[42] This proud claim continued for many decades and was later fostered by Catalan translations of the fourteenth-century *Revelationes* attributed to the saint.[43] Even 150 years after Elisabeth's death, a member of the house of Barcelona,

Historia de la Corona de Aragón, comunicaciones 3-5 (Zaragoza, 1978), pp. 545-555, pp. 551-552. On the descendants of Violant's entourage see Szabolcs de Vajay, "De l'acculturation médiévale a travers le destin d'une famille transplantée: Les ancêtres hongrois et la descendance catalane du Comte Dionis", in *Amics de Besalú*, II assamblea d'estudis del seu comtat (Barcelona, 1973), pp. 231-265.

[40] Josefina Mateu Ibars, "El monasterio de Santa Clara de Lérida. Notas para su historia", *Archivo-Ibero-Americano* 54 (1994), 945-967.

[41] Ronald G. Musto, "Queen Sancia of Naples (1286-1345) and the Spiritual Franciscans", in *Women of the Medieval World. Essays in Honor of John H. Mundy*, eds. Julius Kirschner and Suzanne F. Wemple (Oxford, 1985), pp. 179-214, 190, 208.

[42] *Cronica de los reyes de Castilla desde por maestre Jofré de Loaysa*, ed. Antonio García Martínez (Murcia, 1961), p. 219: "deinde nupsit cum nobilisima infantissa domina Violante, filia domini Jacobi ilustrissimi regis Aragonum supradicti ac nobilis regine domine Violante filie regis Ungarie ac sororis beate Helisabet". *Ex chronico Girardi de Fracheto*, Monumenta Germaniae Historica, Scriptores 26, ed. Oswald Holder-Eggert (Hanover, 1882), pp. 587-590, 589: "Item rex Aragonum filiam suam nomine Ysabellam, neptem beate Elizabeth Theutonicae".

[43] Livarius Oliger, "Revelationes B. Elisabeth. Disquisitio critica una cum textibus latino et catalaunensi", *Antonianum* 1 (1926), 24-83.

prince Peter, pointed out his dynastic relationship to his great-great-aunt.[44]

Peter's reverence for Saint Elisabeth is telling in more than one respect; for the prince did not name any closer, saintly relation. Could he not boast a member of his own family among the canonised? In fact, many men and women of the house of Barcelona in the thirteenth and fourteenth century showed considerable religious zeal. Touched by the spiritual movements of their time, directly related to individuals and circles of strong beliefs and observant inclinations, the princes and princesses of the Catalano-Aragonese crown often walked the narrow line between religious orthodoxy and dissent. It is well known how closely both phenomena were connected, how easily the zealous could slip from one sphere into the other.[45] Various members of the house of Barcelona led intensely spiritual lives, and one of them was even to pass the blurred line between holiness and heresy.

In terms of ecclesiastical history, the thirteenth century may well be termed the century of the mendicants. The four great orders, the Franciscans, the Dominicans, the Carmelites and the Augustinian hermits experienced an extraordinary growth, as did various smaller mendicant orders. These, however, were not lucky

[44] Werner, p. 523; José Pou i Martí, *Visionarios, beguinos y fraticellos catalanes (siglos XIII-XV)* (Vic, 1930), p. 368 and n. 2.

[45] Herbert Grundmann, *Religiöse Bewegungen im Mittelalter. Untersuchungen über die geschichtlichen Zusammenhänge zwischen der Ketzerei, den Bettelorden und den religiösen Frauenbewegungen im 12. und 13. Jh.*, 4th ed. (Darmstadt, 1974). Kaspar Elm, "Die Stellung der Frau in Ordenswesen, Semireligiosentum und Häresie zur Zeit der Heiligen Elisabeth", in *Sankt Elisabeth. Fürstin, Dienerin, Heilige* (Marburg, 1981), pp. 7-28. See also the chapter on "Heretical Saints" in Goodich, pp. 198-206 and Caroline Bynum, *Holy Feast and Holy Fast. The Religious Significance of Food to Medieval Women* (Berkeley, Ca., 1987), pp. 13-30.

enough to be excepted from the papal order of dissolution pronounced in 1215 and repeated at the council of Lyon in 1274. The large number of mendicant saints in the thirteenth century bears witness to the reverence in which the new brethren were widely held.[46] This reverence transcended social boundaries: practically every royal family in Europe had at least one member who was profoundly influenced by the ideals propagated by the *Poverello* of Assisi - individual and common poverty paired with a zeal to imitate the life of the apostles. The house of Barcelona was no exception. Just as queen Violant had done, many of her eight children and step-children extensively patronised the mendicant orders. Foremost among them was Violant, her mother's namesake and wife of Alfonso X of Castile.[47] She not only personally founded the Gallician Clariss monastery at Allaríz, but was also present at the founding of various other houses of the second Franciscan order.[48] Although it seems she was not able to fulfil her vow to enter her nunnery at Allaríz and die in the habit of Saint Claire, Violant's support for the ideal of poverty promulgated by the order exceeded

[46] Goodich, *Vita Perfecta*, pp. 30-31, 147-172; Michael Goodich, "The politics of canonisation in the thirteenth century: lay and mendicant saints", in *Saints and their Culture. Studies in Religious Sociology, Folklore and History*, ed. Stephen Wilson (Cambridge, 1985), pp. 169-189.

[47] Francisco García Oro, *Francisco de Asís en la España medieval* (Santiago de Compostela, 1988), pp. 133-148; Jacobo de Castro, *Del arbol cronológico de la provincia de Santiago I* (Salamanca, 1722), 6. 6.

[48] García Oro, pp. 122, 198, 228, 305, 326, 446. On the history of the Clarisses in Spain and Portugal see the articles and references in *Archivo Ibero-Americano* 54 (1994); on the role of the royal family in Castile see Gregoria Cavero Domínguez, "Monarquía y nobleza: su contribución a las fundaciones de clarisas en Castilla y León (siglos XIII-XV)", ibid., 257-381.

that of other queens. She found a successor in her niece, queen Elisabeth of Portugal (1282-1336).[49]

The daughter of Peter the Great and Constance of Hohenstaufen was married to Dionis I of Portugal in 1282. It was her life's goal to mediate in political and dynastic conflicts between her relatives - the kings of Castile, Aragon and Portugal - as well as between her husband and son, thus fulfilling one of the characteristics of the royal *sanctae modernae* of the thirteenth century.[50] According to her *vita* written shortly after her death, Elisabeth led an exemplary life of charity, personally providing for the impoverished daughters of honourable families as well as for the aged, prostitutes, orphans, and the poor. Her charitable foundations in Coimbra were visible proof of her active care for the weak. She proved to be an ardent defender and patron of the Clarisses, founding the order's monastery at Coimbra and entering it as a *soror* after Dionis' death in 1325. There she is said to have led a life of remarkable austerity marked by frequent acts of renunciation and penitence. Her life, her deeds, and the miracles reported after her death in 1336 led to her late canonisation in 1625, which may have been due - to a greater or lesser degree - to political interests.

In order to find a contemporary member of the house of Barcelona with a life of similarly charitable and spiritual

[49] A. G. Ribeiro de Vasconcellos, *Evoluçâo do culto de Dona Isabel de Aragâo (a Rainha Santa)*, 2 vols. (Coïmbra, 1894); Folz, pp. 145-159. Félix T. Lopes, *Actividades pacificadoras de S. Isabel de Portugal nos dissídios entre Castela e Arago de 1300 a 1304* (Braga, 1967); Félix T. Lopes, "Santa Isabel na contienda entre D. Dinis e o filho 1321-1322", *Lusitania Sacra* 8 (1970), 57-80; Angel San Vicente Pino, *Isabel de Aragón, reina de Portugal* (Zaragoza, 1971); Ivo Carneiro de Sousa, "A rainha D. Leonor e a introduçao da reforma coletina da ordem de Santa Clara em Portugal", *Archivo-Ibero-Americano* 54 (1994), 1033-1070.

[50] Klaniczay, "Legends as life-strategies", pp. 105-106.

characteristics, let us first look at the dynasty *strictu sensu*, that is the rulers of the Catalano-Aragonese Crown and their immediate relatives. Considering the pragmatic and far from zealous nature of king James II (1291-1327), it is slightly surprising that three of his five sons embraced religious life, either as monks or as priests.[51] In the case of prince John, the king himself firmly supported his son's ecclesiastical career - albeit for political reasons. John eventually became archbishop of Tarragona, but although he felt deep devotion for the Franciscan order and his uncle, Saint Louis of Toulouse (d. 1297),[52] he never showed a degree of religious zeal which would have surpassed that of his contemporaries. As to the first-born son of James II, prince James, it is true that he obstinately refused to form part of his father's policy of matrimonial ties and finally succeeded in taking monastic vows, first joining the Cistercians, then the Hospitallers, and finally the order of Montesa. However, his decision does not appear to have been exclusively spiritually motivated.[53] Only *fray Pere d'Aragó*, the fourth-born child, proved

[51] On the king see José M. Martínez Ferrando, *Jaime II de Aragón. Su vida familiar*, 2 vols. (Barcelona, 1948), 1:81-196; Antonio Aragó, "Perfil espiritual de Jaume II, el Just", *Santes Creus* 48 (1978), 431-437. James did however underline his family's close relationship with the Franciscans: Heinrich Finke, *Acta Aragonensia. Quellen zur deutschen, italienischen, französischen und spanischen Kirchen- und Kulturgeschichte aus der diplomatischen Korrespondenz Jaumes II. (1291-1327)*, 3 vols. (Berlin, 1908-1923), 3:16-19.

[52] Pou i Martí, p. 349; Martínez Ferrando, 1:141-151; Marc Dykmans, "Lettre de Jean d'Aragon, Patriarche d'Alexandre, au Pape Jean XXII sur la visión béatifique", *Analecta Sacra Tarraconensia* 42 (1969), 1-26.

[53] Martínez Ferrando, 1:81-106; Joaquím Miret i Sans, *El forassenyat primogènit de Jaume II* (Barcelona, 1957); Eufemia Fort i Cogul, "Una vocació obstinadament interdita", *Studia Monastica* 3 (1961), 357-377; Finke, 3:367-376.

to be truly touched by Franciscan spirituality.[54] Having been given the counties of Ribagorza and Ampurias by his father, Peter governed his possessions as a powerful prince. His marriages to Constance, daughter of Frederick III of Sicily (1296 - 1337), and later to Juana de Foix (d. 1358) consolidated his might. Upon the death of his second wife, at the age of 53, Peter decided to enter the Seraphic order. Until his death in 1381 he not only frequently served the apostolic see as an emissary, but also endeavoured to overcome the schism which shook Christendom at the end of his life. Quite obviously, *Pere d'Aragó* - a princely friar with excellent contacts to influential political circles - was different from the average Minorite. Nevertheless, he was authentically influenced by Franciscan mysticism, as his visions and sermons demonstrate.

The most striking examples of royal piety were not found among the Arago-Catalan branch of the house of Barcelona, but rather among its relatives from the dynasty of Majorca. At the Angevin court at Naples, princess Sancia, a cousin of Elisabeth of Portugal, became famous and was held in great reverence for her religious zeal. Sancia was the eldest daughter of James II of Majorca and Sclaramomda de Foix and was married to Robert of Naples (d. 1343), son of Charles II (1289-1309), in 1304.[55] Robert, a grand-

[54] On the infant see Pou i Martí, pp. 308-396; Martínez Ferrando, 1:158-161; Martin Aurell, "Eschatologie, spiritualité et politique dans la confédération catalano-aragonaise (1282-1412)", in *Fin du monde et signes des temps. Visionnaires et prophètes en France méridionale (fin XIII*e *- début XV*e *siècle)*, Cahiers de Fanjeaux 27 (Fanjeaux, 1992), pp. 199-235, 203-205.

[55] On queen Sancia see Mercedes van Heuckelum, *Spiritualistische Strömungen an den Höfen von Aragon und Anjou während der Höhe des Armutsstreites*, Abhandlungen zur Mittleren und Neueren Geschichte 38 (Berlin and Leipzig, 1912), pp. 36-91; Pou i Martí, pp. 128-144; Gabriel Alomar Esteve, "Iconografía y heráldica de Sancha de Mallorca, reina de Nápoles", *Boletín de la Societat arqueològica lulliana* 35 (1976), 5-36; Musto, "Queen Sancia of Naples", passim.

nephew of Saint Louis (d. 1270) and brother to Saint Louis of Toulouse, was himself an extraordinary example of royal piety and laid down his religious convictions in various sermons and writings.[56] He and his wife converted the court at Naples into a haven for radical Franciscan reformers, a home for dissenters and an open house for religious visionaries like Ramón Llull (d. 1316) and Arnau de Vilanova (d. 1311). They explicitly fostered Clariss and other mendicant foundations in various parts of the Mediterranean - in the kingdom of Naples, in Majorca, in southern France and even in the Holy Land[57] - and surrounded themselves with Franciscan advisors and chaplains. Sancia in particular endeavoured to lead a life of personal austerity and religiosity. She was constantly accompanied by Clarisses and at one time seriously contemplated leaving her husband and entering a convent. However pope John XXII (1316-1334) dissuaded her, and she lived to exercise full regal powers after Robert's death in 1343. A year later, however, she at last was allowed to fulfil her desire: she renounced the world and entered the Clariss convent of Santa Croce in Naples. She died there in 1345 in the odour of sanctity.

[56] St. Clair Baddeley, *Robert the Wise and his Heirs 1278-1352* (London, 1897); Walter Wilhelm Goetz, *König Robert und sein Verhältnis zum Humanismus* (Tübingen, 1910); Romolo Caggese, *Roberto d'Angio e i suoi tempi*, 2 vols. (Florence, 1922-30); Sigismund Brettle, "Ein Traktat des Königs Robert von Neapel 'de evangelica paupertate'" in *Abhandlungen aus dem Gebiete der mittleren und neueren Geschichte und ihrer Hilfswissenschaften. Eine Festgabe zum siebzigsten Geburtstag, Geh. Rat Prof. Dr. Heinrich Finke gewidmet* (Münster, 1925), pp. 200-209.

[57] Joseph Antonio de Hebrera, *Chronica real serafica del reyno y santa provincia de Aragón* (Zaragoza, 1705), pp. 338-382; Musto, p. 192; Patrocinio García Barriuso, OFM, *España en la Historia de Tierra Santa. Obra pía española a la sombra de un regio patronato (estudio histórico-jurídico), vol. 1: siglos XIV, XV, XVI y XVII* (Madrid, 1992), pp. 23-32, 105-110.

Sancia's biography may in itself be indicative of the religious zeal which pervaded the Majorcan branch of the house of Barcelona, but one can only fully appreciate the extent of this family's devotion when one realises that two of her four brothers renounced the world in order to enter religious life. James and Philipp both stepped back from their succession to the throne in order to join the Franciscans. The order's presence on the island was not new. Minorites had accompanied the Christian host during the conquest of Majorca in 1229, a year later a first convent had been founded and in 1256, a house of Clarisses was established. The long-standing and special relationship between the royal family and the friars is clearly expressed in a letter by Sancia to the general chapter of 1334.[58] Towards the beginning of the fourteenth century, the critical voices in the order and among its lay sympathisers were beginning to be heard in the royal palaces in Montpellier, Perpignan and Majorca.[59] Peter John Olivi (d. 1296) and Bernard Délicieux (d. after 1320) seem to have had a strong influence on the young princes, and one of them, Philipp, himself appears to have persuaded his nephew Fernando to renounce secular life. Fernando's father had himself maintained close and friendly contacts to Bernard Délicieux, which had been the cause for violent quarrels and even fights between him and his father, the king of Mallorca.[60]

[58] Pou i Martí, pp. 131-134.

[59] Martí de Barcelona, "L'ordre franciscà i la casa reial de Mallorca", *Estudis Franciscans* 30 (1923), 354-383; Antonio Oliver, "Heterodoxía en la Mallorca de los siglos XIII-XV", *Boletín de la Sociedad Arqueológica Luliana* 32 (1961), 157-176; Duncan Nimmo, *Reform and Division in the Medieval Franciscan Order (1226-1538)*, Bibliotheca Seraphico-Capuccina 33 (Rome, 1987), pp. 109-352.

[60] A vivid description of the conflicts between father and son are to be found in Finke, 2: nr. 59. In spite of his sympathies, Fernando did not join the Franciscan Order (as upheld by Musto, p. 182).

James, the eldest son of James II of Majorca, took the Franciscan habit in 1299, just three years later than his relative and friend, Louis of Anjou, and one year after the future saint's untimely death. It is very probable that both James and Louis first became more intimately acquainted with Franciscan spirituality when the latter was held hostage in Catalonia by James II of Aragon.[61] The latter's note prohibiting the friars from visiting the princes at night is a clear indication of the close ties between the prisoners and the order.[62] While prince Louis was named bishop of Toulouse, James remained in the Minorite convent in Perpignan as a simple friar until the end of his life.

A third son of James II not only sympathised with the radical reformers and Franciscan Joachites, but actually joined them to lead a life of utmost poverty: Philipp of Majorca (d. between 1340 and 1342).[63] Philipp was born in 1288 and raised in Majorca and Paris. The highly gifted prince was soon heaped with praise by such men as Ramón Llull and endowed with lucrative benefices.[64] The winter of 1310/11 radically changed the course of the prince's life. In Vienne, he met Angelo Clareno (d. 1337) and was so impressed by the theologian - who was to become his life-long friend - that he soon endeavoured to defend observant Franciscanism and propagate its ideals before his royal relatives. While his sister supported the moderate, but nevertheless persecuted, observant Franciscans

[61] Pou i Martí, pp. 31-32; Van Heuckelum, pp. 26-36; Jacques Paul, "Der heilige Ludwig von Anjou, Bischof von Toulouse", in *800 Jahre Franz von Assisi* (Krems, 1982), pp. 157-168, p. 161.

[62] Finke, 1: nr. 15.

[63] Jean-Marie Vidal, "Un ascète de sang royale, Phillip de Mallorque", *Revue des questions historiques* n.s. 44 (1910), 361-403; Oliver, pp. 165-170; De Barcelona, pp. 372-379; Pou i Martí, pp. 111-128; Nimmo, pp. 178-180, 265-269, 357-363; Aurell, *Eschatologie, spiritualité*, pp. 200-203.

[64] Oliver, pp. 165-66; Van Heuckelum, p. 54.

around Michael of Cesena (d. 1342), Philip took the side of the more radical, Joachite dissenters around Ubertino de Casale and Angelo Clareno.[65] Pope John XXII repeatedly tried to win the prince back for orthodoxy, first by offering him the see of Mirepoix, then by proposing that he enter an approved order. Philipp, however, had other plans: in 1317, and again in 1328, he requested permission from the papal curia to found an observant branch of the Franciscans. Evidently, Philipp hoped to create a haven for his spiritualist companions with the pope's approval. Not unexpectedly, his pleas went unheard.[66] After a five-year interlude, during which the political situation in Majorca obliged him to act as regent for his nephew,[67] Philipp left Majorca for Naples. At his sister's court, he

[65] Ronald G. Musto, *The Letters of Angelo Clareno* (PhD. Dissertation, Columbia University, 1977), p. 391. Gian Luca Podestà, *Angelo Clareno dai poveri eremiti ai fraticelli*, Nuovi Studi Storici 8 (Rome, 1990), pp. 45-49, 236-239, 287-289. See Sancia's intent to win the general chapter of the Franciscans for the observant movement led by Michael de Cesena (Pou i Martí, pp. 131-134). After Sancia's death, several books by Michael de Cesena were found among her possessions. By order of John XXII, they were brought to Avignon and destroyed. On the radical Franciscan reformers in Catalonia see Pou i Martí; Josep Sanchís Sivera, "Fraticelos catalano-aragoneses", in *Analecta Sacra Tarraconensia* 11 (1935), 23-35; *Western Mediterranean Prophecy. The School of Joachim of Fiore and the Fourteenth-Century 'Breviloquium'*, Studies and Texts 88, eds. Harold Lee, Marjorie Reeves and Giulio Silano (Toronto, 1989), pp. 47-67; Pere Santonja, "Arnau de Vilanova e la seva relació amb els espirituals. Els origens d'aquestes congregacions i llurs ideals religiosos", *Estudios Franciscanos* 91 (1991), 25-53.

[66] Friedrich Ehrle, "Die Spiritualen und ihr Verhältnis zum Franziscanerorden und zu den Fraticellen", *Archiv für Literatur- und Kirchengeschichte des Mittelalters* 4 (1887), 1-190, p. 29; *Bullarium Franciscanum*, eds. J. Sbaralea and C. Eubel, 8 vols. (Rome, 1759-1909), 6:490; cf. Nimmo, p. 357-363.

[67] Guillaume Mollat, "Jean XXII et la succession de Sanche, roi de Majorque (1326-1342)", *Revue d'Histoire et d'Archéologie du Roussillon* 6 (1905), 65-83. Auguste Störmann, *Studien zur Geschichte des Königreiches*

soon attracted a group of loyal followers known as the *fratres fratris Philippi Maioricis*. From the security of the Angevin palace he felt safe enough to openly attack the position pope John XXII had adopted towards the spirituals.[68] In the eyes of the apostolic see, Philipp had now crossed the border between orthodox religiosity and dangerously critical spiritualism. The prince himself was well aware that a reconciliation was no longer possible: he appears to have joined a group of *fraticelli*, the heretical followers of Angelo Clareno, and to have moved to Southern Italy. There, his traces finally disappear.[69] As late as 1362, the memory of the *fratres fratris Philippi Maioricis* lived on among religious dissenters.[70] Although he had endeavoured to follow a model of holiness established by Saint Francis, the prince from Majorca did not meet the understanding the *Poverello* had been fortunate enough to experience in his time. Honoured as a saint by his faithful followers, he died as a heretic without a home. Of all the princes and princesses of the house of Barcelona, Philipp of Mallorca was perhaps the one to draw closest to both heresy and holiness, these two so intimately connected aspects of religious life, both of which were to be found among male and female members of the house of Barcelona.

Mallorca, Abhandlungen zur Mittleren und Neueren Geschichte 66 (Berlin, 1918).

[68] Ehrle, p. 94.

[69] F. Russo, "I fraticelli in Calabria nel secolo XIV", *Miscellanea francescana* 65 (1965), 349-68. After pope John XXII had died, Philipp again requested permission to found a new order and was once again rejected (*Bullarium Franciscanum* 6:123); cf. Nimmo, pp. 362-363. On the *fraticelli* in southern Italy see ibid., pp. 259-272.

[70] Ehrle, p. 100; Antonio Oliver, p. 168; Decima L. Douie, *The Nature and the Effect of the Heresy of the Fraticelli* (Manchester, 1932; repr. Manchester, 1978), p. 229; Pou i Martí, pp. 145-149.

In spite of the exemplary lives of the queens Sancia, Elisabeth and Violant, of princess Sancia or prince James, none of them was raised to the honour of the altars during the middle ages. Don Juan Manuel may have described how the citizens of Acre "fezieron gran onra aquel sancto cuerpo",[71] but Sancia was never revered in her homeland, nor did she receive any form of official recognition by the apostolic see. In fact, no member of the Barcelonese dynasty was canonised before it ended in 1412. On the map of medieval royal holiness, Catalonia and Aragon are desert areas.[72] This was to change only at a later date. Practically every other European country was able to name at least one royal saint of their own.[73] Among others, France could boast Saint Louis (d. 1270),[74] England Saint Edward the Confessor (d. 1066),[75] the German empire Charlemagne (768-814),[76] Hungary Saint Stephen (d. 1038),[77] Denmark Saint

[71] Don Juan Manuel, p. 128.

[72] See the maps (nr. 1 and 2) compiled by Vauchez, pp. 318-319, 320-321.

[73] Robert Folz, *Les saints rois du moyen âge en occident (VI-XIIIe siècles)*, Studia Hagiographica 68 (Brussels, 1984); Goodich, *Vita Perfecta*; Folz, *Les saintes*; Vauchez, *Sainteté*.

[74] Ludwig Buisson, *König Ludwig IX., der Heilige, und das Recht. Studien zur Lebensgestaltung Frankreichs im hohen Mittelalter* (Freiburg, 1954). Jacques Le Goff, "Saint Louis et les corps royaux", *Le temps de la réflexion* 3 (1982), 255-284; Jean Richard, *Saint Louis* (Paris, 1983); Folz, *Les saintes*, pp. 107-113, 148-155.

[75] Bernhardt W. Scholz, "The canonisation of Edward the Confessor", *Speculum* 36 (1961), 38-60; Frank Barlow, *Edward the Confessor* (London, 1970); Janet Nelson, "Royal saints and early medieval kingship", in *Sanctity and Secularity*, ed. Derek Baker (Oxford, 1973), pp. 39-44; Folz, *Les saintes*, pp. 91-101; Susan J. Ridyard, *The Royal Saints of Anglo-Saxon England. A Study of West Saxon and East Anglian Cults* (Cambridge, 1988).

[76] Robert Folz, "La chancellerie de Frédéric Ier et la canonisation de Charlemagne", *Le Moyen Age* 70 (1964), 13-31; Jürgen Petersohn, "Saint Denis

Canute (d. 1086),[78] and Scotland Saint Margaret (d. 1093).[79] The rulers of the Catalano-Aragonese crown could make no such reference to a saint among their forefathers. Neither were they able to experience the cohesive effect local saints may have upon a realm, and they never had the chance to employ holy kinsmen for political ends. The Hungarian Arpads may be the best known example for the able instrumentalisation of sacral kingship and royal sanctity,[80] but they were in no way an exception. The German Hohenstaufen, the Capetians in France, or the Angevins in Naples all consolidated their power by underlining their descent from a

- Westminster - Aachen. Die Karls-Translatio von 1165 und ihre Vorbilder", *Deutsches Archiv für Erforschung des Mittelalters* 31 (1975), 420-454.

[77] Georg Schreiber, *Stefan der Heilige. Eine hagiographische Studie* (Paderborn, 1938); Gábor Klaniczay, "Königliche und dynastische Heiligkeit in Ungarn", in *Politik und Heiligenverehrung im Hochmittelalter*, Vorträge und Forschungen 42, ed. Jürgen Petersohn (Sigmaringen, 1994), pp. 343-364; Folz, *Les saintes*, pp. 76-84.

[78] Erich Hofmann, *Die Heiligen Könige bei den Angelsachsen und den skandinavischen Völkern. Königsheiliger und Königshaus*, Quellen und Forschungen zur Geschichte Schleswig-Holsteins 69 (Neumünster, 1975); Tore Nyberg, "St. Knud and St. Knud's Church", in *Hagiography and Medieval Literature. A Symposium*, ed. H. Bekker-Nielsen (Odense, 1981), pp. 100-110.

[79] Derek Baker, "A nursery of saints. Saint Margaret of Scotland reconsidered", in *Sanctity and Secularity*, ed. Derek Baker (Oxford, 1973), pp. 119-142; Peter Johannek, "'Politische Heilige' auf den Britischen Inseln im 12. und 13. Jahrhundert", in *Überlieferung, Frömmigkeit, Bildung als Leitthemen der Geschichtsforschung. Vorträge beim Wissenschaftlichen Kolloquium aus Anlaß des 80. Geburtstags von Otto Meyer*, ed. Jürgen Petersohn (Wiesbaden, 1987), pp. 77-95.

[80] Klaniczay, "Königliche und dynastische Heiligkeit"; idem, "From sacral kingship to self-representation: Hungarian and European royal saints", in *Continuity and Change. Political Institutions and Literary Movements in the Middle Ages*, ed. Elisabeth Vestergaard (Odense, 1986), pp. 61-86, repr. in idem, *The Uses of Supernatural Power. The Transformation of Popular Religion in Medieval and Early-Modern Europe* (Oxford, 1990), pp. 79-95.

beata stirps.[81] James the Conqueror may have had something similar in mind on shrouding his own descent in an aura of mysticism and sacrality in his *Llibre dels fets* - a notion readily picked up in later Catalan chronicles.[82] In fact, a century after his death he was repeatedly termed "hic sanctus rex" in the work written on behalf of Peter *el Ceremoniòs* known as the *Crónica de San Juan de la Peña*, and even Peter himself spoke of him as a saint.[83] *El Ceremoniòs* seems to have been keenly aware of the deficit his family suffered, for on the death of Peter, the Franciscan son of James II, he informed the *consellers* of Barcelona of the wonders which were reported to have occurred at the grave of his uncle, who had died "en olor de santitat".[84] Perhaps even Don Juan Manuel's words on Sancia are the faint reflex of an attempt by the part of the Catalano-Aragonese rulers to create such a focus of dynastic devotion, the shadow of a saint in the making. If so, none of these plans ever exceeded a preliminary stage.

[81] Folz, *Saints rois*, pp. 137-172; Jürgen Petersohn, "Kaisertum und Kultakt in der Stauferzeit", in *Politik und Heiligenverehrung im Hochmittelalter*, Vorträge und Forschungen 42, ed. Jürgen Petersohn (Sigmaringen, 1994), pp. 101-148; Werner, pp. 523-524; Vauchez, pp. 209-215, 265-272; Gábor Klaniczay, "The cult of dynastic saints in central Europe: fourteenth-century Angevins and Luxemburgs", repr. in idem, *The Uses of Supernatural Power*, pp. 111-129.

[82] François Delpech, *Histoire et légende: essai sur la genèse d'un thème épique aragonais: la naissance merveilleuse de Jacques I le Conquérant* (Paris, 1993), pp. 17-44.

[83] *Crónica de San Juan de la Peña*, ed. Antonio Ubieto Arteta (Valencia 1961), pp. 156-161; *Crónica de San Juan de la Peña* (versión aragonesa), ed. Carmen Orcastegui Gros (Zaragoza, 1985), pp. 94-98; Burns, p. 5, n. 3. In fact, in the beginning of the seventeenth century timid steps for James' canonisation were undertaken, but never continued (ibid.).

[84] Barcelona Arxiu de la Corona d'Aragó, Cancelleria, Reg. 1276, fols. 141r, 145v; Martínez Ferrando, 1:169.

Local saints also served as collective points of reference, at which the spirituality and devotion of medieval nations in formation concentrated. The Catalano-Aragonese rulers had clearly realised this and repeatedly attempted to have compatriots like Ramón de Penyafort (d. 1275), Oleguer of Barcelona (d. 1137), or the Franciscan Martyrs of Ceuta canonised. But unlike their relatives on the thrones of France, England or Hungary, the Catalano-Aragonese rulers had to suffer their requests being constantly rejected.[85] After capturing Marseille in 1423, Alphonso V (1416-1458) had the remains of Saint Louis of Toulouse transferred from the French town to Valencia - apparently, by doing so he intended to legitimise his claims to the Sicilian throne.[86] But the rulers of the Catalano-Aragonese Crown never succeeded in benefiting from the archaic idea that kinship with a saint could sanctify one's own family and ensure divine intercession on behalf of the dynasty and its country. Neither did the notion of sacral kingship, so characteristic for French, German or English monarchies, ever really flourish in the Catalano-Aragonese Crown. Unction and coronation rites never formed an intrinsic part of royal legitimisation south of the Pyrenees.[87] In short, in this respect the house of Barcelona, one of

[85] Vauchez, pp. 82-83. Note the flurry of hagiographic *vitae* of devote Catalans (Pere Nolasc (d. 1249), Oleguer of Barcelona (d. 1136), Maria de Cervelló (d. 1290), Ramón Llull (d. 1315/16), Ramón de Penyafort (d. 1275) written in the fourteenth century (cf. Fernando Baños Vallejo, *La hagiografía como género literario en la edad media* (Oviedo, 1989), pp. 240-248)

[86] Marie Hyacinthe Laurent, *Le culte de S. Louis d'Anjou à Marseille au XIVe siècle*, Temi e testi 2 (Rome, 1954), pp. 97-108.

[87] Marc Bloch, *Les Rois thaumaturges. Étude sur le caractère surnaturel attribué à la puissance royale particulièrement en France et en Angleterre* (Strasbourg, 1924); Ernst Kantorowcz, *The King's Two Bodies: a Study in Medieval Political Theology* (Princeton, 1957); Percy Ernst Schramm, *Herrschaftszeichen und Staatssymbolik*, Monumenta Germaniae Historica, Schriften 13, 3 vols. (Stuttgart, 1954-56); *Coronations. Medieval and Early*

the most powerful dynasties of the late medieval Mediterranean, fell back behind its peers, competitors, and adversaries.

Modern Monarchic Ritual, ed. János M. Bak (Berkeley and Los Angeles, 1990); Richard A. Jackson, "Le pouvoir monarchique dans la cérémonie du sacre et couronnement des rois de France", in *Représentation, pouvoir et royauté à la fin du moyen âge*, eds. Joël Blanchard (Paris, 1995), 237-253; for the Catalano-Aragonese Crown see Bonifacio Palacios Martín, *La coronación de los reyes de Aragón, 1204-1410. Aportación al estudio de las estructuras politicas medievales* (Valencia, 1975). For Castile see Teofilo F. Ruíz, "Unsacred monarchy: the kings of Castile in the later middle ages", in *Rites of Power. Symbolism, Ritual, and Politics since the Middle Ages*, ed. Sean Wilentz (Philadelphia, 1985), pp. 109-144; Peter Linehan, "Frontier kingship: Castile, 1250-1350", in *La royauté sacrée dans le monde chrétien. Colloque de Royaumont, mars 1989*, ed. Alain Boureau and Claudio S. Ingerflom (Paris, 1992), pp. 71-80, as opposed to José Nieto Soria, *Iglesia y poder real en Castilla. El episcopado, 1250-1350* (Madrid, 1988), pp. 56-59.

II ECONOMIC AND CULTURAL EXCHANGES

Pisa and Catalonia between the Twelfth and Thirteenth Centuries

Silvia Orvietani Busch
Los Angeles, California

The first recorded contact between Pisa and Catalonia was the treaty signed in 1113, on the occasion of the joint participation in the crusade against the Muslims of the Balearic Islands.[1] At that moment, besides having a very different political structure and social composition, Catalonia and Pisa were also in two very different stages of commercial evolution. Catalonia, last Christian land before the flourishing territories of Muslim Spain, was constituted by a puzzle of feudal enclaves loosely united and ruled over by the counts of the House of Barcelona.[2] Commerce, in this

[1] The text is published by Carlo Calisse, *Il Liber Maiolichinus* (Roma, 1904), appendix I. On Muslim Majorca and the Balearic Islands see as first references Jaime Busquets Mulet, "Mallorca musulmana", in *Historia de Mallorca* 2 (Palma de Mallorca, 1978), pp. 161-267; Elviro Sans Rosselló, "Los Almoravides", in *Historia de Mallorca* 2 (Palma de Mallorca, 1978), pp. 270-288, with their respective bibliographies.

[2] Josep M. Salrach, "El procés de feudalizaciò", *Historia de Catalunya* 2 (Barcelona, 1987); T. N. Bisson, *The Medieval Crown of Aragon* (Oxford, 1986), pp. 5-57; Santiago Sobrequés, *Els Grans Comtes de Barcelona* (Barcelona, 1961); Michel Zimmermann, "Naissance d'une principauté:

area predominantly agricultural, was a regional exchange of local products and handicrafts. There was also irregular trade to and from the bordering and economically more developed Muslim peninsular kingdoms, as well as with the ultra-Pyrenean Occitan markets.[3] Pisa, lying directly across on the opposite shore of the western Mediterranean, had consistently loosened its ties with the feudal overlords of the region, the Marquises of Tuscany. During the eleventh century the city had started to integrate the surrounding rural aristocracy with the urban elite, creating a ruling class cohabiting peacefully most of the time, and interested in political expansion as well as in commercial development.[4] Consequent upon their political shapes and commercial interests, Pisa and Catalonia were playing very different roles in the Mediterranean power and mercantile network.

While Catalonia was at the margin of the major mercantile routes, Pisa on the contrary was already in 1113 one of the most important maritime powers of the western Mediterranean. Since the

Barcelone et les autres comtés catalans aux alentors de l'an Mil", in *Catalunya i França Meridional a l'entorn de l'any Mil* (Barcelona, 1991), pp. 111-135.

[3] Salrach "Activitates productives i evolució social", in *Historia de Catalunya*, pp. 428-438. See his vast bibliography on this topic, especially the works by Carme Battle i Gallart.

[4] Gioachino Volpe, *Studi sulle istituzioni comunali a Pisa* (Pisa, 1902), to be consulted in the second edition, revised by Cinzio Violante (Firenze, 1970); Gabriella Rossetti, "Storia familiare e struttura politica e sociale di Pisa nei secoli XI e XII", in *Forme di potere e strutture sociali nel medioevo* (Bologna, 1977), pp. 233-291; Gabriella Rossetti, "Ceti dirigenti e classe politica", in *Pisa nei secoli XI e XII: formazione e caratteri di una classe di governo* (Pisa, 1979), pp. 32-33; Cinzio Violante, *Economia, società e istituzioni a Pisa nel medioevo* (Bari, 1980); Marco Tangheroni, "Famiglie nobili e ceto dirigente a Pisa nel XIII secolo", in *I ceti dirigenti nell'età comunale nei secoli XII e XIII* (Pisa, 1981), pp. 328-339. On Pisan and Mediterranean commerce, see M. Tangheroni, *Commercio e navigazione nel medioevo* (Bari, 1996).

beginning of the eleventh century Pisan ships had more frequently crossed western Mediterranean waters, to trade and to impose, with treaties or with its military power, its commerce, from North Africa to southern Italy. That joint expedition of 1113-1115 represented for Pisa the height of its military efforts against the Muslims in the western Mediterranean, as well as its last grand attack.[5]

From this moment on, the Italian port city preferred to establish more peaceful relations with the western Muslims and concentrated its attention on commerce with them.[6] Its more aggressive policy was then reserved mostly for the war long raging with neighbouring Genoa for mercantile supremacy in this area of the Mediterranean. During the twelfth century Pisa better defined its internal political structure, as a consular commune, while its mercantile activity increased quickly; and the city became a major international centre of commerce, creating a specialised port system, based on clever use of the local geomorphology.[7] Its ships were

[5] Giuseppe Scalía, "Epigraphica Pisana. Testi latini sulla spedizione contro le Baleari ed altre imprese antisaracene del secolo XI", *Miscellanea di studi ispanici* (Pisa, 1968), pp. 234-286; Giuseppe Scalía, "Contributi pisani alla lotta anti-islamica nel Mediterraneo occidentale durante il secolo XI e nei primi decenni del XII", *Anuario de Estudios Medievales* 10 (1980), 133-144; Giuseppe Rossi-Sabatini, *L'espansione di Pisa nel Mediterraneo fino alla Meloria* (Florence, 1935), pp. 1-14; Marco Tangheroni, "Pisa, l'Islam, il Mediterraneo, la prima crociata: alcune considerazioni", in *Toscana e Terrasanta nel medioevo* (Florence, 1982), pp. 31-55.

[6] The Pisan ruling class developed steady diplomatic and commercial relations with the North African Muslims, despite its simultaneous support of the Crusader states. In many documents it is the city archbishop himself who leads the diplomatic exchanges (M. L. de Mas Latrie, *Relation et commerce de l' Afrique septentrionale au Magreb avec les nations chrétiennes au moyen age* (Paris, 1886), pp. 63-73).

[7] Gabriella Garzella, *Pisa com'era: topografia ed insediamento, dall'impianto tardoantico alla città del XII secolo* (Pisa, 1990), pp. 171-173. On the system of ports of call of Pisa, see Silvia Orvietani Busch, "An

arriving with frequency in the North African ports, in southern Italy and the Tyrrhenian islands, and in the port cities of the Gulf of Lyon, while Pisan merchants were regularly trafficking with the mercantile centres of Egypt, of the Byzantine empire, and of the Crusader states[8].

Only in the following century would Catalonia achieve a similar mercantile diffusion. And the starting point for the presence of Catalans in the Mediterranean is indeed that same 1113 enterprise organised by the Pisans.[9] There the Catalans participated as an allied contingent in a mission based primarily on Italian organisation and resources.[10] One hundred and twenty years later, in 1229, the

interdisciplinary and comparative approach to northern Tuscan ports in the early and high middle ages", in *Iberia and the Mediterranean World of the Middle Ages,* ed. Larry Simon (Leiden, 1995), pp. 161-184.

[8] Marco Tangheroni, "Sui rapporti commerciali tra Pisa e la Tunisia" in *L'Italia e i paesi mediterranei* (Pisa, 1988), pp. 75-90; Ottavio Banti, "I trattati tra Pisa e Tunisi dal XII al XIV secolo" in *L'Italia e i paesi mediterranei*, pp. 43-74; Marco Tangheroni, "Pisa e il regno crociato di Gerusalemme", in *I comuni italiani nel regno crociato di Gerusalemme* (Genova, 1986); Ottavio Banti, "I rapporti tra Pisa e gli stati islamici dell'Africa settentrionale tra XI e XII secolo", in *Le ceramiche medievali delle chiese di Pisa* (Pisa, 1983), pp. 9-26; David Abulafia, *The Two Italies* (Cambridge, 1977), pp. 59-62, 138-140, and 202-213.

[9] Marco Tangheroni, "Economia e navigazione nel Mediterraneo occidentale tra XI e XII secolo", *Medioevo Saggi e Rassegne* 16 (1992), 21-24. See also his comment on the 1113-1115 expedition.

[10] The role of the Catalans has been widely disputed. Some scholars contend that the Pisan-commanded fleet was thrown on the Catalan coast by a storm (Scalía, "Contibuti pisani", p. 138), as the *carme* written by a Pisan cleric intones (Calisse, vv. 225-260), while Spanish writers opt for the theory of a previous agreement between the Pisans and Ramon Berenguer III - such as Alvaro Santamaria, "Determinantes de la conquista de Baleares", *Mayurqa* 8 (June, 1972), 90 - and of the supremacy of the Catalan count in this enterprise. I believe that some previous contact and request, from Pisa to Catalonia, must have existed, considering not only the careful diplomatic and military

Catalans, by now part of the federated Crown of Aragon,[11] were able to assemble a successful expedition to conquer definitively those islands, which were a Muslim outpost in the northern Mediterranean[12] but also a fundamental mercantile cross-roads. The 1229-1232 mission, in which contingents participated from Occitan city ports, was accomplished independently, without the supervision or even simple contribution of any of the major Italian maritime superpowers. The years between the two enterprises were fundamental for development of Catalan orientation to the sea and for their acquisition of the necessary political, financial, and technical skills. The conquest of the Balearic Islands gains an even greater importance when considered in the light of the following events, which led Catalonia, and the Crown of Aragon behind it,[13] to impose its presence on the markets as well as on the whole political arena of the Mediterranean.

Regarding commercial contacts and exchanges between Catalonia and Pisa during this important phase of their history, direct testimonies are rare. It is specifically the surviving diplomatic correspondence and the political events involving the whole western Mediterranean that reveal the characteristics and the evolution of commercial relations between the two. The first treaty, signed on the

preparation of the Pisans, but also the well organised participation of Occitanian lords with their contingents (see Carme Battle i Gallart, "Els Francesos a la Corona d'Aragó", *Anuario de Estudios Medievales* 10 (1980), 362).

[11] The count of Barcelona Ramon Berenguer IV, son of Ramon Berenguer III, had united in 1137 Catalonia with the kingdom of Aragon. This union created the Crown of Aragon, a confederation of lands destined to grow swiftly in extension and power.

[12] After the attack in 1114 the Balearic Islands had not been settled by the Christians, and in 1116 an Almoravid fleet landed, reclaiming them.

[13] Alvaro Santamaria, "Precisiones sobra la expansión marítima de la Corona de Aragón", *Anales de la Universidad de Alicante* 8 (1990-1991), 211.

occasion of the joint participation in the crusade against the Balearics in 1113, does not have a military character but is a truly commercial agreement. The Pisans were mainly interested in obtaining protection and commercial tax relief in Arles and Saint-Gilles.[14] No specific commercial concession was required in Catalonia, except generic protection and tax facilitations. No port or major commercial place for the Pisans in Catalonia was indicated.[15] After the diplomatic trip of the Catalan count to Genoa and Pisa in 1116,[16] in the following years it was Genoa instead, already a political and commercial rival of Pisa, which secured privileged relationships, commercial advantages, and treaties with Catalonia.[17]

[14] Ramon Berenguer III had married the year before the heiress of Provence, Dolça. But his control, and recognition itself of his claims on Provence, were widely disputed, both by Emperor Henry II, who considered Provence a direct part of the Empire, and by the count of Toulouse, who claimed the inheritance as well (G. de Manteyer, "La Provence du premièr au douzième siècle", *Mémoires et documents publiés par la Société de l'École des Chartres* 8 (Paris, 1908-26) 1:198-328; C. De Vic, J. Vaissète, *Histoire générale de Languedoc* (Toulouse, 1872-1905), 4:57-59).

[15] The text of the document, dated 7 September 1113, was transcribed in the concession by the count-king James I to the Pisans on 8 August 1233 (Calisse, *Liber Maiolichinus*, App. 1).

[16] Ramon Berenguer III's intentions were to reach Rome and ask pope Pascal II to call a crusade against the Muslims of Tortosa. But because of the quarrel with Emperor Henry II over Provence, he decided it was wiser to send his emissaries instead to Rome and wait for them in Pisa (José-Ramon Julià Viñamata, "La situazione politica nel Mediterraneo occidentale all'epoca di Ramon Berenguer III: la spedizione a Maiorca 1113-1115", *Medioevo Saggi e Rassegne* 16 (1992), 69).

[17] In 1126 and in 1227. Both are published by Francisco de Bofarull y Sans, "Antigua Marina Catalana", in *Memorias de la Real Academia de Buenas Letras de Barcelona* 7 (Barcelona, 1901), docs. 3 and 4. The 1227 treaty was generous with the Genoese, and their transit taxes were lowered. See Geo Pistarino, "Genova e l' Occitania nel secolo XII", in *Actes du Ier Congrès Historique Provence-Ligurie* (Aix-Bordighera-Marseille, 1966), pp. 79-81.

During the first years in power of Ramon Berenguer IV (d. 1162), son of Ramon Berenguer III and ruler of both Catalonia and Aragon since 1137, the relations, both commercial and diplomatic, between Catalonia and Pisa are obscure. In 1146 it was once again Genoa, pursuing at this moment a very aggressive policy in the western Mediterranean,[18] which concluded a military treaty with Ramon Berenguer IV, a treaty centred on the conquest of Tortosa and on a projected capture of the Balearic Islands.[19] It was indeed this last Catalan-Genoese project against the islands and the Genoese raid on Minorca which attracted the attention of the Pisans. In a letter to Ramon Berenguer IV the Pisan commune repeated the validity of the shared, Pisan-Catalan, tutelage over the Balearic Islands - a tutelage derived from that first joint expedition in 1113-1115. The Pisans then proceeded to denounce the Genoese interference. This same letter also indicated, for the first time, that direct fighting had occurred between Pisans and Catalans. We cannot know for certain whether these encounters had taken place in Catalan territory or along the Provençal-Occitan coasts, but the

[18] Already in 1109 Genoa had secured a monopolistic treaty, with the count of Toulouse and Saint-Gilles. Then the first known diplomatic document between Genoa and Narbonne is dated 1132. With this treaty Narbonne abandoned its former alliance with Pisa, in a crucial moment in the war between Genoa and Pisa (André Dupont, *Les relations commerciales entre les cités maritimes de Languedoc et les cités méditerranéennes d'Espagne et d'Italie du Xème au XIIIème siècle* (Nimes, 1943), p. 71). The Genoese hold on this coast increased with the multiple treaties with Frejús, Antibes, Marseille, Hyères, and Fos in July 1138. Genoa imposed itself on them as a superior mercantile power and a key player for their commerce with North African states (Pistarino, "Genoa e l'Islam nel Mediterraneo occidentale", *Anuario de Estudios Medievales* 10 (1980), 190-191).

[19] Antonio Imperiale di Sant'Angelo, *Codice Diplomatico della Repubblica di Genova* (Rome, 1936), 1, docs. 168 and 169.

Catalans had already lamented to the Pisan authorities that they had received "unfair" damage.

The tone of the Pisans regarding this matter appears firm but friendly, and they claim to have made inquiries into the accidents and to have done everything possible. Evident here is the determination of the Pisans to better their relations with Catalonia; because of the series of treaties with the Genoese, Catalans must have borne the blows of the vengeful pirate activity of Pisan ships.[20] It is difficult to assess whether this more favourable disposition of the Pisans brought an increase in commercial traffic with Catalonia. Nevertheless, thanks also to a cooling of relations between Genoa and Barcelona after the capture of Tortosa in 1148,[21] relations with Pisa improved sensibly, favoured by a community of interests and alliances in Sardinia.[22] The Tuscan city was at this moment intent upon strengthening its presence in the commercial markets in areas economically more developed, such as North Africa, the Middle

[20] This document lacks a date because it is a copy made in Barcelona of the original letter sent by the Pisans, but it was very probably written between 1147 and 1148. See Blanca Garí, "Pisa y el control del Mediterráneo nordoccidental. Carta de los cónsules de Pisa a Ramon Berenguer IV a mediados del siglo XII", *Acta Mediaevalia* 13 (1992), 14-15, where she discusses also the implications and the situation preceding the letter of the consuls of Pisa to Ramon Berenguer IV regarding the question of the Balearics.

[21] The Genoese, after having obtained one third of Tortosa, concluded a unilateral peace in 1149 with the Valencian ruler, without consulting their Catalan ally (Rossi-Sabatini, 102). From this moment on, Genoa reshaped its previously aggressive strategy towards the western Mediterranean Muslims (Pistarino, "Genova e l'Islam", pp. 193-195). Pisa, which had already quietly de facto implemented a similar less aggressive policy since the end of the expedition to the Balearics in 1113-1115, signed in 1150 a commercial treaty with Valencia as well (Rossi-Sabatini, 6).

[22] F. Artizzu, *Pisani e catalani nella Sardegna medievale* (Cagliari, 1973); Alberto Boscolo, *Sardegna, Pisa e Genova nel Medioevo* (Genova, 1978).

East, and the Occitan coast. But exchanges with Catalonia were not non-existent, and Pisan ships in the port of Barcelona were a frequent sight,[23] having as an incentive also the pilgrim movement to and from Rome, the Holy Land and Santiago de Compostela.

The accession to the throne in 1162 by Alphonse II (1162-1196),[24] the son of Ramon Berenguer IV, and the first to reunite both the titles of count of Barcelona and king of Aragon, coincided with another phase of the struggle between Pisa and Genoa for mercantile supremacy. The principal theatres of the war were now the waters and ports of the Gulf of Lyon. Because in 1166 Alphonse, after the death of the count of Provence, reunited the Provençal domains to Catalonia, his role in the fight grew in importance. In 1167 the Genoese imposed on the count-king, in need of their help against the count of Toulouse, hard conditions against the Pisans, who were not allowed to land in the ports or along the coasts "from Nice to the Ebre" - that is, along all the Mediterranean coast theoretically under the control of Alphonse. Only those Pisan ships used solely to transport pilgrims were excluded from this embargo.[25] Eager to show his own good faith to the aggressive ally, Alphonse had two Pisan ships, surprised in the port of Barcelona, captured; and he granted half of the confiscated

[23] Benjamin of Tudela, "The Travels of Benjamin of Tudela", in *Early Travels to Palestine*, ed. and trans. T. Wright (London, 1848), p. 64.

[24] He was the first to be both king of Aragon (Alfonso II in the Aragonese genealogical line) and count of Barcelona (Alfons I in the Catalan counties). The name difference, also for the following count-kings, is settled here with the use of the English form, in this case Alphonse.

[25] It is dated 7 May 1167. Genoa was trying to establish its mercantile monopoly with the Provençal, Occitan, and, consequently, Catalan coasts. The agreements the Genoese concluded in the 1160s and 1170s with the Occitan coastal cities have in common the total exclusion of Pisa from these ports, as well as Genoa's superiority over them (Dupont, pp. 90-98).

goods to the Genoese consul.[26] Pisan ships had continued therefore to frequent the Catalan ports, carrying both pilgrims and merchandise. The transports must also have been quite frequent, if two Pisan ships could have been caught by surprise by the terms of this agreement while at anchor in the port of Barcelona.

Obviously we should not assume that this treaty completely limited the commercial exchanges of Pisa with Catalonia and the other cities of the Occitan and Provençal coast. Alphonse could control directly only the Catalan coast, and it is not clear how rigidly, even in the same Catalan territories, this total embargo was applied. Regarding trans-Pyrenean lands, application was even more obscure, and was against the interests of the single communities and mercantile centres, which were far more concerned with commercial exchanges with an important economic partner such as Pisa, than with the absolute fidelity to a distant feudal lord. This clause was actually part of the Genoese strategy to limit to the utmost possible the trade of Pisa in all of the western area, as was confirmed by the peace of 1169[27] - in reality a truce of merely one year - between the two Italian cities. But the Genoese, confident in their strong position in that area, did not refrain from concluding two consecutive treaties, in 1171[28] and in 1174, with the great Occitan antagonist of the Crown of Aragon, the count of Toulouse. Aware of the possible consequences of this diplomatic about-face, they required the insertion in the document of 1174 of a clause that invalidated it in case the application of that same treaty would endanger the

[26] Adolf Schaube, *Storia del commercio dei popoli latini del Mediterraneo sino alla fine delle crociate*, ital. trans. Pietro Bonfante (Torino, 1915), p. 544.

[27] One third of the transported merchandise was to be confiscated from all Pisan ships caught in Provençal waters.

[28] 1 May 1171 (Dupont, pp. 103-106).

possessions of the Genoese involved in commerce with the Crown of Aragon.[29] At this time the major Italian commercial partner of Catalonia was Genoa, so worried for the interests, evidently considerable, of its citizens, to the point of protecting them explicitly in a political treaty with a third party.

Alphonse responded to this shifting in Genoese politics with a treaty of friendship and protection with Pisa in 1177, two years after the third peace of Portovenere between Pisa and Genoa. The text of this accord shows how relations between Catalonia and Pisa had evolved in the meanwhile, and it also underscores the increase of activity by Catalan merchants in the Mediterranean. In fact, and it is the first time, the protection required for subjects was reciprocal. The men of the count-king would be safe from Pisan attack from the northern limit of the coast of Catalonia - Salses in the Catalan Roussillon - to its southernmost border. This request shows how the Pisans had abundantly taken a toll, because of the long friendship of the Catalans with Genoa, with pirate attacks even within the very territorial waters of the Crown of Aragon. This document also defined a procedure to settle mutual recriminations and quarrels. The Pisans, in addition, obtained the concession of paying only the commercial taxes agreed upon with Alphonse's predecessors: a clear sign of a recent imposition upon the Pisan merchants of additional, heavy taxation, perhaps as a retaliation for the attacks, or to create an advantage for the Genoese competitors. But once again there is no mention of a specific concession that could highlight the importance of the trade between Pisa and Catalonia: something like a *fonduq*, or the request of complete exemption from commercial dues. For their part the Catalans did not require similar concessions

[29] Both treaties of 1171 and 1174 are in *Liber Iurium Reipublicae Ianuensis* (Torino, 1864), 1, nn. 309 and 310.

in the territories under Pisa, where their traffic must have been scarce. Their major attention is concentrated on obtaining protection from Pisan aggression along their own coasts.[30] This was also the period in which Pisa was focusing on improving its relations with all of the mercantile centres of the north-western Mediterranean,[31] now that the war with Genoa had concentrated in other areas, from Sardinia to the Middle East. The conditions for commercial relations between Pisa and Catalonia were also improving because of the growing aversion of Genoa to the increased dynamism of the Catalans in the Mediterranean[32] and for their never-abandoned plans over the Balearics. The Ligurian city intended to maintain the *status quo* in the western Mediterranean, now that it had a position of supremacy, and it was strongly opposed to any form of

[30] Barcelona, Arxiu de la Corona d'Aragó, Parchment, Alfons I, carpeta 46, n. 214.

[31] Meanwhile Pisa was also busy with decisive diplomatic moves in the Gulf of Lyon. The same Pisan envoy, Ildebrandus Sismondi, who had signed the treaty with Alphonse in January 1177, was in February finalising a treaty with the tutors of Guilhem VIII of Montpellier. The previous treaty had been signed in 1168 and thenceforth relationships between the two cities had remained stable (Dupont, pp. 115-116). At the end of the following month another accord was signed between Pisa and Nice (29 March 1177). In November 1178 a treaty with Grasse was concluded. In this accord there is a clause that obliged the commune of Grasse to notify Pisa in case of hostile acts conducted by the count-king or his representatives in Provence against the Pisans. While it is difficult to know why this request had been made by the Pisans (maybe some minor problems with Catalonia in 1178 that left no trace) this is another proof of the willingness of the citizens to side with a foreign state, if convenient to their interests, rather than with their feudal overlord (Rossi-Sabatini, *L'espansione*, 94).

[32] In 1181-1185 the Ligurean commune signed an agreement with Raimond V of Toulouse and Saint-Gilles, Sanç count of Provence, and Guillaume count of Forcalquier. One of the clauses was indeed the commitment of the three Occitan lords to oppose any attempt by the count-king to dominate Genoa.

strengthening of another Christian power in the area. The war for the succession in the Sardinian judicature of Arborea unsettled the pattern of alliances. One of the consequences was a reconciliation between Genoa and the Crown of Aragon; and in the treaty with the Ligurian city in 1186 Alphonse promised once again to keep the Pisans out of the territories of the Crown and to seize them, if they disembarked on the Catalan coastline. The peace, two years later, between Pisa and Genoa, removed the reason behind this embargo.[33]

During the first years of rule by Peter,[34] son of Alphonse, there were no traces of a marked improvement of relations with Pisa. But we can notice a growth of friction with Genoa, manifested in continuous Genoese pirate attacks against Catalan merchants.[35] Diplomatic exchanges between Pisa and the Crown of Aragon were resumed unexpectedly in 1204, when a Pisan ship arrived, while in pursuit of a Genoese cargo ship, in the harbour of Barcelona. This provided the occasion to conclude right then an agreement between the Pisans and Barcelonese notables. The count-king is never mentioned in the document; and in the text, of Catalan origin, there

[33] Schaube, pp. 769 and 664 (texts of documents in *Liber Iurium Reipublicae Ianuensium*, 1, nn. 360 and 358).

[34] Pedro II (Pere I in Catalonia) ruled from 1196 to 1213.

[35] Pisan ships were probably not directly endangered in Catalonia after the treaty between Pisa and Genoa in 1188 which determined a loosening of the anti-Pisan agreement between the Genoese and Alphonse signed in 1186. Nevertheless, a climate of suspicion must have remained between Catalonia and Pisa. Genoa was still the favourite in commerce with the crown. In 1198 Peter concluded another accord with Genoa. The count-king confirmed the freedom of commerce, and the exemption from taxes for the Genoese in the Realms. But relationships were not at their best, and that same 3 September 1198 agreement shows bitterness over continuous Genoese pirate attacks (Maria Teresa Ferrer i Mallol, "Els Italians a terres Catalanes (segles XII-XV)", *Anuario de Estudios Medievales* 10 (1980), 431). But during his 1204 trip to Rome, Peter stopped in Genoa, where he was received with honour (Schaube, pp. 665-666).

is a continual insistence on the advantage, in protection and security, that this agreement would mean for the Genoese as well, whom the Pisans are obliged not to attack in Catalan waters.[36] The reasoning behind this is the obvious worry about seeming unfaithful to the aggressive ally and the consequent fear of reprisals. After this agreement the Pisans continued a policy of stabilisation of their relations with all the Occitan-Provençal cities, with a series of accords between 1208 and 1211, to increase the volume and the safety of their exchanges in this area.[37] Meanwhile, the mercantile development of Catalonia and its traffic continued.[38] By now the Catalan merchants had no intention of continuing to leave to foreign ships and merchants the monopoly of commerce in their ports and the export of local products, and they called for protectionist measures by the count-king.[39] The old role of commercial mediation between one side and the other of the Mediterranean - a role made

[36] In the Arxiu de la Corona d'Aragó in Barcelona survives a document that recollects the events and the treaty, and it is published by Antonio de Bofarull, *Colección de documentos inéditos del archivo general de la Corona de Aragón* (Barcelona, 1852), 8:95-96.

[37] Profiting from a more peaceful climate with Genoa in this area, Pisa renewed relations with all the western Mediterranean port-cities with a series of treaties: 1208 with Fos, 1209 with Marseille, 1211 with Arles, while with Montpellier and Narbonne they had remained on a stable, cordial, level. All the agreements show reciprocal respect and conditions of parity. Genoa, to compete with the diplomatic strategy of Pisa, was forced to concede to these cities, in the treaties concluded since the end of the twelfth and during the thirteenth century, a position of equality with itself. (Rossi-Sabatini, pp. 95-96; Dupont, pp. 121-122).

[38] Manuel Riu, "El redreç del comerç catalá a l'alta edat mitjana", in *El comerç en el marc economic de Catalunya* (Barcelona, 1980), pp. 55-72.

[39] The count-king James granted to the people of Barcelona, in a document dated 12 October 1227, that a foreign ship could not carry merchandise from Barcelona to North Africa and vice versa if there were a ship of Barcelona about to run the same route (Ferrer, 430-432).

their own by the Italian mercantile city-states in the eleventh and twelfth centuries - was now to be shared with the emerging maritime powers, such as the Crown of Aragon, and with the merchant groups in cities like Narbonne, Arles, and Montpellier.

The point reached by the mercantile, naval, and financial development of the Crown of Aragon became manifest and found its first major external affirmation in the expedition against the Balearic Islands in 1229. Provoked, according to tradition, by pirate attacks against Catalan cargoes and by Catalan awareness of the richness of these isles,[40] this conquest is largely the expression of the anti-Muslim role in the western Mediterranean that the Crown of Aragon claimed, as well as of the continuing claims of the Catalans over the Balearics. Not only Catalan cities and feudal lords, but also Provençal and Occitanian port cities created a politically, socially and geographically varied contingent, very similar, in this aspect, to that gathered by Pisa in 1113.[41] This time however Genoa and also Pisa just observed the situation, without intervention. In 1230, when the Catalan conquest of Majorca had been consolidated, Genoa moved first to obtain substantial commercial facilities in Majorca.[42] Pisa followed suit three years later, with the confirmation of the old treaty of 1113 by the then count-king James. In addition to the old concessions, the Pisans were granted a *fonduq* and fiscal facilities in Majorca. The two Italian cities had already been active in the Balearics since the last years of the twelfth century and had enjoyed

[40] There is documentary proof that Catalan merchants were using Majorca as a commercial stop and port-of-call along their Mediterranean routes (Carme Battle i Gallart, "Les relaciones comerciales de Barcelona con la España musulmana a fine del sigle XII e inicio del XIII", *Anales de la Universidad de Alicante* 6 (1978), 108).

[41] Alvaro Santamaria, "Determinantes de la conquista de Baleares (1229-1232)", *Mayurqa* 8 (June 1972), 65-131.

[42] Schaube, pp. 666-668.

cordial relations with the rulers.[43] Pisa was not yet intensely involved in exchanges with Catalonia: once again there is no mention of commerce with the peninsular part of the Catalan-Aragonese realms.[44]

Commercial relations between Pisa and Catalonia, during the chronological frame here studied, followed closely the oscillations of diplomatic relations, which were in turn tied with the political situation in the western Mediterranean. Besides the lack of direct archival sources for the commercial exchanges, there is never mention of spontaneous commercial accords. The clauses regarding economic matters were always connected to political-diplomatic events and treaties, and are quite vague and unspecified. Pisa remains always satisfied with generic assurances of protection and with moderate fiscal facilities. No specific port or Catalan city is ever explicitly indicated as a major base for Pisan commerce. The only very specific concession is in the last archival testimony of this period, the document of James I to the Pisans in 1233, whereby they obtained a *fonduq* in Majorca (they had already had one before the Catalan conquest) but without asking for any specific concession elsewhere in the territories of the Crown. For their part, the Catalans were never interested in asking for reciprocal conditions for fiscal exemption or commercial advantages in the territories controlled by the Tuscan commune, a sign of the episodic nature of Catalan commerce with Pisa. They only requested protection in their own

[43] Genoa had signed two treaties, in 1181 and 1188, Pisa one in 1184. In 1203 the Banū Ghāniya power was overthrown by an Almohad fleet, commanded by the son of the sultan of Morocco (de Mas Latrie, pp. 98-100).

[44] It is dated 8 August 1233. (Barcelona, Arxiu de la Corona d'Aragó Parchments, Jaume I, 496). It is published by Calisse, *Liber Maiolichinus*, App. 1; and Huici Miranda, Cabanes Pecourt, *Documentos de Jaime I*, 1:318-322).

territorial waters from pirate Pisan attacks, a direct consequence of the hostility of Pisa towards all the allies of the Genoese.

A last consideration concerns the naval, military, and financial techniques, which, in this period, developed at an increasing rate in all of the area of the Crown of Aragon. The 1113-1115 expedition had first exposed the Catalans to direct contact with advanced military and naval techniques, just perfected by the Pisans thanks to their participation in the events subsequent to the conquest of Jerusalem. Moreover, part of the Pisan fleet remained between 1113 and 1114 in the Catalan harbours, for repairs and commerce. As for financial techniques, surely the Catalans benefited from the constant commercial contacts with the Italians, in particular the Genoese, and from their own frequenting of major Mediterranean mercantile places from the second half of the twelfth century. Contact between Catalonia and Pisa was then essentially profitable for the former in this period, as a contact with a more advanced area. Pisa, on its side, never considered Catalonia as a commercial destination of primary importance, both because of its relative backwardness in comparison with nearby areas, such as the city ports of the Gulf of Lyon, and also because of its preference for maintaining relations with Genoa.

Datini and Venice: News from the Mediterranean Trade Network[1]

Eleanor A. Congdon
Gonville and Caius College, Cambridge

On 27 October 1403,[2] Luca di Matteo, a Florentine merchant living in Venice, wrote to one of his associates the latest news circulating within the city.

> Today a report arrived about a clash between the Venetian fleet and Marshall Boucicault's Genoese armada. Apparently, there was a great battle; in the end the Venetians captured three of the eight

[1] I wish to thank those who have helped to bring this project to its present form: the Managers of the Ellen McArthur Fund who awarded me a studentship which allowed me to work in Italy; the Managers of the Prince Consort Thirlwall for a travel grant; and Gonville and Caius College for supporting my presentation at the International Medieval Congress; the archivists and researchers at the Archivio di Stato in Prato, especially Elena Cecchi, and at the Archivio di Stato di Venezia; the presenters and audience for my panel at Leeds; and my Supervisor Dr. David Abulafia for aid, suggestions, and support.

[2] All dates have been modernised in this article.

> Genoese galleys, along with all their men. The rest
> of the Genoese fleet has departed.[3]

By the time he wrote his next letter on 10 November, all of Venice knew that the first reports were basically accurate: a battle had occurred, initiating another period of sea-borne confrontation between the Genoese and Venetians. It had been fought off Modon, at the very mouth of the Adriatic Sea; the Genoese fleet's manoeuvres had suggested to the Venetian commander, Carlo Zeno, that its intent was not simply to enter a port in order to take on fresh water. No matter who attacked first, the result was that the Venetian galleys won and drove the Genoese out of the Ionian Sea. In his second letter, Luca di Matteo adds this comment to a re-statement of events: "and we do not hope that war is the result of this battle because that will be very bad for all the merchants. May God send peace to all those who need it".[4] Other correspondents writing from Venice echo these sentiments, which were the consensus of the entire community of merchants involved in international trade.

Luca di Matteo's letters carrying the tidings of the battle off Modon are examples of the most typical mode by which news spread between merchants throughout the Mediterranean during the middle ages. These documents are reports between two people associated by means of their commercial activities. The letters contain information on accounts, commodity availability and prices, ship movements, money-related services such as banks and

[3] Archivio di Stato, Prato (hereafter, A.S.P.), Datini 928, Carteggio Barcelona, letter Venice to Barcelona, Compagnia Luigi Davanzatti e Luca di Matteo to Compagnia Francesco di Marco Datini e Simone d'Andrea Bellandi, 27 October 1403.

[4] A.S.P., Datini 928, Carteggio Barcelona, letter Venice to Barcelona, Compagnia Luigi Davanzatti e Luca di Matteo to Compagnia Francesco di Marco Datini e Simone d'Andrea Bellandi, 10 November 1403.

exchange rates, summations of old business, instructions for future actions, and notes of personal interest such as deaths and weddings. Each is part of an on-going dialogue between the writer and recipient concerning business matters. "Historic events", such as the Venetian-Genoese encounter off Modon, sometimes created conditions which affected the merchants' business; they are mentioned because of their influence on commerce.

News travelled throughout the medieval Mediterranean markets in several ways. Merchant letters moved specific information between individuals. Word of mouth, collected on the wharves and in merchant houses, brought tales, rumours, and details concerning far-off events and lands. In addition, where possible, merchants collected reports from government officials who had access to the state's information-gathering organs, such as ambassadorial dispatches, other papers, and council debates.

Most "historic events" have significance because they were discussed or prompted by governments whose records - those which were preserved - are now the source material used by most scholars. The battle off Modon is well known for just this reason: the Venetian Senate deliberations are the source for Kenneth Setton's account of it in *Papacy and the Levant*.[5] Such sources are biased by the needs of the government that created them; the principal Venetian evidence is the original draft in the Senate minutes of the

[5] Kenneth Setton, *The Papacy and the Levant*, Vol. 1: *The Thirteenth and Fourteenth Centuries* (Philadelphia, 1976), pp. 382-395. Setton handles the events quite carefully, recognising that the Genoese also had their version of the story. Ashtor is not so careful and paints Boucicault as the aggressor. Eliyahu Ashtor, *Levant Trade in the Later Middle Ages* (Princeton, 1983), pp. 216-220.

letter sent throughout Italy and to the courts of Hungary, Savoy, Burgundy and France with the official version of the events.[6]

Merchant letters, such as the ones written by Luca di Matteo, provide an opportunity for late medieval history scholars to see these events and their impacts in terms of the people who were "outside" the political and military spheres - merchants and other "common people". Unlike account books, which generally only give the end result of endeavours, not reasons for a merchant changing his mind about particular products, and unlike notary books, which record what merchants thought they were about to do, correspondence shows which events received attention as being important to merchants supplying local and international consumers. Unlike judicial records, which were gathered together to prove a person's assertion that an injustice had been committed, merchant letters were only meant to convince the reader that business was moving in a certain direction and that the writer's decisions were sensible and well thought-out.

Merchants throughout the Mediterranean region during the late medieval period were constantly in need of news. They had to know where markets existed, and, within those markets, what goods could be bought, sold or exchanged, what the customs and facilities for commerce were in that locale, whether a company could place a representative there, use a native middle-man, or would be compelled to deal with specific people, and how the local government and populace would react to their presence. They had to know when not to invest in a region because of internal turmoil, when to take advantage of a brief period of peace, when to take precautions against loss because the routes taken by their goods

[6] Archivio di Stato Venezia, *Senato Misti*, reg. 46ii (copia), fols. 380-382; 28 October 1403.

were unsafe, how events in one region would affect another, and when to go about business as if conditions were normal. The information most important to merchants, be they Italian, north European, Catalan, French, Moorish, Greek, Turkish, or anyone else doing business that involved the Mediterranean region, however, was when and how conditions changed. All that was required was one small incident and a market could suddenly close or open, while investments that had seemed safe and conservative could suddenly become terrible disasters - as the events resulting from the battle off Modon were to prove for a number of Italians with capital invested in the western Mediterranean. The speed of reception of news, and timing of reaction to it, could mean the difference between success and bankruptcy. News was the cornerstone of a merchant's prosperity or downfall.

For the late fourteenth century, the papers of Francesco di Marco Datini - the Merchant of Prato - provide a fantastic wealth of information and diversity of authors. Federigo Melis counted over 152,000 individual letters, and around five hundred account books in this archive.[7] No comparable collection for one merchant, tracing the vast majority of his career and mercantile activities, exists for the medieval or early modern periods. Despite the exaggerated claims for its completeness,[8] this archive is in truth only a fraction of the records produced by Datini's seven companies and numerous correspondents. The gaps here can be frustrating and significant; despite the more than 6000 items which he and his companies

[7] Federigo Melis, *Aspetti della vita economica medievale* (Siena, 1962), pp. 30-32.

[8] Iris Origo, *The Merchant of Prato: Daily Life in a Medieval Italian City* (1957; repr. London, 1992), p. 25.

received from Venice,[9] only two dozen letters written to that city by Datini or his dependants survive. In comparison to other archival collections of merchant papers, however, the Datini archive is very complete. Most "historic events" are mentioned by one or more correspondents during their discussions of outside events that might influence business. For example, both the Commessaria di Zanobi di Taddeo Gaddi[10] and Luca di Matteo[11] report the confrontation between Tīmūr (771-807/1370-1405) and the Ottoman Sultan Bayezit (791-804/1389-1402) in Ankara in July 1402. One of the Commessaria's following letters says that Tīmūr's victory brought peace to Turkish lands, that Bayezit's sons had fled to Galipoli, and that merchants in Syria now feared that his next target would be Cairo (although this might not be altogether bad for Christians).[12] Tīmūr's movements remained mysterious and threatening to merchants in Venice throughout the next year; despite persistent rumours to that effect, he did not actually return, not even to take advantage of disruption in Syria and Egypt caused by the Genoese in 1403.

[9] Because none of the recipients in Venice were dependants of Datini's, these letters properly belonged to the archives of the people who received them; they were thus not gathered together in Prato when Datini's companies were liquidated after his death in 1410.

[10] A.S.P., Datini 928, Carteggio Barcelona, letter Venice to Barcelona, Commessaria di Zanobi di Taddeo Gaddi e Antonio di Ser Bartolomeo to Compagnia Francesco di Marco Datini e Simone d'Andrea Bellandi, 14 October 1402.

[11] A.S.P., Datini 928, Carteggio Barcelona, letter Venice to Barcelona, Compagnia Luigi Davanzatti e Luca di Matteo to Compagnia Francesco di Marco Datini e Simone d'Andrea Bellandi, 7 October 1402.

[12] A.S.P., Datini 928, Carteggio Barcelona, letter Venice to Barcelona, Commessaria di Zanobi di Taddeo Gaddi e Antonio di Ser Bartolomeo to Compagnia Francesco di Marco Datini e Simone d'Andrea Bellandi, 6 December 1402.

The contents of the Datini archive demonstrate how, if a merchant wanted information about the far reaches of the Black Sea or the port next door, he would be well served by having a correspondent in Venice. Because Venetian commercial interests and activities were so widespread, merchants on the Rialto had access to information from the whole Mediterranean and all the lands bordering it; they considered all of the reports, whether they were obviously rumours about political figures or were verifiable summations of a year's production for a particular commodity, to be worthy of their attention. For example, Luca di Matteo's first letter describing the Genoese armada's defeat off Modon includes news of a remittance to be made to associates in Bruges, for goods travelling on the Venetian Flanders galley line, and of the movement of ships at Ibiza.[13] His second additionally reports the arrival of ships from the Black Sea with rich cargoes of spices, and that no new reports of disturbances had arrived from Syria and Egypt.[14] People writing from one of the great international ports, especially Venice, had a wider range of information available than people at other locales; they gathered it and then disseminated it through their correspondence. Equally, merchants from one end of the Mediterranean to the other collected and sent intelligence both to people in the great information-redistribution centres, such as Venice, and to locales where it might prove interesting. Although other scholars may or may not want to discuss whether Venice was the premier trading nation at the end of the fourteenth century, it

[13] A.S.P., Datini 928, Carteggio Bareclona, letter Venice to Barcelona, Compagnia Luigi Davanzatti e Luca di Matteo to Compagnia Francesco di Marco Datini e Simone d'Andrea Bellandi, 27 October 1403.

[14] A.S.P., Datini 928, Carteggio Barcelona, letter Venice to Barcelona, Compagnia Luigi Davanzatti e Luca di Matteo to Compagnia Francesco di Marco Datini e Simone d'Andrea Bellandi, 10 November 1403.

certainly was an excellent "listening post" for events from all over which might affect merchants.

The letters from the Datini archive's Venetian collection for the year 1403 are a good example of how, among all the commodity information, the authors felt that non-commercial events were important to their business. As a collection, they record the Genoese armada's entire voyage, with all its stops and accomplishments, and the repercussions for trade arising out of the encounter off Modon. It had sailed in April 1403, almost at the same time as an accord settling a previous dispute between Genoa and Venice was being signed.[15] The Venetians had advance knowledge of Boucicault's intention to punish the Cypriot king, Janus, for trying to return Famaghosta (Famagusta) to native rule.[16] Because they suspected that he also wanted to attack Egypt in the name of "Crusade", they suspended the regular galley-lines to the Levant until the Genoese should return to the west.[17] The Senate dispatched Carlo Zeno and the state fleet to watch Boucicault's movements; the letters from Venice record the Genoese armada passing Modon, stopping at Rhodes, going on to attack the coast of Turkey at Candeloro while the grand master of the Hospitallers negotiated the Cypriot humiliation, and finally their arrival in Cyprus.[18] Venetian fears

[15] A.S.P., Datini 928, Carteggio Barcelona, letter Venice to Barcelona, Compagnia Simone Lappacino to Compagnia Francesco di Marco Datini e Simone d'Andrea Bellandi, 28 April 1403.

[16] A.S.P., Datini 928, Carteggio Barcelona, letter Venice to Barcelona, Compagnia Luigi Davanzatti e Luca di Matteo to Compagnia Francesco di Marco Datini e Simone d'Andrea Bellandi, 20 February 1403.

[17] A.S.P., Datini 928, Carteggio Barcelona, letter Venice to Barcelona, Domenico d'Andrea to Compagnia Francesco di Marco Datini e Simone d'Andrea Bellandi, 18 August 1403.

[18] A.S.P., Datini 928, Carteggio Barcelona, letter Venice to Barcelona, Commessaria di Zanobi di Taddeo Gaddeo e Antonio di Ser Bartolomeo to Compagnia Francesco di Marco Datini e Simone d'Andrea Bellandi, 12 May

about Boucicault's intentions to recoup his honour as a defender of the Christian faith, lost during his humiliating capture by the Turks at the battle of Nicopolis in 1396, were soon realised. In September 1403, the Genoese armada attacked and ransacked the port of Beirut, and also made aggressive gestures at Tripoli, Latakia and Alexandria before sending a haughty message to the Circassian sultan demanding peace. The Datini letters assert, with a mixture of outrage and mourning, that the people who bore the brunt of these attacks were not actually Muslims, but instead Venetian merchants in the ports preparing goods for the next available transport ships.[19] In late September, just six months after he had started, Boucicault

1403, 13 July and 21 July 1403, 10 August and 18 August 1403, 23 August 1403 respectively. Parts of these events are also recorded in A.S.P., Datini 928, Carteggio Barcelona, letter Venice to Barcelona, Compagnia Luigi Davanzatti e Luca di Matteo to Compagnia Francesco di Marco Datini e Simone d'Andrea Bellandi, 1 September 1403; A.S.P., Datini 928, Carteggio Barcelona, letter Venice to Barcelona, Domenico d'Andrea to Compagnia Francesco di Marco Datini e Simone d'Andrea Bellandi, 31 August 1403; A.S.P., Datini 928, Carteggio Barcelona, letter Venice to Barcelona, Paoluccio di Maestro Paolo to Compagnia Francesco di Marco Datini e Simone d'Andrea Bellandi, 10 September 1403.

[19] A.S.P., Datini 928, Carteggio Barcelona, letter Venice to Barcelona, Commessaria di Zanobi di Taddeo Gaddeo e Antonio di Ser Bartolomeo to Compagnia Francesco di Marco Datini e Simone d'Andrea Bellandi, 15 September and 20 September 1403, 29 September 1403; A.S.P., Datini 928, Carteggio Barcelona, letter Venice to Barcelona, Compagnia Luigi Davanzatti e Luca di Matteo to Compagnia Francesco di Marco Datini e Simone d'Andrea Bellandi, 21 September 1403, 6 October 1403; A.S.P., Datini 928, Carteggio Barcelona, letter Venice to Barcelona, Domenico d'Andrea to Compagnia Francesco di Marco Datini e Simone d'Andrea Bellandi, 13 October 1403; A.S.P., Datini 928, Carteggio Barcelona, letter Venice to Barcelona, Paoluccio di Maestro Paolo to Compagnia Francesco di Marco Datini e Simone d'Andrea Bellandi, 22 September 1403.

set sail for the return trip to Genoa, and the fateful encounter at Modon.[20]

The fear of possible war hangs over the letters written in Venice during this period, as does the worry of how any possible entanglement between the Genoese and Venetians would affect commercial enterprises throughout the Mediterranean. The correspondents could almost feel the hostilities that were coming; one, the Florentine Paoluccio di Maestro Paolo, even went so far as to say that the Genoese feared neither the scandal surrounding their actions, nor further confrontation.[21] After the battle off Modon, he noted the Genoese armada's attack on two ships before it even left the Ionian Sea; almost in the same breath, he began to worry about several Venetian ships in Ibiza preparing to sail for Venice.[22]

The fear of possible repercussions after Modon was justified. Antonio Contarini's letter of 21 December 1403 is just one among many that narrates the next developments in the dispute. He reported receiving a letter in which he was advised that the Genoese, upon entering the western Mediterranean in early November, had inaugurated a new spate of state-sponsored piracy. One of their first targets was the Venetian *coche*, the *Coppa*, which they found in the port of Ibiza and relieved of all its cargo, including goods marked

[20] A.S.P., Datini 928, Carteggio Barcelona, letter Venice to Barcelona, Compagnia Tommasso di Giacomino to Compagnia Francesco di Marco Datini e Simone d'Andrea Bellandi, 6 October 1403.

[21] A.S.P., Datini 928, Carteggio Barcelona, letter Venice to Barcelona, Paoluccio di Maestro Paolo to Compagnia Francesco di Marco Datini e Simone d'Andrea Bellandi, 28 September 1403.

[22] A.S.P., Datini 928, Carteggio Barcelona, letter Venice to Barcelona, Paoluccio di Maestro Paolo to Compagnia Francesco di Marco Datini e Simone d'Andrea Bellandi, 10 November 1403.

with the sign of, paid for by, and needed by Contarini.[23] Paoluccio di Maestro Paolo added that he heard through Datini's people in Florence that two Genoese ships had approached the *Coppa*; besides the 100 *fardi* of wool which Contarini bemoaned losing, their haul had included cochineal destined for Paoluccio, and wool marked with signs showing its owners to be a Datini contact in Valencia.[24] His letters over the next few months announced the arrival of the *Coppa* in Genoa, and the stages of the efforts by Datini's Florentine branch to retrieve the goods and bring about a resolution.[25]

The *Coppa* was one of several Venetian-owned ships targeted by the Genoese "pirates". Luca di Matteo noted that, at about the same time, the *Soler* fled from Cartagena out of fear of two arriving Genoese ships. As a result, she returned empty to Ibiza in order to load a substitute cargo.[26] He instructed his associate in Barcelona not to give her a new cargo for two months in order to allow the international situation to stabilise. The *Soler* later returned successfully to Venice with a load of salt. Paoluccio di Maestro Paolo related that the next ship in the western Mediterranean to fall prey to the Genoese was Nicolo Rosso's. She was sailing towards Flanders when the Genoese pirate, Nicolo de Moneglia, caught her

[23] A.S.P., Datini 928, Carteggio Barcelona, letter Venice to Barcelona, Antonio Contarini fo Marino di Ser Pantaleon to Compagnia Francesco di Marco Datini e Simone d'Andrea Bellandi, 21 December 1403.

[24] A.S.P., Datini 928, Carteggio Barcelona, letter Venice to Barcelona, Paoluccio di Maestro Paolo to Compagnia Francesco di Marco Datini e Simone d'Andrea Bellandi, 22(?) December 1403, 31 December 1403.

[25] A.S.P., Datini 928, Carteggio Barcelona, letter Venice to Barcelona, Paoluccio di Maestro Paolo to Compagnia Francesco di Marco Datini e Simone d'Andrea Bellandi, 4 January 1404, 4 February 1404, 23 February 1404, 8 March 1404, 15 March 1404, and 22 March 1404.

[26] A.S.P., Datini 928, from the Company of Luigi Davanzati and Luca di Matteo, to the Company of Francesco di Marco Datini and Simone d'Andrea Bellandi, written at Venice, 22 December 1403.

in the port of Cadiz, at night.[27] Domenico di Andrea also reported to Barcelona that Genoese ships had attacked and disrupted Venetian shipping in the Black Sea, around Constantinople, in the Aegean where Marco Verzoni's ship was seized, and in the Levant.[28] Finally, for several months all of these authors reported that the *Concianave*, which left Ibiza on 22 October, had not arrived in Venice and was long over-due. Had this ship also been plundered? Eventually, the reason for its absence was clarified: it had deviated to "Turpia" in order to avoid corsairs, but was delayed there for a long time owing to the captain's personal troubles.[29] Venetian ships were not safe from attack by the Genoese in the western Mediterranean until several tense months and much negotiation had passed.

The battle off Modon, the events preceding it, and its results, are examples of how merchant letters in general, and those surviving in the Datini collection in specific, relate those events important to merchants. The mention of an incident is enough to prove that the writer felt it might have some significance for his business with the letter's recipient. News-carrying, however, was only one function of these letters: they were an ongoing dialogue between the writer and recipient concerning their particular investments and the conditions which had created them.

[27] A.S.P., Archivio 928, from Paoluccio di Maestro Paolo, to the Company of Francesco di Marco Datini and Simone d'Andrea Bellandi, written at Venice, 26 January 1404.

[28] A.S.P., Datini 928, from Domenico d'Andrea, to the Company of Francesco di Marco Datini and Simone d'Andrea Bellandi, written at Venice, 9 February 1404.

[29] A.S.P., Datini 928, from the Comessaria of Zanobi di Taddeo Gaddi and Antonio di Ser Bartolomeo, to the Company of Francesco di Marco Datini and Simone di Andrea Bellandi, written at Venice, 12 January 1404, 28 January and 4 February 1404, 9 February 1404, and 15 March and 22 March 1404.

These letters are not just conveyors of new information; they are also responses. Each letter sums up the important points from the last received, remarks on action taken as a result of that knowledge, and suggests or commands the actions which should be taken up in the next reply. These documents are not simply curious artefacts suspended in time and space for the modern researcher's enjoyment or bafflement; they were central to the activities of both the sender and the receiver. The recipients of the surviving letters were not passive, they were the writers of the previous and following documents in the series between these two people.

What about the recipients of these letters? For the correspondence used here, the recipients' thoughts and reactions are unfortunately obscured by the absence of their replies to Venice among the Datini papers. The particular documents which form the source-material for this article were all addressed from Venice to Datini's Catalan company in Barcelona. Simone d'Andrea Bellandi, a Florentine by birth, was Datini's chief agent in that city. All the notices concerning ships (and the goods or people they carried) moving to and from the Levant, to and from the Black Sea and Romania, to and from northern Europe's greatest ports at Bruges and London, throughout the Balearic Islands, and along the Iberian coast, though written in Venice and now surviving in Prato, were not written to there or to Datini himself, but instead were sent to Simone, or his representative in Barcelona. Virtually all the letters sent to Barcelona from Venice, however, were themselves responses to reports sent by Datini agents in the Crown of Aragon/Catalonia. As such they can also be used to show how received information informed the commercial decisions of the writers in Venice, and thus also in Barcelona. For example, Antonio Contarini's reaction to the accumulated problems of the *Coppa*, *Concianave*, and *Soler*, was to instruct Simone to delay sending him more wool until the Genoese problem was solved.[30]

The recipients of merchant letters were the ones who put the news to work and, based on knowledge of the wider world and the conditions in their particular locale, made business decisions. In order for Datini's companies in Catalonia to make profits moving Iberian wool and dye-stuffs, they needed to have goods to trade: these came from throughout the Mediterranean and the markets which fed into it such as the Levant, the Black Sea, and northern Europe, by way of Venice. Equally Iberian wool and dyes were distributed throughout the whole Mediterranean in order to pay for the next round of goods. The authors in Venice reported to Barcelona even news which would be local to Simone, such as the attacks on ships in Ibiza, because these events, in combination with the other news-items they related, were all part of the larger context needed for decision-making. As recipients themselves, their letters show that, as a result of the tension between Genoese and Venetians, they were inclined to conclude the investments they currently had in the western Mediterranean and not send new goods, money, or instructions to the region until a lasting peace had been made.

The writers placed information for the eastern Mediterranean in the same letter as news from the west, and from the lands of Italy and beyond. If the merchants considered the far reaches of the Mediterranean to be pertinent to their own every-day activities, then should not modern researchers look at the Mediterranean and the trade crossing it and entering or leaving its proximity as a whole

[30] A.S.P., Datini 928, from Antonio Contarini quod di Marino di Ser Panatelone, to the Company of Francesco di Marco Datini and Simone di Andrea Bellandi, written at Venice, 16 January 1404.

rather than in little regional segments? But if commercial activities throughout the Mediterranean were interdependent; then the question remains, "where are the boundaries of the Mediterranean world, and where are its frontiers?" Braudel was not the first, and certainly should not be the last, to wrestle with the difficulty of talking about this particular region. Many historians use the terms "trading nations" and "spheres of influence" in discussing commerce in the late medieval period, in order to isolate a nation-state and its activities for study. This terminology, however, inherently puts artificial barriers between barriers from different nations, despite the fact that they worked in co-operation with each other. Did merchants really care about nationality and regional dominance when deciding in what regions and commodities they should invest? Certainly Antonio Contarini did not hesitate to employ Simone d'Andrea de Bellandi and the name of the Datini companies in his business. The letters written from Venice to Datini representatives in Barcelona begin to support the idea that international merchants at the turn of the fifteenth century formed a "community", or even a "culture". The sharing of news throughout the Mediterranean was an essential function of their associations with the goal being mutual benefits and member prosperity.

Perceptions of the East in Fourteenth-Century Italian Merchants' Manuals

John E. Dotson
Southern Illinois University

The fourteenth century was a period of crisis in Italy's trade with the Levant. The disintegration of the Mongol state and the accompanying conflict between the Mongols and Mamlūk Egypt introduced instability into an area whose stability had played no small part in the prosperity of European trade in the late thirteenth century. The political impact of the fall of Acre and of renewed calls for a crusade on the oriental trade of the Italian cities has long been known.[1] It is also well understood that trade between the Italian cities and the Levant continued despite political obstacles.[2] These difficulties did not, however, necessarily extend to the whole of the Muslim world.

[1] Wilhelm Heyd, *Histoire du commerce du levant au moyen âge*, 2 vols. (Leipzig, 1885-86), 1:3-64.

[2] See, for example, Eliyahu Ashtor, "Observations on the Venetian trade in the Levant in the XIVth century", *Journal of Economic History* 5 (1976), 533-586.

Three merchants' manuals dating from the first half of the fourteenth century have been published. Two of them are of Venetian origin and anonymous; these are the *Zibaldone da Canal* and the *Tarifa zoè noticia dy pexi e mexure di luogi e teri che s'adovra marcadantia per el mondo*. The third is Florentine in its background. Francesco Balducci Pegolotti's *Pratica della mercatura*[3] was compiled by a representative of the Florentine Bardi bank who had wide business experience in that firm ranging from Flanders and England across Europe and the Mediterranean to Cyprus. These three manuals are sufficiently closely related in time and subject matter to make comparisons among them useful. In the dates of their composition it is likely that the *Zibaldone da Canal* is the earliest of the three, having been mostly composed in the second and third decades of the century. Pegolotti and the *Tarifa* are a little later. Pegolotti probably completed work on his manual sometime shortly after 1340. The *Tarifa* was written about 1345. All of these manuals are compilations of earlier materials taken from a fairly broad chronological span. So, in spite of some differences in dates of compilation, they are all broadly representative of conditions in the first half of the fourteenth century.

There are at least two ways in which to gain some idea of how the compilers of these manuals perceived their world. The first is

[3] V. Orlandini, ed., *Tarifa zoè noticia dy pexi e mexure di luogi e tere che s'adovra marcadantia per el mondo* (Venice, 1925); A. Stussi, ed., *Zibaldone da Canal: Manoscritto mercantile del sec. XIV* (Venice, 1967) and John E. Dotson, ed. and trans., *Merchant Culture in Fourteenth Century Venice: The Zibaldone da Canal* (Binghamton, NY, 1994); Francesco Balducci Pegolotti, *La pratica della mercatura*, ed. Allan Evans (Cambridge, MA, 1936). Here I will use the more familiar name given to Pegolotti's work by his first modern editor, Pagnini, in 1766 and continued by Allan Evans in his 1936 edition. The original title was *Libro di divisamenti di paesi e di misure di mercatantie*. All references to this work will be to Evans's edition and will hereafter be cited as Pegolotti.

indirect: one may examine the amount of text devoted to various locations as an indication of how important the compiler considered each place. This gives a kind of rough index of perceptions of the economic world. Second, there are rare, but revealing, direct references in the manuals to cultural differences or particular business conditions. These references give colour and substance to the rough outline provided by an examination of textual emphasis.

For the purposes of this paper, the amount of text devoted to a place by the compilers of the various manuals was determined by measuring, to the nearest quarter inch, the number of vertical inches of text devoted to each location in the published version, exclusive of footnotes and editor's comments.[4] Each rubric, or other heading, was considered to define the place under consideration. The data was then sorted from least to greatest and divided into categories. For Pegolotti's *Pratica* there was a relatively large number of places (fifty-two) and at the upper end of the scale they fell into obvious groups (See Chart 1). Each group makes up approximately twenty per cent of the total inches of text considered. Divided in this way only two places, Constantinople and Famagusta, constitute the fifth twenty per cent, while forty-one places make up the first twenty per cent. The *Zibaldone da Canal* contains major headings for many

[4] This provides only a coarse measure of importance for several reasons. First, most entries involve more than one place. Every notice of conversion of weights and measures or money of necessity mentions at least two places. In my translation of the *Zibaldone da Canal*, a map of exchange pairs was used to show emphasis of a different kind. Second, the density of information varies according to the format. Entries with many subheadings and lists are less dense than long paragraphs of information. If the goal were to discover fine shadings of emphasis, these considerations would weigh more heavily and some other means of measuring the amount of text, or number of mentions, would be appropriate. Nonetheless, the purposes of this paper are best served by dividing places into a few categories.

fewer places - thirty-one - and a division into groups each of about twenty-five per cent of the total inches of text is most appropriate (See Chart 2). The *Tarifa* considers only twenty-one places and these seemed to fall into four obvious groups that did not represent equal proportions of the total text inches devoted to them (See Chart 3).

The significance of these groupings can be seen more clearly when this information is transferred to maps.[5] We find, for example, that Cyprus appears in the most emphasised category in all three of the manuals and that Nîmes and Montpellier are paired - and receive relatively minor emphasis - in all of them. Of course, the choice of places to include in these manuals was shaped by the business interests of the compiler and the purpose for which the manual was intended. These choices do not necessarily coincide perfectly with the overall importance of places in the economy of medieval Italy. Nonetheless, the manuals do reflect in a broad way what is known from other sources.

It should also be remembered that only a portion of each of the manuals is being considered in the present comparison. All of them contain more than the geographical entries regarding weights, measures, and money that make up the basis for this discussion. The *Zibaldone da Canal* is the most varied in its content, ranging from what appears to be a student's arithmetic workbook to poetry and

[5] While the data is not directly comparable from one manual to another, nonetheless the relative emphasis in each manual is comparable. That is to say, while it would not be possible to build one composite map or table from the data in its present form, it is possible to draw conclusions based on the individual maps and tables. The number of inches of text devoted to a particular topic varies with trivialities, such as the format and typeface of each edition, as well as according to the amount of detail found in each manuscript. Still, the proportions within each edition, when divided into categories of emphasis, can be compared between the editions.

what today might be called "popular science". It may be considered a merchant's manual embedded in a larger commonplace book. The contents of this notebook seem to confirm Ugo Tucci's idea that the Venetian merchants' manuals were intended for the education of young merchants, to acculturate them in the ways of the business elites of that city.[6] Pegolotti's *Pratica* is much more extensive and detailed than either of the Venetian texts. Even allowing for a lack of direct comparability in the data, Pegolotti's guide is an order of magnitude larger than either of the Venetian manuals; this distinguishes it more than the greater number of places considered. The Venetian manuals run to about two hundred and fifty inches of printed text for the geographical entries with the largest entries running to thirty or forty inches of text. Pegolotti gives over fifteen hundred inches of such material and the largest entry contained in his manual is nearly one hundred and sixty inches long.

All three of the manuals show a strong interest in eastern ports and markets. In them the categories of the longest entries are heavily weighted toward the eastern Mediterranean. This emphasis is most evident in the *Tarifa*. An area encompassing Venice and the eastern locations mentioned in this work accounts for almost ninety per cent of the place-oriented text. All of the places included in the two most emphasised categories (Groups 3 and 4, see Map 1) and all but one of the places in Group 2 are within the indicated area. An area chosen from Pegolotti that includes all of the places in the two most emphasised groups extends from Italy east (Groups 3 and 4, Map 2). Only the *Zibaldone da Canal* includes places in its most emphasised groups that are not in either Italy or the Levant (Groups 3 and 4, Map 3). Tunis has more text devoted to it than any other place

[6] Ugo Tucci, "Tariffe veneziane e libri toscani di mercatura", *Studi Veneziani* 10 (1968), 65-108.

discussed in the *Zibaldone*. Even considering that fact, an area that includes all the places in the two most emphasised categories of the *Zibaldone da Canal* definitely extends mostly to the east.[7] Even Pegolotti, that representative of the Bardi bank whose extensive involvement in English wool is so well known, devoted much more space in his manual to Italy and the east than to any other areas.[8]

The importance of Cyprus (and especially its northern port of Famagusta after the fall of Acre) for the very profitable trade in oriental goods is well established.[9] This importance is reflected in the manuals by the fact that Cyprus is found in the most emphasised category in all three of them. In the *Zibaldone* it is second, after Tunis, while in both the *Tarifa* and in Pegolotti's *Pratica* it is given more inches of text than any other place.

Both the compiler of the *Zibaldone da Canal* and Pegolotti, though they include Acre, speak of it in the past. There is no separate section for Acre in the *Zibaldone da Canal*, but it is mentioned at various places in the text. At one point that has no particular heading, Acre is discussed along with Limassol. The compiler of the *Zibaldone* reports, "Now I would have you know that, at the time Acre was standing, for the merchants who wanted to go outside Acre to buy cotton ...", and so forth. This choice of words implying the destruction of Acre (not merely its capture as Pegolotti reported) may not be accidental. The *Zibaldone* as noted

[7] The method of determining emphasis by measuring text within each rubricated passage underestimates the importance of Venice in the *Zibaldone*. Another method, counting exchange pairs, shows Venice to be the most emphasised place in this manual (Dotson, pp. 15-16).

[8] Pegolotti was, himself, director of the Bardi operations in England for four years between 1318 and 1321 (Pegolotti, p. xviii).

[9] See, for example, Heyd, 2:3-23, and David Jacoby, "The Rise of a new emporium in the eastern Mediterranean: Famagusta in the late thirteenth century", *Μελεται και Υπομνηματα* 1 (1984), passim.

earlier, unlike either of the other manuals, contains much material that is not strictly mercantile in nature.[10] In this material there is a fragmentary chronicle in which is found an exaggerated report of the fall of Acre:

> During the year 1291, on the 19th day of May, the city of Acre was taken by the sultan Saladin Menisaldar .... And when he had taken it, he had everything torn down and destroyed to the foundations, and left nothing of it, neither house, nor palace, nor church, save one bell tower, or mosque, in order to shout out his cruel laws.[11]

It is only in these non-mercantile portions of the *Zibaldone da Canal* that there is any evidence of the clash of two worlds that modern students often expect from the "Age of Crusades". Nonetheless, even in this part of the *Zibaldone*, only this passage contains what may be considered a pejorative reference to Muslim actions, while there are several more or less extensive and proud tales of Venetian victories over the Genoese.[12]

Pegolotti heads his section on Acre, "Acre in Syria, for itself when it was in the hands of the Christians". There follows a long series of subsections on the conversion of the weights of Acre with other places in the Mediterranean ranging from Tunis, Sicily, and Puglia to nearby Tripoli, Antioch, and Damascus. The section headed "with Famagusta of Cyprus when Acre belonged to the Christians" shows that - at least for those conversions that Pegolotti gives here - weights and measures of the two were identical. The last part of the Acre section: "Acre for itself after it passed into the

[10] Dotson, pp. 11-15.
[11] Dotson, p. 153.
[12] Dotson, pp. 152-54.

hands of the Saracens, with Cyprus" indeed shows that measures changed when the city changed hands.[13] The older material may have been included simply because it was available, but there is an effort made to distinguish between current and dated information. This suggests that current information had some utility; that in spite of prohibitions, some trade with that area continued.[14]

It is possible to see certain developments in the Levant trade reflected in the manuals. To do this requires a use of evidence from other sources to explain the manuals rather than vice versa. For example, many more places along the coast of Syria are included in the *Zibaldone da Canal* than in either Pegolotti or the *Tarifa.* Both the latter manuals include much information relating to places in the Black Sea that does not appear in the *Zibaldone*. This difference reflects the decline of direct trade with Syria and the increasing importance of the Black Sea trade between the early fourteenth century when the *Zibaldone* was compiled and the 1340s when Pegolotti's *Pratica* and the *Tarifa* were assembled. Similarly, there is a visible shift in the relative prominence of Limassol and Famagusta in three passages in the *Zibaldone da Canal* that appear to be derived from different sources. This is probably the result of the decline of Limassol after the fall of Acre and the rise of Famagusta which was better positioned to trade with Ayas and the northern Syrian ports. The *Tarifa* makes no reference to Limassol, and concentrates entirely on Famagusta in its consideration of Cyprus. By mid-century Famagusta had become the chief port of the

[13] Pegolotti, pp. 63-69.

[14] Bruno Dini suggests that the outdated material was included for sentimental reasons and as a reflection of a merchant culture that valued a certain historical perspective (Bruno Dini, *Una pratica di mercatura in formazione (1394-95)*, Serie I, Documenti (Florence, 1980), 2:3).

island, a fact that is reflected in the way it is treated in the manuals.[15]

If commercial relations between the Italian cities and the Levant were unsettled by political strains, there is evidence in the manuals for smoother interaction with another part of the Muslim world. All the manuals contain advice on business conditions, tariffs, fees to be paid and so forth. Most of this information - and there is comparatively little of it as a proportion of the whole - is straight-forward, informative, and neutral in tone. One such passage from Pegolotti's manual speaks of "Tariffs on merchandise that one pays at Safi (Morocco)". Here he explains the tariffs that had to be paid on bringing goods into the kingdom. The "mangona", a sixteenth of the estimated value of the merchandise, was paid only once, but the *decima* had to be paid in each of the major cities. Then he cautions, "And if you carry it (i.e., merchandise) from one town to another, then you must carry an *albara'a* (*barā'a* - a licence or patent), that is, a certificate from the lord's customs service, to be able to show whence you brought it".[16] Explanations such as this of the costs and regulations for doing business are fairly common in the manuals, at least for the major markets. Additionally, there are occasionally more general comments on conditions that a merchant might encounter. In the *Zibaldone da Canal* there are several very favourable references to localities in North Africa west of Tunis. The description of Collo is nearly gushing: "I would have you know that Collo is not a city, but is a village .... And it is one of the good places in Barbary, the best except for Tunis and Bugia, and it is a place where everyone wants to go".[17] Djidjelli also receives praise,

[15] Dotson, pp. 17-18.

[16] Pegolotti, p. 274.

[17] Dotson, p. 91.

"You ought to know that Djidjelli is a good place for merchandise, and does not have tax farms; everyone who wants to go there can buy and sell in Djidjelli .... And there are good people in this place".[18] Bugia, still farther to the west, is described as "a very beautiful city and the best in Barbary, save Tunis, but there are better men in Bugia than in Tunis".[19] On balance, the image of the Barbary coast in the *Zibaldone da Canal* is very positive.

Positive assessments were not always the case. The compiler of the *Zibaldone* showed his frustration with conditions in the Christian kingdom of Lesser Armenia in his discussion of the grain trade in Ayas:

> In Ayas wheat and barley are sold by a measure that is named *marzipane*, and by the wish of the Armenians no one can truly tell from one month to another (what this measure is) because no measure converts with this one; that is because it increases and decreases at their wish, and so the merchants get out of it many times what they give.[20]

Occasionally, though, there is information that speaks to more complex interactions, at least in Pegolotti and the *Zibaldone*. Tunis, both agree, had a five per cent tariff on precious metals. The *Zibaldone* points out, in what seems to be an approving fashion, that one could avoid paying this charge by concealing the gold when it was imported - that is, by smuggling it. The context makes it evident that gold is the commodity in question since later passages calculate the difference between having *dopla* coins, which are gold coins,

[18] Dotson, p. 92.

[19] Dotson, p. 93.

[20] Dotson, p. 111 and note. Pegolotti explains that the *marzipan* was a measure used in retail trade. In the wholesale trade grain was sold by the *moggio* (Pegolotti, p. 59).

minted from bullion on which the duty has been paid and that which was smuggled.[21] Pegolotti gives a much more detailed account. He reports that, in addition to the five per cent import duty, it was necessary to provide "wine for the Saracens and the factors" amounting to an additional ¼ per cent so that the total cost was 5¼ per cent. (This matter of wine raises other questions about cultural differences that will be addressed shortly). He, too, observes that one can smuggle goods and avoid paying the tariff and explains that this is easy to do with gold "because it occupies little space", but is more difficult with silver because of its greater volume for a given value. Pegolotti, however, also makes a further, crucial point: "And whoever brings it in concealed, so that it may not be found, or later known, pays nothing; and if he were discovered on entering it carries no penalty, save to pay the duty as explained above ...". The obvious course would seem to be that one should smuggle gold into Tunis, as the *Zibaldone* appears to advise. But, like many things that seem too good to be true, there turns out to be a catch in this advice for penalty-free smuggling as well. Pegolotti reveals it when he says, "Although you may be found trying to hide things in order to avoid paying the duty, and being found out, you pay nothing except the duty; nonetheless you lose faith and honour by it, so that they will never trust you as before your crime was found out".[22] This may simply reflect Pegolotti's fuller explanations of almost everything the two manuals discuss in common. But, it may also reflect the difference between a mature, thoughtful businessman and diplomat and an untried youth just beginning a career as a merchant.

Pegolotti's comment about the provision of wine for customs officials in Tunis raises the question of dietary restrictions in Islamic

[21] Dotson, pp. 85-86.

[22] Pegolotti, pp. 130-131; Dotson, p. 86 and note.

territories, a point that can shed some light on the perception of cultural differences. In the merchants' manuals the importation of wine into this Muslim city is accepted without comment. Immediately preceding the discussion of smuggling, Pegolotti states: "Wine is sold by the *mezeruole*". The *Zibaldone da Canal* says, "Also, you ought to know what it takes to make a *mezarolla* of wine at Tunis, because wine is sold at Tunis by the *mezarolla* ...".[23] From this it may seem that Italian merchants were indifferent to Muslim dietary laws. However, wine is not mentioned as an import commodity into any other Muslim community. It seems likely, then, that this wine was imported into Tunis for consumption by the substantial Christian commercial community in that bustling port.[24]

This assumption is strengthened by comments on the importation of oil into Tunis. The *Zibaldone da Canal* notes that "Everyone who carries oil to Tunis must empty it out and have it measured in jars, and one cannot have this done unless the oil stevedores of the foreigners' warehouse are there to see it put into the jars". It is easy to assume that this was done merely to assure fair measure by local standards.[25] Again, Pegolotti's more extensive comments clarify the situation.

[23] Pegolotti, p. 130; Dotson, p. 88.

[24] Tunis, very near the same site of ancient Carthage, had a native Christian population well into the middle ages, but by the thirteenth century that community had almost completely vanished except for a few small remnants in the countryside. By the end of the thirteenth century there was again a considerable Christian population, but it consisted of Europeans, mostly Italians, established and protected by treaties with the Ḥafṣid rulers of the city. See Ronald A. Messier, "The Christian community of Tunis at the time of Saint Louis' crusade, A.D. 1270", in *The Meeting of Two Worlds: Cultural Exchange between East and West during the Period of the Crusades*, ed. Vladimir P. Goss and Christine Verzár Bornstein (Kalamazoo, MI, 1986), pp. 241-243.

[25] I made this assumption in my translation of the *Zibaldone da Canal* (Dotson, p. 88, n. 126).

> And whoever carries it (oil) to Tunis should not carry it in old casks, because it can happen that the casks may have held wine or fat, and if you may be accused that they held wine, or fat, or pork bones, then you will be refused, and you will be fined by the court, and more than that, the court could put you in prison, and it may happen that you could be deported from the country. And therefore, whoever carries it (oil) there should carry it in new casks so that there can be no accusation of any wrongdoing. And remember that nowadays oil in casks is decanted in Tunis; the court wants it to be taken from the casks and put in jars, and if, while it is being poured into the jars, there is found in it any bones of pig or rat, that is to say, a dead rat, then be certain that the court will refuse it in the manner described in this chapter. And for that reason whoever carries it to Tunis, or anywhere in the Saracen lands, you want to be very careful that you cannot be accused of any of the said misdeeds.

The seriousness of ignoring the religious sensibilities of Islam could scarcely be more firmly put. Still, the tone of this passage, while strict, is not hostile. Any suggestion of blame, as in the matter of smuggling (which carried no religious overtones), is on the Christian merchant who should know and respect local laws and customs.

On the whole, the attitude found in the merchants' manuals of the early fourteenth century may be described as rational, businesslike, and often well-disposed toward Muslims. Occasionally even, they reveal an attitude of understanding toward the laws and sensibilities of their hosts. Considering the tensions of the era, including renewed calls for crusades by pope John XXII in the mid-1320s, the manuals are important in helping to develop a more rounded understanding of European attitudes in the late middle ages. The papal call for a crusade was directed at the Egyptian government, while the more approving passages of the merchants' manuals refer to Tunisia. Nonetheless, the attitudes revealed in the manuals suggest the existence of a true business community reaching across cultural differences usually perceived as barriers. This is especially noticeable when the attitudes suggested in the merchants' manuals are considered in the light of other sources not included here, such as notarial documents and merchants' correspondence. There may have been another dimension - besides greed and insubordination - to the resistance by Christian merchant communities to the embargo of Egypt and Syria in the second quarter of the fourteenth century.[26] And that dimension may have been the awareness of another, more inclusive community.

[26] For a discussion of trade with Egypt and Syria in the fourteenth century, see Ashtor, pp. 533-586.

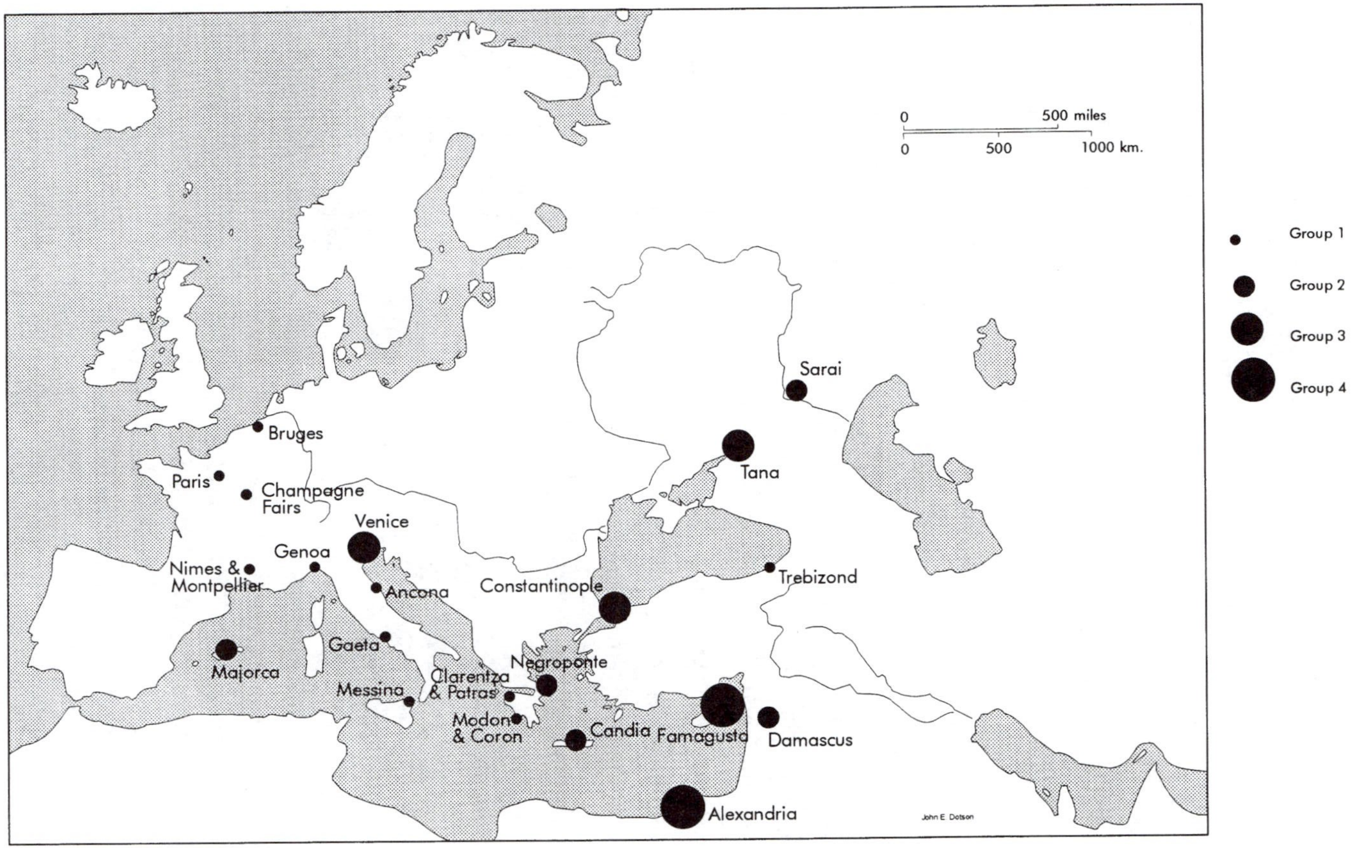

Map 1: Relative Importance of Places in the "Tarifa zoè noticia . . ."

Chart One

Place	Text Inches
Fairs of France	1
Paris	1.5
Modon & Coron	2.25
Gaeta	2.5
Nîmes & Montpellier	3
Genoa	3
Ancona	3.25
Messina	3.5
Trebizond	3.75
Bruges	5.25
Clarentza & Patras	6
Negroponte	9
Sarai	10
Candia	10.5
Majorca	10.75
Damascus	13.75
Venice	25
Tana	29.75
Constantinople	30.75
Alexandria	44.75
Famagusta	47.25

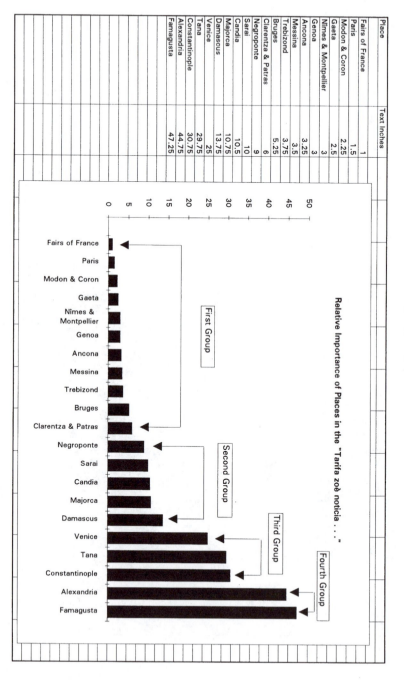

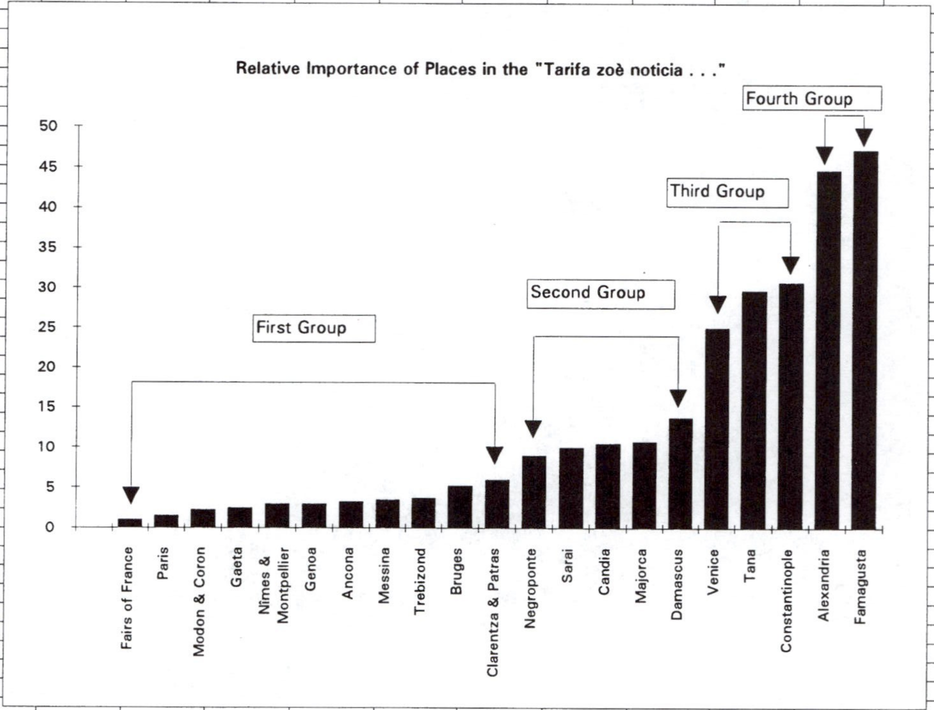

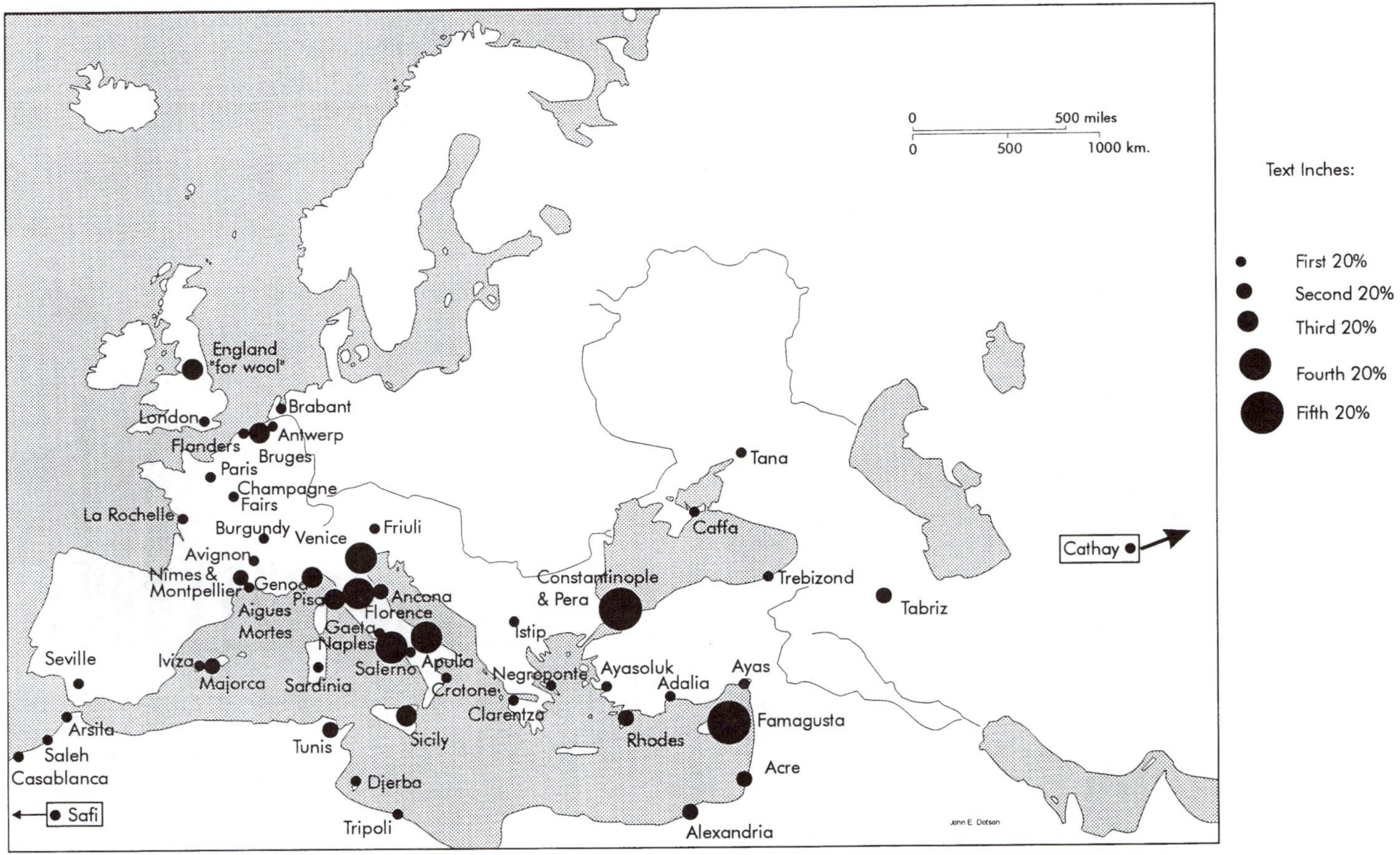

Map 2: Relative Importance of Places in Pegolotti's *Pratica*

Chart Two

Place	Text Inches
Crotone in Calabria	0.50
Negroponte	1.00
Brabant	1.00
Istip (Serbia)	2.50
Paris	2.50
LaRochelle in Gascony	2.50
Saleh (Morocco)	2.50
Avignon	2.75
Tripoli in Barbary	3.00
Djerba	3.00
Iviza	3.75
Caffa	4.25
Salerno	4.50
Gaeta	5.25
Casablanca (Morocco)	5.50
Flanders	6.25
Trebisond	6.50
Arsila (Morocco)	7.00
Adalia	7.25
Morocco	8.50
Burgundy	9.50
Fruili	10.50
Aigues Mortes	11.00
Tana	12.00
Ayasoluk (Ephesus)	13.00
Fairs of Champagne	15.75
Cathay	17.50
Sardinia	18.00
Clarentza	18.50
Seville in Spain	22.00
Antwerp in Brabant	23.00
London in England	25.50
Ayas in Armenia	26.00
Tabriz	29.25
Nimes & Montpellier	29.50
Rhodes	31.00
Ancona	31.00
Acre in Syria	38.25
Tunis in Barbary	38.50
Alexandria	44.70
Majorca	49.00
Sicily	60.75
Pisa	60.75
Genoa	61.50
England for wool	64.75
Bruges in Flanders	74.50
Naples	75.75
Florence	82.50
Apulia	95.50
Venice	101.00
Constantinople and Pera	137.25
Famagusta in Cyprus	158.50

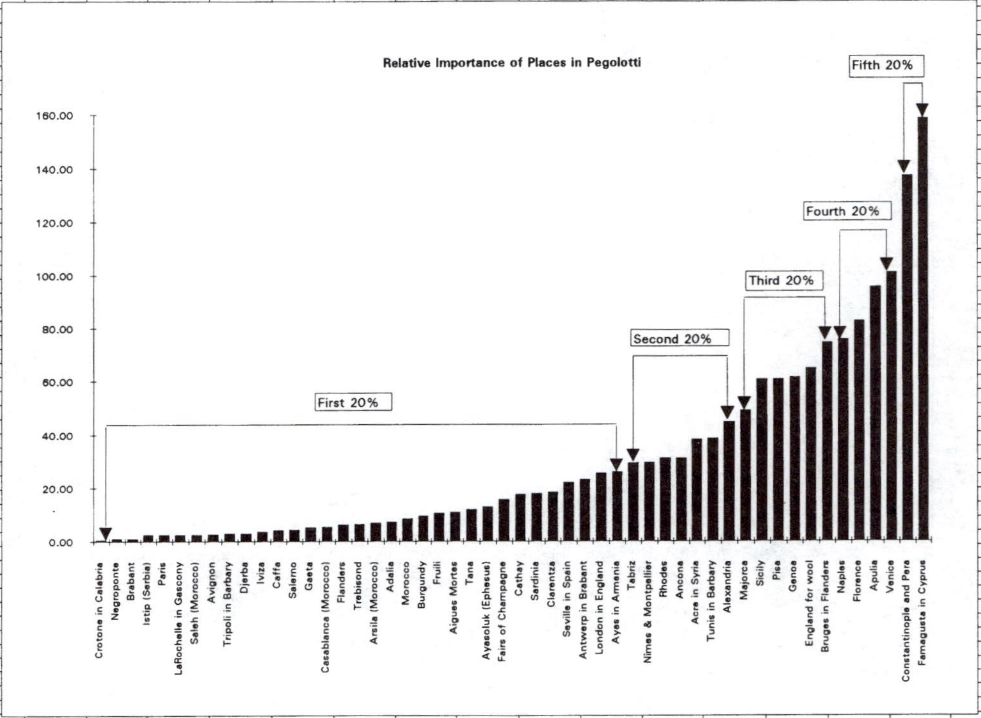

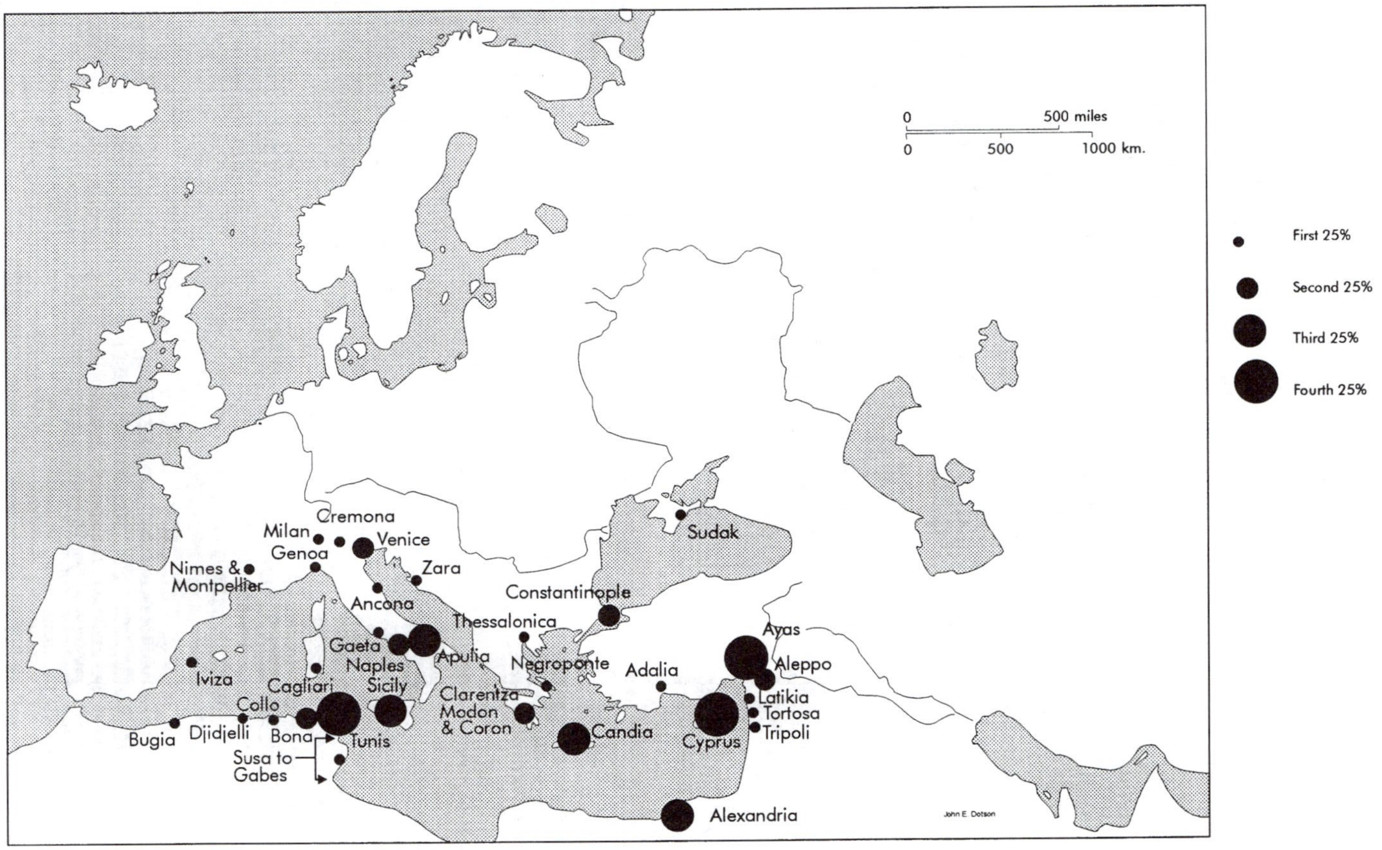

Map 3: Relative Importance of Places in the Zibaldone da Canal

Chart Three

Place	Text Inches
Cagliari	0.50
Iviza	0.50
Ancona	0.75
Tortosa	1.00
Nîmes & Montpellier	1.75
Genoa	2.00
Latakia	2.00
Zara	2.75
Cremona	2.75
Thessalonica & Sudak	3.25
Tripoli in Syria	3.50
Djidjelli	4.00
Susa to Gabes	4.25
Milan	4.25
Bugia	4.50
Collo	5.00
Adalia	5.25
Negroponte	5.50
Clarentza, Coron & Modon	5.75
Venice	6.25
Bona	7.00
Naples	8.25
Aleppo	9.50
Constantinople	10.00
Candia	13.50
Sicily	15.75
Alexandria	18.50
Apulia	20.50
Ayas	23.00
Cyprus	23.50
Tunis	28.50

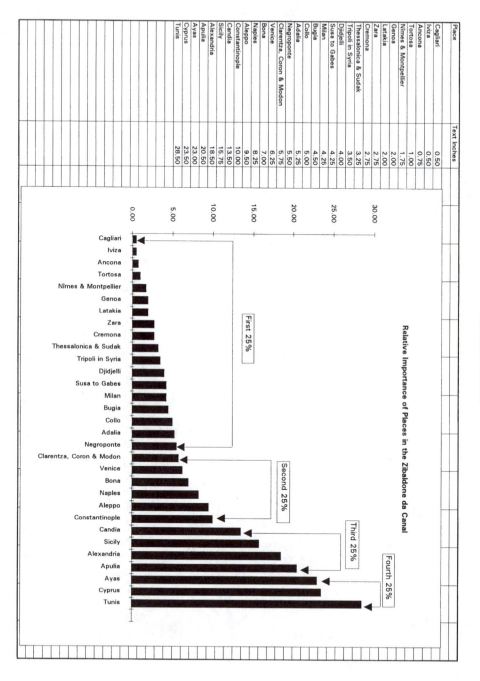

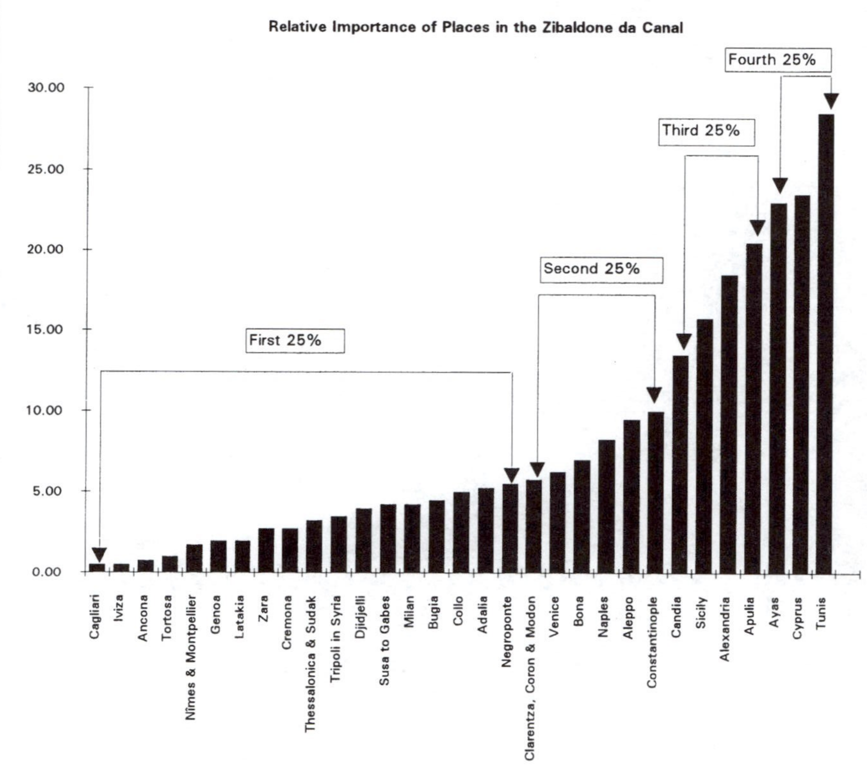

III ISLAMIC AND WESTERN POLITICS: RELIGIOUS THOUGHT

Averroes' *Commentary on Plato's Republic*, and the Missing *Politics*

Oliver Leaman
Liverpool John Moores University

Many philosophers in the Islamic world held Aristotle (d. 322 BC) in great respect. He was frequently called the "first master", lesser masters being those who were capable of interpreting his works. An extensive and efficient translation service had translated into Arabic, generally via Syriac, much of Greek philosophy, and especially of Aristotle. Although Plato (d. 347 BC), and to a certain extent Socrates (d. 399 BC), were also admired in Islamic philosophy, there is no doubt that among the Peripatetic thinkers, Aristotle came first. In any case, there were fewer platonic texts with which to work, and Plato's works lacked the structure of an organon, an organisation which very much impressed the *falāsifa*. The one major work by Aristotle which did not appear in Arabic, apparently, is his *Politics*. The *falāsifa* knew of its existence, and some parts of it turn up in books by al-ᶜĀmirī (d. 381/992), for example, but there does not appear to have been any translation of the text as a whole. Had there been such a text, there is little doubt that it would have been fallen upon with glee by his admirers, and I think we can be sceptical of the suggestion by even such a distinguished scholar as

Muhsin Mahdi that they may have had it, but preferred not to use it because of the dangers which existed in it.[1]

The main thinker who may be assumed to have been disappointed by the absence of the text is Ibn Rushd (Averroes) (d. 595/1198). He was, after all, working on an official commission to comment on all the works of Aristotle, and he knew of the *Politics*, but implies that it had not reached the western regions of the Islamic world. He had no compunction, then, in using Plato's *Republic* as the book which completes, as it were, Aristotle's *Nicomachean Ethics*. This may strike us as rather strange, yet it would not have seemed so in the sixth/twelfth century when he was working. There was a long and distinguished tradition of regarding Plato and Aristotle as basically in agreement on the major philosophical issues, a tradition which owed much to the work of al-Fārābī (d. 350/961) some centuries earlier. Yet we should be careful about assuming that Averroes went along with this view. Indeed, in his writings he is often careful to distinguish between what he took to be the real Aristotle, and the neoplatonic accretions which had built up over the centuries of Hellenism and Avicennan commentary. Averroes is scathing throughout his works about these accretions, and it is highly unlikely that he was unaware of what were genuinely Aristotelian views, and which views owed more to Plato and his followers.[2]

How, then, does the *Republic* fit onto the *Nicomachean Ethics*? Averroes argues that the latter is the theoretical part of politics, while the former is the practical part. To get the *Republic* to fit onto the *Nicomachean Ethics*, he had to change both texts. The *Ethics* comes to acquire far more of an explicitly political tinge,

[1] Muhsin Mahdi, "Philosophy and political thought: reflections and comparisons", *Arabic Sciences and Philosophy* 1 (1991), 9-29.

[2] Oliver Leaman, *Averroes and his Philosophy* (Oxford, 1988).

which then allows the *Republic* to complete it, as it were. Politics is the art which provides the end which is most desirable for its own sake. Politics orders all the activities of the *polis*, and all such activities are directed towards an end, so politics has to order all the activities to bring about a more attractive end than any one activity could do by itself. As we know, in the *Ethics* Aristotle concentrates on the nature of the end to which activities are directed, but Averroes interprets this to mean that the main subject of the text about ethics is the organisation of the city and the good to be derived from such organisation.

An interesting aspect of Averroes' commentary on the *Ethics* is its almost total neglect of the more contemplative and religious passages, those parts which address the nature of happiness as compared with the aims to which human life points. For him, the *Ethics* is all about how to train people to lead lives of virtue, and how those lives can be aggregated acceptably within a community. So the book is really about the principles of legislation, and the assumption he makes is that the *Politics* must be about the particular laws which those principles embody. Averroes interprets Aristotle to have argued that theoretical knowledge has the role of guiding practical issues, and on this he was surely wrong, but given that interpretation it becomes easier to continue the investigation with the *Republic*, in which, according to Averroes, Plato deals with the perfect ruler as the person with theoretical knowledge who can use that knowledge to direct practical matters, and in particular knows how to convey his points to different groups of people in different ways.

One of the key changes that Averroes makes to the *Republic* is to exclude from his discussion everything which he thinks is dialectical, as compared with demonstrative. This results in a wholesale excision of much of the platonic text, which Averroes obviously thinks is superfluous. The only role which he sees for dialectical reasoning, and it is an important role, is as part of the educative process, but it is not necessary when it is a matter of explaining the sort of reasoning which is appropriate to the logicians, *ahl al-burhān.* Here demonstrative reasoning alone suffices. It is obvious that what Averroes finds acceptable about the *Republic* is its ability to be Aristotelianised, which hardly means providing a faithful account of the text, its concerns and structure. In a sense, Averroes takes the attitude to the text of the Oxford philosophy don of the 1950s. He is going to look at the text in so far as it raises issues which he regards as important and interesting, and he is going to ignore those parts which are irrelevant or only of historical interest. We have to remember here that we are talking about books which are middle commentaries, and these are not intended to provide a complete picture of the text under discussion. While they are not as free as the paraphrases, they are nonetheless often quite loose in their readings, being written to present something of the flavour and importance of the original text. Hence we get contemporary references, references which often raise issues such as whether Averroes himself was advocating particular solutions to practical political problems.

Some commentators on Averroes suggest that it is possible to derive his own opinions on politics from the discussion of the *Republic*. One of the most astute commentators, Charles Butterworth, even suggests that Averroes "continues to speak in his own name" when he "accepts the idea that equality between men and women requires the women to join the men in exercising without clothing and the notion that children should be held in common".[3] There are certainly passages in the commentary in which

[3] Charles Butterworth, "Ethics and classical Islamic philosophy: a study of Averroes' *Commentary on Plato's Republic*", in *Ethics in Islam*, ed. R.

Averroes does seem to be pointing to contemporary political parallels in the nature of the state, but it would be extraordinary were he to be an advocate of mixed gymnastics in the nude! This was an idea which rather shocked the Athenians, and it is difficult to see how Averroes could recommend it for the Andalusian society of his day. He does report throughout his commentary on the various passages in which Plato refers to the necessity of equality between men and women, and the common possession of women and children, and there is nothing in his description of these views which shows that he disagrees with them. Yet there is also nothing which suggests that he agrees, despite the clever ways in which Butterworth, Lerner and Rosenthal all seek to manipulate the forms of language in which he expressed himself.[4] Perhaps Averroes was an early feminist, but we cannot derive this from his mere reporting of the *Republic*. He might much more plausibly be taken to be describing what he takes Plato's views to be, without making any judgement about them at all. One might assume that such a proposal was so weird in the context of the Andalus of his day that it was especially worth reporting, to give a flavour of the unusual which exists in the *Republic*. Again, if one sees the middle commentary as proceeding like an old-fashioned philosophy lecturer, one would expect its author to produce evidence of the rather strange views of the author whom he is discussing. One should not take at face value Averroes' claim to reproduce the scientific views of Plato, as though

Hovannisian (Malibu, 1985), p. 40. See also his "Ethics in medieval Islamic philosophy", *Journal of Religious Ethics* 11 (1983), 224-39, "Medieval Islamic philosophy and the virtue of ethics", *Arabica* 34 (1987), 221-50 and "New light on the political philosophy of Averroes", in *Essays on Political Philosophy and Science*, ed. G. Hourani (Albany, 1975), pp. 118-127.

[4] Ralph Lerner, *Averroes on Plato's "Republic"* (Ithaca, 1974); E. I. J. Rosenthal, *Political Thought in Medieval Islam* (Cambridge, 1958), p. 191 and his *Averroes' Commentary on Plato's "Republic"* (Cambridge, 1969).

this meant all the views with which his commentator was in agreement.

What did Averroes miss through not having the *Politics*? The arrival of this text in Christian Europe is often supposed to have heralded a conceptual revolution, in that it established a form of political naturalism, the idea that political association arises directly out of the attributes of human nature as opposed to having its origins in God or convention. The *Politics* demonstrated that political theory was more than a branch of jurisprudence, but rather is an autonomous system of investigation. It brought to an end the dominance of the Augustinian-Platonic notion of politics as merely a highly dependent part of the study of virtue. The Aristotelian tradition did see politics as the most important area of study within practical knowledge (*NE* 1094a18-1094b11). The art of politics is not directly based on individual virtue, nor is it based on an extension of the skills required for the efficient management of the household, and it has a secular direction which argues for its independence as a subject of study.

How would Averroes have reacted to such an idea? Quite happily. According to his commentary on the *Republic*, we live together because no one of us can acquire all the virtues by himself or herself. It is only if we coexist that we can hope to acquire more than just one or two of the virtues. We understand this, and so we live together. We are political animals because we realise that our happiness is dependent upon social life, not to mention our physical wellbeing. This is how Averroes starts his commentary on the *Republic*, and it is supposed to set the stage for using this text to complete, as it were, the work of the *Nicomachean Ethics*. Although in his commentary on the *Nicomachean Ethics* he discusses at some length the different kinds of virtues, he seizes on Plato's *Republic* to argue that the virtues are to be organised hierarchically, with theoretical reason at the apex of them all and their ultimate end. In the *Nicomachean Ethics* morality is identified with ethical habits and character traits, and so with the sorts of actions we can train ourselves to perform. We can use the notion of the mean as a guide to enable those activities to become habitual and allow rationality to control our passions. While Averroes does report on this discussion quite accurately, it is clear that for him there is not much point in the laborious analysis of the different virtues and the forms of training which are appropriate to them. What is important, for him, is the end to which all the virtues point, and this, in true platonic style, he argues is theoretical wisdom, an area of virtue for which the mean has no relevance. We have to raise the question again, what did he miss through not having the *Politics* to hand? Would he have produced this rather platonic account of the relationship between the virtues had he been aware of the argument of the *Politics*? One might be tempted to say that the *Republic* is actually more amenable to the sorts of religious agenda which an Islamic philosopher would have than is the *Politics*, and so it is more than just fortuitous that the latter was replaced by the former. Politics as an independent science might not be able to find a place within the context of Islamic philosophy, and so the *Politics* might have been ignored, even were it to have been available. This is a tempting suggestion, but surely just wrong. After all, it was the Ashᶜarite thinker Ibn Khaldūn (d. 808/1406-7) who developed a view of politics within the context of Islamic history in an entirely areligious sort of way. What we can observe in the dominance of the *Republic* over the *Politics* in the thought of Averroes is the reassertion of a basically platonic, or perhaps better, neoplatonic, view of politics, as ultimately dependent upon an understanding of the nature of *sophia*, of theoretical wisdom, or at least some all-encompassing rational principle.

But was not Averroes a fierce critic of neoplatonism, especially as practised by Ibn Sīnā (Avicenna) (d. 428/1036-7)? Did he not try throughout his writings to get back to the real Aristotle and so cleanse the neoplatonic detritus which had attached itself over the centuries to the thought of his hero? This is true, but it is also true that Averroes, in spite of himself, was operating within a context in which neoplatonism was the way in which philosophy was done. There were limits, then, in how far he could go in rejecting it, and he stayed within those limits. To have done otherwise would have been to stray beyond the realms of intelligibility. The *Republic* does, for a neoplatonist, work nicely with the *Nicomachean Ethics*. The *Republic*, with its detailed discussion of education, of different ways of talking to different sorts of people, and its emphasis upon justifications for inequalities, represents a philosophical enquiry into the notion of *hierarchy* in the state. If there is one principle which can be said to characterise neoplatonism, it is that of hierarchy, and although we are far more familiar with its implications for metaphysics and ontology in Islamic philosophy, it also had a major impact upon political theory. So the *Republic* is for Averroes a far more suitable conclusion to the *Nicomachean Ethics* than the *Politics* could ever have been.

Although the context within which Averroes worked seems very distant to us now,[5] there are some interesting general issues which arise when examining this aspect of intellectual history. One is that we must never forget that we are dealing with a thinker who was commenting on texts which he could not read in their original language, and which had been translated into Arabic some time in the past. Also, we ourselves do not have the text which Averroes

[5] It is nicely explored by Hans Daiber, "Political Philosophy", in *The History of Islamic Philosophy*, ed. S. H. Nasr & O. Leaman (London, 1995), 841-885.

produced, but only a translation of that text into other languages, in this case Latin (the *Middle Commentary on the Nicomachean Ethics*) and Hebrew (*Commentary on the Republic*). On the other hand, as I suggested above, we have quite a modern approach to the texts in question. Averroes did not set out just to comment on these texts. Rather, he wanted to give his readers the flavour of the texts, but he also wanted to relate those texts to issues which Averroes thought were important and interesting. Many writers on Averroes would imply that there must be a religious agenda here to which he was responding. Yet there is no reason to think this is true. There was a philosophical agenda to which he was responding, and that is, I argue, a neoplatonic agenda, one which fits the *Republic* far more snugly than the *Politics*. Again, this is not unfamiliar to us today. We select and relate texts in political philosophy which seem to us to go well together, which raise interesting points and suggest important solutions. What seems to us to be strange about what Averroes was doing nine centuries ago is its proximity to what we see political philosophers doing today.

Al-Ghazālī, Metaphor and Logic

Salim Kemal
University of Dundee

Any Muslim religious philosopher must account for the status and seriousness of figurative language since it occurs frequently in the Qur'ān. Perhaps surprisingly, given his reputation for rejecting philosophy and for a commitment to mysticism, al-Ghazālī (d. 505/1111) finds logic crucial to this explanation. In the space available in this paper[1] my intention is to sketch out al-Ghazālī's account of figurative language, to show how he deals with truth, and thereby to identify some of the issues this raises that need further consideration.

REASON, LOGIC, COMMUNITY

To sketch out the conception of the relation between reason, logic, and the community, we may begin with al-Ghazālī's affirmation of the importance of reasoning. Where some people want to promote

[1] I undertook the research of material in this paper while I was a Research Fellow at the Oxford Centre for Islamic Studies, and am grateful to the centre, its director, and registrar for their help and support.

behaviour "that is in following, not in the reasoning of intellects", al-Ghazālī prefers that "intellectual reasoning ... be a guide to knowledge of the object of reasoning", a knowledge we gain by "following this path of reasoning and assuming it".[2] Those who cannot accept a basis in reason, who fail even to acknowledge the "basis of existence ... [i.e. that there must be a reason for the existence of a thing]", would contradict themselves in the fact of their very existence, and put themselves beyond the domain of arguments and reasonable conviction.[3] Their rejection of the premises may at best be treated, since it has a non-rational cause, and cannot be reasoned with.[4] Moreover, al-Ghazālī thinks that reasoning is the basis of a community. He says that "those who reason, if they agree on the reasoning, on the proof and on specifying one proof for each question and stop at the latter, opposition among them is inconceivable".[5]

These citations also introduce considerations of premises, suggesting that there are two kinds of motivation in understanding, one existential and the other rational. The latter consists in the rules of logic we use to think clearly; the existential motive comprises our

[2] Al-Ghazālī, *Freedom and Fulfillment*, trans. and ed. R. McCarthy (London, 1972), p. 233. The pagination given in the following notes refers to this translation and edition.

[3] In *Faḍā'iḥ al-Bāṭiniyya wa Faḍā'il al-Mustaẓhariyya* (pp. 175-286, in *Freedom and Fulfillment*, op. cit.) al-Ghazālī begins by asserting that people must accept certain obvious and undeniable premises such as "basis of existence ... [i.e. that there must be a reason for the existence of a thing]". Of anyone who denies this premise al-Ghazālī says "your treatment should be in the hospital, for this is due to a bad mixture of humours. For one who doubts about the basis of existence has indeed doubted first of all about his own existence", McCarthy, p. 254.

[4] By contrast, al-Ghazālī implies, he has successful arguments and so can enter the domain of reason and argumentation.

[5] ibid., p. 257.

existence in this world and includes an awareness of the next. Now, reason turns out to be indispensable to this too. First, human beings attain truths by relying on imagination, estimation, and other faculties, whose successful operation provide the objects about which we might reason. And, second, when considering the consistency of the Qur'ān, al-Ghazālī proposes that "oneness is the indication of the true, and multiplicity is the indication of the false".[6] The implications of these proposals are as follows. We may take it that logic depends on supposing that there is a set of theorems or axioms that forms the basic operation of reasoning, regardless of the content, of what the set of premises is, etc. In terms of the distinction between form and content, or logical procedure and premises, the consistency of the Qur'ān at issue in the quotation must concern the content of the arguments rather than their form, must describe the premises at work. The quotation, in part, says that insights into the nature of things must be consistent and not arbitrary. Arguably this consistency must include reason. If the truths and imperatives the Qur'ān contains must find purchase in our lives, action, and beliefs, the book can neither plausibly enjoin actions that contradict central beliefs nor promote contradictory beliefs. If we understand behaviour as the rule governing actions of individuals, then an inconsistent belief or imperative would promote self-thwarting actions, expecting people to follow mutually conflictive imperatives.[7] But this would destroy the community.

[6] ibid., p. 221.

[7] Here logic need not control every aspect of life and behaviour. It may not be a positive criterion such that to determine whether any action can be undertaken at all the actor must first derive the rule of action from some core of established permissible actions and cannot perform any action unless it can be so derived. Consistency may only be a negative criterion here, in that actions are permissible unless they can be shown to contradict given rules, so that the community is made up of actions that, first, do not thwart each other always, and

Conversely, the most secure community is one based on reason and truth.

TRUTH, INTERPRETATION, AND EXISTENCE

From the basis in truth and reason sketched out above, al-Ghazālī goes on to propose that the community with its concern for truth is also the basis of interpretation. He is certain that everyone is "compelled to use interpretation - unless one exceeds the bounds in stupidity and ignorance".[8] The suggestion is that since we can establish what is true, we must be able to establish what is not true and, by extension, what cannot be known to be true because the conditions for arriving at consensus have not been met. These conditions set out the space for interpretation. Al-Ghazālī expects that agents can agree about the truth. In this context he does not contrast interpretations with more straightforward literal propositions on the grounds that they are false whereas the latter are true. Rather, interpretations too are a variety of knowledge and are capable of grasping truth. They are not qualitatively distinct from unproblematic truth claims; their imperfection consists only in their less clear expression of the truth and a commensurately less powerful call on agreement from other subjects.[9]

second do not contradict the basic rules. This leaves a large range of permissible behaviour that is pragmatically consistent internally even if its logical status is not clearly defined. Nor, alternatively, must its pragmatic status always be testable by strict logical consistency with a central core of rules of behaviour. Nonetheless, the internal pragmatic consistency of that permissible behaviour can be expressed as rules of behaviour that are compatible with each other.

[8] ibid., p. 157.

[9] In addition to expecting that the need for interpretation is capable of being proved, again suggesting that there is a continuity between levels of

First, al-Ghazālī identifies differing degrees of *existence*, that yield distinct levels of truth and interpretation. He cites a "law of interpretation" which says that

> the allowability of [interpretation] rests on solid apodictic proof of the impossibility of the literal sense. The first literal meaning is that of essential existence. If this is sure, it generates what comes after it. But if it be impossible, then sensible existence; for if this is sure it is guaranteed against what comes after it. And if this be impossible, then imaginative or mental existence. And if this be impossible, then analogical existence .... Nor is it permissible to turn from one degree to what is

interpretation based on their grasp of the object, al-Ghazālī also expects that the polyvalence of meanings that gives rise to the need for interpretation will make it difficult for every interpretation to be accepted universally. The issues involved here are distinct from another set of issues centring on the way in which different sects insist on the literal truth of certain claims that, by al-Ghazālī's account, are really matters of interpretation. Such sects make a category mistake, and the demands they make of members of the Muslim community, the exclusions they wish to practice, cannot claim the apodictic certainty that accrues to literal truths, ibid., p. 157. The issue arising from the polyvalence of meanings and the need for interpretation implies that agents cannot be excluded from the community for failing to accept any given interpretation because, first, interpretations of meanings lack the authority that extends over the whole Muslim community, which rests on access to truth, and so cannot expect to speak for the whole community, and, second, where an interpretation does extend over the whole community, the possibility of other meanings makes it impossible to claim authority for any single meaning and, therefore, cannot exclude any members of the community who propose other meanings.

> beneath it except because of the necessity deriving from the apodictic demonstration.[10]

LEVELS OF EXISTENCE DETERMINE LEVELS OF INTERPRETATION

This is not the occasion to develop further his complex explanation of the levels of existence.[11] For our concern with metaphor, we may look at his account of analogical existence. Al-Ghazālī distinguishes analogical existence by reference to a mental content that denotes an object, the "thing in itself", by means of some resemblance to "one of [the object's] properties and one of its qualities".[12] Mental existence, he argues, is informed by some essential quality of the object, even though the concept does not resemble the particular objects it orders. The concept of a pen, which has a mental existence, relates to the image of a particular reed and metal pen because it identifies the essence of the actual pen's purpose to write. Imaginative existence relies on an ability to bring to mind an image of an absent particular. Sensible and essential existence denotes the original grasp of that particular. All these depend on the object,

[10] Al-Ghazālī also proposes both that "the allowability of [interpretations] rests on solid apodictic proof of the impossibility of the literal sense", ibid., p. 157, and "that it is not permissible to turn from one degree [of interpretation] to what is beneath it except because of the necessity deriving from apodictic demonstration", ibid., p. 157.

[11] Al-Ghazālī sometimes writes as if the first were true, at other times, the second. It would take us too far off our topic to discuss this in detail, but clearly there must be some hierarchy of grasp of the object if he is to talk coherently of moving from one state to the next by necessity.

[12] ibid., p. 152.

seeking to grasp it and relate to it as fully and fundamentally as possible for each capacity.[13]

By contrast, analogical existence depends on securing an indirect relation to aspects of an object. Al-Ghazālī cites as an example ascriptions of

> anger and yearning and joy and patience and other such things in what has reached us regarding God most high. For the real meaning of anger, for example, is that it is the ebulation of the blood of the heart due to the desire for revenge. But this is not free from imperfection and pain. So one who has solid apodictic proof of the impossibility of real anger's abiding in God most high essentially, and sensibly, and imaginatively, and mentally reduces it to the abiding of another attribute from which proceeds what proceeds from anger, like the will to punish. But the will does not correspond to anger in the reality of its essence, but in one of the qualities which goes with it and one of the effects which proceeds from it, viz. the infliction of pain.[14]

Some things to note are, first, that al-Ghazālī seems to identify the mental existence, the real meaning of anger with an explanation of its physiology: it is an ebulation of the blood of the heart due to

[13] The image that invokes an absent particular is systematically connected to other images of the same particular, where all the possible images, for example, of a mosque in Samarkand, relate to each other in ways determined by the nature of the object. The mental existence seeks to abstract and acquire a concept or rule that grasps whatever is definitive about an object and to relate that quality to other similar particulars.

[14] ibid., p. 155.

the desire for revenge. This identification is not necessary. Previously he has described the real meaning of the pen by reference to its function, which suggests that we should stress "due to the desire for revenge" because that is the function of anger in the present example. In effect, that becomes its essence. Second, such a function "is not free from imperfection and pain" and therefore cannot be ascribed to God. Given apodictic proof "of the impossibility of real anger's abiding in God most high essentially and sensibly and imaginatively and mentally", anyone who ascribes the emotion to God must be speaking metaphorically, indicating the presence of some other attribute that plays the role that anger usually plays for us. Whereas for human beings anger generates a will to revenge, to punish an agent who has transgressed against some rights, the same will to punish cannot have a similarly profane origin in God, and an ascription of anger must, therefore, be a shorthand way of denoting that feature of God's will. But that "will does not correspond to anger in the reality of its embrace, but in one of the qualities which goes with it and one of the effects that proceeds from it, viz. the infliction of pain". God does not seek to inflict pain; but his concern for justice leads to punishment that seems to parallel our search for revenge over some slight or insult. Or so al-Ghazālī seems to be arguing.

Anger generates the desire for revenge, to seek to punish by causing pain to a transgressor; such pain seems to afflict the person who transgresses against God's laws and will, and we move from the similarity this bears with the former case to ascribe anger to God, even though we know certainly that essentially, in his very concept, sensibly, in our experience, imaginatively, in the images we may evoke of him, and mentally, in what we understand of his meaning, there is no basis for ascribing to God the anger, an ebulation of blood, or a search for revenge.[15] By this account, then, the structure of analogies seems to be that: A-->B in object O_e in our experience and B occurs in object O_1 in our experience; therefore we ascribe A to O_1. The generalisation that "all punishment and revenge are generated by anger", cannot find anything like the inductive proof it would require for truth. However, its metaphorical use accepts that the generalisation does not apply to God but that the analogy is still fruitful in bringing to attention some feature of our complex relation to a world that owes everything to God. Only by misusing arguments by analogy, by failing to recognise the problematic epistemological status of the underlying generalisation, do we mistake metaphors for truth.

Al-Ghazālī also proposes that there are grounds of certainty whose violation leads us from the level of essential knowledge through successive stages to metaphor. He suggests two kinds of consideration. The first diagnoses that disagreement and uncertainty over the truth of essential existence, a failure of proof, can result from a number of sources including

> (1) an inability to grasp completely conditions [for sound arguments]; or (2) in connection with their resorting in their speculation to simple innate bent and nature divorced from weighing with the balance [of reason] ... or (3) because they differ about the cognitions which serve as the premises of the apodictic proof ... or (4) because of mixing up judgements of imagination with those of reason, or (5) because of mistaking sayings which

[15] For example, revenge may arguably be something we can seek against someone who is comparable to us in power and conscience, who is human or can be anthropomorphised without deficit, whereas no exercise of our abilities could balance and oppose an omnipotent and omniscient divinity.

> are accepted and esteemed for analytical judgements and primary truths.[16]

People may fail to gain the certainty that apodictic proofs are capable of for these reasons, but the fallibility of the people who provide apodictic proofs does not show any weakness in the proof procedures itself; existence of these obstacles does not, conversely, imply that certainty is impossible. Rather, in every case, presumably critics must be able to identify the particular errors that infect the soundness of any putative apodictic proof.

The second consideration is more than just a failure of proof but suggests a positive account of the impossibility of literal sense.[17] Al-Ghazālī says

> it is, for example, like saying: this jewel is many times a horse - i.e. in the sense and meaning of financial worth which is perceived mentally, not in its [physical] size which is grasped by sensation and imagining.[18]

[16] ibid., pp. 154-155.

[17] Self-contradictory statements would also seem to be obvious candidates for such problematic status.

[18] At p. 154 al-Ghazālī provides examples of how propositions fail literal sense and gain imaginative or mental existence. He cites as mental existence the

> utterance of the Apostle - God's blessings upon him - "He who is brought forth from the fire will be given a portion of the garden equivalent to ten times this world". The literal meaning of this points to its being ten times in length and breadth and surface, and this is sensible and imaginative difference. Then one may be astonished and say: "The garden is in the heaven, as the literal meanings of the tradition have indicated: how then can the heaven be broad enough to be ten times the world when the heaven also is part of this world?" The interpreter may surmount his astonishment and say: "What is meant is an abstract and

To explain: the truth of the proposition (1) "the jewel is many times a horse" depends on (2) "many times" is only apparently meant as a comparison of spatial position since as such it would plainly be false. Rather (3) "many times" is better understood as a more abstract comparison of values, so that the proposition is really (4) "The jewel is many times the financial worth of the horse", (3) sets out the comparison that is the interpretation linking (1) to (4), while (2) sets out the need to move from (1) to (4), motivated by the principle of veracity and its assumption that these propositions seek to make sense. Similarly, in another example, al-Ghazālī proposes to move from (5) "God most high leavened the clay of Adam with his hand for forty days" to (9) "God made Adam", the move being instigated by (6) that "the hand of God" is only apparently affirmed of him since this can only be true at the level of sensible or imaginative existence but is false at the level of essential existence, (and we suppose that (5) is capable of being true), and following the interpretation (7) that "the spirit and meaning of the hand" is "that by which one strikes and effects and gives and holds back", and (8) that "God most high gives and holds back by means of the angels".[19]

This procedure assumes what we might call a principle of veracity, by which, first, al-Ghazālī supposes that the proposition is meaningful at some level or is part of a rational enterprise of grasping the nature and order of the world and, second, takes it that the different levels of existence are all attempts to gain as "truthful" a grasp of the nature of reality as is possible - that the degrees of interpretation are degrees of interpretation of the truth of reality. In both cases the move to seek the levels of essential existence depends

mental difference, not that which is sensible and imaginative".

[19] ibid., p. 154.

on the failure of sense at some other level. The character of the intervening interpretations, the level or levels of existence it refers to, will establish the kind of statement it is and the level at which it exists.

By this account, we set out in a series the axioms, propositions, and comparisons that reduce the interpretation to a clear expression of an essential or sensible existence. In this procedure, reasoning, logic, and rules of interpretation cannot yield truth. They denote procedures for right thinking, they do not determine what the truths are or what we must accept for that reason. But we can insist, and al-Ghazālī too insists, that the truth cannot be internally inconsistent. No community could survive as a unity on the basis of mutually contradictory or exclusive rules of behaviour.[20] The truth cannot be irrational, it does not exist as a result of the procedures of logic and interpretation, but its development and transmission depend on these procedures.

Those procedures and their basis in existences al-Ghazālī takes to be exhaustive. Any interpretation that does not fit these rules must be irrational and cannot generate any significant agreement about meanings. This axiomatic status, the use of those procedures and existences as the basis for all thought, is not arbitrary. Just as Aristotle (d. 322 BC) took the first figure of the syllogism to be obvious and undeniable, and defended this status by showing how all other argumentative forms were ultimately reducible to the first figure through a series of generalisations and basic categories, so too al-Ghazālī seems to propose a parallel structure whereby the different levels of interpretation find their ultimate justification by reference to essential existence and rules of interpretation. In effect,

[20] The presence of such contradictions and their implications may not always be clear, but that does not imply that they can continue and have an effect.

essential existence plays the same fundamental role as the first figure of the syllogism does for Aristotle, and for al-Ghazālī refers to the roots of faith and given traditions. In that case, disagreement with the existences proposed by al-Ghazālī would take a particular form, for example requiring the critic to produce new categories by extrapolation, showing why or how a recalcitrant instance does not fit the given categories yet still seems to make sense. The intuition of sense and of its lack of fit needs to be justified by showing how an alternative new category works better than the old one. An intuition that some meaning does not find a satisfactory home in any of the given existences must be capable of being translated into an argument showing that some additional existence is necessary. No intuition by itself can be a justifiable basis for accepting or rejecting the given existence, as if it were an independent source of knowledge of essences, but must be explained by extrapolating from a given existence to show why and how a new one will order elements that otherwise do not completely fit the given divisions yet still make sense. And given this possibility, al-Ghazālī is not claiming that his conception of the existences and their nature is immutable. Such a claim would be dogmatism - a charge he is as quick to reject as he is to seek a rational faith. Similarly, although al-Ghazālī does not clearly aim for it, an inference we might draw from the crucial role of consensus is that figurative language and metaphor must make comparisons that engage others as well. A private metaphor, a comparison that has value only to the particular individual, seems unlikely to succeed as an interpretative rule since it fails to generate the consensus necessary to its truth and validity.

Now al-Ghazālī explains metaphors further by characterising the comparisons at work in their analogical structure, but this development seems to raise a problem. Metaphorical uses of concepts bear some resemblance to the concept of their object, but are

> the most bizarre of interpretations and the furthest removed from reality, [where] you make what is said a trope [*majāz*] or a metaphor [*istiʿāra*], these being mental existence and analogical existence.[21]

As mental existence, figurative language still uses or relies on concepts that grasp and relay meanings at some level, but their reference is mediated through a comparison that does not closely bear on the image and imaginative existence usually associated with an object. A "pen" has form and meaning, the first of which occurs as a mental image that we can invoke even when the object, the pen itself, is absent. The relevant mental existence, the concept that constitutes the meaning of "pen", does not need to look like, in the sense of being visually comparable to, the image of the object, the pen, but we may expect the concept to order and relate all particular images of the forms of pens, including the one made of a cane body and metal nib, another made of wood, another of bone, and so on. Although no particular image need necessarily and sufficiently embody the meaning of a pen, there will be certain functions the form or image must include in order for it to be a pen. Or, conversely, a commonly used kind of pen, or its image, may serve to evoke the concept of the pen and can be used to stand for the function the pen serves. Thus, the image of a particular kind of pen, a quill, can stand for the concept of a pen and the use to which pens are put, of expressing thought and reflection, where the fragility of the quill can embody the ease with which free reflection can be stifled or cut down. Similarly, a sword may stand for power and its attendant violence, especially where its exercise is unjust and,

[21] ibid., p. 155.

therefore, irrational or unthinking, and does not brook reasoning in matters of knowledge, action, or faith, and may be counterpoised in a particular relation to the quill, with all its attendant meanings and images, to constitute the claim that "the pen is mightier than the sword". The proposition is literally (usually) false but, assuming a principle of veracity, leads us to seek out comparisons based on images and analogies, meanings and oppositions, to make good sense of it.

The comparisons are indirect and somewhat extended, and depend for their plausibility on finding acceptance with their audience. Whatever the particular images, meanings, comparisons and oppositions involved, none of these elements in their juxtapositions works unless they generate consensus. Where they do, where their sense is shared, the comparisons make sense and can share that interest in truth which makes metaphors interesting and insightful about reality, perhaps consolidating a range of feelings and unarticulated attitudes and imprecise meanings without seeking to be literally true.

TWO SENSES OF CONSENSUS?

However, al-Ghazālī's reference to consensus here seems problematic. This kind of consensus seems to differ from the consensus previously ascribed to truth. The consensus of metaphors seems to establish meanings and coherence rather than truth, and does not clearly participate in the authority claimed for consensual truth by citing the prophet's caution that "the *umma* cannot be mistaken". Metaphors not only cannot gain the same certain grasp of truths as their more prosaic and precise counterparts, but their attachment to the truth also does not seem so close as to be warranted by the prophet's caveat. The comparisons are too imprecise to gain that justification.

The contrast suggested above is not entirely satisfactory, and explaining its inadequacy may help clarify the role of consensus in metaphorical and figurative language. Al-Ghazālī maintains that analogous existence falls within the compass of reason, and so must have some relation to reason and to its dealings with known truths. The central truths that he is concerned with, to which the community gives warrant through consensus, are the objects of knowledge: that which we came to know. Given in a apodictic revelation, they cannot be inconsistent, and do not validate a false consensus. They may come to be known in diverse ways, and interpretation of them in cases remains unavoidable, even if people differ over exactly what needs interpretation and of what kind. The problem, for al-Ghazālī, is that some people form themselves into sects and accuse others of misrepresenting the given truths when, in particular cases, truths are available only in interpretations, and therefore no one is in a position to claim certainty. Consequently, no sect can dismiss another's claim as simply false by contrast with their allegedly true knowledge. Over some things there is only interpretation available, and those who claim absolute certainty are simply making an impossible claim.

To explain the certainty we may expect, al-Ghazālī set out his theory of interpretation, which he explains by reference to the five levels of existence. These set out the contributions to gaining truths that we are capable of, given our faculties or capacities for receiving the truth. Metaphors, and figurative speech, as part of this battery of modes of grasping truth, of interpreting its details and making them accessible to each other, are varieties of access to the truth - over which the *umma* cannot be mistaken. Of course, by its nature interpretation cannot claim the certainties available to a direct grasp of the truth because the very concept allows room for uncertainty, for an interpretation being unable to grasp the truth fully, of being only a possible approach to the truth. Therefore, there are limits to the demands we can make of others in the community for consensus. Apodictic certainty has a stronger claim on agreement from the community than interpretation does, and interpretation itself has numerous divisions according to levels of existence, the structures of interpretative rules and the status of axioms. The further along the scale of division, the weaker the demand an interpretation can make on the community for agreement because the less direct is its grasp of the truth. This is because a metaphor makes a more ambiguous claim about its object, deals with it in a less direct, less explicit, more polyvalent way, where its claims, so to speak, have wider resonances than a strict, precise reference to the object in an essential existence can afford. The precision of the expression, the directness of the claim, makes for a more explicit and exactly calibrated demand for agreement from the community, since its implications and nature can be clearly set out. The metaphor, by contrast, has a less precise nature.

But the lack of precision involved here, the polyvalence a metaphor possesses, is not vagueness. The metaphor is ambiguous not in the sense of having no clear meaning at all but rather polyvalent in the sense of having a set of possible meanings, interconnected with each other, where we lack any criteria for showing preference for some of those possible meanings over others. Their interpretative excess over, say, mental existence is not a greater vagueness, an amorphous "reasonableness" that lacks detail, but a richness of meanings and interconnections that is irreducible to some single univalent terms.

Without this polyvalence, if metaphors were only vague expressions rather than an interrelated set of mutually-determining meanings, figurative language would fall outside the compass of reason and could not claim any grasp of truth because it could not clearly articulate any grasp of anything at all. By contrast, because of their polyvalence, metaphors still claim the authority ascribed to truth, but because of the mutual determinations of meanings, their polyvalence, these demands can be met by a number of different responses, and so they do not provide a precisely calibrated guide to action and therefore cannot clearly reject a range of actions as unguided or false either. Nevertheless, there are limits to the openness of metaphors: some meanings will clearly be beyond their scope. Talk of polyvalence is intended to suggest just that: that there may be a set of mutually-determining meanings, but there is a determining set.

Polyvalence is not ambiguity or sheer open-endedness but a determinate set of meanings. And the determinateness of that set will justify the strength of the demand analogical existence can make on the community. It does not permit just any behaviour in response, though it does define those behaviours much less thoroughly than, say, essential existence. Thus its demand is less precise, less detailed, but it is no less authoritative than the compulsion embodied in essential existence. In this sense, figurative language occurs within the compass of reason or bears the noose of reason.

FURTHER ISSUES

This explanation of al-Ghazālī's conception of metaphor and figurative language leaves a number of issues uncharted. For example, we need to consider in more detail the source and nature of the premises about which we reason and which we can develop in figurative language. Given his mysticism, we may have to accept that some premises occur as intuitions or insights into the nature of reality. This is entirely compatible with the use of logic as a tool of reason, however, in that the insights and premises cannot be self-contradictory if they are to be taken seriously, regardless of whether their expression is precise or relies on figurative language. This comparison also requires us to consider further how al-Ghazālī understands the sources of premises - an issue that is clearly connected with the nature of essential and other existences and the issue of how fully it is possible to set out the rules and conditions for particular levels of existence. In any case, what I wanted to emphasise in this paper is that reason has an important role to play in al-Ghazālī's work, and it would be unfortunate if we were to reject its place for the sake of ascribing a merely irrational mysticism to this philosopher.

The Influence of the Arabic Pseudo-Empedocles on Medieval Latin Philosophy: Myth or Reality?

Daniel De Smet
Katholieke Universiteit, Leuven

An inadvertent lack of criticism, when animated by euphoric enthusiasm, may easily become a serious threat to any scientific research, as one takes for granted what originally was only hypothetical, based on apparently evident but tentative premises. Soon there follows a concatenation of conjectures and new hypotheses which are not doubted any more, but are exalted to become real dogmas. This way myths and legends are created, many of which prove to be extremely persistent.

In the case I want to present, I propose myself to demystify the story about the Arabic pseudo-Empedocles, in particular his alleged influence on Latin scholasticism by way of Jewish philosophical texts of Spanish origin. For the present time I shall limit myself to a negative approach, by challenging older theories; a solution of the problem will appear in the monograph I am preparing, with the support of the Belgian-Flemish Fund for Scientific Research (NFWO), about the Arabic pseudo-Empedoclean tradition.[1]

As far as I can see, the image of the Arabic Empedocles prevailing in western research for nearly a century and a half was shaped, at least in its broad outlines, by Salomon Munk. He cites the following remark made by Shēm Ṭōb b. Joseph b. Falaqēra (d. c. 689/1290) in the introduction to his Hebrew translation of Ibn Gabirōl's (Avicebron, d. 450/1058-9) *Fons Vitae*:

> Having studied the book composed by the learned Rabbi Salomon b. Gabirol and entitled *The Source of Life*, it appeared to me that the author's doctrines followed the system of some ancient philosopher, such as the one exposed in the work of Empedocles (fl. 450 BC) about the Five Substances.[2]

Munk further refers to Empedocles' theory as presented by Shahrastānī (d. 548/1153-4):[3] amidst the neoplatonic doctrines that Shahrastānī attributes to the philosopher of Akragas, Munk discovered a real similarity to Ibn Gabirōl's neoplatonic philosophy. This would confirm Ibn Falaqēra's statement. The conclusion

[1] For some preliminary results, see Daniel De Smet, "De geschiedenis van de Griekse filosofie volgens laat-antieke en islamitische auteurs", *Handelingen van de Koninklijke Zuidnederlandse Maatschappij voor Taal- en Letterkunde en Geschiedenis* 48 (1994), 57-69; idem, "Héraclite, philosophe de la guerre, dans la tradition arabe", *Acta Orientalia Belgica* 9 (1994), 131-140.

[2] Salomon Munk, *Mélanges de philosophie juive et arabe* (Paris, 1859), p. 3.

[3] Al-Shahrastānī, *Kitāb al-Milal wa l-Niḥal*, ed. Muḥammad Sayyid Kaylānī, 2 vols. (Beirut, s.d.), 2:68-73; see the French translation by Jean Jolivet and Guy Monnot, *Shahrastani. Livre des religions et des sectes*, 2 vols. (Louvain, 1986-93), 2:193-200.

seemed obvious: Ibn Gabirōl would have been influenced by some apocryphal neoplatonic text that the Arabs ascribed to Empedocles.[4]

How Ibn Gabirōl could have had access to this Arabic Empedocles was given a simple explanation by Munk. Here he could invoke Ibn al-Qifṭī (d. 646/1248-9), who in his chapter on Empedocles reports that a fraction (*firqa*) of the *Bāṭiniyya* followed the doctrine of this ancient sage, as did Ibn Masarra (d. 319/931), the *bāṭinī* of Cordoba: this heretic used to study and to teach the philosophy of Empedocles.[5] To Munk the matter was perfectly clear. At the beginning of the fourth/tenth century the Andalusian mystic Ibn Masarra would have collected on his journeys through the oriental regions of the Muslim world some Arabic texts attributed to Empedocles, which he introduced into Spain (a fact not mentioned by any source); one of these texts, a "Book about the Five Substances", would have circulated in Spain until the days of Ibn Gabirōl, the philosopher of Malaga, who would have made use of it while elaborating his own philosophy.[6]

The brief statements by Ibn Falaqēra and Ibn al-Qifṭī, as interpreted by Munk, form the two premises on which the whole theory about the Arabic pseudo-Empedocles was built.

Munk's conclusions were accepted and reiterated by David Kaufmann, who by chance discovered fragments of a Hebrew translation of this "Book about the Five Substances" attributed to Empedocles, in two Kabbalistic works of the eighth/fourteenth century, the *Yesōd ʿOlām* by Elḫanan b. Abraham and an anonymous commentary on the Pentateuch, as well as in a collection

[4] Munk, pp. 240-45.

[5] Ibn al-Qifṭī, *Ta'rīkh al-Ḥukamā'*, ed. J. Lippert (Leipzig, 1903), pp. 15-16; after this statement, the author gives some biographical notes about Ibn Masarra.

[6] Munk, pp. 241-242.

of notes by Jo̱hanan Allemanno (d. after 1504), the preceptor of Pico della Mirandola (d. 1494).[7] Encouraged by this discovery, Kaufmann overestimated the influence of the pseudo-Empedocles on Jewish and Muslim philosophy in Spain: thus Ibn Masarra would have introduced, along with pseudo-Empedoclean texts, the seed of enlightenment ("Aufklärung") in a country ravaged by Muslim fanaticism. Although he considers Ibn Falaqēra's remark as being beyond any doubt, he becomes really embarrassed when comparing the *Fons Vitae* with the fragments of the "Book about the Five Substances", as he too has to admit that the two doctrines are not as identical as one would expect. But to Kaufmann, this could easily be explained by the fact that only some loose fragments of the pseudo-Empedoclean work have come down to us.[8]

The image of the Arabic Empedocles, as shaped by Munk and Kaufmann, owes its most complete though somehow imaginative elaboration to Miguel Asín y Palacios. In his inaugural lecture held before the Real Academia de Ciencias Morales y Políticas in 1914,[9] the famous Spanish scholar tried to reconstruct what he calls "the pseudo-Empedoclean system", using Shahrastānī and Shahrazūrī[10]

[7] David Kaufmann, *Studien über Salomon Ibn Gabirol* (Budapest, 1899), pp. 13-15; edition of the fragments, ibid., pp. 17-51.

[8] Kaufmann, pp. 1-12, 52-8.

[9] Miguel Asín y Palacios, *Abenmasarra y su escuela. Origenes de la filosofía hispano-musulmana* (Madrid, 1914); Elmer H. Douglas and Howard W. Yoder, Eng. trans. *The Mystical Philosophy of Ibn Masarra and his Followers* (Leiden, 1978). The publication of this translation, which does not reconsider Asín y Palacios' study in the light of recent research, gave new life to the myth of pseudo-Empedocles, but met at the same time with some serious criticisms, as in the reviews by Bernd Radtke, *Der Islam* 58 (1981), 330-331 and Paul E. Walker, *Journal of the American Oriental Society* 103 (1983), 761-762.

[10] Shams ad-Dīn al-Shahrazūrī, *Nuzhat al-Arwāḥ wa Rawḍat al-Afrāḥ*, ed. Sayyid Khurshīd Aḥmad, 2 vols. (Hayderabad, 1976), 1:50-55. The text of

as his main sources. This "system" would have consisted in no less than seventeen parts. However, most of them are but general topics, common to any neoplatonic doctrine, such as the inaccessibility of the first principle, the generation of plurality by emanation from an absolute unique source, and the cosmological hierarchy represented by the hypostases of intellect, soul and nature. In fact, only the notion of matter as the first creature and of love and strife as contradictory principles might be specific to the Arabic Empedocles.[11] Nevertheless, Asín y Palacios projected this whole system into the scarce information about Ibn Masarra's thought as given by Ibn Ḥazm (d. 456/1063) and Ibn al-ᶜArabī (d. 638/1240) and, not content with this, he argued that in the fifth/eleventh century the "Empedoclean" doctrine of Ibn Masarra was adopted by the Ṣūfī school of Almeria and as such inspired Ibn al-ᶜArabī directly, who propagated it through the whole Muslim world, as far as Persia and India.[12] Moreover, pseudo-Empedocles was made one of the major sources for Jewish philosophy in Spain: Judah Halevi (d. shortly after 535/1140-41), Joseph b. Ṣaddīq (d. 544/1149), Moses b. ᶜEzra (d. 561/1165), Samuel b. Tibbōn (d. c. 627/1230) and, of course, Ibn Gabirōl presented as his disciples. Ibn Gabirōl was even held responsible for a real invasion of "pseudo-Empedoclean thought" in Latin scholasticism since the beginning of the twelfth century: the Franciscan school, to which belonged Alexander of Hales (d. 1245), St. Bonaventura (d. 1274), Roger Bacon (d. c. 1294), William of Auvergne (d. 1299), Duns Scotus (d. c. 1308) and Raymundus Lullus (d. 1316), followed the doctrine of the pseudo-Empedocles, whereas Dominicans such as Albertus

this edition differs sometimes considerably from the Leiden Manuscript 1488 used by Asín y Palacios.

[11] Asín y Palacios, pp. 47-57.

[12] Asín y Palacios, pp. 73-129.

Magnus (d. c. 1280) and Thomas Aquinas (d. 1274) continued the Aristotelian tradition, in Islam represented by Ibn Sīnā (Avicenna) (d. 428/1037) and Ibn Rushd (Averroes) (d. 595/1198). Even Dante (d. 1321), Pico della Mirandola and Marcilo Ficino (d. 1499) inherited from the Arabic pseudo-Empedocles, whose influence only decreased with the advent of modern philosophy.[13]

It is quite easy to prove that Asín y Palacios' statements are largely exaggerated, as he simply identifies every kind of neoplatonic or Gnostic thought with his "pseudo-Empedocles", who tends to become a sort of passe-partout. The links he established lack every probability on the historical, as well as on the philosophical and doctrinal level. Nevertheless, his book had a considerable influence on many historians of Latin scholasticism and medieval Jewish and Arabic philosophy.[14] Only a few Arabists, such as Affifi and Arnaldez,[15] formulated some objections against a number of Asín y Palacios' most hazardous theses, but they

[13] Asín y Palacios, pp. 129-145.

[14] Asín y Palacios' theses were uncritically repeated, for instance, by Max Horten, *Die Philosophie des Islam in ihren Beziehungen zu den philosophischen Weltanschauungen des westlichen Orients*, Geschichte der Philosophie in Einzeldarstellungen I/4 (Munich, 1924), pp. 66, 237, 347; ᶜAbd al-Raḥmān Badawī, *Histoire de la philosophie en Islam*, Etudes de philosophie médiévale 60 (Paris, 1972), pp. 697-698; Henri Corbin, *Histoire de la philosophie islamique. I. Des origines à la mort d'Averroës* (Paris, 1964), pp. 305-311; Miguel Cruz Hernandez, *Historia del pensamiento en el mundo islamico*, 2 vols. (Madrid, 1981), 1:92; Isaac Husik, *A History of Medieval Jewish Philosophy* (Philadelphia, 1946), pp. 61-64; Eliyahu Ashtor, *The Jews of Moslem Spain*, 3 vols. (Philadelphia, 1984), 3:46.

[15] A. E. Affifi, *The Mystical Philosophy of Muḥyid Din-ibnul ᶜArabi* (Cambridge, 1939), pp. 178-183; Roger Arnaldez, "Ibn Masarra", *Encyclopaedia of Islam. New Edition*, 8 vols. 2nd ed. (Leiden, 1971), 3:868-72. Both authors reject the connection between Ibn al-ᶜArabī and Ibn Masarra.

refrained from contesting the essence of his theory. Obviously the myth of the Arabic pseudo-Empedocles was too firmly established.

In reality, the theory is only based on two premises which do not resist critical examination: Ibn al-Qifṭī's statement about the relationship between Ibn Masarra and Empedocles, and Ibn Falaqēra's judgement on the similarity between the doctrines of Ibn Gabirōl and Empedocles. If we could succeed in unsettling these two remarks, the whole construction would inevitably collapse.

It is an already well-known fact that Ibn al-Qifṭī borrowed most of his information about Empedocles, the link with Ibn Masarra included, from Ṣāᶜid al-Andalusī (d. 462/1070)[16] who, in his turn, relies on Abū l-Ḥasan al-ᶜĀmirī (d. 381/992). As ᶜĀmirī's work has now been made accessible, it has become clear that he did not mention Ibn Masarra at all: he only states that a fraction of the *Bāṭiniyya* (*ṭā'ifa min al-bāṭiniyya*) follows Empedocles' teaching, without giving any name.[17] From this new evidence we may conclude that Ṣāᶜid has added his reference to Ibn Masarra in order to discredit this notorious heretic who had a very bad reputation in Spain. The link between Empedocles and Ibn Masarra begins to appear very weak.[18]

Moreover, when we compare the few elements we know about Ibn Masarra's doctrine to the Arabic Empedocles, it soon becomes

[16] Ṣāᶜid al-Andalusī, *Kitāb Ṭabaqāt al-Umam*, ed. Louis Cheikho (Beirut, 1912), pp. 21-22.

[17] Abū l-Ḥasan al-ᶜĀmirī, *Kitāb al-Amad ᶜalā l-Abad*, ed. Everett K. Rowson, *A Muslim Philosopher on the Soul and its Fate*, American Oriental Series 70 (New Haven, 1988), p. 70.

[18] See also Samuel M. Stern, "Ibn Masarra, follower of pseudo-Empedocles - an illusion", in *Actas do IV Congresso de Estudos Arabes e Islāmicos (Coimbra/Lisboa 1968)* (Leiden, 1971), pp. 325-328. Unfortunately, Stern's sudden death prevented this eminent scholar from achieving a projected monograph about the Arabic pseudo-Empedocles.

obvious that there is no objective relationship between them.[19] If Ibn Masarra, as well as Spanish Ṣūfism and Ibn al-ᶜArabī have nothing to do with the Arabic pseudo-Empedocles, how then could they have transmitted his doctrine to Jewish philosophers such as Ibn Gabirōl?

Of course, we still have Ibn Falaqēra's remark. But an attentive reading of his text reveals that the Hebrew translator does not actually assert that Ibn Gabirōl borrowed his doctrine in the *Fons Vitae* from Empedocles' "Book about the Five Substances": he only remarked a certain similarity between the two works.[20] Even a superficial examination of the *Fons Vitae* immediately shows that this similarity does not go much further than some very general topics common to most neoplatonic thinkers.[21] Only Ibn Gabirōl's notion of spiritual matter as the first created being could appear, at first sight, as an undeniable pseudo-Empedoclean element.[22] But

[19] I could not find even the slightest similarity as to the doctrine and terminology between, on the one side, the remnants of Ibn Masarra's thought conserved in Ibn Ḥazm, *al-Fiṣal fī l-Milal wa l-Ahwā' wa l-Niḥal,* 5 vols. (Būlāq, 1899-1903), 2:99, 4:150-1 and Ibn al-ᶜArabī, *al-Futūḥāt al-Makkiyya*, 4 vols. (Būlāq, 1876), 2:581 and, on the other, the pseudo-Empedoclean doctrine transmitted by Shahrastānī and the Hebrew fragments.

[20] See also Jacques Schlanger, *La philosophie de Salomon Ibn Gabirol. Etude d'un néoplatonisme*, Etudes sur le judaisme médiéval 3 (Leiden, 1968), p. 88.

[21] See, for instance, the confrontation of the *Fons Vitae* with Shahrastānī's pseudo-Empedocles and the Hebrew fragments in Schlanger, pp. 77-94. Although Schlanger still maintains that amidst a lot of other Arabic Neoplatonic texts the fragments of the "Book about the Five Substances" are very close to the doctrine of the *Fons Vitae*, he had to admit that they cannot be considered as the major source used by Ibn Gabirōl (Schlanger, p. 94).

[22] This was stressed by Munk, p. 245, Kaufmann, pp. 52-53, Asín y Palacios, pp. 130-131, Schlanger, pp. 91-92 and Colette Sirat, *La philosophie juive médiévale en terre d'Islam* (Paris, 1988), pp. 89-90.

even in this case we have obviously two different traditions before us.

Indeed, and without being able to go into details here, the *Fons Vitae* linked universal matter, as a principle of potentiality, in an inseparable way to universal form: both are situated on the same ontological level.[23] We are here in the presence of a doctrine relatively common to later Neoplatonism, as it is professed, for instance, by Proclus (d. 485), who claims that Aristotelian hylemorphism is not limited to material things, but also characterises the constitution of the spiritual worlds: at every level of the cosmic hierarchy the spiritual entities display a hylemorphic structure, being composed of form and intelligible matter. Proclus presents these two principles as separate hypostases, universal form and universal matter, situated at the same level and forming an indivisible unity. He identifies them with Plato's dyad of the unlimited and the limited.[24]

To the Arabic pseudo-Empedocles, however, matter is in itself a hypostasis, which is not directly associated with form: in its quality of first created being, it stands between the creator and the intellect, which emanates from it. Matter is the initial potentiality; it is the seed of all subsequent beings, out of which the entire creation

[23] Ibn Gabirōl (Avicebron), *Fons Vitae*, ed. Clemens Baeumker, Beiträge zur Geschichte der Philosophie des Mittelalters I/2-4 (Münster, 1892-5), IV, 10, p. 233, V, 31, pp. 314-315, V, 42, p. 333; cf. Schlanger, pp. 216-272; Jean Jolivet, "La matière d'en haut", *Annuaire de l'Ecole Pratique des Hautes Etudes. Sciences Religieuses* 96 (1987-1998), 41-42; John Dillon, "Salomon Ibn Gabirol's doctrine of intelligible matter", *Irish Philosophical Journal* 6 (1989), 59-81.

[24] Proclus, *In Timaeum*, ed. Ernest Diehl, 3 vols. (Leipzig, 1903-1906), 1:263, 384-385; idem, *In Parmenidem*, ed. Victor Cousin (Paris, 1864), pp. 1119-1120, 1123; cf. Jean Trouillard, "La genèse de l'hylémorphisme selon Proclos", *Dialogue. Revue canadienne de philosophie* 6 (1967-1968), 1-17.

is to be generated by the antithetic action of love and strife.[25] As this is a totally different conception, it is improbable that Ibn Gabirōl would have used it to elaborate his own doctrine on spiritual matter.

If there exists no real connection between the Arabic pseudo-Empedocles and Ibn Gabirōl, Ibn Falaqēra's remark being merely a personal judgement, the supposed influence of pseudo-Empedocles on Latin scholasticism becomes dubious, as Ibn Gabirōl would have been the principal mediator. So we may conclude that Asín y Palacios' impressive construction does not resist a critical examination. But this does not mean that the chapter on the Arabic Empedocles should hereby be closed. On the contrary, the question has again to be thoroughly studied, but on different grounds. It will be necessary to obtain a clear image about the contents of the Arabic Empedocles, his sources and the intellectual circles in which he originated, before dealing with his possible influence on later Muslim, Jewish or Christian philosophers.

[25] See the pseudo-Empedoclean texts collected by Jolivet, pp. 28-39.

The Paradise and the City: Preliminary Remarks on Muslim Sacral Geography

Jan M. F. Van Reeth
Katholieke Universiteit, Leuven

In a series of late medieval paintings, of which the Ghent altarpiece by Van Eyck is the most famous, the worldly or heavenly city of Jerusalem appears as the Dutch town of Utrecht, immediately recognisable by its typical, lofty tower. Yet its symbolic value remains unexplained; we only know that the reformists of the Modern Devotion directed their invectives against it,[1] as if it were some modern counterpart of the biblical tower of Babel.

Some centuries before, however, during the episcopacy of Bernold (1027-1054), a cross of churches was built in the same town of Utrecht: crossways around the cathedral in its centre, four churches were founded: St. John, St. Peter, St. Mary and the abbey

[1] See our article: "Het Lam Gods-retabel en de relatie van Byzantium en Florence met onze gewesten", *Millennium. Tijdschrift voor Middeleeuwse Studies* 2 (1988), 133, n. 37; J. Huizinga, "De Kunst der Van Eyck's in het leven van hun tijd", *De Gids* 80/6 & 7 (1916), 440-462, 52-82 = *Verz. W.* (Haarlem, 1948), 3.1:447; J. G. J. Tiecke, *De Werken van Geert Groote* (Nijmegen, 1941), pp. 228-231; M. van Vlierden, *Utrecht een hemel op aarde,* Clavis Kunsthistorische Monografieën 6 (Zutphen, 1988), pp. 33; 42, n. 88; 70.

of St. Paul. Utrecht thus followed a tradition dating from a few decades earlier: in some imperial German cities, a similar cross of churches was erected, at Bamberg and Paderborn.[2] These crosses leave us with the impression that they represented an even larger cross on the surface of the globe: it was an old German tradition indeed, to establish four margraviates at the four corners of the empire, representing the quadripartite structure of the cosmos.[3] Utrecht was thus situated in the north-west, whereas Bamberg was considered to be the centre of the state, founded and ornamented as such by the emperor Henry II (1002-1024) in 1007:[4] in front of its cathedral a pillar was dressed with an image of Christ the Saviour on it. A comparable representation has been preserved on an ivory binding from the Schnütgen-Museum: Christ, surrounded by angels and saints sits on a globe on top of a pillar, symbolising the column of the world.[5]

Undoubtedly this column in Bamberg referred to a similar column in Jerusalem. It was well known in Europe through one of the most important old descriptions of Jerusalem: the travel-record by the seventh-century monk Arculf, with his sketches and maps, redrafted by Adamnan, abbot of Iona (d. 704).[6] It appears from his account that the column was a relic of an old solar cult, for he remarks that the pillar does not cast any shadow at the summer-

[2] Van Vlierden, p. 26.

[3] ibid., p. 16; M. Müller, *Die heilige Stadt. Roma Quadrata, himmlisches Jerusalem und die Mythe vom Weltnabel* (Stuttgart, 1961), pp. 97-100, 222.

[4] Van Vlierden, pp. 16, 26.

[5] Köln, Schnütgen-Mus. Inv. Nr. B 98; J.-H. Baumgarten, in *Ornamenta Ecclesiae. Kunst und Künstler der Romantik in Köln*, ed. A. Legner, 3 vols. (Köln, 1985), 2:238 f. (E 32); Van Vlierden, pp. 26; 55, nr. 29.

[6] Vienna, Öst. Nationalbibl., MS 458, fol. 4v & MS 609, fol. 4r; J. Wilkinson, *Jerusalem Pilgrims Before the Crusades* (Warminster, 1977), pp. 10, 195 f.; O. Mazal, in *Ornamenta Ecclesiae*, 3:77-79.

solstice. Adamnan deduced from this that Jerusalem had to be the centre, the navel of the earth.[7] We have demonstrated elsewhere the close parallelism that must have existed between the conception of the basilica of the Holy Sepulchre, the Dome of the Rock and the memorial church of St. Symeon at Qalᶜat Simᶜān, as indeed we argued that the pillar of the Stylite had a similar cosmological and astral connotation.[8]

It is therefore as if the column's umbra in the occident, whilst the sun is at its zenith above the holy city, is shown, petrified, in the three cities with their cross of churches, as a huge silhouette spread all over the map of Germany: a cross of light with Jerusalem (or Rome) as its base and oriented towards the north-west.

With the accession of a new dynasty on the throne of the holy Roman empire in 1024, in the person of Konrad II (d. 1039) as the

[7] F. Niehoff, "Umbilicus mundi - Der Nabel der Welt. Jerusalem und das Heilige Grab im Spiegel von Pilgerberichten und -karten, Kreuzzügen und Reliquiaren", in *Ornamenta Ecclesiae*, 3:53, 54, 57; M. Werner, "The Cross-Carpet page in the Book of Durrow: the cult of the True Cross, Adamnan, and Iona", *The Art Bulletin* 72 (1990), 202, 205 (my attention was directed to this important article by Ms. H. Pulliam, in a discussion following her contribution at the International Medieval Congress, Leeds); cf. J. Jeremias, "Golgotha und der heilige Felsen. Eine Untersuchung zur Symbolsprache des Neuen Testaments", *Angelos. Archiv für NT Zeitgesch. und Kulturkunde* 2 (1926), 74 f.; H. Adolf, "Christendom and Islam in the middle ages: new light on 'Grail Stone' and 'Hidden Host'", *Speculum* 32 (1957), 110.

[8] See my article: "Symeon Stylite l'Ancien. Le Saint qui s'est fait colonne", in *Acta Orientalia Belgica* 10: "La Fête" (1996), nn. 57, 107-108. St. Symeon was known in the west already during his life: Gregory of Tours, *Historia Francorum*, 8:15; *Vita Genovefae Virginis Parisiensis*, 27, in B. Krusch, ed., *Passiones Vitaeque Sanctorum Aevi Merovingici et antiquiorum aliqot*, Monumenta Germaniae Historica, Scriptorum Rerum Merovingicarum (Hannover, 1896), 3:226; H. Delehaye, "Les Stylites. Saint Syméon et ses imitateurs", *Revue des questions historiques* 13 (1895), 80 f.; J. Ebersolt, *Orient et occident. Recherches sur les influences byzantines et orientales en France avant et pendant les croisades* (Paris, 1928-1929), pp. 15 f.; nn. 10, 24 f.

first Salic emperor, a new imperial ideology was developed. The concept of a circular state around an *umbilicus*, a central pole, resounds in his motto: *Roma caput mundi regit orbis frena rotundi.*[9]

As early as 1030, the bishop of Paderborn, Meinwerk (1009-1036), sent abbot Wino von Helmarshausen to Jerusalem, to make a survey of the *Anastasis*-church, as he intended to copy it for the *Busdorfkirche* which he was about to build in his town.[10] The mission must have reflected eschatological expectations linked to the concept of Jerusalem as the *Umbilicus Mundi,* for the second coming of Christ was considered to be imminent.[11] Remarkably, it was the same bishop Meinwerk who founded the cross of churches at Paderborn.[12]

These eschatological ideas were expressed in a series of apocalyptic texts. The *Sibyl of Cumae*, as composed in the late eleventh/early twelfth century, clearly points to the Salic emperors; even the older Tiburtine version from the middle of the eleventh century briefly indicates the first *rex Salicus.*[13] Similarly, Benzo of Alba, around the same time, applies the prophecy about the last

[9] Th. Schieffer, "Konrad II", in *Lexikon für Theologie und Kirche* 6 (1961), col. 466; cf. L. Genicot, *Les lignes de faîte du moyen âge* (Tournai, 1975), pp. 123; 327, n. 21.

[10] See the *Vita* of Meinwerk, ed. G. H. Pertz, *Vita Meinwerki Episcopi Patherbrunnensis,* Monumenta Germaniae Historica (Hannover, 1854), 11:158 f.; cf. H. A. Erhard, *Regesta Historiae Westfaliae* (Münster, 1851) 2: nr. 127; D. G. Dalman, *Das Grab Christi in Deutschland,* Studien über christliche Denkmäler 14 (Leipzig, 1922), p. 36; R. Wesenberg, "Wino von Helmarshausen und das kreuzförmige Oktogon", *Zeitschrift für Kunstgeschichte* 12 (1949), 30 f.; M. Wittig, "Busdorf", in *Lexikon für Theologie und Kirche* 2, 3rd ed. (1994), col. 819.

[11] Niehoff, pp. 58-59.

[12] Van Vlierden, p. 26.

[13] C. Erdmann, "Endkaiserglauben und Kreuzzugsgedanke im 11. Jahrhundert", *Zeitschrift für Kirchengeschichte* 51 (1932), 394, 400.

emperor to Henry IV (d. 1106); he announces a military expedition to Jerusalem.[14] This theme ultimately goes back to an apocalypse of Syrian origin: the so-called pseudo-Methodius, according to which the last emperor, coming from the west, will go on to Jerusalem and deposit his crown at the *Umbilicus Mundi,* at the spot where the holy cross had stood.[15] Once again, we see how this form of eschatology goes back to Syrian sources. Eventually, the idea became one of the leading themes in the Crusades, for the appeal of pope Urban II (1088-1099) at Clermont clearly states: *Jerusalem umbilicus est terrarum ... civitas regalis, in orbis medio posita.*[16]

In autumn 1064, a few decades after Wino's expedition, one of the strangest pilgrimages ever held departed for Jerusalem, led by the archbishop of Mainz, Siegfrid I (1060-1084), with Gunther, bishop of Bamberg (1057-1064), and Wilhelm, bishop of Utrecht (1054-1076), among its participants. They travelled in the form of a regular army, but their number was too small really to challenge the Muslims. They were nevertheless attacked, just as one could have expected,[17] their expedition thus taking on a kind of suicidal overtone, as if they would have wanted to provoke the final combat that was to inaugurate the end of time, as if the idea of the holy

[14] Erdmann, p. 403.

[15] P. J. Alexander, *The Byzantine Apocalyptic Tradition* (Berkeley & Los Angeles, 1985), p. 50; Niehoff, p. 57.

[16] Robert de Reims, *Historia Jherosolymitana*, 1.2 Recueil des historiens des croisades, Occident, 3 vols. (1866), 3:729; E. Lamirande, "Jérusalem céleste", *Dictionnaire de spiritualité* 8 (Paris, 1974), col. 953; Müller, p. 53.

[17] W. Besant and E. H. Palmer, *Jerusalem. The City of Herod and Saladin*, 2nd ed. (London, 1888), pp. 149-151; S. B. J. Zilverberg, "(231.) Guillaume", *Dictionnaire d'histoire et de géographie ecclésiastiques* 22 (Paris, 1988), col. 1037; Lampert von Hersfeld, *Annalen*, Ausgewählte Quellen zur Deutschen Geschichte des Mittelalters, eds. O. Holder-Egger and W. D. Fritz, 13 (Darmstadt, 1973), pp. 94-105.

empire, cosmically blessed by the sign of the cross, was now finally leading to its completion.

As already suggested, the concept of the cross of churches seems to continue an old Syrian religious tradition. As a matter of fact, the description by Adamnan of the entrance of the Tomb of Christ reflects a similar representation on the cover of the famous Vatican Sancta Sanctorum Reliquary dating from the sixth or seventh century.[18] Its central Crucifixion-scene is very similar to its counterpart in the well-known Rabbula-codex, and thus its Syrian, Palestinian provenance is evident. In the upper left corner we recognise the resurrection: the sepulchre is depicted just as in Adamnan's description. Above the tomb appears a dome; even the stone which closed the grave seems to follow his wording.[19] The same stone, broken into two parts, has been countlessly represented on Byzantine *Anastasis*-icons; ultimately the representation goes back to the resurrection as described in the Syrian *Cave of Treasures.*[20] According to its legend, the remains of Adam were

[18] Vatican City, Museo Sacro Inv. Nr. 1883a-b; D. Talbot Rice, *Art of the Byzantine Era* (London, 1963), p. 39 f.; ill. 29; K. Weitzmann, "*Loca Sancta* and the representational arts of Palestine", *Dumbarton Oaks Papers* 28 (1974), 49; A. Legner, *Ornamenta Ecclesiae* 3:80 f. (H 8); Werner, 183 n. 30.

[19] Niehoff, pp. 55, 80 f. Cf. the description of the two gates of the sepulchre in al-Idrīsī, who also attaches great weight to the directions of the monuments in Jerusalem: J. Wilkinson, J. Hill and W. F. Ryan, *Jerusalem Pilgrimage 1099-1185* (London, 1988), p. 224, referring to the translation of G. Le Strange, *Palestine under the Moslems. A Description of Syria and the Holy Land from A.D. 650 to 1500* (London, 1890), p. 206 s.q., who translates the edition of J. Gildemeister, "Beiträge zur Palästinakunde aus arabischen Quellen", *Zeitschrift des Deutschen Palaestina-Vereins* 8 (1885), 117-145.

[20] C. Bezold, *Die Schatzhöhle* (Leipzig, 1883-1888; Amsterdam 1981), p. 69 f. (trans.); A. J. Wensinck, *The Navel of the Earth,* Verhandelingen der Koninklÿke Akademie van Wetenschappen te Amsterdam, Afdeling Letterkunde, Nieuwe Reeks 17.1 (Amsterdam, 1916), p. 17.

buried in the middle of the earth, which had opened itself in the form of a cross into four parts, like a door with four leaves,[21] whereupon this navel of the earth closed itself again, enveloping the body. It was this grave that was to be called Golgotha, for it contained the skull of Adam; there too Jesus would suffer and deliver man by reopening the doors of limbo:[22] the gate to the netherworld which was at Jerusalem's centre, in the middle of the universe.

Almost a century earlier, there had already arrived in the west, in the monastery of Bobbio in the Apennines, possibly as a gift of pope Gregory the Great (590-604) to its benefactor, a series of Syro-Palestinian mud ampullas, or "eulogies", with a picture of the holy sepulchre on them, while others represented Symeon on his pillar, that other transfiguration of the column of the world.[23] From the beginning, Bobbio was closely related to the Irish tradition, for its founder and first abbot originated from Bangor.[24]

All these images must have been developed around the same time, closely related to the reconstruction of Jerusalem by Heraclius (610-641). Indeed, they do not represent as such the historical form it had in new testament times, but rather its ideal, transcendent

[21] Wensinck, p. 17. For Tree of Life symbolism in the western tradition, see Werner, 182; nn. 22, 192.

[22] Bezold, p. 28 (trans.). Accordingly, Adam is depicted as a cosmic man, englobing the four cardinal points that encompass creation (A. C. Esmeijer, *Divina Quaternitas. A Preliminary Study in the Method and Application of Visual Exegesis* (Assen, 1978), pp. 60, 64), an idea that has also many ramifications in the east (see my article on "Symeon", nn. 95-96). According to Glaber, the number 4 indicates the *divina quaternitas* of the earthly and heavenly worlds (Esmeijer, p. 61; Wensinck, 21).

[23] C. Cecchelli, "Note iconografiche su alcune ampolle Bobbiesi", *Rivista di archeologia cristiana* 4 (1927), 115-139; A. Grabar, *Ampoules de Terre Sainte (Monza-Bobbio)* (Paris, 1958); Niehoff, p. 55.

[24] Werner, 194 f., 200 f.

archetype, which the emperor most probably intended to imitate.[25] It is most striking how much the city, as it is depicted by Arculf,[26] resembles the outlines of Hiraqla, a strange monument which stands close to the town of Raqqa on the Euphrates, which Herzfeld, and many after him, has dated under Hārūn al-Rashīd (786-809), but which may follow - according to its name - a much older example.[27] Moreover it was remarked in a recent archaeological survey that the castle, "basé sur le principe de la pièce centrale et des quatre *iwâns* qui lui sont perpendiculaires, rappelle le plan du Palais Doré construit par al-Mansûr .... Elle est la miniature de Bagdad la ronde qui a disparu sous la ville moderne".[28]

These early medieval pictures of Jerusalem were intended to illustrate orthodox (or in the case of Heraclius, monothelete) Christology, combined with the cult of the true cross, which had already originated in the days of Constantine (324-337), resulting in the type of the *Crux Gemmata* as a glorification of the tree of life. As early as the first half of the seventh century, it found its way to Hiberno-Saxon miniatures and monumental crosses, along with its theological background.[29] Indeed, the veneration of the tangible wood of the cross and of the materiality of the place where Christ

[25] ibid., 181, 201.

[26] Vienna MS 458 fol. 4v; Mazal, *Ornamenta Ecclesiae,* 3:78; Werner, 202.

[27] Q. Tweir, "L'Hiraqla de Hârûn al-Rašîd à Raqqa", in *La Syrie de Byzance à L'Islam,* Publications de l'Institut Français de Damas 137, ed. P. Canivet (Damas, 1990), p. 179 f.; fig. 1. According to Yāqūt, *Muʿjam al-Buldān,* ed. F. Wüstenfeld, 4 vols. (Leipzig, 1866-1873), 4:961 f., al-Rashīd captured the city; so it must already have existed: he may have reconstructed it to give it its actual form. See also: A. Frolow, "La Vraie Croix et les expéditions d'Héraclius en Perse", *Revue des Études Byzantines* 11 (1953), 88-105.

[28] Tweir, pp. 184, 185.

[29] Werner, pp. 180 f., 190 f.

suffered and subsequently rose from the dead, was a most efficient weapon of popular propaganda against the Arians, who denied the possibility that a truly divine saviour could have suffered, as one could presently rely on what appeared to be physical evidence.[30] At the same time, the new devotion was liturgically underlined in Jerusalem, just as it was in the commemoration of St. Symeon (d. 592) at Qalʿat Simʿān, in the consecration-service of the Dedication of the Holy Sepulchre and the Finding of the Holy Cross,[31] which quickly found its way to Constantinople and Rome as a part of the Holy Week services. Also shaped after its example was the ceremony of altar consecration, during which the bishop applies chrism to the middle and the four corners of the altar, thus representing the four Evangelists (as in the *Book of Durrow*),[32] the four rivers of Paradise, or even the five wounds of Christ. The latest interpretation is traditionally given to the so-called Jerusalem-

[30] ibid., pp. 184-187.

[31] J. Hani, *Le symbolisme du temple chrétien* (Paris, 1962), p. 115 and my study about "Symeon", n. 109; H. Ashworth, "Urbs beata Ierusalem", *Ephemerides Liturgicae* 70 (1956), 238-241 (stanza 5 of the hymn refers to the theme of the corner-stone); Lamirande, "Jérusalem céleste", col. 953-955; R. J. Zwi Werblowsky, "Jérusalem dans la conscience juive, chrétienne et musulmane", *Jaarbericht Ex Oriente Lux* 23 (1973-1974), p. 432; Werner, 188 f.

[32] The ceremony also has an oriental origin: P. de Puniet, "Dédicace des églises", in *Dictionnaire d'archéologie chrétienne et de liturgie* 4 (Paris, 1920), col. 387 & figs. 3635, 397, referring to the seventh-century *Vita S. Vulframni episcopi Senonici,* eds. B. Krusch and W. Levison, *Passiones Vitaeque Sanctorum Aevi Merovingici*, Monumenta Germaniae Historica, Scriptorum Rerum Merovingicarum 5 (Hannover-Leipzig, 1910), 665; Werner, 175, 177, 208-210; cf. the "hieroglyph" of the Logos Cosmocrator in the intersection point of the cross on the episcopal cathedra of the Cathedral at Torcello: H. P. L'Orange, *Studies on the Iconography of Cosmic Kingship in the Ancient World,* Institutet för Sammenlignende Kulturforskning, Serie A 23 (Oslo, 1953), pp. 196-197.

Cross,[33] which again leads us directly to the time of the Crusades and to the symbolism of Utrecht: the city was dedicated to Christ so as to become an immense consecrated altar, a transposition of Golgotha. Possibly the underlying idea was already introduced at Utrecht in Merovingian times, when St. Willibroard (d. 739) respectively founded and refounded the churches of St. Salvator and of the Holy Cross.[34]

Fundamentally however, the central cross corresponds to the foundation-stone of the Temple of Jerusalem (the *'eben šetayyâ* of the Jewish tradition) and, in its Christian adaptation, to the spot where Christ suffered on earth, the altar of the church, where the divine communicates with the material world underneath,[35] while the four little crosses around it are its virtual, spiritual projections, crystallised in the four corner-stones (*'eben pinnâ*) which link together the walls of the Temple, signifying "que le Christ a racheté les quatre parties du monde",[36] thus illustrating Eph. 2:20: "and ye are built upon the foundation of the apostles and prophets, Jesus Christ himself being the chief corner stone". This quoin is at the same time the keystone which holds together the vault of temple, church and heaven, corresponding perpendicularly to the foundation-stone right under it, as its terrestrial counterpart. The

[33] J. Sauer, "Kreuz. II. Christl. Kreuzesformen", *Lexikon für Theologie und Kirche* 6 (1961), col. 606 f.

[34] M. van Vlierden, *Willibrord en het begin van Nederland,* Clavis Kunsthistorische Monografieën 15 (Utrecht, 1995), pp. 47 f. Merovingian coins found at the Domplein in Utrecht itself (Van Vlierden, p. 77, nr. 43), in Dorestad nearby (ibid., p. 94, nr. 74) and in Remmerden (ibid., p. 68, nr. 28) have the typical design of a cross with a horizontal base or a cross surrounded by four dots, which one also finds in the Anglo-Saxon world; Werner, 179, 181.

[35] The *bīr al-arwāḥ* under the *qubbat al-ṣakhra* in Jerusalem according to Islamic legend: Hani, p. 116; Adolf, p. 110; Jeremias, pp. 91, 94-98, 105; and my article "Symeon", n. 110.

[36] Hani, pp. 118-119.

celestial dome is once more repeated in the ciborium or baldachin which, supported by its four columns, covers the altar in eastern churches.[37]

Thus western iconography developed a typical plan of Jerusalem as a circular town, divided into four parts with a cross of two streets going through it and with four gates on its periphery,[38] giving it an ideal form, according to what was considered to be the image of heavenly and eternal Jerusalem. It resembles the pictures of eternal Jerusalem in Carolingian manuscript commentaries on the Apocalypse of St. John.[39] There the city is built in twelve concentric circles of different colours for the twelve tribes of Israel; to the north, south, west and east, there are each time three gates, their total number being twelve again.[40]

The historical city of Jerusalem, even in its Heraclean form, could only partially conform to this abstract plan, just as the mount of Golgotha was necessarily idealised in the *Cave of Treasures*. In the west, from where deliverance was to be expected according to

[37] ibid., p. 120.

[38] Niehoff, pp. 55 f., 74-79; W. Müller, *Die heilige Stadt. Roma Quadrata, himmlisches Jerusalem und die Mythe vom Weltnabel* (Stuttgart, 1961), pp. 53-114; Esmeijer, p. 74.

[39] M.-Th. Gousset, "La représentation de la Jérusalem céleste à l'époque carolingienne", *Cahiers archéologiques* 23 (1974), 48-50; Van Vlierden, pp. 53 f.; cf. the *Beatus-Apocalypse,* Esmeijer, p. 59; figs. 49, 61.

[40] Valenciennes, Bibl. Meur., MS lat. nouv. acq. 1132, fol. 33r; Gousset, pp. 49 f.; Esmeijer, pp. 73; 156, n. 2 & fig. 59. Gousset notes that these illustrations may follow an insular style, perhaps having as common source the manuscript(s) that Biscop, founder of the Abbey of Wearmouth, brought from Rome, and that inspired the frescoes he had made for its church: as such they might have an oriental origin too. The doctrinal influences have given rise to a huge historical debate: L. Bieler, "The Island of Scholars", *Revue du moyen âge latin* 8 (1952), 213-234; R. E. McNally, "The 'Tres linguae sacrae' in early Irish bible exegesis", *Theological Studies* 19 (1958), 395-403.

the contemporary Apocalypses, the German emperors could found such planned cities in order to conform them to an eschatological perspective. In their view, the powers of evil were to be located in the opposite direction, in the east, on the other side of Jerusalem, focused in its biblical, apocalyptic prototype: Babylon. Indeed, Adso, in his *De Ortu et Tempore Antichristi,* knows that the Antichrist will be born in Babylon, the *radix omnium malorum.*[41] Using the same wording as the Carolingian commentator Haymo of Auxerre (d. c. 855) of the ninth century, he depicts the Antichrist as a native of Babylon who will assemble the Jews in the holy city.[42] In his Commentary on the Apocalypse, Haymo develops the theme of the two cities: the city of the blessed, Jerusalem, and the city of evil, Babylon, a motif which ultimately goes back to St. Augustine (d. 430)[43] and his immediate predecessor Tyconius (d. before 400), of whose Commentary on the Apocalypse only fragments have survived,[44] but who must have influenced many of his successors, among them Caesarius of Arles (d. 542)[45] and Haymo. As for St. Augustine, he was clearly following oriental sources, among them Origenes (d. c. 254) who had already exerted an enormous influence

[41] E. Sackur, *Sibyllinische Texte und Forschungen. Pseudomethodius, Adso und die tiburtinische Sibylle* (Halle, 1898), pp. 107, 111; Adso Dervensis, *De Ortu et Tempore Antichristi*, ed. D. Verhelst, Corpus Christianorum. Continuatio Mediaevalis 45 (Turnhout, 1976), pp. 24, 27 (cf. Sackur, p. 102).

[42] Dervensis, p. 27, referring to Haymo, *In epist. II ad Thess.,* PL 117, col. 780B.

[43] Haymo, *Expositio in Apocalypsim,* ed. G. Hittorpius, (Cologne, 1531), PL 117, 4:1108, 5:1137, 6:1139, 1152 f.; J. van Oort, *Jeruzalem en Babylon. Een onderzoek van Augustinus' de Stad van God en de bronnen van zijn leer der twee steden (rijken)*, 3rd ed. ('s Gravenhage, 1987), pp. 99 f.

[44] Van Oort, pp. 214 f.; J. Ratzinger, "Ticonius", *Lexikon für Theologie und Kirche* 10 (1965), col. 180.

[45] Van Oort, p. 222.

on Syrian writers[46] and, of course, the Manichaean tradition to which St. Augustine had adhered in his early years, as is obvious from the dualistic interpretation of history culminating in the theory of the two empires.[47] The oriental and Syrian ramifications are once more undeniable.

It is important to remark that the theory of two opposite empires is balanced in Augustine and others by the introduction of a *tertium quid.* The principles of good and evil are placed on an eschatological level; in this world they are practically always mingled together: in the city of our *saeculum,*[48] in view of its ultimate realisation in eternal, divine Jerusalem. The concept of the pilgrimage, of the *miʿrāj* of Islam, is connected to this: there is a temporal empire somewhere (for the Latin church it is the Christian state in the west) that prefigures the ideal city of Jerusalem, to which one has to make pilgrimage spiritually until the completion of this *aeon.* There are therefore always two good cities: the ideal one, Jerusalem, and its earthly prefiguration.

Eastern apocalyptic literature shows how the Arabic Islamic tradition could develop a similar division: at one time Babylon is identified with Jerusalem, at another with historical Babylon in Mesopotamia as the town where the adherents of the false Messiah shall assemble from the seventy-two tribes, then again it is identified with Makka.[49] Babylon is further explained as *al-Madīna,* the city of

[46] ibid., pp. 70, n. 364; 101, 236-238 and my article "Symeon", n. 73.

[47] Van Oort, pp. 180-188.

[48] ibid., pp. 127-129; cf. Zwi Werblowsky, pp. 429-431.

[49] For this transfer of ideas from Jerusalem to Makka as centre of the world, see Wensinck, pp. 21, 25; for the tribes distributed to the different sectors of the town: L. Massignon, "Explication du plan de Kufa (Irak)", in *Mélanges Maspéro* III, Mémoires de l'Institut Français d'Archéologie Orientale du Caire (Le Caire, 1935), 337-360 = Y. Moubarac, ed., *Opera Minora* 3 (Beirut, 1963), p. 35.

Islam, the one that was founded as the capital of the ᶜAbbāsids: Baghdād.[50]

It is remarkable indeed that there is only one city where the concept of the ideal town as described in oriental apocalyptic texts, and especially in the *Cave of Treasures,* has been fully realised: not in Jerusalem itself, not in the west, but in the ᶜAbbāsid capital, Baghdād, which continued, as a kind of refoundation, the millennial capital city of Babylon and Ctesiphon nearby.
According to ancient descriptions, the ᶜAbbāsid round city was conceived of two surrounding walls, each preceded by two glacis (*fuṣlān*), the inner wall being higher than the outer.[51] In each of these walls four gates were made, that is to say eight in total, corresponding to the street-cross that divided the city in four equal sections, pointing to the north-east (the Gate of Khurāsān), the north-west (Shām-Gate), the south-west (Kūfa-Gate) and the south-east (Baṣra-Gate).[52] Whereas lodging, administrative and service

[50] R. W. Cowley, *The Traditional Interpretation of the Apocalypse of St. John in the Ethiopian Orthodox Church* (Cambridge, 1983), pp. 127-138. Similarly, the traditional presentation of the plan of the mosque of the Kaᶜba resembles the figure of the court of the tabernacle in MSS of Cosmas Indicopleustes (MS Vat. gr. 699, fol. 49r) and Cassiodorus (MS Flor., Laur. Am. I, fols. 2v, 3r), which seem to follow an older Alexandrian type, connected to the exegesis of Philo: Esmeijer, p. 73 & figs. 62, 63.

[51] Ṭabarī, *Ta'rīkh al-Umam wa l-Mulūk* 3/1:321, year 146; H. Kennedy, trans. & annot., *The History of al-Ṭabarī: Al-Manṣūr and al-Mahdī* 29(New York, 1990), p. 6; al-Khaṭīb al-Baghdādī, *Ta'rīkh Baghdād* (Cairo, 1931), 1:73; J. Lassner, *The Topography of Baghdad in the Early Middle Ages* (Detroit, 1970), p. 52; D. Sourdel, "Bagdâd, capitale du nouvel empire 'abbâside", *Arabica* 9 (1962), 254; J. Lassner, *The Shaping of ᶜAbbāsid Rule,* Princeton Studies on the Near East (Princeton, 1980), pp. 185, 188.

[52] Ṭabarī, 3/1:321, year 146, Kennedy, p. 5; Sourdel, p. 254; L'Orange, p. 12; Ch. Wendell, "Baghdād: *Imago Mundi,* and other Foundation Lore", *International Journal of Middle East Studies* 2 (1971), 116.

quarters were located along the surrounding walls, the large esplanade inside was reserved for the caliph's residence: the Gold Palace (*Qaṣr al-dhahab*) with a green dome and, next to it, the mosque, *Jāmiᶜ al-Manṣūr.*[53]

Different origins have been suggested for this concept, even when Arab sources stress that there were no antecedents.[54] Creswell has already pointed to ancient Egyptian and Assyrian traditions; L'Orange developed a similar thesis.[55] Wendell endeavoured to demonstrate that the sources were to be looked for still further to the east, in Zoroastrianism and Buddhism: the plan would be an adaptation of a fire temple or a Buddhist *stûpa*[56] and would have been proposed to the caliph by his advisor Khālid b. Barmak (d. 165-166/781-782), who indeed was a member of an old family of priests of the temple of Nawbahār.[57] But the evidence for his role is rather meagre and thus the theory has been refuted by Lassner, who proposes a more practical explanation.[58] There is still another possible advisor: the court astrologist Nawbakht, who according to Yaᶜqūbī (d. 278-279/891-892) was assisted by a Jew, Māshā'llāh b. Sāriyya, and who was a leading twelver shīᶜite, a member of the

[53] K. A. C. Creswell, *Early Muslim Architecture* (Oxford, 1940), 2:9; Lassner, *Shaping*, p. 189; A. A. Duri, "Baghdād", *Encyclopaedia of Islam*, 2nd ed. (1960), 1:922.

[54] Al-Yaᶜqūbī, *Kitāb al-Buldān*, Bibliotheca Geographorum Arabicorum 7, ed. M. J. De Goeje (Leiden, 1892), p. 238; Khatīb, *Bagdād,* 1:67; Lassner, *Topography*, pp. 46; 232, n. 6.

[55] Creswell, pp. 18-21; L'Orange, pp. 12 f.; Lassner, *Shaping*, pp. 169 f.

[56] Wendell, p. 124; cf. Lassner, *Shaping*, pp. 172 f.

[57] Wendell, pp. 123-125; W. Barthold and D. Sourdel, "al-Barāmika", *Encyclo-paedia of Islam*, 2nd ed. (1960), 1:1064 f.

[58] Lassner, *Shaping*, pp. 176-179.

famous Banū Nawbakht. Massignon has emphasised the importance of his astrological predictions.[59]

One of the most characteristic details linking Baghdād to the foregoing period is reported by Ṭabarī: caliph al-Manṣūr (136-158/754-775) took the iron gates from the city of Wāsiṭ and transported them to Baghdād; again he used a gate from Pharaonic times and still another from the Umayyad period,[60] thus following the example of the founder of Wāsiṭ, al-Ḥajjāj b. Yūsuf (d. 95/714), who had the same doors, allegedly made by the demons, removed from al-Zandaward, a town that would have been built by Sulaymān b. Dāwūd (the biblical Solomon).[61] This removal of doors as a symbolic expression of conquest - just as al-Nāṣir Muḥammad (693-694/1293-1294, 699-700/1299- 1309, 710-742/1310-1341) would do again with the portal of the Cathedral of Acre for his mosque in Cairo[62] - establishes a connection further stressed by the close parallelism between the Green Domes of Wāsiṭ and Baghdād: even the dimensions are identical.[63]

[59] Yaʿqūbī, p. 238; Khaṭīb, 1:67; Masʿūdī, *Murūj al-Dhahab,* ed. C. Barbier de Meynard, *Maçoudi, les Prairies d'Or*, 9 vols. (Paris, 1874), 8:290; Lassner, *Topography*, pp. 46; 232, n. 7 (cf. G. Monnot, *Penseurs musulmans et religions iraniennes. 'Abd al-Jabbâr et ses devanciers,* Etudes musulmanes 16 (Paris-Beyrouth, 1974), pp. 53-55; L. Massignon, "Le mirage byzantin dans le miroir bagdadien d'il y a mille ans", in *Mélanges H. Grégoire,* III, *Annuaire de l'Institut de Philologie et d'Histoire Orientale et Slave* 10 (1950), 429-448 = *Opera Minora* 1:435 f.

[60] Tabarī, 3/1:321, year 146, Kennedy, p. 5; Lassner, *Shaping*, pp. 180; 288, n. 52.

[61] ibid., p. 287, n. 51.

[62] Wendell, p. 114; n. 4; Lassner, *Shaping*, p. 181; R. B. Parker, R. Sabin and C. Williams, *Islamic Monuments in Cairo*, 2nd ed. (Cairo, 1985), p. 202.

[63] Wendell, pp. 117-119; Lassner, *Shaping*, pp. 181 f.; 288, n. 54, referring to O. Grabar, "Al-Mushatta, Baghdad and Wāsiṭ", in *The World of*

The dome certainly had a symbolic function: in one of the few explanations given by our Arabic sources, al-Khaṭīb tells us that the city had to be round, in order that the monarch could be in the middle of it, for in a square, some districts would be closer to him than others.[64]

The ideal Islamic city has a concentric and hierarchical structure. In the case of Baṣra, for instance, this planning was linked to the tribal origin of the inhabitants, just as in the afore-mentioned Christian apocalyptic tradition the ideal city of Jerusalem was conceived in twelve concentric circles for the twelve tribes of Israel. In the centre of the town (as was the case in Baghdād), there was the mosque with the official buildings, then there were the commercial and artisanal quarters, and around them the residential townships; the following circle was semi-rural, which was finally surrounded by the necropolis.[65] Thus the city was given the aspect of Paradise, which the caliph al-Manṣūr emphasised by giving it the name Madīnat al-Salām,[66] a title that refers to a Qur'ānic name for Paradise, as in Sūra 6:127 and 10:26: "and God called to the *dwelling of peace* and guided whom He will into a right way".

The already-mentioned Green Domes all appear to follow the example of *al-Qubbat al-Khaḍrā'* of Muᶜāwiya (41-661) in Damascus; it was also imitated by the dome of the palace of Hishām

Islam: Studies in Honor of P. K. Hitti, ed. J. Kritzek & R. B. Winder (New York, 1959), pp. 99-108.

64 Ṭabarı, 3/1:321, Kennedy, p. 6; Lassner, *Topography*, pp. 52; 238, n. 19, who notes that according to Creswell, p. 21, its form had only an economic purpose.

65 X. De Planhol, *Fondements géographiques de l'histoire de l'Islam* (Paris, 1968), pp. 49 f.; idem., *Le monde islamique: essai de géographie religieuse* (Paris, 1957), pp. 13, 26.

66 Duri, 1:921.

b. ᶜAbd al-Malik (106-126/724-743) in Ruṣāfat al-Shām.[67] It is clear from our sources that the *qubba* in Baghdād was considered a symbol of sovereignty, which had been transferred from the Umayyads to the ᶜAbbāsids.[68] According to Islamic tradition the *qubba* represented the hemisphere (just as the ciborium in Christian eastern churches), the shape of the earth,[69] which in its turn was covered by a still larger dome, the sphere of the lowest heaven, as is well illustrated by the cupola of the Umayyad Quṣayr ᶜAmra, whereupon the zodiac has been depicted as a helical system evolving around its navel, the centre of the earth, where the caliph stands.[70] The walls encircling the round town of Baghdād are like Mount Qāf which according to Islamic cosmology encompasses the world, whereas the central axis is "surrounded by alternating rings of mountains and oceans ... like a gigantic circular platter with a rim".[71]

Not only is there the orientation - *qibla* - which links the "symbolic world center of Baghdād with the actual world center of Mecca",[72] but also the sequence of the Qaṣr with the Jāmiᶜ al-Manṣūr behind it[73] (still underlined by the form of the *majālis* adjoining the four gates as a kind of reduction of the central hall, expressing the caliph's authority over the four quarters of the world)[74] follows the pattern of the church of the Holy Sepulchre, which also precedes a grave, like the palace standing close to the

[67] Wendell, p. 117; Lassner, *Shaping*, p. 182.

[68] Lassner, *Shaping*, pp. 182 f.; Wensinck, p. 65.

[69] Wensinck, pp. 38, 50, referring to Masᶜūdī, 1:269.

[70] Wensinck, p. 45; Wendell, p. 118; L'Orange, p. 13.

[71] Wendell, pp. 121, 126; Wensinck, p. 45.

[72] Wendell, p. 122, cf. Lassner, *Shaping*, p. 174, and the concept of the *masjid al-ḥarām* as opposed to the *masjid al-aqṣā* in the Qur'ān, Sūra, 17:1.

[73] Creswell, pp. 9, 22; Lassner, *Shaping*, p. 167.

[74] Lassner, *Shaping*, p. 194.

mosque in Baghdād. Similarly Theodore of Mopsuestia wrote that the Tabernacle is an image of the world, while the apsis symbolises heaven. The tombs of Adam and of Christ are the divine throne, which is represented in this world by the seat of the caliph.[75] It is the place for the *minbar,* the pole of the universe,[76] the most elevated spot on earth[77] which, just as the episcopal cathedral at Utrecht, links our world to heaven.

[75] Wensinck, pp. 52, 54 f.
[76] ibid., pp. 55, 57.
[77] ibid., p. 47.

The Basic Postulates of Ṣūfism in the Poetry of Yūnus Emre

Xénia Celnarová
Slovak Academy of Sciences, Bratislava

On the territory of Asia Minor, the first literary works in the Turkish language were born in the seventh/thirteenth century. They originated thanks to Ṣūfism, and so indirectly also ancient Greek thought, which was one of the two basic sources of Islamic mysticism.

The theosophy of the medieval Muslim world developed in parallel with Arab philosophy, and like it arose from two sources. The first of these was the Islamic religious tradition, connected with the tradition of Judaism and Christianity. For Ṣūfis, the Qur'ān and *sunna* represented the basic steps on the path *(ṭarīq)* to knowledge of God. However, behind the exoteric *(ẓāhir)* content of the verses of the Qur'ān, they sought their esoteric, internal *(bāṭin)* meaning.

The second source for speculative Islamic mysticism was connected with the orientation of the leading thinkers of medieval Islam to the Greek west.[1] This derived both from the occupation of

[1] G. E. Grünebaum, *Classical Islam: A History 600-1258* (London, 1970), cited in the Russian translation: *Klassicheskiy islam* (Moscow, 1986), pp. 91-92.

the centres of Hellenic culture in Syria, Mesopotamia and Iran, and from the accessibility of the works of the Greek philosophers through translations into Arabic.[2]

Although contact with the cultures of Iran and the Indian subcontinent, where mysticism had an old and rich tradition, also made an immense contribution to Ṣūfism, its theosophy most significantly showed the influence of neoplatonism. Finally the idea of the neoplatonists about knowledge of the divine factor, about penetration into the essence of being by means of love, undoubtedly contributed to the emergence of Ṣūfism from simple asceticism in the true mystic's aim of spiritual communion with God. This also occurred within the Christian church with the contribution of the same factor. Beginning in the third/ninth century, Ṣūfism was formulated into an independent religious-philosophical teaching, although it never acquired the form of a firmly defined system.[3]

As far as it concerns pragmatic mysticism, it gathered a whole complex of religious ideas, rituals and practices of the ethnic groups with which Islam was progressively coming into contact, into specific methods of advance on the mystical path. This syncretic character of the religious practice of the Ṣūfis, together with their ecstatic, exalted approach to faith in one God, so very different from the rigorous doctrines of the theologians, gained the settled population and nomadic tribes for Islam.

In Asia Minor in particular, the Ṣūfis were extraordinarily successful in spreading Islam and its culture. When the victory of

[2] Concerning translations of Greek philosophers into Arabic see: J. L. Kraemer, *Humanism in the Renaissance: The Cultural Revival during the Buyid Age,* Studies in Islamic Culture and History Series 7 (Leiden, 1986).

[3] O. F. Akimushkin, "Sufiyskiye bratstva. Sloshniy uzel problem" (Ṣūfi brotherhoods. A complicated knot of problems) in J. S. Trimingham, *Sufiyskiye ordeny v islame* (The Ṣūfi Orders in Islam) (Moscow, 1989), p. 4.

the Saljūqs at Manzikert in 464/1071 opened the road into the peninsula to the Oghuz tribes from the area between the Caspian and Aral Seas, many Ṣūfis came with them. The nomads treated them with reverence, comparable to that enjoyed by the shamans.

These smaller or larger groups of dervishes belonged to pragmatic Ṣūfism. They devoted themselves more to winning new territory and more believers for Islam than to meditation. They participated in military actions,[4] and developed extensive missionary and charitable activities. They received support from the Saljūq rulers and feudal lords, who were aware of their great influence on the masses.

However the golden age of Ṣūfism in Asia Minor began in the seventh/thirteenth century. It was a paradox that the unprecedented flourishing of Islamic culture in this region was caused by the same factor which struck an almost fatal blow at this culture in the Islamic east.

This factor was the Mongol invasion, which not only caused a strong movement of Turkic tribes towards the west, but also a mass migration of the settled population from the areas devastated by the Mongols. This migration also significantly strengthened the ranks of the Ṣūfis in Asia Minor, this time not only with dervishes carrying out missionary activity among the nomads, but also with theosophers from the traditional centres of culture and education of eastern Islam.

The dervishes who came to Asia Minor from Turkestan and Khurāsān were bearers of a tradition connected with the name of Aḥmad Yasawī (d. 562/1166). Authorship of religious poems consisting of several four-line strophes in syllabic metre is attributed

[4] These dervish-fighters, *alperenler*, fought with wooden swords. Fuad Köprülü, *Türk Edebiyatında İlk Mutasavvıflar* (The First Mystics in Turkish Literature) (Ankara, 1984), pp. 253-254.

to this founder of the Yasawiyya Ṣūfi brotherhood. The *Dīwān-i Ḥikmet*, as Yasawī's pupils named these poems, interpreted the basic postulates of Islam in eastern Turkic dialect. Aḥmad Yasawī's successors interpreted the poems accompanied by a stringed instrument. Thanks to this kind of interpretation, taken over from folk poetry, they fulfilled their mission among the nomads in eastern Turkestan, Transoxania and Khurāsān with great success.[5] This genre also met with a positive response in Asia Minor, where a special form called *ilāhī*, very similar to early Christian hymns,[6] developed from it.

Many representatives of the Persian branch of Ṣūfism, at this time representing its core, also found shelter in Asia Minor. Its territory remained free of the Mongol yoke until 641/1243. In particular Konya, the capital of the Saljūqs under the rule of ʿAlā' al-Dīn Qayqubād (616-634/1219-1236) experienced an unprecedented flowering. Some important personalities of Islamic culture found there an asylum for a longer or shorter period.

Mawlānā Jalāl al-Dīn Rūmī (d. 672/1273) found his new home and place of final rest in Konya. In the work of this genial Persian mystic, Ṣūfi theosophy and literature reached its zenith. The personality and work of Rūmī had far-reaching importance, not only for strengthening the position of mysticism in Asia Minor, but also for the development of Turkish literature in this territory.

[5] Fuad Köprülü holds that this specific kind of Turkic religious lyrics was already born in the fifth/eleventh century, and was associated with the tradition of wandering minstrels. Dervishes in Turkestan started to fill the poetical form of the tribal poets with a religious content. They also took over the style of interpretation with accompaniment of stringed instruments from wandering minstrels. Köprülü, p. 18.

[6] See J. R. Walsh, "Yunus Emre: a 14th century Turkish himnodist", in *Yunus Emre and his Mystical Poetry*, Indiana University Turkish Studies 2, ed. T. S. Halman (Bloomington, 1981), pp. 111-126.

Muḥīy' l-Dīn b. al-ᶜArabī (d. 638/1240), known as Ibn al-ᶜArabī, also lived and worked in Konya for some time. This Arab theosopher and poet, born in Murcia in Spain, re-evaluated the development of speculative Ṣūfism over almost five centuries, and summarised it into a compact whole on a high intellectual and aesthetic level. The doctrine of monism, *waḥdat al-wujūd* (the unity of being), formulated by Ibn al-ᶜArabī, gained a significant response in Asia Minor, thanks to his pupil Ṣadr al-Dīn al-Qūnawī (d. 672/1273). This conception found its poetic expression in the work of Rūmī[7] and in the poetry of many generations of mystics from Asia Minor. It is also one of the central themes of the poetry of Yūnus Emre, which arose in connection with the creative work of Rūmī, and at the same time in the tradition of the poetry of Aḥmad Yasawī.[8] The mystic poet, Yūnus Emre (d. 721/1321) left a permanent mark on the thoughts and feelings of the people of Asia Minor. His poetry lived in the memory of the people, and was spread by oral tradition from generation to generation. The oldest manuscript collection (*Dīwān*) of the poetic message of Yūnus, consisting of about 300 poems, dates from the eleventh/seventeenth century.[9]

The figure of this unique medieval poet remains a veiled mystery. The poems of Yūnus contain no mention of his belonging to any specific brotherhood. However the motif of continual travelling frequently occurs in them. If we were to interpret this motif literally, we could judge that it concerned a wandering

[7] Rūmī contacted Ibn al-ᶜArabī personally during his stay of a few years in Damascus. E. de Vitray-Meyerovitch, *Rúmí a súfismus. Úvod do islámské mystiky* (Rūmī and Ṣūfism. Introduction to Islamic Mysticism) (Bratislava, 1993), pp. 13-14.

[8] Köprülü, p. 255.

[9] ibid., pp. 287-291.

dervish, such as the Qalandar dervishes, who came to Asia Minor from Persia in the seventh/thirteenth century. However it is necessary to understand the motif of wandering more as a symbol of the advance of the mystic on the long and difficult journey to *tawḥīd* (oneness) with *ḥaqīqa* (divine reality). The adjectives *ummī* (untaught, illiterate) and *miskīn* (poor) cannot be taken literally either. They are traditional symbolic epithets which are applied to the personality of the prophet himself.

Actual lack of education, on which many great Ṣūfis placed emphasis, has a parallel in the *docta ignorantia* of Christian mystics. Empirical knowledge, *ᶜilm,* acquired by way of rational learning, is different from an unlimited knowledge, *maᶜrifa,* which is intuitive and goes beyond the intellectual. This true knowledge begins with knowledge of oneself.

According to St. Augustine (d. 430) a man should not look outwards, but into himself, for the truth dwells within. Like Christianity, Islam was committed to Greek thinking, with the idea of deeper knowledge of oneself as a starting point for the journey to virtue and understanding of the essence of being.[10] The great Ṣūfis understood self knowledge as introspection aimed at researching their consciousness, and through mystical intuition also subconsciousness. If a person was to release himself from his physical, personal "I", and discern in himself the true being connected with God, through the self-reflection of God in man, he first had to free himself from the ballast of empirical knowledge. This idea is also aptly expressed in the verses of Yūnus Emre:

> Knowledge should mean a full grasp of know-
> ledge:

[10] Grünebaum, p. 124.

Knowledge means to know yourself, heart and soul.
If you have failed to understand yourself,
Then all of your reading has missed its call.

Don't boast of reading, mastering science
Or of all your prayers and obeisance.
If you don't identify Man as God,
All your learning is of no use at all.[11]

In this context, the Qur'ān and *sharī'a* form a special chapter. They cannot be a means of knowledge, since a person who relies on dogmas remains on their surface. He does not attempt to penetrate to their essence, to grasp it:

God's truth is an ocean and the dogma is a ship.
Most people don't leave the ship to plunge into the sea.[12]

Those who set out on the journey of knowledge understand the hidden meaning of the Qur'ān only when they dive like a duck to the bottom of the ocean and bring the jewel (*gevher*) to the surface. The "jewel" is understood as meaning the essence, and he who finds it must also be able to determine its value. The first "jeweller" in this sense of the word was the prophet, who perceived the reflection of the absolute truth (*ḥaqq*) in himself:

[11] For Yūnus Emre's quoted verses translated from Turkish to English, see "Selected poems translated by Talât Sait Halman", in *Yunus Emre and His Mystical Poetry,* ed. T. S. Halman (Bloomington, 1981), p. 144.

[12] ibid., p. 181.

We have turned into the Wise Men [13]
To find pearls in the depths again;
Only the jeweller would know
How valuable those pearls might be.

Muhammad came to perceive God,
And saw God's truth in his selfhood.
Providence exists everywhere
So long as there are eyes to see.[14]

Another important doctrine of Ṣūfism also penetrated into these verses. According to it, God created Muḥammad as the archetype of all human beings. The prophet possesses all the attributes of God, which existed in the preceding ages, just like the Qur'ān.

The question of the relationship between the divine creative spirit and the multiplicity of creation, between ideal things and their material form, excited the Muslim theosophers just as it did the philosophers. In the fourth/tenth century, the members of a secret philosophical association from Baṣra, called Ikhwān al-Ṣafā', had already attempted to answer this question. They set the aim of "removing the errors which penetrated into Islam by means of philosophy".[15] However their own teaching derived from the

[13] In the original the first two verses of the quoted strophe are: "Gine biz bahri olduk / derinden gevher alduk", where *bahri* is from Arabic *baḥrī* and means "a species of sea-duck". See Sözlük [Vocabulary] in the following editions of *The Dīwān* of Yūnus Emre: *Yunus Emre Divanı* (Dīwān of Yūnus Emre), ed. K. Timurtaş (Ankara, 1986), p. 271; A. A. Bolel, *Yunus Emre Hazretleri. Hayatı ve Divanı* (His Holiness Yūnus Emre. His Life and Dīwān) (Eskişehir, 1983), p. 486.

[14] Halman, p. 151.

[15] Y. E. Bertels, "Proiskhozhdeniye sufizma i zarozhdeniye sufiyskoy literatury" (The origin of Ṣūfism and beginning of Ṣūfi literature), in Y. E.

philosophy of Empedocles (fl. 450 BC), Plato (d. 347 BC), Aristotle (d. 322 BC), Plotinus (d. 270 AD) and the neoplatonists. This especially applied to their solutions to metaphysical problems. Space arose by emanation from primeval essence, its evolution going round in circles. Emanation of the primeval essence has a declining tendency, going through the human, animal, vegetable and mineral, then returning by re-emanation back to the primeval essence.

In Asia Minor, this conception of the essential unity of the creative and created principle, rooted in Hellenic culture, fell on soil saturated with the spirit of this culture. Rūmī developed it in innumerable images in the spirit of Persian poetry. On a more modest level, Yūnus Emre inserted the basic principles of this conception into images and notions closely understood by the Turks. Whole generations of Turkish poets took over the message of these two great mystics.

The introductory verses of Rūmī's *Mathnawī* express in a unique way the longing of all living and inorganic elements in the universe to return to the primeval essence of being. Yūnus Emre also speaks in his verses about the return to God as the return to the true homeland. In the eternal cycle of emanations of the absolute, the poet had already been the star in the sky, the snake, Abraham and the burning rose bush. He passed through hundreds of thousands of forms before he became the mystic Yūnus, who found God in himself, and identified himself with God.

The verses by Yūnus in which he speaks of his own deification can be interpreted as meaning that at the time of their origin, the poet had already reached the aim of the mystical path, that in a state

Bertels, *Izbrannyye trudy. Sufizm i sufiyskaya literatura* (Selected Works. Ṣūfism and Ṣūfi Literature), ed. M. N. O. Osmanov (Moscow, 1965), p. 26.

of enlightenment he was aware of his substantial unity (*tawḥīd*) with the supreme being (*ḥaqīqa*).

The unity of everything which exists in this world also flows from the unity of God and the world. Man as the mediating link between the creator and the created world also has to be aware of this unity in relation to religion. Plotinus had already expressed the idea that different people may have different routes to God. Meister Eckhart (d. 1327), who declared that there is no difference between Christians and pagans, since all achieve knowledge of God, also emphasised this idea, essentially connected with neoplatonism.

Beginning with al-Ḥallāj (d. 310/922), through al-Fārābī (d. 339/950) and others up to Rūmī, we find the idea that different religions are manifestations of the absolute truth (*ḥaqq*). Yūnus Emre also repeatedly expressed this idea, connecting it with an appeal to true love:

> We regard no one's religion as contrary to ours,
> True love is born when all faiths are united as a whole.[16]

As in other mystical systems, love is also the central notion in Ṣūfism. It represents a mobilising principle, a cosmic force controlling all forms of movement. At the same time, it is a purifying force, which enables a person to release himself from his earthly existence and raise himself to God.

True love is metaphysical love. However Ṣūfism also accepts love for the beings and beauties of the real world, since the beauty of God is reflected in them as in a mirror. Earthly love has its place in the ethics of Ṣūfism. For a person to reach divine love and beauty, he must learn to love himself and his neighbours. It is also important for a man to behave in a way that will make his neighbours love

[16] Halman, p. 14.

him. Yūnus also speaks of love in these ways. He speaks of having a mission as a proclaimer of love:

I am not here on earth for strife,
Love is the mission of my life.
Hearts are the home of the loved one.
I came here to build each true heart.[17]

Mystical moral enthusiasm and a fervent relationship with God are fully reflected in the poems of Yūnus Emre. Yūnus Emre and his followers were able to address a wide range of the population of Asia Minor with their poems. In this way, the wealth of thought, created through the centuries by the greatest thinkers of the Hellenic and Islamic worlds, penetrated into the minds of the people. This wealth of thought participated in forming the world-view and moral ideals of the Turks of Asia Minor.

[17] ibid., p. 176.

IV WORK AND WARFARE IN THE MEDITERRANEAN: ACROSS THE FRONTIERS

The Genoese Art of Warfare

Gabriella Airaldi
Università di Genova

This paper forms the point of departure for a series of studies into the theme of war in the history of Genoa and attempts to illustrate the fundamental part warfare itself appears to play in the life of the individual.

At the end of the twelfth century, Caffaro, the first and most famous chronicler of medieval Genoa, took part in the first crusade. This and later experiences in the Mediterranean area led him to write two separate works both on his experience in the eastern Mediterranean crusade and on the war waged by the Genoese against Almeria and Tortosa (which were still under Muslim rule) in the western Mediterranean about forty years later.[1]

In the first case, which involved one of the most famous international acts of war of the time, he subtly linked the creation of the municipality of Genoa with the most important war of the era,

[1] L. T. Belgrano and C. Imperiale di Sant'Angelo, eds., *Annali genovesi di Caffaro e dei suoi continuatori* (Rome, 1890-1929); particularly the *Annali* of Caffaro, and *Lyberatio Orientis* and *Ystoria captionis Almerie et Tortuose* by the same author.

thus underlining the consolidation of the city's political and institutional revolution by means of that particular act of war. And since his was an official chronicle, this choice must be considered significant.

Caffaro also describes an act of war in the other interesting work, "Ystoria captionis Almerie et Tortuose". In both cases, he testifies to the dual direction of Genoese economic expansion towards east and west - a trend which was already noticeable at the very beginning of Genoa's history and which would continue and intensify over the coming centuries.

It is clear that the Genoese intended to follow a global policy of opening up commercial markets and that they were ready to fight to defend this purpose not only throughout the Mediterranean but also in nearby areas, which is to say in the regional territory as well as on the islands of Corsica and Sardinia - as is witnessed by contemporary events and as Caffaro himself reports.

From the very beginning of the city's early medieval history, war was evidently a recurring theme in the life of the Genoese and certainly to a much greater extent than in the case of the other maritime powers of the time - Pisa, Venice and the crown of Aragon. Although these powers engaged in sporadic warfare at sea, the Genoese were forced to fight all three rivals over the entire Mediterranean area and would regularly do so throughout the middle ages.

Yet war also played a central role in Genoese life for other reasons. In addition to facing its enemies at sea, there were the difficulties involved in establishing dominion over the regional territory and the nearby islands of Corsica and Sardinia. This situation was also aggravated by the violent internal strife which is unique in Italian civic history.

However, it is interesting to note that Genoese military strength seems to have weakened in the face of the Saracens. After the early phase of war, the Genoese clearly opted for a policy of negotiation. In this case, and whenever it was subsequently possible (during the struggle with the Turks, for example), the Genoese adopted an extremely flexible position in order to benefit their trading policy. In fact, their supply of ships for the crusaders' expedition was merely formal or an outright act of self-interest.[2]

When relating the conquest of Jerusalem, Caffaro describes the way in which Guglielmo Embriaco ("Caput mallei") used the wood of the ships in which the Genoese had come to the aid of Geoffrey de Bouillon to build "ballistas" (an ancient form of catapult) for the siege, which contributed to victory. The technological skill of the Genoese in such matters was of contemporary renown, for the Milanese also used the same machinery for the siege of Como in 1116.

Caffaro gave a detailed description of the military operations carried out in Liguria by the Genoese to bring the local feudal landowners to obedience. He also described Genoese resistance to Frederick I. The city ambassadors, he reported, told the emperor that they would not pay the taxes that had fallen due because

> for a long time they had been defending the coast from the pagan invaders who plagued the seas from Rome to Barcelona, so that people could doze peacefully under their fig trees and vines.[3]

[2] See G. Airaldi, *Genova e la Liguria nel Medioevo* (Turin, 1986): the quotations and references to Genoa may be found here. Specific research on this topic is currently underway using published and unpublished sources.

[3] R. Lopez, "Le marchand génois. Un profil collectif", *Annales* 13.3 (July/September, 1958), 506; now in R. Lopez, *Su e giuu per la storia di Genova* (Genoa, 1975), p. 26.

The specific role of the Genoese was therefore different from that of other Italian cities which opposed the emperor - the role of imperial warriors. In any case, the Genoese prepared themselves to fend off any assaults by the imperial troops: in 1155, they built a mighty city wall in just one night, on which they carved a Latin inscription as a warning to those who approached: *si pacem portas, licet tibi has attingere portas; si bellum quaeres, fractus victusque recedes* ("if you come in peace, you may approach these walls; if you bring war, you will depart broken and defeated").[4]

During those times, the Genoese were already selling their technological know-how and their services in war and peacetime. In 1112, a Genoese called Ogerio used his skills to work with his own sailors on building ships for the bishop of Santiago de·Compostela: the "Cronica compostelana" tells the story of the acts of war in which these military seafarers defeated the Saracens on numerous occasions.[5]

The codex containing these "Annals" of Genoa contains small illustrations marking the centres gradually conquered on the reproduction of a castle, as well as a variety of ships in the parts relating to exploits at sea. Together with the documentary evidence which has come down to us, these annals bear interesting witness to the advanced skills of the Genoese in the construction and use of sea-going vessels. The galley is known to have been the favourite ship of the Genoese for use in the Mediterranean. This was replaced by the carrack when they started to sail out northwards along the Atlantic coast in the late thirteenth century. Nevertheless, the galley

[4] ibid., p. 26.

[5] See G. Airaldi, "Genoa, i regni iberici e l'Oceano tra XIV e XVI secolo", in *La Costruzione di un nuovo mondo. Territorio, città, architettura tra Europa e America Latina dal XVI al XVIII secolo*, ed. G. Rosso Del Brenna (Genoa, 1994), pp. 13-20.

was preferred since it was suited both for commerce and war, being well equipped with crossbow-men and other combatants.[6]

Galleys were used in all the major Mediterranean battles. One outstanding example of naval strategy is the definitive victory of the Genoese at Meloria in 1284 over their ancient and dangerously nearby rival, Pisa. The leading figure in the final phases of this battle was the famous Benedetto Zaccaria, who subsequently became an admiral in the service of the House of Castille (and victorious in the battle of Tarifa in 1291). Zaccaria would later be employed as admiral in the service of the French crown and drew up a small treatise on naval war strategy for Philip the Fair of France in view of a possible naval blockade of England.

Zaccaria was well known for his skills throughout the Mediterranean - from Byzantium to the kingdom of Aragon (the overthrow of the Angevins in Sicily in 1282 was partly due to his diplomacy). His, indeed, is one example among many of the behaviour of the Genoese, who were ready to make private use of skills and capital throughout the known world. Nor should it be forgotten that he owned the first ships to make the voyage from the eastern Mediterranean to Flanders, where they first carried shipments of the Focea alum which had been given as a monopoly concession to the Zaccaria family by the Byzantines. This remains the earliest evidence of the wide-scale outgoing merchant traffic which was soon to involve Venetians and Florentines and saw a

[6] R. Lopez, *Storia delle colonie genovesi nel Mediterraneo* (Bologna, 1936), pp. 41-74; L. Gatti, *L'arsenale e le galee* (Genoa, 1990); L. Gatti, *Navi mediterranee tra Medioevo ed Età Moderna* (Genoa, 1992); V. Vitale. ed., *Le fonti del diritto marittimo ligure* (Genoa, 1951).

change in direction, with non-Italian ships sailing towards the Mediterranean only much later on.[7]

Maritime commerce opened up the world and war was often the instrument for this. Technical skill frequently led to unusual challenges: it was for this reason that Ugolino and Vadino Vivaldi made their courageous attempt in 1291 to sail "ad partes Indie". Their venture was unsuccessful but can be easily understood: the Genoese had already sailed north through the Straits of Gibraltar and had reached the Atlantic coast of Morocco at Safi and Saleh in 1160 - as is testified by Giovanni Scriba, the notary whose register (the oldest of its type in the world) is still preserved in the Genoa State Archives.[8]

For obvious reasons, the Genoese, at the same time capitalists, seafarers and soldiers always ready to undertake profitable ventures, were employed as admirals in the imperial and royal navies of the time.

In Castille, therefore, we find not just Zaccaria, but also Ugo Vento (though he did not complete his task) and, a little later, the renowned Egidio Boccanegra, who will be discussed below. The exploits of Zaccaria in France have already been mentioned, while Manuele Pessagno put his ships and experienced seamen at the disposal of Portugal in 1317. Indeed, his family was to remain almost constantly at the head of the fleet, take an occasional part in commerce and even carry out pirate raids. Such exploits

[7] R. Lopez, *Benedetto Zaccaria ammiraglio e mercante* (Messina-Milan, 1933).

[8] R. Lopez, "I genovesi in Africa occidentale nel Medio Evo", in *Studi sull'economia genovese nel medioevo* (Turin, 1936), pp. 1-61; G. Airaldi, "Da Genova al Maghreb nel Basso Medioevo", in *Italia e Algeria. Aspetti storici di un'amicizia mediterraneo*, ed. R. H. Rainero (Milan, 1982), pp. 69-80; G. Jehel, *Les Génois en Méditerranée Occidentale* (Paris, 1993).

characterised the history of those times, in which the cruelty of the Genoese was rivalled only by that of the Catalans, though only from the fourteenth century onwards.

It would also be of great interest to analyse the various contracts stipulated between the admirals and various kingdoms (including the Empire, which from Frederick II's (1198-1250) time had a series of Genoese admirals, despite there being no lack of capable seamen in the Sicilian region). Such an analysis would aid further understanding of the importance of the role and the power of these men and the forces which they commanded.[9]

All of these activities were possible because private initiative dominated over public enterprise from the very beginning of Genoa's history. This, of course, led to great difficulty in consolidating the state itself and later caused weakness in facing attacks from the outside: there was private enterprise in the commercial sector and private initiative was also predominant in the making of political decisions. This meant, as Roberto Lopez pointed out many years ago, that individualism and action by groups and families was strongly encouraged to an extent which was unequalled in medieval times and which remains a characteristic of modern Genoese society.[10] Thus, the history of local government as a driving force in the political sphere pales before a myriad of individual actions, whereas in Venice, for example, political action and structures were decidedly more monolithic. This partly explains not only the behaviour described, but also the sense of calculated risk, the concepts of risk-sharing and profit and loss applied to ship-owning and the birth and growth of company systems - in both

[9] C. Manfroni, *Storia della marina italiana*, 2 vols. (Livorno, 1899), 2:449-490, and op. cit. R. Lopez and G. Airaldi.

[10] R. Lopez, "Le marchand", p. 17.

commerce and war - which are well-documented by the mass of notarial documents which have been preserved.

It also explains the wide-ranging nature of the activities in which the Genoese were involved. These included the early creation of "maone" (companies formed for the conquest and exploitation of specific colonial areas) and participation in the Portuguese colonisation of the Atlantic islands. Genoese colonisation itself was aimed more at the establishment of commercial bases or districts, rather than at creating military settlements, which were only required in areas of strategic importance. These activities led to the rise of potentates such as Alamanno da Costa at Syracuse and Enrico Pescatore in Malta.

Unlike the Venetians, the Genoese certainly preferred to obtain commercial bases, contracts and monopolies or to provide loans to monarchies which were constantly short of funds, but in many cases they also exploited their ability in the construction of fortresses and the organisation of port landing-stages. Thus, they built the arsenal at Rouen for the French monarchy, just as the "Captain of the People", Guglielmo Boccanegra, built the town of Aigues Mortes when in exile from Genoa. In the field of colonial control, there were areas over which they were obliged to exercise military dominion - above all, Corsica, Chios and the northern coast of the Black Sea. In such cases, the Genoese always adopted a precise policy which was again quite different from that of the Venetians - great constructors of isolated fortresses along their trade routes and throughout their territory. The Genoese sought places where harbours were already protected by hilly areas, where they then built the fortress which was to defend the settlement.[11]

[11] G. Airaldi, "Genovesi guerrieri e mercanti", in *Le vie del Mediterraneo. Idee, uomini, oggetti (secoli X-XVI)* (Genoa, 1997).

The small amount of literary output by the Genoese (which reflects the rural conciseness of their character) offers several interesting examples. The majority of Italian poets writing in "langue d'oc" were actually Genoese. One of the most famous was Percivalle Doria, who wrote of war. His works certainly conform to the cultural dictates of chivalry, as Doria was himself of noble extraction and belonged to one of Genoa's most ancient families. He was a man of arms, deputy to Frederick II and Manfredi and governor of many Italian and Provençal cities. His family sent three hundred members to the battle of Meloria and obtained the right to hang the trophies from this battle on the walls of the family church of San Matteo rather than leave them (as would have been logical) to the glory of the city council. However, it should not be forgotten that this family was also very active in all areas of Genoese commercial development, from Sardinia to the west and east, and that the battle of Meloria was actually the conclusion of a long trade war.[12]

The important battles of Meloria (1284) and Curzola (1291) were even celebrated by the austere author of the "Legenda aurea", who not only went into great detail but also openly praised the martial ability of his fellow citizens and their skill in naval battles. Furthermore, despite being a pious Dominican, Jacopo da Varagine described some of the harshest aspects in his "Chronicle" of the city, and it is curious to note the way in which the Genoese archbishop dwelt upon details such as the following:

> As for the city of Venice, it must be said that the Venetians once caused a lot of damage to the Genoese. This was because our citizens did not

[12] G. Bertoni, *Trovatori d'Italia* (Modena, 1915); P. Lingua, *I Doria* (Rome, 1994).

> have good judgement at that time and had men from Lombardy on their galleys, who were not good seamen and had no experience of naval battles. Therefore, just as they were unable to row, they were useless during battles and were generally unskilled and clumsy in all matters. People like that are better at hoeing the earth than at sailing the seas and better at driving carts than at sailing boats. When at sea, they have headaches and upset stomachs and just start complaining like children; rather than tackling the enemy they just fall to the ground, when they should stop complaining and help the wounded.[13]

One anonymous poet of the fourteenth century wrote a famous encomium of the city, following the example of other contemporaries. His work not only underlines port and mercantile work, but also the ability to face the sea and the perils encountered there in the form of battles or pirates. The anonymous writer goes to great lengths to describe the ability in war of his fellow citizens, who also fight well on land against enemies arriving by sea or coming down from the surrounding mountains.[14]

Of the fighting elements, he refers many times to the crossbow-men, who were always present in battle and often decisive in particularly difficult situations. These soldiers do, in fact, constitute a separate chapter in the history of Genoese warfare in their own right.

They are to be found throughout the history of medieval warfare, but among Italian soldiers only Genoese crossbow-men

[13] G. Monleone, ed., *Jacopo da Varagine e la sua cronaca di Genova* (Rome, 1941), p. 137.

[14] L. Cocito, ed., *Anonimo Genovese, Poesie* (Rome, 1970).

were always present to a massive extent because of the private nature of supply at an international level: they fought in European armies and for the Saracens and the Turks. Political refugees or war merchants frequently offered capital, ships and sailors, as well as trained units of crossbow-men for service in international conflicts. The city of Genoa was not well organised for defence: the fortresses surrounding the city were not well equipped and were often in private hands; the city did not have a public fleet until modern times and limited itself to arming a few ships to control the coastline and would seek private supplies in the event of war. Yet there is much evidence to show that even the city council paid special attention to the crossbow-men: a large public space was dedicated to preparation and training for this kind of military skill.

A great deal of information is still available on the varieties of Genoese crossbow and the techniques used to perfect it, as well as prices, shapes and measures. Deeds of apprenticeship also still exist. Much is known about what was to be found in a crossbow-maker's workshop and in Genoese fortresses. The art of making crossbows definitely existed as early as 1275. They were made of wood until 1460, when some foreign craftsmen imported iron crossbows, which were replaced by the arquebus in 1529. Not only Genoa but the entire region was involved in training these specialised combatants, and competitions were held with large silver cups as prizes. The town council and private enterprise paid very high salaries to crossbow-men - comparable to the cost of building a ship or to the annual salary of a teacher. The fame of these soldiers was obviously a reflection of their quality: the chroniclers report that it was the Genoese crossbow-men who saved Richard the Lionheart (1157-1199) from an attack by the Egyptian cavalry during the third crusade. Even Ramon Muntaner, the Catalan annalist and ferocious enemy and denigrator of the Genoese, recognised the superiority of their crossbow-men over the Catalans. Naturally, the risks were also proportional to the profit. In 1245, Frederick II ordered that those captured should have their left hand cut off and their right eye gouged out.[15]

Things did not always go well for the Genoese, as is documented by the English and the French. Those who traded in England were also known for their readiness to supply services. The galley-men took part in the Anglo-Scottish conflict of 1310-17 - in the shadow of such famous Genoese figures as Pessagno, Doria, Usodimare, Dentuto and Mangiavacca - and supplied ships to both the English and the Scots. While their lives were often at risk during times of growing xenophobia, their virtue as traders is recalled by the "Libelle of Englysche Polycie". Working in London, Sandwich and Southampton, they played a direct and important part in the Anglo-French war. The chronicles of Froissart (d. c. 1410), Holinshed (d. c. 1580) and Stow (d. 1605) and certain poems by Laurence Minot (d. c. 1352) (official bard of the victories of Edward III [1312-1377]) make various mention of them. The chroniclers were inclined to underline the skills of the Genoese in battle, while Minot was less laudatory since those particular Genoese figures always fought for the French.

Of the many references which survive, two deserve special mention here. These involve the battle of Sluys (1340), which saw the presence in the French ranks of Egidio Boccanegra (mentioned earlier). Brother of the Doge Simon Boccanegra, and known as "Blackbeard", he was renowned, feared and hated by the English for his strategic fighting skills at sea. The battle of Sluys was lost by the French because the other admirals did not carry out Boccanegra's orders. The English even made an unsuccessful attempt to buy his

[15] N. Calvini, *Balestre e balestrieri medievali in Liguria* (Sanremo, 1982).

services in 1344. In the same year, he was already serving in the Castillian navy and fought in the victorious battle of Algeciras. The English again found him fighting for the enemy in the battle of Winchelsea in 1352. He fought on the Earl of Pembroke's side in his claim of the Castillian crown. For the services rendered to Castille he was rewarded, as was usually the case, with a manorial estate - Palma del Rio - although his participation in the Castillian civil war eventually brought him to a violent end. He was beheaded.

The other, more famous, example relates to the battle of Crécy in 1346, in which thousands of Genoese crossbow-men are reported to have taken part (although this number is probably an exaggeration) under the leadership of a Ranieri Grimaldi (fl. Fourteenth century) who had fled his homeland for political reasons. Although the English undoubtedly won the battle on the grounds of their superiority and skill, the French are reported to have blamed the Genoese crossbow-men for a defeat which was really due to strategic errors which are of no relevance here.[16] The chroniclers report many other naval and land battles in the Mediterranean area in which Genoese ships and assault towers played a decisive role.

The fame of the Genoese as an aggressive and daring people remained unaltered. In his sixteenth-century text for commercial traders, Benedetto Cotrugli reports that whenever Genoese

[16] G. Warner, ed., *Lybelle of Englishe Polycye* (Oxford, 1926), pp. 17-19; J. A. Buchon, ed., *Les chroniques de sire Jean de Froissart*, 5 vols. (Paris, 1838-1942), 1:759-762; W. Stokes, ed., *J. Stow, Annales* (London, 1873), p. 385; W. Stokes, ed., *Holinshed, Chronicle* (London, 1875), pp. 358-360; "How Edward the King come in Braband and take Homage of the Land", "The Batail of Inglish-men and Normandes in the Swin", "The Bataille of Crécy", "How King Edward and his Menche met with the Spaniardes on the See", in *War Ballads*, ed. D. C. Stedman (Dublin, 1917). On Egidio Boccanegra, see *Dizionario Biografico degli Italiani* (Rome, 1970) under the same heading, and the comment in D. Stedman, op. cit.

merchants suffered a reversal of fortune they were quite ready to become pirates.[17] It is not known whether or to what extent codes of honour and truces of God played a part in naval history, which is rather less easy to follow than events occurring on land. However, there is no doubt that the special Genoese interpretation of the market economy and their unbridled individualism were elements destined to strengthen rather than weaken their aggressiveness, without which their history would have been quite different. At the end of the middle ages and during the modern era, they principally became financiers, although they did not completely abandon trading and warfare - areas in which they continued to display their natural aggressiveness. In conclusion, to quote Roberto Lopez, "in the Middle Ages, the Genoese had all the courage they needed".[18]

[17] B. Cotrugli, *Della mercatura et del mercante perfetto* (Venice, 1573), p. 168.

[18] R. Lopez, "Le marchand", p. 25.

Repercusiones de la Piratería Mediterránea y Atlántica en el Comercio Exterior Castellano a Finales de la Edad Media

Juan Manuel Bello León
Universidad de La Laguna

La comunicación que presentamos, forma parte de un trabajo de investigación que por sus características y amplitud no podemos reproducir dentro de los límites impuestos a esta edición. Con él he pretendido acercarme al análisis de dos actividades, la del corsario y la del pirata, consideradas como uno de los elementos que entorpecían de forma más grave las relaciones comerciales y diplomáticas de los distintos Estados europeos a finales de la Edad Media. En ese trabajo al que aludimos[1] se analizan tres zonas que a grandes rasgos coinciden con los ámbitos comerciales más importantes con los que se relacionaba la España de finales del siglo XV: en primer lugar el Atlántico andaluz, la Berbería de poniente y las Islas Canarias; en segundo, la amplia fachada marítima que va desde la costa gallega hasta el Canal de la Mancha, y por último el Norte de Africa y el Mediterráneo Occidental. Cada uno de ellos

[1] La versión íntegra del mismo se publicará próximamente en la revista Historia. Instituciones y Documentos de la Universidad de Sevilla.

presenta un tratamiento distinto en función de la documentación disponible y de los estudios que nos permitan conocer diversos aspectos de la actividad marítima de cada zona. Así, es al ámbito Mediterráneo al que hemos prestado mayor atención dado el temprano desarrollo que en sus aguas conocieron ambas actividades, la gran cantidad de mercaderes, ciudades y reinos que en ellos estaban implicados, y el importante volumen de fuentes catalanas y valencianas, además de genovesas y venecianas, con las que hoy en día contamos. En el ámbito Atlántico nuestro interés se centró en las alteraciones que provocó la violencia marítima en el tráfico mercantil que unía a los distintos puertos castellanos con los de Francia, Ingalterra o Países Bajos. Por último, en el Atlántico Medio destacaron los enfrentamientos que se localizan en las aguas próximas al Estrecho y costa occidental africana debido a lucha que mantuvieron castellanos y portugueses en sus respectivos procesos de expansión por aquella zona.

LAS FUENTES Y ALGUNOS DE SUS PROBLEMAS

Dos problemas han preocupado de forma especial a todos aquellos que se han acercado a una historia de la piratería en cualquier época y ámbito geográfico. El primero ha sido establecer una distinción entre el corsario y el pirata. Se suele definir al pirata como aquel individuo que actua por su cuenta y riesgo, atacando a todo navío que se encuentra en su ruta sin importarle su nacionalidad, mientras que el corsario se va distinguiendo progresivamente de aquel ya que su actividad es ocasional y casi siempre ceñida a unos objetivos muy concretos (supuestamente un enemigo). Lo que termina de diferenciar al corsario del pirata es que el primero entra en los planes políticos de los Estados, de tal forma que cuando la estructura militar y los problemas económicos de los distintos reinos no permiten afrontar los costes de la defensa marítima, el corsario presta un servicio a los Estados con la condición de respetar a los navíos aliados e indemnizar a los afectados en caso de error.[2] No obstante, lo que estas definicones más o menos ambiguas no aclaran es que, en muchos casos, la documentación medieval no permite distinguir en la práctica la actividad del corso de la del pirata, puesto que lo que se suponía era un ejercicio con cobertura legal en el caso del corso,[3] se transforma en numerosas ocasiones en simple piratería al no respetarse las treguas y las paces acordadas por los Estados.

El segundo problema lo constituyen las fuentes que permitan trazar las características de aquella violencia marítima. La extensión

[2] Estas observaciones se han puesto de manifiesto en los numerosos trabajos que se dedican al corso y la piratería. Ambas definiciones pueden seguirse con amplitud en los trabajos presentados el XV Colloque International d'Histoire Marítime: *Course et Piraterie* (San Francisco, 1975). También en los de Michel Mollat, "Essai d'orientation pour l'étude de la guerre de course et la piraterie (XIII-XV siècles)", *Anuario de Estudios Medievales* 10 (Barcelona), 743-749; en el de Anna Unali, *Mariners, pirates i corsaris catalans a l'época medieval* (Barcelona, 1985); y en el de J. Guiral-Hadziiosif, *Valencia, puerto mediterráneo en el siglo XV (1410-1525)* (Valencia, 1989), pp. 137-140. Como obras generales que superan el marco temporal de la Edad Media me remito a los trabajos de Philip Gosse, *Los corsarios berberiscos. Los piratas del norte (Historia de la Piratería)* (Madrid, 1947); A. Masia de Ros, *Historia general de la piratería* (Barcelona, 1959); J. Hernandez, *Piratas y corsarios. De la antiguedad a los inicios del mundo contemporáneo* (Madrid, 1995); y al ya clásico trabajo de J. L. Azcarraga y Bustamante, *El corso martítimo* (Madrid, 1950).

[3] En el caso castellano las acciones de corso estaban reguladas y autorizadas por la Corona; de los beneficios que se obtenían con estos ataques el rey se beneficiaba con la quinta parte, del cual participaba su almirante (el "quinto" se repartía en dos tercios para el rey y uno para el almirante). La figura y la institución de los almirantes de Castilla ha sido estudiada por F. Perez Embid en su trabajo "El almirantazgo de Castilla hasta las capitulaciones de Santa Fe", *Anuario de Estudios Americanos* 1 (1944), 1-170.

geográfica de la actividad de corsarios y piratas es tal que hace necesario, como indica M. Mollat en el artículo ya citado, un plan internacional que lleve a los investigadores a los cuatro puntos cardinales de los distintos mares y océanos que recorrían los hombres del medievo para proporcionos el material requerido. Con todo, y este trabajo desde luego que no lo pretende, es difícil hallar los documentos que ofrezcan la suficiente calidad como para elaborar las fichas estandar que propone el citado profesor.

Esta dispersión de los documentos ya plantea un grave problema. Empezaré reconociendo que si en el suceso interviene algún extranjero se hace difícil acceder a las fuentes directas, tanto si es la víctima como si es el que cometió el acto de violencia. Los registros hasta ahora publicados indican que los archivos ingleses, franceses o italianos guardan colecciones documentales[4] que sin duda complementarían la visión de las denuncias que conocemos a través de las fuentes castellanas y catalano-aragonesas. En ambos casos la documentación que más abunda - para este tema y especialmente en el caso castellano - es la que procede de las denuncias elevadas a la Corona por los robos, asaltos y usurpaciones, presentadas generalmente por la víctima o un representante legal del mismo.[5] En

[4] Tanto los fondos de la Torre del Tombo, estudiados a través de los catálagos publicados correspondientes a "Las Gavetas" y la "Monumenta Henricina", como los procedentes de Inglaterra, analizados a través de la edición de los Calendar of Patent Rolls, indican que los archivos extranjeros custodian una documentación muy interesante para la influencia de la violencia marítima en las relaciones comerciales de ambos países con España.

[5] Nuevamente los límites impuestos a esta publicación no nos permite describir las fuentes utilizadas en este estudio. Además de los datos que proporcionan la abundante bibliografía, señalar únicamente que proceden del Archivo General de Simancas, de varios archivos locales andaluces (Sevilla, Sanlúcar, etc.) y de las colecciones documentales de tres obras fundamentales para el análisis del gobierno de los Reyes Católicos. Me refiero a los trabajos de Antonio de la Torre y Luis Suarez Fernandez. Del primero son los seis

todos los casos lo que obtenemos es la versión unilateral del suceso, lo que sin duda distorsiona la realidad de los hechos. En muchos carecemos de los resultados de la investigación que se abría o del proceso seguido contra los acusados, si es que el denunciante tenía la fortuna de que el asunto no se enquistara en las distintas instancias judicales. Si el pleito no "moriría" a través de los años y se llegaba dictar algún tipo de sentencia tampoco sabemos mucho del grado de cumplimiento de la misma o de la efectividad de las penas impuestas.

En todo caso, es al hilo de las declaraciones de las víctimas de donde podemos obtener un perfil aproximado de las circunstancias que rodearon a los actos de violencia. Su seguimiento no siempre es sencillo. A las dificultades propias de una grafía siempre cambiante en el caso de los nombre extranjeros, hay que añadir la situación de que en muchas ocasiones sólo conocemos los hechos a través del propio rey que ordena a alguno de sus embajadores que proteste ante la cancillería genovesa, veneciana o inglesa por el asalto que sufrió alguno de sus súbditos.

Veamos algunos problemas que ha presentado la documentación manejada. Un primer hecho a destacar es el elevado número de reclamaciones que se presentan. Como se puede observar en el cuadro, entre los años 1477-1499 se documentan más de 200 denuncias a las que le acompañan múltiples documentos que van desde la naración de los hechos por parte de la víctima hasta las resoluciones tomadas por la Corona, pasando por las protestas de municipios y comerciantes ante la proliferación de las cartas de marca para todos aquellos casos en los que los afectados no lograban

volúmenes de los *Documentos sobre las relaciones internacionales de los Reyes Católicos* (Barcelona, 1949-1966): del segundo el monumental trabajo (6 vols.) sobre la *Política internacional de Isabel la Católica* (Valladolid, 1965-1972). De ambos son los tres volúmenes dedicados a los *Documentos referentes a las relaciones con Portugal durante el reinado de los Reyes Católicos* (Valladolid, 1956-1963).

satisfacer las pérdidas. He intentado comparar todos y cada uno de los casos para no repetir alguna denuncia; aún así es posible, dado el número de afectados y el ya mencionado cambio en la grafía de los nombres, que algún caso aparezca más de una vez.

Determinar la fecha exacta de la agresión suele ser una tarea imposible. Son muy pocos los casos que expresan la fecha en la que sufrieron el asalto, y cuando lo hacen lo señalan con una vaga referencia que situa los hechos años atrás (algunos hasta 15 y 20 años) sin especificar el mes ni el día.[6] Por ello he optado por clasificar las agresiones según la fecha de la primera denuncia que aparece. Reconozco que siguiendo este criterio se plantea un grave problema si queremos relacionar los ataques piráticos con una coyuntura política determinada, pero era el único medio de clasifircar con cierto orden cronológico los distintos episodios de violencia.

Andamos sobre mejores bases para tratar de conocer a los hombres que han participado en los hechos. En todos los documentos - hay pocas excepciones - se expresa el nombre de los afectados (que suele ser el denunciante) y el de los agresores. En algunas ocasiones se añade el nombre del patrón o capitán de los barcos que participaron en el suceso. Son más parcos los documentos a la hora de expresar el orígen geográfico de la víctima y el acusado, si bien algunos nombres y apellidos denotan una procedencia muy clara.

Hay que caminar con mucha cautela en todo lo que se refiere a las condiciones económicas y técnicas que rodean a las agresiones. En primer lugar siempre hay que tener presente que las circunstancias económicas en las que vivían algunos pueblos costeros obligaba a sus

[6] Casi todos los casos que incluyen la fecha aproximada de la agresión aluden a unos hechos que ocurrieron hace dos o tres años; en el extremo opuesto se encuentran aquellos casos que hacen referencia a agresiones ocurridas hace 17, 20, 30 o más años. De estos últimos véanse algunos ejemplos en Simancas. Registro General de Sello, 13-VI-1485, fol. 187; 3-V-1490, fol. 244; 24-V-1490, fol. 267.

habitantes a procurarse las necesidades alimenticias básicas acudiendo al asalto de los navíos que, cargados de cereales, se acercaban al litoral en una escala voluntaria u obligado por dificultades metereológicas o de navegación. Tampoco podemos olvidar que las acciones de piratería entraban dentro de las actividades de aquellos mercaderes, e incluso pescadores,[7] que por cualquier circunstancia acudían a la agresión como medio de obtener ganancias o sufragar pérdidas. La proleferación de aquellos hechos situaban a todos los que navegaban ante la posibilidad de ser pirata o víctima.

La misma precaución hay que tomar en lo que se refiere a las mercancías y a las pérdidas que declaran las víctimas. En este punto creo que no exagero si afirmo que sus denuncias siempre estan sobredimensionadas. Los documentos suelen generalizar cuando describen los productos que transportaban los barcos que sufrían la agresión reduciéndolos a la ambigua expresión de "mercaderías". La excepción se presenta cuando entre las pérdidas se encuentran esclavos o dinero. En cualquier caso todos afirman tener grandes pérdidas que sin duda evalúan por encima de la realidad. A esta evalución monetaria de las pérdidas - que no siempre aparece - se le añaden dos problemas: el primero es que en muchos casos se expresa en moneda extranjera, y aunque se conocen tablas que permiten convertir a alguna de ellas a las que comúnmente se empleaban en Castilla, lo cierto es que las contínuas devaluaciones y la distancia entre el curso legal de las monedas y la realidad económica de cada país hacen que no siempre sea fácil buscar la equivalencia en moneda castellana. En segundo lugar el valor monetario de las pérdidas recoge en algunos casos no sólo la parte correspondiente al daño que

[7] Pueden verse algunos ejemplos de navíos que se vieron afectados cuando estaban pescando en aguas del Atlántico Medio en Simancas. Registro General del Sello: 20-XI-1477, fols. 340 y 345; 12-XII-1498, fol. 284.

se ha sufrido en las mercancías sino también el quebranto económico que le supone a la víctima todas las diligencias necesarias para denunciar al agresor. Si el documento no lo expesa claramente resulta imposible deslindar la cuantía de ambos conceptos.

En cuanto a los aspectos técnicos, de forma especial aquellos referidos al tipo de navío, al tonelaje del mismo y al armamento que participó en las distintas agresiones, es poco lo que podemos decir. Es común la aparición del término nao o navío para designar a los barcos que forman parte de los hechos, especificandose en algunos casos el tipo (carabela, balliner, fusta, etc.) y tonelaje de la embarcación. En cualquier caso, en todos ellos se evidencia la estrecha conexión entre los autores del comercio y la piratería ya que en todos los ejemplos conocidos se revela una identidad entre las embarcaciones empleadas en usos mercantiles y las empleadas en los hechos violentos. A través de la documentación que he manejado poco o nada se puede intuir acerca de la modalidad del ataque; tan sólo la simple mención al abordaje sin especificar ningún tipo de dispositivo táctico que preparase la agresión.

Un último aspecto a destacar, dentro de esta breve relación de la características de los documentos, es aquella que se refiere a la localización geográfica del acto de violencia. Como se observa en el cuadro algo más del 15% de los casos no declara el lugar de la agresión, mientras que un porcentaje considerable lo deja en una vaga referecian que engloba a espacios tan amplios como "allende", "viniendo de Berbería" o "camino de Inglaterra". También hay que destacar que buena parte de los actos de piratería no se localizan en alta mar sino que, más bien hay que buscarlos en los puertos o bahías que acogen a los navíos, aprovechando el momento de la descarga de los productos o la entrada y salida al mismo.

En síntesis, las grandes líneas de la evolución cronológica y localización geográfica de la violencia marítima pueden verse en el siguientes cuadro:

CUADRO I

Años	Atlant. Medio	Atlant. Norte	Mediterr.	Sin localizar	**Total**
1477-1480	9	9	6	6	30
1481-1485	8	9	10	12	39
1486-1490	7	16	15	10	48
1491-1495	13	14	29	8	64
1496-1499	--	7	13	7	27
%	**10,7**	**20,5**	**30,5**	**15**	

LA VIOLENCIA Y ALGUNAS DE SUS CONSECUENCIAS

Sin duda la consecuencia más grave a la que se veían sometida las víctimas de una ataque marítimo era la pérdida de su propia vida. A lo largo de numerosos ejemplos se puede observar como el asalto a un navío comportaba generalmente el saqueo de toda la carga, del aparejo del barco y de los bienes pertenecientes a la tripulación y mercaderes que iban a bordo. Cuando los hechos se desarrollaban de esta manera siempre se podía confiar en que recurriendo a la corona se podría obtener algún tipo de compensación para las pérdidas. Sin embargo no es extraño que, para eliminar cualquier testimonio del suceso y de esta manera evitar las represalias, el pirata o el corsario quemen el navío, arrojen al mar a los tripulantes o simplemente maten a sus víctimas. Veamos dos casos que pueden considerarse como ejemplos significativos. En 1477 Juan Suárez, vecino de Sevilla, denunciaba el asalto que unos años antes había sufrido su padre cuando se dirigía desdes el Puerto de Santa María a Inglaterra con un carracón cargado de vino, hierro y otras mercancías que valoraba en más de 6.000 coronas de oro. Al llegar cerca de la costa de Francia le atacaron tres navíos de esta nacionalidad que no dudaron en matar a 6 hombres y herir a otros 25, llevandose a los que habían sobrevivido hasta una una isla inglesa donde fueron abandonados. Esta vez la fortuna quiso que poco tiempo después pasara cerca de allí un barco de pescadores que pudo rescatarlos.[8] Tampoco tuvieron mucha suerte los tripulantes de la carabela del vizcaíno Martín de Raelga que en 1499, cuando regresaba desde Bretaña a España, sufrió el ataque de cierta armada procedente del ducado. Tras matar a alguno de los

[8] Simancas. Registro General del Sello: 26-IX-1477, fol. 497. Se trata de un largo documento en el que se narra las quejas ante el rey de Francia y las diligencias emprendidas ante Enrique IV de Castilla para obtener justicia. Finalmente se le concedió una carta de marca y represalia.

marineros y apoderarse de la mercancía, hundieron la carabela y abandonaron al resto de tripulantes ("desnudos") en la costa.[9]

Sin llegar a la trascendencia de la pérdida de vidas pero tambièn con graves consecuencias para los que se encuentran a bordo de los navíos que padecían la violencia del corso y la piratería, estan los casos de aquellos que son reducidos a la condición de esclavos o son detenidos hasta que logren pagar su rescate. Generalmente la primera de estas situaciones afecta a las empresas dirigidas contra las naves musulmanas o contra aquellas capturas consideradas como de "buena guerra", mientras que la segunda puede englobar a cualquier enemigo.[10]

En muchos casos estos cautivos servían para intercambiarlos por los cristianos que los musulmanes podían tener en su poder. Para facilitar el canje, además de las limosnas públicas y privadas destinadas al pago del alto precio de los "rescates", se había promulgado una ley en las Cortes de 1462 mediante la cual se regulaba la entrega de esclavos musulmanes a todas aquellos que los

[9] Simancas. Registro General del Sello: 8-I-1499, fol. 131. Poco tiempo antes Martín de Raelga había perdido a manos de ciertos franceses otra carabela cargada de hierro. Estos dos casos no son los únicos. En 1483 Arthur de Lili, mercarder bretón, denunciaba la pérdida de dos hombres en el ataque que había sufrido en la costa del sur de Portugal (Simancas. Registro General del Sello: 5-XII-1483, fol. 107); en 1485 García de Escalante y López Ibáñez denunciaban el asalto y posterior arrojo al mar que habían sufrido la tripulación de sus tres carabelas junto a la costa de Flandes (Simancas. Registro General del Sello: 8-XI-1485, fol. 97).

[10] Al respecto de ésto último véase un buen ejemplo en Simancas. Registro General del Sello: 2-IV-1487, fol. 75. Describe el ataque que sufrió una carabela propiedad de unos vecinos de San Vicente de la Barquera cerca de la costa de Bretaña, la captura de 13 de sus tripulantes y el coste del rescate de cada uno de ellos.

necesitaran para recuperar a sus familiares.[11] La aplicación de la norma no siempre contó con el acuerdo del propietario de los esclavos, que en todos los casos intentó obtener el precio más alto posible.[12]

En cuanto a otro tipo de pérdidas, en este caso las correspondientes a las mercancías embarcadas en el navío capturado, indicar que esos productos variaban en función de la ruta que se seguía. Así en el caso de los ataques que se registran en el Atlántico Medio predominan los más comunes en el comercio de la zona, de tal forma que esclavos y el oro procedentes del Cabo de Aguer, el trigo y los caballos que vienen de Azamor o Fadala, y la plata, la seda y una serie de productos vedados que por pate castellana se exportan hacia Arcila, Mazagán, Tánger, Safi, etc. forman parte de las mercancías obtenidas en los distintos ataques. Como caso especial dentro de este ámbito se encuentra los bienes obtenidos a partir del asalto que sufrió alguno de los navíos que llevaba la paga de las guarniciones portuguesas en el norte de Africa, o los procedentes de los bienes de algunos judíos que emigraban de Portugal con destino al citado continente.[13]

En el ámbito del Golfo de Vizcaya y Canal de la Mancha la variedad de productos que forman parte de los apresamientos se corresponde con la diversidad e intensidad de tráfico marítimo en la zona. Así la fruta, el hierro, el vino, el aciete, la sal y sobre todo los paños importados a Castilla estan presentes en casi todos los ataques. A ellos hay que añadir el valor que podía alcanzar la nave y aparejos

[11] La ley establecía que el precio a pagar sería una tercera parte más si el propietario lo hubiese tenido un año; la mitad más si lo hubiere tenido por más tiempo, y lo que el propietario quisiere si era él mismo quien lo había capturado.

[12] Véanse diversos ejemplos en Simancas. Registro General del Sello: 24-IV-1480; 8-VI-1491; 11-V-1492; 22-X-1499.

[13] Simancas. Registro General del Sello: 3-XI-1490, fol. 36 y 26-X-1493, fol. 64.

en aquellos casos en los que el ataque se saldaba con el apresamiento del navío. En el ámbito Mediterráneo el botín guarda la misma variedad; así las especias, los esclavos, o el alumbre procedente del Oriente, los cereales que salen de Sicilia, o el aceite, los cueros, la fruta seca, y el vino de Valencia y Cataluña, forman parte de los bienes transportados por las embarcaciones que sufren la piratería en este mar.

En el primer epígrafe de este trabajo ya advertía las dificultades que plantea la documentación para conocer el valor de las pérdidas que ocasionaba a los mercaderes y a los tripulantes un ataque pirático. Una vez más sirvan como testimonio algunos ejemplos que afectaron tanto a españoles como a extranjeros. En 1491 varios mercaderes burgales denuncian la pérdida de una serie de mercancías valoradas en unos 5.475.000 maravedís tras el asalto que sufrió la nao que habían fletado en Inglaterra a Martín de Guía;[14] unos años antes, en 1484, cinco naves bretonas ocasionaron un duro golpe a Juan de Arbolancha cuando cargaba en un puerto inglés paños, cueros, plomo, estaño y otras mercancías, valorando sus pérdidas en 5.904.000 maravedís.[15] En 1490 aún continuaba el pleito entre Diego Simón, vecino de Palos, y Alonso Pérez, regidor del Puerto de Santa María, por la carabela que el primero le había tomado a Fernando Pérez cuando regresaba desde el Cabo de Aguer con 105 esclavos "moros" además de cierta mercancía, valorando todas sus pérdidas en algo más de 1.000.000 de maravedís.[16]

[14] B. Caunedo, *Mercaderes castellanos en el Golfo de Vizcaya (1475-1492)* (Madrid, 1983), p. 192.

[15] Suarez, 3:325-338.

[16] Simancas. Registro General del Sello: s.d. noviembre de 1490, fol. 211. En 1488 el citado Pedro Pérez declaraba que había perdido a 72 esclavos y 1.500.000 mrs. por asalto sufrido a manos de Antonio Quintero y Martín Rodríguez. Véase Simancas. Registro General del Sello: 28-IX-1488, fol. 136.

La mayor parte de los bienes apropiados en estos ataques suelen venderse rápidamente en los puertos y ciudades próximas al lugar del asalto. Sin embargo, también se documentan algunos casos en los que el agresor se dirige hacia su lugar de origen con la intención de vender allí los productos del botín; en esos casos es presumible que los funcionarios locales o los representantes de la corona sean parte muy interesada en el negocio ya que no suelen poner grandes dificultades para que distrubuyan los bienes procedentes del asalto.

La indemnización que podía esperar la víctima de alguna de estas agresiones suele convertirse en una operación larga, difícil y costosa. Las más de las veces las negociaciones con la corona o las autoridades extranjeras no reflejaban el resultado esperado, por lo que los afectados, tras esperar un determinado tiempo, no dudaban en acudir a la represalia como medio de obtener la compensación que la maraña de instancias judiciales le había negado.

El desarrolo de la autoridad monárquica y el propio interés de los Estados en mantener abiertos los circuitos de intercambio fueron canalizando estas acciones hacia la concesión de las llamadas "cartas de marca y represalia", con las que se pretendía, a través de una serie de normas que no siempre se cumplían, atender a las personas perjudicadas por un ataque. Para el reinado de los Reyes Católicos se conocen pocas cartas de marca,[17] casi todas ellas concedidas contra mercaderes extranjeros. La autorización regia, concedida para un tiempo y cantidad de dinero limitados previamente, guardaba ciertos requisitos como eran los de obligar a los patrones de los barcos armados a acudir después de las operaciones al puerto más cercano, donde, tras la inspección de las autoriades, vender en "pública almoneda" todo lo capturado, quedando obligados en ese momento a

[17] Algunas de ellas han sido analizadas por Caunedo, pp. 234-257.

entregar el "quinto" correspondiente a los reyes.[18] De todas formas estas medidas tampoco se mostraron muy eficaces; de un lado porque teóricamente se podía evitar la aplicación de una de estas licencias amparandose en algún salvoconducto o seguro, de tal forma que no es extraño que los reyes ordenen la devolución de lo capturado cuando la carta de marca se aplicaba sobre algún mercader, generalmente extranjero, que disfrutaba del seguro real. De otra, porque el abuso en su utilización podía alejar a los comerciantes extranjeros de los puertos españoles. Como reflejo de ambas circunstancias sirvan los casos del pronunciamiento de los almojarifes de Sevilla ante la proliferación de este tipo de acciones y la conocida reacción de diversos concejos del Norte de España ante el asunto de la carta de represalia concedida a Juan de Arbolancha.

En el primero de los casos los perceptores de esta renta aduanera se dirigen a los reyes debido a que se consideran unos de los más perjudicados al entender que se obstruía el comercio exterior por las arbitrariedades cometidas en el uso de las cartas de marca.[19] Esa impresión se corrobora en el ámbito de los puertos andaluces si tenemos en cuenta que entre los más afectados por la aplicación de las cartas de marca se encuentran los mercaderes genoveses, de los que tanto dependía el desarrollo económico de la Baja Andalucía.[20] Del segundo caso sólo recordaré que el mercader bilbaíno había permutado su carta de marca por un recargo del 3% sobre los diezmos de la mar que abonasen los mercaderes bretones en los puertos

[18] Un buen ejemplo de estas características puede verse en la carta de marca concedida a Juan Iñiguez de Bermeo y los herederos de Fortín Sánchez contra unos franceses. Simancas. Registro General del Sello: 7-II-1497, fol. 10.

[19] Simancas. Registro General del Sello: 15-VI-1485, fol. 217 y 5-VII-1491, fol. 147.

[20] Sirvan de ejemplo los siguientes documentos: Simancas. Registro General del Sello: 10-VIII-1487, fols. 343 y 344; 5-II-1488, fol. 221; 6-IV-1491, fol. 77.

españoles. La aplicación de este acuerdo, que se puso en práctica desde 1484, encontró serias resistencias en los concejos de La Coruña, Ferrol, Vivero, Bermeo, Santander y otros del Cantábrico. El concejo coruñés alegaba a su favor el hecho de que el acuerdo sólo afectaba a vizcaínos y bretones, y que además el cobro de este recargo terminaría por alejar de su puerto a los mercaderes del ducado.[21] Sin duda la dependencia de todos aquellos puertos del comercio con Francia, Inglaterra y Flandes condicionaba la acogida al acuerdo entre Arbolancha y los bretones. Tras varios años el concejo de La Coruña logró que su protesta surtiera efecto, de tal forma que fue anulada la autorización que permitía a los factores de Arbolancha percibir la mencionada sobrecarga.

Los seguros y salvoconductos son la cara opuesta a las cartas de marca y represalia. Concedidos por la corona con el fin de garantizar la navegación y proteger a los mercaderes, su causística es casi tan amplia como los documentos que se conocen.[22] Podían ser generales, como los concedidos a los genoveses en distintas fases de su enfrentamiento con el almirante de Castilla, si bien eran más comunes los individuales, englobando en éste último caso tanto a extranjeros como a castellanos. En cualquier caso he de recordar que el salvoconducto no siempre podía impedir que se ejerciera la violencia sobre aquellos que disfrutaban de él.

Para terminar con esta relación de algunas de las consecuencias del corso y la piratería quisiera hacer referencia al efecto que causaba en las poblaciones costeras la presencia más o menos permanente de

[21] Puede verse el desarrollo de este proceso en las obras de J. A. Garcia de Cortazar, *Vizcaya en el siglo XV. Aspectos económicos y sociales* (Bilbao, 1966), pp. 250-52; y en el de E. Ferreira, *Galicia en el comercio marítimo medieval* (La Coruña, 1988), pp. 540-541.

[22] En breve análisis sobre los seguros concedidos a los extranjeros en las últimas décadas del siglo XV puede verse en mi trabajo *Extranjeros en Castilla (1474-1501)* (La Laguna, 1994), pp. 26-31.

barcos armados que recorrian el litoral, especialmente cuando éstos pertenecían a musulmanes norteafricanos. Y es que el impulso que había adquirido la actividad corsaria de los norteafricanos en las décadas finales de la Edad Media hizo que se constituyeran en un peligro tanto para la navegación como para las villas costeras debido a que muchas de sus acciones terminaban en verdaderas operaciones de invasión.

Las dos medidas más comunes y eficaces de cuántas se tomaron para proteger la costa fueron la de edificar una amplia red de atalayas y torretas que tuvieran como función más inmediata la alerta ante la presencia de cualquier barco enemigo, y el armar una serie de barcos encargados de proteger a los navíos mercantes, a los cuales se aconsejaba que navegaran en convoyes para evitar los peligros.[23] Ambas medidas tuvieron una incidencia desigual ya que el equipamiento de los navíos y el esfuerzo financiero necesario para el mentenimiento de la red de defensa costera era muy considerable, especialmente para las ciudades, las más interesadas y últimos responsables del coste de la protección.

[23] Jacqueline Guiral y José Hinojosa ofrecen múltiples ejemplos referidos al armamento de navíos por parte de la ciudad de valencia destinados a salvaguardar el tráfico marítimo. Véanse Guiral-Hadziiosif, pp. 176-183; y "Piratas y corsarios en Valencia a principios del siglo XV (1400-1409)", *Cuadernos de Historia* 5 (Madrid, 1975), 103-106. No podemos detenernos en un estudio pormenorizado del funcion-amiento de la alerta costera, especialmente la utilizada en el Mediterráneo y costa andaluza, por lo que me remito a los trabajos de M. A. Ladero Quesada, "Defensa de Granada a raiz de la conquista (1492-1501)", en *Homenaje a Elías Serra Ráfols*, Tomo 4 (Universidad de la Laguna, 1973); J. E. Lopez De Coca, "Finaciación mudéjar del sistema de vigilancia costera en el reino de Granada (1492-1501)", *Historia Instituciones Documentos* 3 (1976), 397-415; A. M. Vera Delgado, "La readaptación del sistema de defensa costera en el obispado de Málaga (1501-1511)", *Baética* 4 (1981), 193-208; de la misma autora *La última frontera medieval: la defensa costera en el obispado de Málaga en tiempos de los Reyes Católicos* (Málaga, 1986).

Algo más difícil de medir o comprobar es lo que podríamos llamar el efecto "psicológico" (aunque quizás no sea el término más adecuado) que causaba la alerta permanente en la que vivían algunas de estas villas costeras. Voy a emplear un ejemplo tardío, aunque entiendo que significativo, para este propósito. Me refiero al clima de inquietud que se respiraba en Sanlúcar de Barrameda en las primeras décadas del siglo XVI cuando se esperaba un posible ataque, primero de piratas franceses y años después de corsarios musulmanes.

La primera medida que tomaba el concejo sanluqueño ante una amenaza era informarse mediante una serie de correos y mensajeros de la veracidad de las noticias de un posible ataque. Así ocurrió en el verano de 1512 cuando se enteró de la presencia en la costa andaluza de una armada francesa compuesta por 12 galeras y 4 navíos y envió a Rota y el Puerto de Santa María unos mensajeros para que confirmasen o se informasen de la presencia de dicha armada y de su amenaza sobre Cádiz.[24] Las precauciones fueron aún mayores cuando en mayo de 1524 el Cabildo ordenaba, ante la llegada de unas embarcaciones moras cerca de la villa de Chipiona, a todo aquel que tuviera un esclavo musulman en su poder que por la noche lo custodiase en su casa atado con grilletes hasta el amanecer de tal forma que no se pudieran soltar. Si en su vivienda no dispusiera de "prisión" se le ordenaba que lo trajese a la cárcel pública.[25] Cinco días después se presentaba ante el concejo García de León, caballero de la Casa del duque de Medina Sidonia, para encargarse de la custodia de la ciudad ante un posible ataque moro. La primera medida fue la de designar a ocho hombres que rondarían por la playa para ver si los moros llegaban a desembarcar. En 1526 se reiteran las medidas

[24] Archivo Municipal Sanlucar de Barrameda, Actas Capitulares, 22-VII-1512, fol. 33.

[25] ibid., Actas Capitulares, 23-V-1524, fol. 202; 27-V-1524, fol. 204; 14-VI-1524, fol. 296.

empleadas en los últimos días de mayo de 1524 y otras de carácter más preventivo, de tal forma que se ordena vigilar a todos los esclavos moros y se exige a todos los propietarios de barcas grandes o pequeñas que cada noche llevan a su casa los mástiles, remos y velas para impedir que las embarcaciones pudieran navegar.[26] Un año después el temor aún persistía, sobre todo al saberse a través de un mensajero enviado por Jerez de la Frontera que los moros habían salido desde sus puertos norteafricanos y podían dirigirse hacia la villa de Sanlúcar.[27]

Quizás sea un poco desmesurado afirmarlo, pero lo cierto es que entre mayo de 1524 y agosto de 1527 la población de Sanlúcar de Barrameda se vió condicionada por la amenaza de un desembarco berberisco que nunca llegó a producirse. Y aunque el fenómeno no es exclusivo de esta ciudad andaluza creo que puede ser un buen ejemplo de cómo el miedo a las flotas corsarias y a un ataque pirático impregnaba la mentalidad colectiva de los habitantes de la costa y condicionaba la acción de los mercaderes en los años finales de la Edad Media. Cuando a comienzos del siglo XVI se inicie el apogeo de la piratería argelina, inglesa y flamenca la flota castellano-aragonesa llevaba varios siglos sufriendo el acoso de regiones y hombres más desfavorecidos debido a un hecho indudable: la progresiva pujanza del comercio exterior español amplía los intereses marítimos lo que sin duda suscita todo tipo de problemas comerciales con otras potencias mercantiles. Y es que, como reconocen todos los historiadores, si no hay comercio marítimo no hay corso ni piratería.

[26] ibid., Actas Capitulares, 8-VI-1526, fol. 255.

[27] ibid., Actas Capitulares, 5-VIII-1527, fol. 302.

Historical-Linguistic Reliability of Muqaddasī's Information on Types of Ships

Dionisius A. Agius
University of Leeds

INTRODUCTION

1.0

Two principal sources exist for the identification of medieval Muslim ship-types. The first consists of a scattered collection of references by Muslim geographers, travellers and historians and the second is navigational literature. Neither of them affords a wholly reliable basis for reconstruction of the authentic types of ships that were used in the Islamic provinces and the neighbouring territories. One unique contribution in this field is that of Muqaddasī (d. 378/988-9) who supplies a list of thirty-six types of ships and boats which he claims to have existed in his times.[1] How far is this claim true?

Abū cAbd Allāh al-Bashshārī, better known as al-Muqaddasī (or al Maqdisī) wrote a geographical work, *Aḥsan al-Taqāsīm fī*

[1] Muḥammad b. Aḥmad al-Muqaddasī, *Aḥsan al-Taqāsīm fī Macrifat al-Aqālīm*, ed. M. J. de Goeje, Bibliotheca Geographorum Arabicorum, 8 vols. (Leiden, 1906; first edited 1877), 3:31-2.

Maᶜrifat al-Aqālīm designed for the travellers and the merchants, the professionals and the commoners. In it, he laid down the foundations of a scientific method for a human geography, written in an elegant style, often in rhymed prose, and containing some fables for their popular appeal. It is a good example of an *adab* (polite literature) work with the aim to instruct and entertain.

Personal experience in fact-finding was fundamental for Muqaddasī and it formed the basis of his work.[2] His experiences in travelling and collecting information over a period of twenty years are remarkable.

> I could not write anything until I had travelled through the whole kingdom and visited the territories of Islam ... I had been present at the assemblies of narrators of stories and public preachers ... and associated with people of all classes, paying careful attention to the particulars of this science until I came to have a good grasp of it. I examined likewise into the condition of climate and water. In doing this, I had to spend a great deal of money and put in much labour.[3]

This statement emphasises the fact that Muqaddasī did not compile his material haphazardly, nor construct it in any random fashion. Of all his experiences, what instigated my curiosity was his inquiry into seamanship:

> I was thrown in to the company of men - captains, pilots, ... agents and merchants, - who, bred and born upon it, possessed the clearest and fullest knowledge of this sea, its anchorages, its winds and its islands. I plied them with questions

[2] ibid., 3:43.

[3] ibid., 3:2-3.

> concerning its position, physical peculiarities and its limits. I have also seen in their possession sailing directories (*dafātir*) which they constantly study and follow with implicit confidence.[4]

One would have expected that this report would be followed by some nautical information; no such data exist and therefore questions regarding nautical skills are lacking, nor do we have information on ship-building. The nomenclature of names of types of ships or boats was another disappointment insofar as he does not give any description of the types he lists. He proposes to investigate them thoroughly according to each clime, but in fact he does not discuss these terms in their relevant usage in any part of the book. Reconstructing, therefore, the history of Muqaddasī's nomenclature becomes an extremely difficult exercise.

The starting point of the present inquiry into the classification of ships and boats is based on the premise that Muqaddasī would not have mentioned one type of ship or boat had it not been of common usage in his time.[5] This paper, therefore, attempts to look at the names of ship-types supplied by Muqaddasī comparing, historically and linguistically, information on their usage with data found in contemporary works of Muslim geographers, travellers or historians and wherever possible to establish the geographical area in which such ships or boats were in use.[6]

[4] ibid., 3:10-11; George Fadlo Hourani, *Arab Seafaring in the Indian Ocean in Ancient and Early Medieval Times* (Beirut, 1963), p. 107.

[5] The term used by him is *ta^cāruf*, an approach which he applied to religious arguments, according to the Ḥanafite school of thought: Muqaddasī, *Aḥsan al-Taqāsīm fī Ma^crifat al-Aqālīm*, partially trans. André Miquel (Damascus, 1963), p. 163/11-2.

[6] For classification on the etymology of these terms I generally relied on M. de Goeje's *Indices, Glossarium ed addenda et emendanda*, Bibliotheca Geographorum Arabicorum, 8 vols. (Leiden, 1879), 4, the *Annales. Introductio,*

2.0

Muqaddasī was the last of the geographers who constituted the Classical School with ideas based on metaphysics and geometry, the significant contribution of which was a set of twenty maps outlining the world. Al-Balkhī (d. [?] 322/934) was the originator of these maps but his work *Ṣūrat al-Aqālīm* was lost. His followers Iṣṭakhrī (d. c. 350/961), Ibn Ḥawqal (d. c. 380/990) and Muqaddasī claimed that they had consulted his work. Both Ibn Ḥawqal and Muqaddasī broke new ground in looking at the science of geography not merely from a physical point of view but also including a socio-economic description of the regions they visited, thus turning this science into both a physical and human geography.

Muqaddasī's topographical information was applied with a more methodical, systematic and scientific approach than his predecessors of the Classical School. The reliability of his work was due to his method of collecting data from libraries, eminent scholars and ordinary people, both of good judgement. He scrutinised the works of learned men through a chain of authorities (*isnād*) and acknowledged them whenever he cited them. He admitted that his work was not devoid of any error but he was confident that in the course of his travels he recorded what he witnessed and experienced and took pains to note what the tradition, custom and usage was in the particular region he described.

2.1

A small but unique section of Muqaddasī's work was an inventory of material-cultural terms used by the people of different climes.[7] In itself the list is lengthy, containing several categories of cultural

glossarium, addenda et emendanda (Leiden, 1901) and other glossaries which throw light on difficult passages.

[7] Muqaddasī, 3:30-2.

terms, such as household furniture, kitchen utensils, textiles, weights and measures, inns and markets, and cultivated plants. For ships and boats, he has a list of thirty-six types used, apparently, in ᶜIrāq, the Arabian/Persian Gulf, the Indian Ocean and the Mediterranean: *barᶜānī, barka, bīrajh, burākiyya, burma, dūnij, ḥamāma, ᶜirdās, jāsūs, jabaliyya, kārwāniyya, khayṭiyya, makkiyya, malqūṭa, markab, miᶜbar, musabbaḥiyya, muthallatha, qārib, raqqiyya, safīna, shabūq, shadhā, shalandī, shamūṭ, shankūliyya, shīnī, sūqiyya, talawwā, ṭayyār, ṭayra, wāsṭiyya, walajiyya, zabzab, zabarbādhiyya, zawraq* (numerically itemised in the chart at the end of the article). Some of these terms were listed a century later by Abū l-Qāsim al-Baghdādī (fl. c. fifth/eleventh century),[8] perhaps independently or simply copied from what Muqaddasī had earlier recorded. Al-Azdī, writing about al-Baghdādī, pointed out that all the types of ships but one mentioned by Muqaddasī were used in ᶜIrāq.[9]

If this statement is correct it would be surprising to find that *shīnīs* and *shalandīs*, both Mediterranean types, were sailing in ᶜIrāq. Some of Muqaddasī's names of ship-types were discussed in the light of medieval sources by Kindermann in his dissertation *"Schiff" im Arabischen Untersuchung über Vorkommen und Bedeutung der Termini* (Bonn, 1934) though little attempt was made to analyse the obscurer types. An insight into medieval warships was covered by A. M. Fahmy's study on *Muslim Sea-Power in the Eastern Mediterranean from the Seventh to the Tenth century AD* (Cairo, 1966). But the early history of Muslim navigation is still

[8] Abū l-Muṭahhar Muḥammad b. Aḥmad al-Azdī, *Ḥikāyat Abī l-Qāsim al-Baghdādī (Abulḳāsim ein bagdâder Sittenbild),* ed. A. Mez (Heidelberg, 1902), p. 107.

[9] ibid.

vague and questions as to size, weight, shape and function of these ships are mere guess-work.

3.0

We know from Muqaddasī's nautical experience that his knowledge on ships was not restricted to ᶜIrāq.[10] He noted places of danger with reefs such as Jubaylān, at the entrance of the Suez Canal. Fārān, where the Gulf of ᶜAqaba and the Red Sea meet and the winds from Egypt and Syria blow in opposite directions. Ships can sail only when the winds calm down. At the port of Ḥawrā', on the North Arabian coast, the rocks are in abundance. The old port of Jār on the west of Madīna has perilous reefs which can wreck ships. Between Jār and Jābir on the west coast of Arabia lies the Island of Ṣilāb which strikes terror in all passing ships. Further catastrophes are mentioned of ships sailing by Jābir, Kamarān and Mandam to the south of the Red Sea on the Arabian coast. In the Arabian Sea wrecks are said to be frequent between ᶜAdan and ᶜUmān.[11]

The physical conditions of the province of ᶜIrāq changed during the first centuries (second-third/eighth-ninth) of the ᶜAbbāsid caliphate. One fact mentioned by Muslim geographers was the existence of the "Great Swamp", covering an area of 50 miles across and some 200 miles in length, which came down to Baṣra and the consequent change in the courses of both Euphrates and Tigris. According to the historian Balādhuri (d. 279/892-3), the beginnings of the swamp dated as far back as during the reign of Qubādh (end of fifth century AD), the Sassānid king.[12] Irrigation

[10] Muqaddasī, 3:10, 15.

[11] ibid.

[12] Aḥmad b. Yaḥyā l-Balādhurī, *Kitāb Futūḥ al-Buldān*, ed. M. de Goeje (Leiden, 1866), p. 292; Yāqūt b. ᶜAbd Allāh al-Rūmī, *Kitāb Muᶜjam al-Buldān*, ed. F. Wüstenfeld, 6 vols. (Leipzig, 1866-1870), 1:669.

canals were in abundance on the Tigris from one hundred miles below Baghdād down to sixty miles below Wāsiṭ. As navigation was possible down through a line of lagoons connected by open channels, cargo-boats sailed from Baghdād to Baṣra with ease.

The system of canalisation inherited by the Arabs after conquering the Persians was of great importance and the distribution of water supply was the chief factor for the fertility of ^{c}Irāq. One would question, however, Ibn Ḥawqal's claim that in the Baṣra district there were over one hundred thousand canals and that twenty thousand of these were navigable for boats.[13] The ideal way to travel from Baghdād to Baṣra was by boat down the Tigris river into the Great Swamp through which boats sailed into Baṣra and eventually the open sea.[14] Several towns on the rivers had bridges of boats or skiffs, such as at Ḥilla on the pilgrim route from Baṣra to Kūfa on the eastern bank of the Euphrates,[15] at Nahrawān on the route from Baghdād to Khurāsān and Zawāriq on the Kūfa road.[16]

4.0

Muqaddasī's list of ships and boats is perhaps a unique record in any geographical, travel or historical account; his decision to mention types of sea craft of common usage (on the criterion of *ta^{c}āruf*) offers good credentials for the authenticity of the

[13] Abū l-Qāsim Ibn Ḥawqal, *Kitāb al-Masālik wa l-Mamālik*, ed. M. de Goeje, Bibliotheca Geographorum Arabicorum, 8 vols. (Leiden, 1873), 2:159-60.

[14] Aḥmad b. Abī Ya^{c}qūb b. Wādiḥ al-Ya^{c}qūbī, *Kitāb al Buldān*, ed. M. de Goeje, Bibliotheca Geographorum Arabicorum, 8 vols. (Leiden, 1892), 7:320.

[15] Yāqūt, 2:322; 3:861, 4:123; Abū Isḥāq Ibrāhīm b. Muḥammad al-Iṣṭakhrī, *Kitāb al-Masālik wa l-Mamālik*, Bibliotheca Geographorum Arabicorum, 8 vols. (Leiden, 1870), 1:85-6; Ibn Ḥawqal, 2:166, 168; Ya^{c}qūbī, 7:309.

[16] Ibn Ḥawqal, 2:167.

information. But several questions arise from this inventory as to changes in form and meaning of terms. To what influences was the meaning subjected during its development? How many of these words can be listed as Arabic or non-Arabic in origin? What role would those that are identified as non-Arabic play when they become arabicised? Arabic, as Kindermann rightly pointed out, has an astonishing capacity for absorbing foreign words into the language so as to make them almost unidentifiable, making any attempt at etymology all the more difficult.[17] The answers to these questions cannot be found only on the linguistic level. Historically and technically, the researcher is faced with other problems as to which terms listed by Muqaddasī are synonymous; which of them are boats, ocean-faring ships, galleys etc. How widespread were they in the Islamic provinces, let alone the non-Islamic world, and in exactly which waters did they sail?

An attempt is made here to identify the ships by placing each term, linguistically and historically, in the context of both Muqaddasī's time and the credibility of his experience. The chart at the end of this article illustrates the type, place and period of the occurrence of the term followed by the source of reference; the last two columns include the origin, synonymy and variation of the term in question. Those asterisked are purely guess work.

4.1

Broadly describing ships in Muqaddasī's time we have two categories: (a) the sewn type, a technique used until fairly recently; these are referred to as *khayṭiyya*, a generic term.[18] The *marākib*

[17] Hans Kindermann, *"Schiff" im Arabischen Untersuchung über Vorkommen und Bedeutung der Termini* (Bonn, 1934), p. 101.

[18] Muqaddasī, 3:32.

khayṭiyya (sewn ships),[19] were stitched together with coconut cord by the shell-first method (i.e. the hull first then the ribs inserted later), a technique applied to the Greek galley, (b) the nail type were those ships that were nailed together with ribs first and then had the planks attached to them, a technique called the skeleton method. It is difficult to ascertain which of Muqaddasī's ships were built using either technique, though it is assumed that the *marākib khayṭiyya*, i.e. *dūnij, sha(n)būq, shadhā* adopted the first method while the *shīnīs, shalandīs, musa(ṭṭ)aḥiyya, sūqiyya* were constructed by the second method. Several arguments as to which method applied was the strongest are found among Masᶜūdī (d. 345/956-7), Idrīsī (d. 561/1165-6), Ibn Jubayr (d. 614/1217-8), Ibn Baṭṭūṭa (d. 779/1377-8) and Marco Polo (d. 1323); none of their arguments seems to hold water and Hourani is of the opinion that for economic reasons "iron-fastening was more expensive than stitching, the raw material for which was at hand".[20] The process of mining, smelting and manufacturing the nails in regions of India, Iran and Sudan was on a much smaller scale and therefore expensive compared to in the Mediterranean area. Interestingly enough, the sewn hulls, from what Ibn Jubayr and Ibn Baṭṭūṭa observed, were flexible, and the chances of getting wrecked by high waves were slimmer than for nailed ships.

4.2

Of the list *ᶜirdās, shamūṭ* and *zabarbādhiyya* are of obscure origin. *Burākiyya* is possibly "a large rowing boat", a variant of *barka* "a small boat", both of which could be related to the post-classical Latin term *barca* (< Gr βᾶρις "a small Egyptian boat"). Only *barka*

[19] Yaᶜqūbī, 7:390.

[20] Hourani, p. 96.

is noted by Iṣṭakhrī[21] and appears to be similar to *zawraq* (< [?] Aram or [?] Per) "a boat, skiff, barque"[22] or *dūnij* (< Per *dūnī* "long swift vessel" < Hind *dingi/ dengī/ dongī* "small boat") "barque, skiff, sloop, canoe, coastal boat".[23] One assumes that *jabaliyya* and *wāsṭiyya* are *nisbas* probably for transport ships named after the town they originated from, i.e. Jabala, a north west Syrian town in the Mediterranean, and the ᶜIrāqī town Wāsiṭ on the Tigris river, while *makkiyya* could be a ship for the transport of pilgrims to Makka, as Kindermann understands it.[24]

4.3

A few ship-types have Greek connections and it is difficult to establish geographically where some were located, e.g. *qārib* (< Gr κάραβος, κάραβιον) "an escort boat, ferry boat, coastal boat" is mentioned by Maqrīzī (d. 845/1441-2) in his account around the year 53/673 and several times by Ibn Baṭṭūṭa, but much later during the eighth/fourteenth century.[25] The word *shabūq* "a small boat" is possibly *sanbūk/q, sanbuq, ṣanbuq* or *sunbūq* (either < Gr

[21] Iṣṭakhrī, 1:139.

[22] Muqaddasī, 3:31; Ibn Ḥawqal, 2:159; Abū Jaᶜfar Muḥammad b. Jarīr al-Ṭabarī, *Ta'rīkh al-Rusul wa l-Mulūk*, eds. M. de Goeje *et al.*, 15 vols. (Beirut, 1965; first published Leiden 1879-1901), 3:1168, 2074; Iṣṭakhrī, 1:80; Kindermann, p. 37.

[23] Muqaddasī, 3:32; De Goeje, 4:240; Yāqūt, 4:216; Abū ᶜAbd Allāh Muḥammad al-Sharīf al-Idrīsī, *Description de l'Afrique et de l'Espagne*, ed. M. de Goeje (Leiden, 1866) 1:374; Kindermann, p. 28.

[24] Kindermann, p. 103.

[25] Aḥmad b. ᶜAlī l-Maqrīzī, *Khiṭaṭ*, 2 vols. (Būlāq, 1270 AH), 2:180; Abū ᶜAbd Allāh Muḥammad Ibn Baṭṭūṭa, *Riḥla or Tuḥfat al-Nuzzār fī Gharā'ib al-Amṣār wa ᶜAjā'ib al-Asfār. Les Voyages d'Ibn Batoutah*, ed. and trans. C. Defémery and B. R. Sanguinetti, 4 vols. (Paris, 1853-1859), 2:181, 241, 244, 420, 431; 3:1, 154; 4:119, 287.

σαμβύχη or most probably Per *sunbuk* or Skt *çambūka*), a common ship and synonymous to *zawraq*, quoted by Maqrīzī in the year 264/877 and Rāmhurmuzī (fl. c. fourth/tenth century) found in the Arabian/Persian Gulf, the Red Sea and the Arabian Sea.[26]

4.4

Other types of transport are possibly *shankūliyya* (< [?] Per *shankūl* "elephant's trunk"), *malqūṭa* (Ar. for *laqaṭa* "to collect, pick up from the ground") and *ḥamāma*, the latter mentioned by Maqrīzī.[27] Two odd terms are the *muthallatha* (Ar *muthallath* "triangular") implying a lateen-rigged boat on a single mast and *talawwā* (< [?]), a small boat or an escort boat like the *qārib*. Of particular interest is the *barᶜānī* (< [?] Hind *be'ra* "large boat, raft") stitched together in reed bundles as the *burma*, synonymous with *quffa* made of reeds. *Burma* in Arabic is a kitchen receptacle term meaning "jug, vessel or pot" with cognates in Syriac *būrmā*/ *burmtha* "a store jar", Akkadian *burmāḫu* "container" and ultimately traced to Sumerian *burmaḫ*.[28] It seems that the *burma* was a round-shaped boat made of reed and like the *quffa* had rowers sitting in pairs in opposite directions. All of these types were used on the canals and rivers of ᶜIrāq. One suspects that the *walajiyya*, as recorded by Muqaddasī, may be a variant of the present Bahraini *wāriyya* (/j/ is phonetically /r/ and the liquid /l/ is assimilated to /r/), a canoe or a coaster used

[26] Maqrīzī, 2:180; Buzurg b. Shahriyār al-Rāmhurmuzī, *Kitāb ᶜAjā'ib al-Hind (Le livre des merveilles de l'Inde)*, ed. P. A. van der Lith and trans. L. M. Devic (Leiden, 1883-1886), p. 190.

[27] Maqrīzī, 2:180.

[28] Dionisius A. Agius, *Arabic Literary Works as a Source of Documentation for Technical Terms of the Material Culture*, Islamkundliche Untersuchungen, Band 98 (Berlin, 1984), p. 135.

for fishing. Similar to the *wāriyya* is the Emirati or Omani *shāsha*, a beach boat (see Plate One).

4.5

In his *Ta'rīkh*, Ṭabarī (d. 310/922-3), who was a contemporary of Muqaddasī, was unusually informative on ships and boats. Of Persian origin, he lived and worked in Baghdād. He made use of all the sources available in his time and divided his material chronologically according to caliphs' reigns. Two important events of note are the ᶜAbbāsid upheaval (247-256/861-870) and the Zanj movement and its uprising (255-270/869-883). Ṭabarī's information on their military expeditions is very detailed and mention of war vessels is of particular interest. A typical warship *bīrajh* is mentioned during the ᶜAbbāsid caliphal confrontation against the Turks in 215/865.[29] One recalls that the introduction of Turks brought by Muᶜtaṣim (218-227/833-842) from central Asia as soldiers and officers marked a new event in ᶜAbbāsid history. They were recruited in their thousands and their arrival was the beginning of military uprisings and political intrigues in the palace, rendering the power of the caliphs precarious.[30] *Bīrajh* is understood to be a "pirate ship",[31] a variant of *bārija* (pl. *bawārij*), probably of Sanskrit origin. It is conventionally, but probably wrongly related to the Arabic root /b.r.j/ "to be fortified with towers".[32] Muqaddasī uses the term *bawārij* (no singular given) in a reference on 'Usqūṭra

[29] Ṭabarī, 3:1582.

[30] Dionisius A. Agius, "A selfish pursuit in a slave uprising of third/ninth century Iraq", *Slavery and Abolition* 4, i (1983), 8.

[31] Balādhurī, p. 435; Abū l-Hasan ᶜAlī b. al-Ḥusayn al-Masᶜūdī, *Kitāb al-Tanbīh wa l-Ishrāf*, ed. M. de Goeje, Bibliotheca Geographorum Arabicorum, 8 vols. (Leiden, 1894), 8:55; Yāqūt , 3:102.

[32] Agius (1984), pp. 208-9.

(Soqotra); he reports that the island is "a *sadd* for the *bawārij* of which sailing-ships were afraid", in the context that Soqotra may have been a barrier against pirate ships or warships.[33]

In connection with the Zanj revolution Ṭabarī records *shadhā* (pl. *shadhāwāt/ shadhā'āt*) "a light war vessel" (< Gr σχεδία or [?] Aram).[34] A common term in the accounts of Ṭabarī, it is often listed with *sumayriyyāt* (< [?]) between the years 255/819 to 270/884.[35] In one instance a reference is made to *al-shadhā(wāt) al-jannābiyyāt*, specifically war vessels imported from Jannāba on the north of the Iranian coast.[36] Also included in his accounts is *safīna*[37] (< Gr σαγήνη or Aram *cephîynâh* "sea-going vessel" < Akk *sapī[a]tu*) which was used to signify "transport ship" for cavalry, troops, weapons and equipment of war.[38]

One warship not recorded by Ṭabarī is *ṭayyār* (pl. *ṭayyārāt* from Ar *ṭāra* "to fly") localised in and around Baghdād and Baṣra; *ṭayyārāt* are mentioned from 207/822 to 315/927 on different events,[39] one of which is during the Carmathians' threat on Baghdād. The caliphal troops crossed the Euphrates on *ṭayyārāt* in 315/927.[40] The war fleet included *zabāzib* (s. *zabzab* < [?] Aram)

[33] ibid., p. 209.

[34] Siegmund Fraenkel, *Die Aramäischen Fremdwörter im Arabischen* (Hildesheim, 1962; first published Leiden, 1886), p. 220.

[35] Ṭabarī, 3:1948-49, 1961, 1965-66.

[36] ibid., 3:1844.

[37] ibid., 3:1550, 1844, 1965, 1968.

[38] ibid., 3:1965, 1968, 2074.

[39] Yāqūt, 3:888; ᶜArīb b. Saᶜd al-Qurṭubī, *Ṣilat Ta'rīkh al-Ṭabarī. Tabari continuatus*, ed. M. de Goeje (Leiden, 1897), p. 37.

[40] ᶜArīb, p. 133.

which were considered to be small or large warships[41] and *sumayriyyāt* and *shadhāwāt*.[42]

Maᶜābir (s. *miᶜbar* from Ar "to cross over") "cargo or transport ships" are mentioned alongside with *shadhāwāt* on the Tigris canals;[43] they were used to ferry troops, infantry and high-ranking officers during the years 258/872, 267/880, 269/882-3 of the Zanj uprising.[44] *Zawraq* "a small vessel, skiff, barque" was frequently mentioned with *jarībiyyāt* "flat-bottomed vessels" in connection with the Zanj in Baṣra in 255/869, 256/870 and 269/882-3.[45] Both vessels are indispensable on the ᶜIrāqī rivers and canals; as a matter of fact Iṣṭakhrī and Ibn Ḥawqal saw countless *zawraqs* on the canals of Baṣra.[46] One peculiar term recorded along with *shadhāwāt*, *sumayriyyāt* is *raqqiyyāt* to ferry horses across. Kindermann associates the word with Raqqa, a north Syrian town on the Tigris,[47] probably fabricated there.

The nomenclature of Ṭabari's ship terms illustrate clearly the function of *bīrajh* (*bārija*) and *shadhā* as warships, *safīna*, *miᶜbar*, and *raqqiyya* as cargo or transport ships and *zawraq* as a small boat ferrying people or even used, though it is not specifically stated, for reconnaissance purposes as the names *jāsūs* (< Aram *gasosā* "spy") and *kārwāniyya* (< Per/ Tur *qarāwul* "scout" or Rom (Port) *caravel*

[41] Yāqūt, 3:888.

[42] Masᶜūdī, *Murūj al-Dhahab wa Maᶜādin al-Jawhar. Les prairies d'or*, ed. and trans. C. Barbier de Meynard and Pavet de Courteille, 9 vols. (Paris, 1861-1877), 8:345.

[43] Ṭabarī, 3:1871, 1948, 1961, 1968.

[44] ibid., 3:1871, 1948.

[45] ibid., 3:1836, 2074; Kindermann, p. 17.

[46] Iṣṭakhrī, 1:80; Ibn Ḥawqal, 2:159.

[47] Kindermann, p. 32.

"trading vessel; exploration vessel") given by Muqaddasī may suggest.[48]

4.6

One geographical area covered by Muqaddasī was Baḥr al-Rūm (the Mediterranean Sea), though he seems more familiar with the coastal towns of Shām (the Greater Syria).[49] One generic term for ship is *markab* (pl. *marākib* from Ar *rakiba* "to travel, board") like *safīna*. The understanding of this term as a merchant or transport ship may be more accurate in Muqaddasī's times though the possibility of it being a galley is noted by Ibn Jubayr in 581/1185 alongside with *jafn* (< [?]) and *ṭarīda* (< Gr ταρίτα), both war galleys.[50]

We have no knowledge of how Muslim warships were constructed in the Mediterranean; it is safe to assume that ship-building techniques were learnt by the Arabs from the conquered people, the Byzantines. Some modifications may have been made but it seems that Muslim warships were similar to Byzantine ones and not technically inferior.[51] Interestingly enough Ibn Ḥawqal, when writing about *shalandī* (pl. *shalandiyyāt* < Gr χελάνδιον, Lat *celandra/ celandria/ celandrium*), refers to it as a Byzantine warship not a Muslim one.[52] On the siege of Damietta in 238/852-3 Ṭabarī calls the warships specifically *al-sha(r)andiyyāt al-ḥarbiyya*

[48] Muqaddasī, 3:31; Kindermann, pp. 15, 88.

[49] Muqaddasī, 3:151-92.

[50] Abū l-Ḥasan Muḥammad Ibn Jubayr, *Riḥla. The Travels of Ibn Jubayr*, ed. W. Wright and revised M. J. de Goeje, E. J. W. Gibb Memorial Series, Volume 5 (Leiden: E. J. Brill, 1907; first edition 1852), p. 337.

[51] John H. Pryor, *Geography, Technology and War. Studies in the Maritime History of the Mediterranean, 649-1571* (Cambridge, 1992; first published 1988), p. 62.

[52] Ibn Ḥawqal, 2:132.

(note scriptorial error /r/ for /l/) meaning "war *shalandīs*", which were used to transport troops.[53] In his *Al-Kāmil fī l-Ta'rīkh*, Ibn al-Athīr (d. 630/1232-3) mentions these vessels in the siege of Sicily in 244/858-9.[54] There is no indication as to whether these warships had two or three banks such as the Greek *biremes* and the *triremes*. In any case this method of classification is not totally correct because some Greek galleys had up to seventeen banks. Some other method must have existed but no written records of the method is available.

One other galley confused by Muslim medieval authors was the *shīnī* (pl. *shawānī* < [?] Per [*shānā* "swimming"] or [?] Gr); it is a common term in the accounts of the Crusade period.[55] Idrīsī indicates some varying degree of difference between *ḥarābā* (Ar *ḥarb* "war") "warships" and *shawānī* "galleys".[56] Nothing is known about the vessel *sūqiyya* which may be related to Greek σαγήνη, but most unlikely to Arabic *sūq* "market", as Kindermann indicated.[57] Similar to *shīnī* is the *musaṭṭaḥ* and Muqaddasī's term *musabbaḥiyya*[58] is very probably a scriptorial error for *musa(ṭṭ)aḥiyya*, where the diacritical dot for /b/ was missing and edited by the copyist to mark the consonant /t/ with two dots instead.

[53] Ṭabarī, 3:1417-8.

[54] ᶜIzz al-Dīn Abū l-Ḥusayn ᶜAlī b. Abī l-Karam Ibn al-Athīr, *Al-Kāmil fī l-Ta'rīkh*, 12 vols. (Beirut, 1965; first published Leiden, 1862-1876), 7:41-2.

[55] Ibn Ḥawqal, 2:132; Muqaddasī, 3:177; Maqrīzī, 1:351; Ibn al-Athīr, 8:70.

[56] Idrīsī, p. 112.

[57] Kindermann, p. 45.

[58] Muqaddasī, 3:32.

CONCLUSION

5.0

A general weakness of the medieval accounts lies in their brevity, mutual dependence and repetition and their tendency to exaggeration. Muqaddasī offers no explanation with the word-list, unique as it stands in the history of medieval Muslim types of ships and boats. His scientific approach based on consultation with eminent scholars and libraries, his careful observation and his interviewing of professional and non-professional people alike in several regions of the Islamic caliphate over a period of twenty years, ranks him as one of the most reliable geographers and travellers of the period. The long inventory of material-cultural terms used by people of different climes is in itself a testimony to his keen observation in terms of language and society. Unfortunately, Muqaddasī fails to analyse the terms semantically and historically. Equally frustrating is the fact that medieval lexicographers found it difficult to analyse and describe material-cultural terms. The only existing pure language for them was that which they perceived as "Classical Arabic". Meanings of names of types of ships and boats were not defined, since they held that such words were *ma^{c}rūf* "well known" in the language among the commoners and the professionals. Furthermore, lexicographers omitted loan-words (in the case of Muqaddasī's list of ship-types, two-thirds) as they were not considered "pure" Arabic. Muqaddasī, though an *adīb*, did not belong to the circles of philologists; he collected data from the professionals of all walks of life but also relied on the commoners where necessary and consequently his contact with them was looked down upon by the purists of the language who regarded dialectal words as dubious and contaminated, in particular, those that were compiled from the coastal towns which were peopled by non-Arabs. In this respect, for the modern researcher, Muqaddasī offers a unique list of terms most of which were not recorded in medieval lexica and it is only by consulting other geographical, travel and historical accounts that we can authenticate the existence of the ships and boats of his time.

It is obviously illusory for the student of maritime history to identify meanings and concepts with the present ones. On one hand medieval lexicographers went in circles searching for what the root or form meant, giving no synchronic, and for that matter diachronic, meaning of the word concerned; while on the other hand authors, such as geographers, travellers and historians, referred to ships and boats *en passant* with little or no comments at all. What the researcher is looking for is what meaning did the name of the type of ship or boat convey in the context of the speakers of the time. Language and culture, for Muqaddasī, were dynamic; he recognised this dynamism because he looked at geography as a "human" living science where language played an inseparable role. For him, language evolved with society and with a change of environment and his intention was to investigate the classification of ships according to each clime. This he never did or if he did the manuscript was lost.

Our conclusions on the classification of the types of ships listed by Muqaddasī are drawn from information given by Ṭabarī, Iṣṭakhrī, and Ibn Ḥawqal and the fact that the majority of the fourth/tenth-century ships and boats mentioned by Muqaddasī are related to ᶜIrāq. Only a few of these ships are of Arabic origin, i.e. *markab*, *miᶜbar*, *musa(ṭṭ)aḥiyya*, *muthallatha*, *ṭayyār*, *ṭayra*; some have apparently an underlying layer of the long established Aramaic language of ᶜIrāq, i.e. *jāsūs, khayṭiyya, zabzab, zawraq* or earlier

Semitic languages such as *burma, shadhā and safīna*. Others have seemingly a Persian, Hindi or Sanskrit origin, i.e. *bar*ᶜ*ānī, bīrajh, dūnij, sha(n)būq, shankūliyya*, and Greek or Latin, e.g. *barka, burākiyya, kārwāniyya, qārib, sha(n)būq, shadhā, shalandī, shīnī and sūqiyya*.

It is possible to identify the size and function of some ships. We have classified them, as far as it was possible, under three general categories: (a) ferry and transport, (b) warships, (c) boats, canoes, skiffs, reed boats and rafts (see appendix). It appeared quite impossible to determine precisely the meaning of any single form as such, but it has been possible to determine the limits of the self-contained structural-semantic system by which the analysis was conducted. Some of the findings, however, remain hypothetical.

A possible remnant of the *walajiyya* is the *shāsha*, a beach boat that could not have changed since Muqaddasī's times; made solely of date sticks bound together with coir, and pointed at the stern as well as the bow. (Photograph: fisherman with *shāsha* at Khorfakkan, United Arab Emirates, April 1996, D. A. Agius).

name	type	place	period	source	origin	comments
1 *bar^{c}ānī*	* large boat	^{c}Irāq		Mq 3: 32; Kd 6	Hind *be'ra* "large boat; raft"	ps. variant of *bireme* "galley"
2 *barka*	small boat	Mediterr-anean		Mq 3: 32; Goe 4: 188; Ist 1: 139; Kd 3	Lat *barca*; Gr βᾶρις "a small Egyptian row-boat"	cf. *zawraq*
3 *bīrajh*	pirate ship; war vessel	Arabian/ Persian Gulf; Arabian Sea; Indian Ocean	251/865 (Tab)	Mq 3: 14, 32; Bal 435; Mas (Tan) 8: 55; Yaq 3: 102; Tab 3: 1582; Kd 3	Skt (?)	ref. *marākib al-hind*; ps. *bīraja*/ *bārija*
4 *burākiyya*	* large rowing boat	Mediterr-anean		Mq 3: 31; Kd 4	Lat *barca*	ps. variant of *barka*
5 *burma*	* rowing/ paddling boat	^{c}Irāq		Mq 3: 32; Kd 7	Syr *būrmā* "store jar"; *burmtha*; Akk *burmāhu* "contain-er"; Sum *burmah*	syn. *quffa* "a reed basket-shaped boat"

6 *dūnij*	barque; skiff; canoe; coastal boat; life boat	^{c}Irāq; Arabian/ Persian Gulf; Indian Ocean		Mq 3: 32; Goe 4: 240; Yaq 4: 216; Id 1: 374; Kd 28	Per *dūnī* "long swift vessel; Ur *do'ngā*/ *do'ngi* "small boat"; Hind *dingi*/ *dengī*/ *dongī* "small boat"; Tam *thoṇī* "sailing vessel"; Skt *drona* "trough"	cf. *qārib;* ps. Hind *dingi* (/g/ > /c/ > /j/)
7 *ḥamāma*	*transport ship		264/877 (Maq)	Mq 3: 32; Maq 2: 180; Kd 24		ps. *ḥammāla*
8 ^{c}*irdās*	(?)			Mq 3: 31; Kd 64		
9 *jāsūs*	* reconnaissance ship			Mq 3: 31; Goe 4: 231; Kd 15	Aram *gasosā* "spy"	
10 *jabaliyya*	* ferry boat	Mediterranean		Mq 3: 32; Goe 4: 202; Mas (Mur) I: 282; Kd 15		nisba Jabala (Syrian coastal town)
11 *kārwāniyya*	* reconnaissance ship	Mediterranean		Mq 3: 31; Goe 4: 337; Kd 88	Per/Tur *qarāwul* "scout"	ps. Rom (Port) *caravela* "trading vessel; exploration boat"

12 *khayṭiyya*	ocean-faring boat	Arabian/ Persian Gulf; Indian Ocean; China		Mq 3: 32; Goe 4: 231; IJ 69; Ya 7: 390; Kd 26	Aram (?)	generic term ref. *marākib khayṭiyya*
13 *makkiyya*	* ferry boat	ᶜIrāq		Mq 3: 32; Goe 4: 355; Kd 103		nisba Makka
14 *malqūṭa*	* ferry/ cargo boat	ᶜIrāq		Mq 3: 32; Goe 4: 349; Kd 104		participial form laqaṭa "to collect, pick up from the ground"
15 *markab*	cargo ship; galley	Mediterr-anean		Mq 3: 32; IJ 337; Kd 95-6		mīmī term, rakiba "to board; travel"; generic term; syn. *safīna* cf. *jafn*; *ṭarīda*
16 *miᶜbar*	ferry boat; transport / cargo boat; pontoon	ᶜIrāq	258-69/ 872-83 (Tab)	Mq 3: 32; Goe 4: 295; Tab 3: 1871, 1948, 1961, 1968, 2001, 2074; Kd 102		mīmī term ᶜabara "to cross"; cf. *shadhā*, *sumayriyya*; *safīna*
17 *musabba-ḥiyya*	war galley	Mediterr-anean		Mq 3: 32; Kd 98		ps. *musaṭṭa-ḥiyya*; syn. *shīnī*, *ghurāb*
18 *muthallatha*	* trading vessel			Mq 3: 31; Kd 94		muthallath "triangular" (lateen-rigged on a single mast)

19 *qārib*	escort boat; auxiliary boat; small ship; pontoon; ferry boat; coastal boat	Mediterr-anean; Arabian/ Persian Gulf	53/673 (Maq)	Mq III: 32; Maq II: 180, 190; Id 193; IB II: 181, 241, 244, 420, 431; III: 1, 154; IV: 119, 287; Kd 76-7	Gr κάραβος/ κάραβιο ν "a small boat"	ref. *qawārib al-khidma* cf. *ḥamāma*
20 *raqqiyya*	* ferry boat	Syria; ᶜIrāq	269/882 (Tab)	Mq 3: 31; Tab 3: 2074; Kd 32		<u>nisba</u> Raqqa (N.E. Syria) cf. *shadhāwāt*; *sumayriyyāt; jarībiyyāt*
21 *safīna*	transport ship; ocean-going ship; pontoon	ᶜIrāq; Mediterr-anean; Arabian/ Persian Gulf	pre-Islamic (Tab); 251/865; 257-267/870-880 (Tab)	Mq 3: 31; Tab 3: 1550, 1844, 1965, 1968; IJ 337; Kd 40	Gr (?) σαγήνη; Syr/ Aram/ Heb *cᵉphîy-nâh* "sea-going vessel" Akk *sapīn-(a)tu*	generic term; syn. *markab*
22 *shabūq*	small boat	Red Sea; Arabian Sea; Arabian/ Persian Gulf; Indian Ocean; China Seas	264/877 (Maq)	Mq 3: 32; Ram 190; IB 2: 17, 181, 183, 198, 251; Maq 2: 180; Kd 43	Gr σαμβύχη ; Per *sunbuk*; Skt *çambūka*	ps. variant of *sanbūq;* syn. *zawraq;* var. *sanbūk/q*, *sanbuq*, *ṣanbūq*, *sunbūq*

23 *shadhā*	small ship; war vessel	^{c}Irāq; Arabian/ Persian Gulf	198/813; 257/870-1 (Tab); 329/940-1 (Mas); 303/915-6 (Arib)	Mq 3: 32; Tab 3: 1844, 1860, 1948-49, 1960, 1965-6; Mas (Mur) 8: 345; Kd 48	Gr σχεδία "light-craft"; [?] Aram/ Heb	cf. *sumayriyyāt*; *al-shadhāwāt* *al-jannābiyyāt* (< Jannāba N.E. of the Persian Gulf); ref. *zawraq*
24 *shalandī*	war galley; transport ship	Mediterr-anean	238/852-3 (Tab); 244/858-9 (IA)	Mq 3: 32; IH 2: 132; Tab 3: 1417-8; IA 7: 41-2; Kd 51	Lat *celandra*, *celand-ria*, *celand-rium*; Gr χελανδ-ιον; Syr (?)	ref. *al-sharandiyyāt* *al-ḥarbiyya* (note interchange of liquids /r/ with /l/); syn. *shīnī*
25 *shamūṭ*	(?)			Mq 3: 32; Kd 52		
26 *shankūliyya*	* ferry boat			Mq 3: 31; Goe 4: 277; Kd 52	Per (?) *shankūl* "elephant trunk"	
27 *shīnī*	war galley	Mediterr-anean	fourth/ tenth (Mq, IH); [sixth/ eleventh (Id, IA)]	Mq 3: 32, 177; IH 2: 132; Id 112; Maq 1: 351; IA 8: 70; Kd 53	Per (?) *shīnā* "swim-ming"; Gr (?)	cf. *shalandī*, ref. *marākib ḥammāla*; *ḥarāba*; syn. *musaṭṭaḥiyya*
28 *sūqiyya*	war galley			Mq 3: 32; Kd 45	Gr (?) σαγηνη	
29 *talawwā*	* small boat			Mq 3: 31; Goe 4: 198; Kd 15		
30 *ṭayyār*	warship; swift vessel	^{c}Irāq; Arabian/ Persian Gulf	207-30/822-913-4 (Yaq); 315/911-2; 329/941; 333/945 (Arib)	Mq 3: 31; Goe 4: 231; Yaq 3: 888; Arib 37, 133; Mas (Mur) 8: 345-77; Kd 60		syn. *zabzab*; *shumayliyyāt*; cf. *sumayriyyāt* ; *shadhāwāt*

31 *ṭayra*	* swift boat			Mq 3: 32; Kd 61		
32 *wāsṭiyya*	(?)	ᶜIrāq		Mq 3: 31; Kd 107		nisba Wāsiṭ (SE Iraq)
33 *walajiyya*	* coaster; reed-bundles canoe	ᶜIrāq; Arabian/ Persian Gulf		Mq 3: 32; Goe 4: 379; Kd 107	Per (?)	ps. *wāriyya* (in present day Bahrain)
34 *zabzab*	small and large warship		329-33/941-5 (Mas)	Mq 3: 31; Goe 4: 231; Mas (Mur) 8: 345; Kd 33	Aram (?)	cf. *shadhāwāt*; *ṭayyārāt*; *sumayriyyāt*
35 *zabarbādhi-yya*	(?)			Mq 3: 32; Kd 33		
36 *zawraq*	small vessel; boat; skiff; barque	ᶜIrāq	269/883	Mq 3: 31; IH 2: 159; Tab 3: 1168, 2074; Ist 1: 80; Kd 37	Per (?); Aram (?)	cf. *jarībiyyāt*; *sumayriyyāt*

ABBREVIATIONS

(i) Authors

Arib	^{c}Arīb	IH	Ibn Ḥawqal	Mq	Muqaddasī
Bal	Balādhurı	IJ	Ibn Jubayr	Ram	Rāmhurmuzī
Goe	De Goeje	Ist	Iṣṭakhrī	Tab	Ṭabarī
IA	Ibn al-Athīr	Maq	Maqrīzī	YA	Ya^{c}qūbī
IB	Ibn Baṭṭūṭa	Mas (Mur)	Mas^{c}ūdī (Murūj)	Yaq	Yāqūt
Id	Idrīsī	Mas (Tan)	Mas^{c}ūdī (Tanbīh)		

****

(ii) Languages

Akk	Akkadian	Hind	Hindi	Sum	Sumerian
Ar	Arabic	Lat	Latin	Syr	Syriac
Aram	Aramaic	Per	Persian	Tam	Tamil
Gr	Greek	Rom	Romance	Tur	Turkish
Heb	Hebrew	(Port)	(Portuguese)	Ur	Urdu
		Skt	Sanskrit		

****

(iii) Other

cf.	compare	<	originally from
ps.	possibility	(?)	doubtful origin
syn.	synonymous	>	becoming
ref.	reference	*	description not certain

V ISLAMIC SOURCES AND TRANSMISSION

Para una Nomenclatura Acerca de la Indumentaria Islámica en Al-Andalus

Dolores Serrano-Niza
Universidad de La Laguna

INTRODUCCION

Las palabras que siguen pretenden, tal y como se indica en su título, establecer las bases para la realización de una nomenclatura sobre la indumentaria islámica en un contexto geopolítico y cultural bien preciso, al-Andalus. Sin embargo, dicho título requiere que hagamos dos salvedades.

La primera de ellas es que si entendemos el vocablo "nomenclatura" como un lista de términos técnicos relacionados - en este caso - con la indumentaria islámica, entramos de lleno en el terreno de la lexicografía árabe (*lugha*) por lo que es necesario advertir que tanto ésta como la gramática (*naḥw*) tenían como objeto de estudio la descripción de un sistema colectivo previamente establecido y aceptado al que llamaron con diversos nombres: *kalām al-ʿarab* o *al-lugha l-ʿarabiyya* ambos con el mismo equivalente español 'lengua árabe'.[1]

[1] El *kalām al-ᶜarab* ha sido definido como "un estado de la lengua árabe en el que se ha hecho abstracción de diferencias dialectales, diacrónicas y

Quiere esto decir que en la historia de la lexicografía árabe primero se registró el material léxico hasta componer un determinado corpus[2] que incluirá exclusivamente aquellas realizaciones de árabes considerados puros desde una perspectiva lingüística. Después, los lexicógrafos se limitarán a una tarea de recopilación de trabajos anteriores por lo que las obras lexicográficas, con independencia de dónde fueran escritas, están contínuamente remitiendo a idéntico estado de lengua y los diccionarios árabes clásicos trasladan literalmente (o con escasas matizaciones) las definiciones de sus precedentes.

En el caso de la indumentaria - y por lo que sabemos - la mayoría de los vocablos recogidos se refieren a tejidos o prendas de vestir propios de la vida beduína del desierto dejando a parte aquellos términos vinculados a la vida urbana. En cuanto a las definiciones, éstas no son precisamente prolijas en detalles como veremos en el curso de este trabajo.

Por otra parte, podríamos entender el vocablo "nomenclatura" como un mero listado donde figuren las prendas de vestir que a lo largo de toda su historia fueron propias de los musulmanes. Y ésta es la segunda salvedad al título porque, en este caso, sería preciso recurrir a una historia de la indumentaria islámica que, no sólo está por hacer, sino que, además, resulta una empresa de gran envergadura para quien pretenda llevarla a cabo, pues en general, su elaboración viene marcada por la dificultad de encontrar fuentes de

diafásicas, y que resulta de la suma de todas las realizaciones - efectivas o posibles - atribuidas a un grupo de hablantes bien definido, los *ᶜarab*; esto es, los árabes puros o auténticos, que, por no haber estado sometidos a ningún tipo de mestizaje cultural, hablaban una lengua exenta de corrupción (*fasād*) Salvador Peña, "El corpus de los lingüístas musulmanes y la noción de autoridad", *Miscelánea de Estudios Arabes y Hebraicos* 37 (1988), 195.

[2] Para la composición de las fuentes que componen el corpus de la descripción lingüística, Peña, 197-200.

diversa naturaleza con las que conformar una noción general de lo que la comunidad denominada arabe islámica utilizó - y utiliza - en materia de tejidos y vestidos. La complejidad del trabajo aumenta conforme se pretenda cubrir todos los países islámicos en todos los periodos de su historia.

En el caso concreto del vestido en al-Andalus, la escasa documentación existente para los siglos que van desde el emirato omeya de Córdoba hasta el reino de Granada contrasta - como ya han señalado algunos autores[3] - con la que conocemos sobre la indumentaria *naṣrī* y morisca.

Nos hacemos cargo de que la ausencia de tal información resulta una dificultad insalvable. Especialmente, la carencia de fuentes iconográficas capaces de mostrarnos la referencia de aquellos vocablos sobre indumentaria que aparecen en los textos jurídicos, históricos y literarios de la época donde apenas si aparece esbozada una descripción de tales prendas.

Así las cosas, el objetivo principal de este trabajo será el de estudiar la indumentaria islámica tomando como base una obra lexicográfica del siglo IX - que pasamos a describir inmediatamente - y como conclusiones ofreceremos lo que los datos obtenidos pueden aportar para la elaboración de una nomenclatura que exponga el modo de vestir de los musulmanes andalusíes.

[3] Rachel Arié, "Acerca del traje musulmán en España desde la caída de Granada hasta la expulsión de los moriscos", *Revista del Instituto de Estudios Islámicos* 13 (1965-1966), 103.

LA OBRA

La obra que nos ha servido de punto de partida para nuestro estudio pertenece al llamado género lexicográfico de *gharīb*[4] y lleva por título *Gharīb al-Muṣannaf*, procede de la pluma del oriental Abū ᶜUbayd al-Qāsim b. Sallām al-Harawī al-Bagdādī (m. 224/838)[5] quien es también autor de otras dos conocidas obras pertenecientes al mismo género: *Gharīb al-Qur'ān* y *Gharīb al-Ḥadīth*.

El *Gharīb al-Muṣannaf* se clasifica entre los diccionarios onomasiológicos en los que el léxico se ordena desde el significado (*maᶜnā*) al significante (*lafẓ*). Para su composición, Abū ᶜUbayd tuvo en cuenta una serie de trabajos monográficos en los que se recogían las palabras relativas a un mismo tema, como la obra de su maestro al-Aṣmaᶜī (m. 213/828) y de otros autores precedentes y contemporáneos que quedan citados rigurosamente para dar autoridad al contenido de su obra, en consonancia con lo que es tradicional en el marco de la historia de la lexicografía árabe.

La totalidad del material léxico recogido por Abū ᶜUbayd quedó ordenado en libros (*kutub*) y capítulos (*abwāb*) relativos a temas tales como el ser humano, los alimentos, los vestidos, las mujeres, las enfermedades, los caballos, las armas, las aves, las palmeras, los camellos, los vientos etc.

De esta obra consta en nuestro poder el microfilm de uno de sus manuscritos. La copia, fechada en 601/1205, se encuentra en la Biblioteca de San Lorenzo de El Escorial (nº1650).[6] En ella, los

[4] S. A. Bonebakker, "Gharīb", *Encyclopédie de l'Islam*, nouvelle édition (Leiden/Paris, 1960 y ss), 2:1034-1035.

[5] H. L. Gottschalk "Abū ᶜUbayd", *Encyclopédie de l'Islam*, op. cit., 1:161-162.

[6] H. Derenbourg, *Les manuscrits arabes de l'Escurial*, 3 vols. (Paris, 1884-1928), 3:183-184.

vocablos que hacen referencia al atavío se encuentran reunidos bajo el título *ḍurūb al-thiyāb min al-burūd wa l-raqīq wa-naḥwihā* aunque en nota marginal y escrita por otra mano se especifica que es un *kitāb al-libās*. Efectivamente, en los folios 18v a 21v se concentran los capítulos referidos a prendas de vestir, como los mantos (fols. 18v-19r), los tocados y las calzas (fol. 19r), la camisa y las partes que la componen (fol. 19v) y los colores de los vestidos (fol. 20r). De igual manera se menciona a las pieles y su curtido (fol. 20v) el calzado (fol. 20r), y, además, se incluyen apartados donde se recopilan vocablos sobre la manera de ponerse los vestidos (fol. 19r) o el corte y confección de éstos (fol. 20r).

Por otra parte, dentro del *kitāb al-nisā'* (fols. 14v-18r), el autor dedica un capítulo dedicado a la ropa de la mujeres (fol. 16v) donde también se recogen algunas referencias a vestidos de niños.

He aquí los vocablos referidos a indumentaria que se encuentran en el *Gharīb al-Muṣannaf* y que hemos seleccionado para nuestro estudio sobre la indumentaria islámica. Lo presentamos tal y como aparecen ordenados en la obra con el fin de dar cuenta al lector de la macroestructura que presenta la misma. Junto a cada término aparece su localización en nuestro manuscrito y a continuación la definición - si la hubiera - que acompaña al vocablo, prescindiendo del aspecto morfológico.

1. CAPÍTULO ACERCA DE LA INDUMENTARIA FEMENINA

itb (fol. 16v): prenda de vestir confeccionada a partir de una pieza de tejido con una abertura que queda en el cuello de la mujer; no tiene mangas ni abertura por la parte anterior (*jayb*)

bukhnuq (fol. 16v): velo (*burquʿ*) pequeño; pieza de tela zafia con la que la mujer cubre su cabeza

nifāḍ (fol. 16v): prenda de vestir (*izār*) de los niños

ṣiqāᶜ (fol. 16v): harapo que se coloca bajo el velo (*khimār*) para preservar a éste del ungüento del cabello
ghifāra (fol. 16v): [similar al] *ṣiqāᶜ*
waṣwaṣ (fol. 16v): velo peqeño; velo que está próximo a los ojos
burquᶜ (fol. 16v): velo pequeño
lifām (fol. 16v): velo que se coloca sobre la punta de la nariz
lithām (fol. 16v): velo que se coloca sobre la boca
niqāb (fol. 16v): velo que se coloca por debajo de los ojos
khayᶜal (fol. 16v): *qamīṣ* sin mangas; manto (*burd*) que lleva cosido uno de sus dos costados
naṣīf (fol. 16v): velo (*khimār*)
shawdhar (fol. 16v): [semejante al] *itb*
ᶜilqa (fol. 16v): primera prenda de vestir que se le pone al niño
rihṭ (fol. 16v): piel (*jild*) abierta que visten los niños y las mujeres
baqīr & *baqīra* (fol. 17r): [semejante al] *itb.*

2. CAPÍTULO ACERCA DEL *ṬAYLASĀN* Y *KISĀ'*

sadūs (fol. 18v): es el *ṭaylasān*
miṭraf (fol. 18v): tejido o vestido (*thawb*) de forma cuadrada [confeccionado en] seda cruda (*khazz*) que tiene bordados (*aᶜlām*)
jinniyya (fol. 18v): manto circular que tiene bordados. Lo visten las mujeres
mustaqa (fol. 18v): prenda de vestir (*jubba*) de piel con mangas largas
khamīṣa (fol. 18v): vestido (*kisā'*) negro cuadrado que tiene dos cenefas
subja & *sabīja* (fol. 18v): vestido (*kisā'*) negro; es de piel (fol. 19r)
batt (fol. 18v): tejido o vestido (*thawb*) de lana gruesa semejante al *ṭaylasān.*

3. CAPÍTULO ACERCA DEL *QALĀNIS* Y *TUBBĀN*

qalansiya (fol. 19r)
diqrār (fol. 19r): es el *tubbān*
tubbān (fol. 19r).

4. CAPÍTULO ACERCA DEL *QAMĪṢ*

banīqa (fol. 19v)
dhaladhil (fol. 19v): parte inferior del *qamis*
niṭāq (fol. 19v): falda de mujer doblada a la mitad y ceñida mediante un cinturón de manera que la parte superior caiga sobre la inferior
nuqba (fol. 19v): semejante al *niṭāq* pero lleva cosido el cinturón a modo de alforza como en el *sarāwīl*
ṣanīfa (fol. 19v): cenefa (*ṭurra*)
qunn (fol. 19v)
rudn (fol. 19v)
jayb (fol. 19v)
zirr (fol. 19v)
ʿurwa (fol. 19v).

LA INDUMENTARIA SEGUN LA OBRA DE ABŪ ʿUBAYD

A la terminología que el *Gharīb al-Muṣannaf* nos proporciona sobre indumentaria, le hemos sumado la información de otros diccionarios.[7] Con esta base lexicográfica y la de los estudios que

[7] Hemos tenido en cuenta dos diccionarios clásicos en lengua árabe: Ibn Manẓūr, *Lisān al-ʿArab*, 20 vols. (Būlāq, 1300/1922-1308/1930); Ibn Sīda, *Al-Mukhaṣṣaṣ*, 7 vols. (Būlāq, 1316/1898-1321/1903) y diccionarios bilingües de

nos preceden elaboramos un esquema en el que se refleja, a grandes trazos, el modo de vestir islámico. Para ello, en primer lugar, hemos hecho tres grandes grupos que corresponden al atavío masculino, femenino e infantil.

Con los datos que tenemos y dentro de las anteriores divisiones, consideramos que en función de su uso, las prendas de vestir se pueden agrupar en:

1. los tocados
2. los vestidos interiores
3. los vestidos exteriores
4. los mantos.

Según esto, observamos que muchas prendas fueron comunes a hombres y mujeres, especialmente las prendas interiores. Entre éstas se encuentran las calzas o pantalón y que Abū ᶜUbayd denomina de manera genérica *tubbān* y nos ofrece un sinónimo, *diqrār*.

Tanto la palabra *tubbān* como su significado parece tener origen persa[8] aunque fue muy pronto adoptada por los árabes pues el vocablo aparece recogido en la tradición donde se indica que un hombre hizo la oración vistiendo uno de ellos.[9] Es probable que su largo no revasara la rodilla.

Un tipo de calzón de cuero es el que cita Abū ᶜUbayd como *riḥṭ*, usado por mujeres y niños aunque no hemos encontrado más datos que nos lo describan.

alto uso en la traducción: R. Dozy, *Supplément aux dictionnaires arabes*, 2 vols. (Beirut, 1968); A. B. Kazimirsky, *Dictionnaire arabe-français*, 2 vols. (Paris, 1860; reimp. Beirut, s. d.); E. W. Lane, *Arabic English Lexicon*, 8 vols. (Londres, 1863-1893; reimp. New York, 1955-1956).

[8] R. Dozy, *Dictionnaire détaillé des noms des vêtements chez les arabes* (Amsterdam, 1845; reimp. Beirut, s. d.), pp. 93-94.

[9] A. J. Wensinck, *Concordance et indices de la tradition musulmane*, 4 vols. 2ª ed., (Leiden/New York/Köln, 1992), 1:264.

Otra prenda de las denominadas interior y usada por ambos sexos, fue el *qamīṣ* a la que nuestro autor debe considerar bien conocida puesto que no la define; ahora bien, le dedica un capítulo completo explicando las partes de la que ésta se compone. El vocablo *qamīṣ* aparece recogido ampliamente en los hadices especificando, en ocasiones, su color blanco.[10] Creemos que esta prenda, en los primeros tiempos del Islam, debió ser un tipo de túnica amplia y larga que se confeccionaba en tejidos ligeros como el algodón, o bien en lana. Aunque también las hubo de excelente lino[11] e incluso de seda.[12]

Como hemos dicho, Abū ᶜUbayd se detiene a nombrar una por una las partes de las que se compone gracias a las cuales sabemos que el *qamīṣ* tenía mangas (*kumm*) con puños (*rudn*) y que éstas podían ser ampliadas a la altura de la axila mediante una pieza triangular llamada *banīqa*. Podía tener botones (*zirr*) y ojales (*ᶜurwa*) y llevar una abertura frontal o un pliegue (*jayb*) que partía del cuello y si el *qamīṣ* se ceñía con un cinturón tal abertura servía de bolsillo. Probablemente se vistiera sobre el pantalón debido a su largura y su parte baja (*dhildhil*) se decorara mediante una cenefa (*ṣinf*).

Una variante femenina del *qamīṣ*, según nuestro autor, era el *khayᶜal* al que describe como vestido que lleva cosido uno de sus dos lados o bien, un *qamīṣ* sin mangas.

Sobre las ropas interiores se vestían distintos tipos de prendas a los que hemos llamado vestidos exteriores. A éstas se las denominaban de manera genérica *kisāʼ*, caracterizándose por ser prendas holgadas confeccionadas en distintos tejidos y colores, en

[10] Wensinck, 5:468-469.

[11] R. B. Serjeant, *Islamic Textiles (Material for a History up to the Mongol Conquest)* (Beirut, 1972), p. 53.

[12] Serjeant, p. 203.

ocasiones adornadas mediante cenefas o bordados, según la posibiliades de su propietario.

Entre los vestidos de estas características que usaban los hombres, tenemos uno, llamado *khamīṣa*, que era de color negro, de forma cuadrada y que se adornaba con dos cenefas, a menudo, de distinto color. Es otra de las prendas de antigua tradición en el Islam, pues en los hadices se menciona que el Profeta poseía uno de ellos.[13] En opinión de Dozy, con el vocablo *khamīṣa* se hace referencia a un manto de uso tanto femenino como masculino.[14]

En este grupo de vestidos se incluyen también los que están confeccionados con piel, el denominado *mustaqa*, con mangas largas y el llamado *subja* y *sabīja*, al que Abū ʿUbayd define primero como una prenda exterior (*kisāʾ*) negra y luego añade que es de piel. Por su parte, Kazimirski amplia la definición de esta misma palabra diciendo que no tiene mangas ni cuello.

Como vestidos exteriores femeninos nuestro autor cita el *itb* confeccionado a partir de una pieza de tejido con una hendidura que queda en el cuello de la mujer. Esta prenda no tiene mangas ni abertura por la parte anterior (*jayb*). Según Dozy, la simplicidad de este vestido parece indicar que ya lo usaban las mujeres en los primeros tiempos del Islam[15] a lo que añade que, de manera general, este vocablo indica un vestido cuyo largo no sobrepasa la mitad de la pierna o una túnica sin mangas o un tipo de calzas sin abertura para meter las piernas.[16]

Semejante al *itb*, nos dice Abū ʿUbayd, son los vestidos llamados *baqīr* (o *baqīra*) y *shawdhar* aunque este último también

[13] Wensinck, 2:85.

[14] Dozy, *Dictionnaire détaillé*, p. 174.

[15] ibid., p. 22.

[16] ibid., p. 23.

tiene el sentido de un gran manto que puede ser de distintos tejidos y colores con el que las mujeres se cubren cuando salen a la calle.[17]

Y con esta segunda acepción de la palabra *shawdhar*, pasamos a describir otro tipo de vestido exterior que - de manera general - llamaremos mantos. De éstos sabemos que hay algunos propios de mujer, otros que sólo usaron los hombres y otros cuyo uso no aparece especificado aunque suponemos que fueron comunes a ambos. Como en el caso del *kisā'*, se confeccionaron en lana, seda, algodón y lino y los había bordados y de distintos colores.

Abū ᶜUbayd sólo menciona uno como propio de mujer el denominado *jinniyya* al que describe como circular y con bordados. Es muy probable que fuera éste propio del estrato social alto puesto que Kazimirski indica que era un tipo de mantón de seda.

En cuanto a los que consideramos que sólo fueron usados por los hombres, se encuentra el *ṭaylasān* al que nuestro autor no define aunque dicho vocablo le permite referirse a sinónimos como *sadūs*[18] o a prendas similares como el manto denominado *batt* del que dice estar confeccionado en lana gruesa[19] y el *miṭraf*, pieza de tejido de seda cruda (*khazz*), de forma cuadrada con bordados.

Para muchos autores, el *ṭaylasān* era una especie de gran velo que sólo los hombres de ciencia y ley utilizaban, echándolo sobre la cabeza y sobre los hombros[20] adquiriendo, por tanto, en ocasiones el significado de tocado.

No es este el caso del autor del *Gharīb al-Muṣannaf*, para quien los tocados masculinos vienen representados por un único

[17] ibid., pp. 216-219.

[18] ibid., p. 201, lo define como manto verde y apunta la posibilidad de que lo usaran las mujeres según se desprende de un verso de Abū ᶜUbayda.

[19] O de piel de oveja que usan lon derviches: ibid., p. 54.

[20] ibid., pp. 278-280.

vocablo, *qalansiya*. Esta palabra de origen persa,[21] al parecer, se introdujo en el atavío islámico con los Omeyas y designa, en general a un tocado de hombre que sufrió distintas modificaciones a lo largo de los siglos. En la época de los abbasíes fueron altos y negros y los usaban los cadíes llegando a ser junto al ya mencionado *ṭaylasān*, un tocado oficial.

En cuanto a los tocados femeninos, éstos se reducen al uso del velo que podían ser, según Abū ᶜUbayd, telas de poca calidad que se colocaban en la cabeza bajo el velo exterior para preservar a éste del ungüento del cabello (*bukhnuq*; *siqāᶜ*; *ghifāra*). Velos de distintos tamaños destinados a cubrir partes muy concretas del rostro: *waṣwaṣ* velo peqeño y también un velo que está próximo a los ojos; *burquᶜ*; velo pequeño; *lifām*, velo que se coloca sobre la punta de la nariz; *lithām*,[22] velo que se coloca sobre la boca y *niqāb*, velo que se coloca por debajo de los ojos. Y velos de mayor tamaño que cubrían, además de la cabeza, los hombros: *naṣīf*; *khimār*.

Por último, sobre la ropa usada por los niños, constan en el *Gharīb al-Muṣannaf* sólo tres referencias: el nombre del primer vestido que se le pone a éstos, *ᶜilqa*, una pieza de tejido, a modo de *izār*, en el que son envueltos que lleva como nombre, *nifāḍ* y una prenda que comparte en el uso con las mujeres y que ya hemos descrito, *riḥṭ*.

[21] Para todo lo relativo a esta prenda, véase W. Björkman "*Kalansuwa*", *Encyclopaedia of Islam,* 9 vols., (Leiden, 1987; repr. of 1st ed., 1913-1924), 4:677-678.

[22] Sobre este tipo de velo, véase Björkman "*lithām*", *Encyclopédie de l'Islam*, op. cit., 5:775-776.

CONCLUSIONES:
ACERCA DE LA INDUMENTARIA ISLAMICA EN AL-ANDALUS

La información que la obra de Abū ᶜUbayd ofrece es una aportación indiscutible para establecer una nomenclatura sobre el atavío andalusí desde las dos perspectivas diferentes. Una de ellas es la lexicográfica, puesto que nos permite conocer las definiciones de esos vocablos en la lengua árabe clásica - lo que resulta imprescindible, por ejemplo, para el conocimiento de la poesía clásica que se escribió en al-Andalus.

La otra perspectiva es la histórica. En este caso, los términos recogidos en el *Gharīb al-Muṣannaf* son un buen punto de partida para la realización de una historia de la indumentaria arabe islámica dada la conocida pervivencia de ciertos vocablos a lo largo de los siglos.

Este es el caso de determinadas palabras como *qalansiya*, *qamīṣ*, *tubbān*, *ṭaylasān*, *miṭraf*, *ghifāra*, *lithām* o *khimār*, vistas en el transcurso de este trabajo y que se usaron, así como las prendas a las que denominaron, en al-Andalus.

Como es natural, esas prendas a las que se refieren debieron sufrir transformaciones. Sin embargo, explicar y documentar las variaciones que sufrió el atavío andalusí debe ser labor del historiador dispuesto a elaborar esa "reclamada" historia de la indumentaria andalusí.

Ibn Baṭṭūṭa y las Escuelas Jurídicas en los Países del Mediterráneo

María Arcas Campoy
Universidad de La Laguna

La abundante y variada información aportada por Ibn Baṭṭūṭa (m. 770/1368-69 ó 779/1377) en su célebre *Riḥla*[1] es una rica cantera de la que puede extraerse aún interesante material para la investigación de muy diversas facetas del mundo árabo-islámico y de otros países ajenos al Islam en la Edad Media, concretamente en el siglo XIV.

En esta comunicación presento la visión del viajero tangerino sobre las escuelas o doctrinas (*madhāhib*) jurídicas[2] en los países

[1] Ibn Baṭṭūṭa, *A través del Islam*, ed. y trad. de S. Fanjul y F. Arbós (Madrid, 1987), pp. 17-19, ofrece una completa bibliografía sobre el autor y la obra entre la que figuran las principales ediciones y traducciones: H. A. R. Gibb, *The Travels of Ibn Baṭṭūṭa* (1325-1354). Translated with revisions and notes from the Arabic text edited by C. Defrémery and B. R. Sanguinetti (Cambridge, 1958), 4 vols. (reimpr. de Wiesbaden, 1972); F. Gabrieli, *I viaggi di Ibn Baṭṭūṭa* (Florencia, 1961); C. Defrémery y B. R. Sanguinetti, *Voyages d'Ibn Baṭṭūṭa*, ed. y trad. (Paris, 1854), 4 vols. (reed. Paris, 1969, con una introducción de V. Monteil); Ibn Baṭṭūṭa, *Riḥla*, ed. de K. al-Bustānī (Beirut, 1964). Hay que añadir otra edición más reciente: Ibn Baṭṭūṭa, *Riḥla*, ed. Ṭalāl Ḥarb, 2ª ed. (Beirut, 1992), con magníficos índices.

[2] G. H. Bousquet, "Ibn Baṭṭūṭa et les institutions musulmanes", *Studia Islamica* 24 (1966), 81-106, presenta un estudio sistemático y global del texto de

islámicos del Mediterráneo por él visitados: Argelia, Túnez, Egipto, Palestina, Siria, Anatolia y al-Andalus, de donde partió hacia Mali para regresar definitivamente a Marruecos, su país de origen.

Las noticias sobre la práctica jurídica y la actividad judicial es constante a lo largo del relato. Ibn Baṭṭūṭa se muestra siempre muy interesado sobre esta cuestión, sin duda por que él mismo, seguidor de la doctrina de Mālik b. Anas (m. 179/795), fue alfaquí e incluso desempeñó el cargo de cadí, como se verá más adelante. Es lógico, pues, que manifestase una especial sensibilidad al tratar temas relacionados con el Derecho Islámico y con el funcionamiento de las escuelas jurídicas de los que él era buen conocedor.

Paso a exponer la información acerca de las instituciones jurídicas en países islámicos del Mediterráneo, siguiendo el mismo orden que ofrece la *Riḥla* a cuya edición realizada por *Ṭalāl Ḥarb (Riḥla, Dār al-kutub al-ʿilmiyya*, 2ª edición, Beirut, 1992) hacen referencia las páginas citadas en adelante. Asimismo, me resta señalar que dada la profusión de nombres de cadíes, alfaquíes y otros cargos relacionados con la teoría y la práctica del *fiqh* cuya mencion completa haría pesada la redacción de este trabajo, me limito a mencionar sólo aquellos que en el relato tienen mayor relevancia o protagonismo.

la *Riḥla* en relación con varios aspectos de la organización religiosa y social de la comunidad musulmana, así como de la personalidad del propio viajero; véase también Ibn Baṭṭūṭa, *A través del Islam*, pp. 47-48 de la intr. de S. Fanjul y F. Arbós.

DE TÁNGER A ALEJANDRÍA

Ibn Baṭṭūṭa inicia su viaje para cumplir el precepto islámico de la peregrinación (*ḥajj*) el 2 de *Rajab* de 725/14 de Junio de 1325, fecha en que sale de Tánger, su ciudad natal.

La información sobre la administración de la justicia y las personas relacionadas con la misma en el Norte de Africa es muy escasa, si bien aporta algunos datos de interés.

A su llegada a Tremecén (p. 32), Ibn Baṭṭūṭa fue recibido por el cadí de matrimonios (*qāḍī l-ankiḥa*) de Túnez, quién se había desplazado a tal efecto como enviado del sultán tunecino, y en Bugía (p. 33) se hospedó en la casa del cadí de la ciudad. En Túnez (pp. 34-35) conoció al cadí de la comunidad (*qāḍī l-jamāᶜa*) cuyo padre, oriundo de Valencia, había desempeñado el mismo cargo. Asimismo menciona a dos alfaquíes que anteriormente habían ejercido el cadiazgo. Uno de ellos era el alfaquí y muftí, Abū ᶜUmar b. ᶜAlī b. Qaddāḥ al-Hawārī, del que se cuenta que, recostado en una columna de la mezquita al-Zaytūna, tenía por costumbre emitir los dictámenes jurídicos (*fatāwī*) que le solicitaban hasta llegar a un límite de cuarenta.

En este tramo del viaje se produjo un hecho importante que afectó al propio Ibn Baṭṭūṭa, pues a la salida de Túnez, fue nombrado cadí por los miembros de su caravana, que eran *ma ṣmūda*[3] en su mayoría.

[3] Una de las principales familias étnicas beréberes asentada en el extremo occidental del Magreb. Junto con los *ṣinḥaya* constituyen la rama de los *barānis*: *Encyclopédie de l'Islam*, nouvelle édition, 8 vols. (en curso) (Leiden, 1960 y siguientes), 6:730-733 (G. S. Collin, s. v. "Maṣmūda").

Por último menciona en Sfax el sepulcro del alfaquí mālikí, Abū l-Ḥasan al-Lakhmī,[4] autor del *Kitāb Tabṣira fī l-Fiqh*.

En el año 749/1349, tras realizar la cuarta peregrinación y pensando ya en regresar a Marruecos, Ibn Baṭṭūṭa volvió a Túnez (p. 665). De esta estancia en la ciudad recuerda a varias personas vinculas al derecho y a la administración de la justicia.

En ningún caso indica el *madhhab* al que pertenecían los alfaquíes y cadíes citados, sin duda porque el único implantado con fuerza en el Magreb, al igual que en al-Andalus, era el *mālikī*, al que él pertenecía y conocía perfectamente. Por este mismo motivo, el relato de Ibn Baṭṭūṭa es más breve y menos detallado que el que dedica al funcionamiento de la justicia en otros países.

DE ALEJANDRÍA A EL CAIRO

El viajero de Tánger menciona a tres cadíes de la ciudad de Alejandría (p. 41), entre ellos, Fakhr al-Dīn b. al-Rīghī b. al-Miskīn, perteneciente a la doctrina *shāfiʿī*, la más fuerte y extendida en Egipto. De este cadí alguien le contó a su paso por Damanhūr, donde por aquel tiempo desempeñaba el cadiazgo, que había obtenido el cargo mediante el pago de veinticinco mil dirhams, es decir, mil dinares de oro. Años atrás, su abuelo, igualmente llamado Fakhr al-Dīn al-Rīghī, también fue nombrado cadí de Alejandría,

[4] Sobre Abū l-Ḥasan ʿAlī b. Abī Bakr al-Lakhmī (m. 498/1104-05), jurista *mālikī* que vivió y murió en Sfax, véase M. García Arenal, "Algunos manuscritos de *fiqh* andalusíes y norteafricanos pertenecientes a la Real Biblioteca del Escorial", *Al-Qanṭara* 1 (1980), 12, nº 1082.

pero la causa de su designación no fue el dinero sino su conducta austera y ejemplar.[5]

En el trecho de Alejandría a el Cairo (pp. 46-53) Ibn Baṭṭūṭa menciona a los cadíes de Taruja (p. 46), de Damanhūr (p. 46), de Naḥrāriyya (pp. 47-48), de Ibyār (p. 48), de al-Maḥalla al-Kabīra (pp. 48-49), de Manūf (p. 48) y de Damieta (pp. 51-52), señalando en algunos casos la doctrina jurídica a la que pertenecían. Así, encontramos dos cadíes *shāfiʿíes*, el de Damanhūr - Fakhr al-Dīn b. al-Righī al-Miskīn, antiguo cadí de Alejandría citado anteriormente - y el de Ibyār, al que el propio Ibn Baṭṭūṭa acompañó en la ceremonia de observación de la luna nueva de Ramadán. En cambio, eran seguidores de la doctrina *mālikí* el cadí de Naḥrariyya, hombre destacado entre los *mālikíes*, que viajó a Iraq como embajador de al-Malik al-Nāṣir,[6] y el sustituto (*nāʾib*) del cadí supremo (*qāḍī l-quḍāt*) de al-Maḥalla l-Kabīra, como se deduce de su nombre, Abū l-Qāsim b. Banūn al-Mālikī.

[5] Despúes de hacer la peregrinación a La Meca, este personaje regresó a Alejandría sin medios económicos. Se aplicó en el estudio del Corán en una *madrasa* y su fama de hombre honesto, sabio y asceta llegó al soberano egipcio quien lo nombró cadí de Alejandría.

[6] Al-Malik al-Nāṣir Muḥammad b. Qalāwūn, sultán mameluco de Egipto y Siria, tuvo tres reinados entre 694/1294 y 741/1341; Ibn Baṭṭūṭa lo conoció personalmente en su tercer reinado (709/1310-741/1341). Véase ᶜA. Ibrāhīm Ḥasan, *Dirāsāt fī ta'rīkh al-Mamālik al-Baḥriyya fī ʿAṣr al-Nāṣir Muḥammad bi-wajh khāṣṣ* (El Cairo, 1948); *Encyclopédie de l'Islam*, op. cit., 6:307 (P. M. Holt, s. v. "Mamlūks").

EL CAIRO

En la capital del reino de los mamelucos, bajo el gobierno de al-Malik al-Nāṣir, la actividad jurídica era lógicamente superior a la de otras ciudades de menor categoría.

Antes de pasar a relatar sus impresiones sobre esta cuestión, Ibn Baṭṭūṭa menciona la *zāwiya* en la que el *imām* Abū ᶜAbd Allāh al-Shāfiᶜī (m. 179/796), el fundador de la doctrina de su nombre, se dedicaba al estudio, así como su sepulcro en el gran cementerio de El Cairo (pp. 56, 58).

Entre las personalidades próximas al monarca mameluco destaca el cadí Fakhr al-Dīn al-Qubṭī (p. 62), un copto islamizado de buena reputación en el ejercicio de su cargo. Además, la ciudad de El Cairo contaba con cuatro cadíes supremos (*qāḍī l-quḍāt*), uno de cada escuela jurídica (p. 62). El de más alto rango y mayor consideración era el cadí *shāfiᶜī* y así queda reflejado en la descripción del tribunal que al-Malik al-Nāṣir presidía los lunes y los jueves con los cuatro magistrados sentados a su izquierda.[7] Dicho cadí ocupaba el lugar más destacado, seguido por el *ḥanafī*, el *mālikī* y por último, el *ḥanbalī*. A la muerte del representante *ḥ anafī* ocupó su puesto, es decir el segundo, el cadí de la escuela *mālikī*, restableciéndose así el orden seguido antiguamente.

Otros sabios y alfaquíes del Cairo aparecen en la *Riḥla*, entre ellos un nieto de al-Shādhilī[8] que era sustituto (*nāᵓib*) del cadí supremo.

[7] Tribunal para las reclamaciones e injusticias (*maẓālim)*; véase E. Tyan, *Histoire de l'organisation judiciaire en pays d'Islam*, 2ème éd. (Leiden, 1960), pp. 433-446.

[8] Abū l-Ḥasan ᶜAlī b. ᶜAbd Allāh al-Jabbār al-Sharīf al-Zarwīlī l-Shādhilī (m. 656/1258), fundador de la *ṭarīqa* de su nombre. Enseñaba a sus discípulos la meditación como medio de unión con Dios. Véase *Encyclopaedia of Islam*, 9

RECORRIDO POR EL NILO

Tras su estancia en El Cairo, Ibn Baṭṭūṭa remontó el Nilo hasta Edfu, desplazándose de allí a la costa del mar Rojo, para después repetir el camino en sentido inverso y volver al Cairo de donde partió hacia Palestina y Siria. En este recorrido menciona al cadí de Bahnasa (p. 66), al de Munyat Ibn Khaṣīb (p. 67), *mālikī*, y al de Manlawī (p. 67), *shāfiʿī*, según indican sus respectivas *nisbas*.

El cadí de Asyūṭ (pp. 67-68) era Sharaf al-Dīn b. ʿAbd al-Raḥ mān, apodado "No hay fondos" (*ḥāṣil mā tamma*), pues así acostumbraba a responder a los caminantes (*abnāʾ al-sabīl*) que le solicitaban una ayuda a cargo de las fundaciones pías (*awqāf*)[9] y de las limosnas bajo su administración.

En su viaje hacia el alto Egipto, Ibn Baṭṭūṭa conoció a los cadíes de Akhmīm (p. 69), Qūṣ (p. 70), Armant (p. 70) e Isnā (p. 71), cuya categoría era de juez supremo. En Qūṣ, además, destacan dos alfaquíes (*fuqahāʾ*), uno de ellos profesor de la *madrasa mālikī*.

DE EL CAIRO A DAMASCO

Tras regresar de su viaje por el Alto Egipto, Ibn Baṭṭūṭa salió de El Cairo a mediados del mes de *Shaʿbān* del año 726/1326. En el relato de su paso por Palestina y Líbano cita a un cadí y a un muftí de Jerusalem (p. 79), así como al maestro (*mudarris*) de la *madrasa*

vols. (Leiden, 1987; reprint of first edition, 1913-1924), 7:246-247 (A. Cour, s. v. "Shādilī").

[9] En el Magreb se les denominaba *ḥabus pl. aḥbās*. Véase *Encyclopaedia of Islam*, 9 vols. (Leiden, 1987; reprint of first edition, 1913-1924), 13:1096-1103 (Heffening, s. v. "Wakf").

mālikī de esta ciudad, el granadino Muḥammad b. Muthbit. También menciona a un alfaquí de Ramla (p. 81) y en Trípoli (p. 85) al juez supremo y al cadí al-Qirimī, dueño de uno de los baños de la ciudad.

En el camino a Alepo otros dos cadíes se incoporan al repertorio: el de *Ḥiṣn al-Akrād*[10] (p. 85) y el de Ḥimṣ la antigua Emesa (p. 86), probablemente de origen andalusí según indica su nisba al-Sharīshī, es decir, el de Jerez.

En la ciudad siria de Alepo (pp. 91-92), había cuatro jueces, uno de cada una de las escuelas ortodoxas. El más destacado era el representante *shāfiʿī*, quien fue llamado por al-Malik al-Nāṣir para desempeñar el cargo de cadí supremo de la capital de su reino, pero murió cuando se dirigía a El Cairo. Ibn Baṭṭūṭa indica el nombre de los cadíes *ḥanafī* y *ḥanbalī*, pero no quiere hacerlo en el caso del *mālikī*, a quien reprocha haber alcanzado el cargo sin merecerlo. También recuerda en su relato a dos alfaquíes, uno de ellos el más importante de los emires del sultán mameluco.

Antes de emprender el viaje de la cuarta peregrinación, Ibn Baṭṭūṭa volvió a Alepo en el año 1348 (p. 659). De su estancia en la ciudad recuerda un veredicto de pena de muerte que emitieron los cadíes de las cuatro escuelas ortodoxas. Los condenados eran un maestro y su discípulo acusados del delito de blasfemia.[11]

De nuevo en la ruta de la primera preregrinación, en el trecho de Alepo a Damasco, la *Riḥla* menciona a los cadíes de Tizīn (p.

[10] Es decir, Fortaleza de los kurdos, pequeña localidad situada entre Trípoli y Ḥimṣ, según el relato. En *Encyclopédie de l'Islam*, op. cit., 6:306 (P. M. Holt, s. v. "Mamkūks"), se identifica con Crac des Chevaliers, tomada y restaurada por Baybars.

[11] El maestro, que vivía retirado del mundo, dijo en cierta ocasión que el Profeta no podía prescindir de las mujeres, pero él sí. Algunos dieron testimonio de su manifestación y junto con su discípulo, que estaba de acuerdo con él, fue procesado y condenado a muerte.

93), Shugrubukās (p. 94, nota 60), Ṣahyūn (p. 94), Latakia (p. 100) y Ḥiṣn al-Marqab (p. 101). De todos ellos destaca el cadí de Latakía por su protagonismo en un proceso judicial en el que, a instancias del emir Ṭaylān y estando ocultos los testigos, obtuvo la confesión de Ibn Mu'ayyad, acusado de hablar en términos agnósticos de la religión. El cadí ordenó su detención y encarcelamiento, pero finalmente fue sacado de la prisión y murió estrangulado. Más tarde, sus familiares llevaron ante el sucesor de Ṭaylān al cadí y a sus testigos, quienes estuvieron a punto de ser también estrangulados, pero se salvaron en el último momento por la intercesión de los emires que iban a presenciar la ejecución.

DAMASCO

El 9 de *Ramaḍān* del 725/1326 llegó Ibn Baṭṭūṭa a Damasco y se hospedó en la *madrasa* de los *mālikíes* (p. 104).

La *Riḥla* ofrece una extensa y detallada descripción de la ciudad y, entre otras muchas facetas de la vida de ésta, da abundante información sobre las escuelas jurídicas y el funcionamiento de la justicia. El orden del relato es el siguiente: a) la mezquita de los Omeyas; b) relación de los cadíes; c) las *madrasas*.

a) En la aljama (*al-jāmi'*) de Damasco, la célebre mezquita de los Omeyas, las escuelas jurídicas estaban representadas por sus respectivos *imāmes* (p. 108). El *imām shāfi'ī* dirigía la oración desde la gran *maqṣūra*, donde prestaban juramento los deudores y los demandados. A su izquierda estaba el *mihrāb* de los *mālikíes*, a su derecha el de los *ḥanafíes* y, a continuación, el de los *ḥanbalíes*. A la salida de la puerta oeste se encontraba una *madrasa* de los *shāfiʿíes.*

El número de *imāmes* de esta mezquita ascendía a trece (p. 111). De ellos, el *shāfiʿī*, que también era alfaquí y cadí supremo, gozaba de mayor categoría.[12] Del *imām mālikī*, refiere Ibn Baṭṭūṭa, como en otras alusiones a personas de origen magrebí o andalusí, que era un alfaquí oriundo de Córdoba, pero nacido en Granada.

Muy interesante es la información sobre los notarios (*shuhūd*/*ʿudūl*) de Damasco (p. 110) cuyas sedes (*dukkān*) se ubicaban junto a la puerta oriental de la gran mezquita, muy próxima a los zocos de los papeleros que vendían papel, cálamos y tinta, elementos indispensables para realizar las escrituras. En cada local, dos de ellos pertenecientes a la doctrina *shāfiʿī*, había cinco o seis notarios, además de un representante del cadí para formalizar matrimonios (*qāḍī al-ankiḥa*). El resto de los notarios estaban repartidos por toda la ciudad.

Asimismo, la gran Mezquita de Damasco contaba con un afamado elenco de maestros (pp. 111-112) de las distintas escuelas, entre los que Ibn Baṭṭūṭa destaca al *shāfiʿī* y al *mālikí.*

b) Los cuatro cadíes supremos de Damasco son mencionados en el relato (p. 112). El representante de la docrina *shāfiʿī* era el *imām* de la aljama anteriormente mencionado, y el *mālikí*, que contaba con un sustituto en la madrasa Shamsiyya, destacaba como jeque de los *ṣūfíes*. Curiosa e interesante es la información sobre el representante de los *ḥanafíes*, ʿImād al-Dīn al-Ḥawrānī, ante el cual comparecían los cónyuges con desavenencias. Tan colérico era su carácter que muchos maridos, con sólo oir su nombre, rectificaban su conducta antes de llegar a su presencia.

[12] Postertiormente fue cadí supremo en Egipto.

En el relato dedicado a los cadíes de Damasco Ibn Baṭṭūṭa refiere los acontecimientos que causaron la condena y muerte de Ibn Taymiyya (m. 728/1328), acusado de antropomorfismo.[13]

c) Gran parte de las muchas y afamadas *madrasas* de Damasco (pp. 114) pertenecían a los *shāfiʿíes*. Entre ellas destaca la *ʿĀdiliyya* cuyo cadí supremo, Jamāl al-Dīn b. Jumla, fue destituído por el monarca a instancias del cadí supremo de la doctrina *mālikī* que le acusaba de haber llevado a cabo un proceso fuera de las normas de su *madhhab*.[14]

Igualmente eran numerosas las *madrasas* de los *ḥanbalíes* y de los *ḥanafíes*, en cambio los *mālikíes* sólo contaban con tres, siendo la llamada *Shamsiyya* la residencia y lugar de actuación de su cadí supremo.

También cuenta Ibn Baṭṭūṭa que durante su estacia en Damasco entabló amistad con el maestro (*mudarris*) de la *madrasa mālikī*, quien lo instaló y cuidó en su casa mientras estuvo enfermo, además de proporcionarle medios y víveres para proseguir su viaje (p. 123), que tendría lugar el 1 de *Shawwāl* del 723 (1 de septiembre de 1326). Entre los miembros de la caravana había un cadí cuya doctrina no se especifica y un profesor *mālikī*.

[13] Sobre el jurista *ḥanbalī*, Taqī l-Dīn Aḥmad b. Taymiyya, y su proceso, véase *Encyclopédie de l'Islam*, op. cit., 3:976-979 (H. Laoust, "Ibn Taymiyya"); Ibn Baṭṭūṭa, *Riḥla*, ed. S. Fanjul y F. Arbos, p. 189, n. 58, recoge las opiniones de Monteil, Hrbek y Gibb sobre la imposibilidad de que Ibn Baṭṭūṭa asistiera al sermón por el que fue procesado Ibn Taymiyya.

[14] Según el relato de Ibn Baṭṭūṭa, este cadí impusó un castigo de doscientos azotes y un paseo a lomos de un asno a quien le había llamado mentiroso. La dureza y exceso del castigo no correspondían a las normas de su escuela y por ello fue destituído.

Años después, en 748/1348, antes de su cuarta y última peregrinación, Ibn Baṭṭūṭa vuelve a dar información sobre la actividad judicial y las escuelas jurídicas de Damasco (pp. 656-657). Menciona entre otros personajes a los cadíes supremos *mālikī* y *shāfiʿī*, así como a un alfaquí tangerino, residente en la Ẓāhiriyya, por el que supo de la muerte de su padre en Marruecos.

ANATOLIA

Tras la tercera peregrinación a La Meca, Ibn Baṭṭūṭa llega a Anatolia (*bilād al-rūm*) en 1332. En su relato destaca que la totalidad de sus habitantes eran *sunníes* y seguidores de Abū Ḥanīfa, y le extraña que fueran consumidores habituales de hachis (*ḥashīsh*), si bien entre ellos no lo consideraban un vicio (p. 299). En su recorrido por este país menciona a cadíes, alfaquíes y muftíes de Ālāyā (p. 299), de Lādhiq (p. 305), de Mīlās (p. 307), de Qūniya (p. 309), de Sīwās (p. 312), de Birkī (p. 314), de Burlū (pp. 327-328), de Qaṣṭamūniya (p. 331) y de Ṣanub (pp. 331-332).

En todas estas ciudades Ibn Baṭṭūṭa fue siempre bien recibido y honrado por sus juristas y jueces, todos ellos *ḥanafíes*. Los habitantes de Ṣanub no conocían la manera de orar los *mālikíes*, con las dos manos caídas sobre el costado. Algunos de ellos habían visto rezar de forma parecida a los *rāfiḍíes*[15] en Iraq y el Ḥiyāz, por lo que sospecharon que el viajero de Tánger y sus acompañantes también

[15] Seguidores de la *rāfiḍa*, nombre que se le dió al principio a los *šiʿíes*, es decir, los protestantes, los que rechazaban los gobiernos ilegítimos. Los *rāfiḍíes*, por los cuales muestra gran adversión Ibn Baṭṭūṭa, destacaban por sus posturas intransigentes y extremistas. Cf. F. M. Pareja, *Islamología* (Madrid, 1952-1954), pp. 592, 727; G. H. Bousquet, "Ibn Baṭṭūṭa", p. 83; Ibn Baṭṭūṭa, *A través del Islam*, intr. de S. Fanjul y F. Arbós, p. 411, n. 198.

lo eran. Para aclarar la situación no bastó con decirles que pertenecía a la doctrina de Mālik b. Anas, pues tuvieron además que superar una prueba. El lugarteniente del sultán les mandó una liebre, quedando uno de sus criados encargado de vigilar lo que hacían. El grupo de Ibn Baṭṭūṭa degolló, cocinó y se comió el animal, quedando la incógnita despejada, pues los *rāfiḍíes* no comen jamás liebre.

AL-ANDALUS

Tras cumplir la cuarta peregrinación y regresar a Marruecos, el incansable viajero se dirigió al vecino país de al-Andalus. El primer cadí mencionado es el de Gibraltar (*jabal al-fatḥ*) (p. 675), de donde partió con destino a Ronda (p. 678). En esta ciudad conoció a dos cadíes, uno de los cuales era su primo paterno, Abū l-Qāsim Muḥ ammad b. Yaḥyā Ibn Baṭṭūṭa.

Las últimas referencias a personas relacionadas con el derecho y la administración de la justicia se sitúan en Málaga (p. 679) y en Granada (p. 679-680). En la capital del reino nazarí, como en tantos otros lugares por los que pasó, Ibn Baṭṭūṭa gozó de la hospitalidad de las personas más distinguidas. Entre ellas figura un alfaquí, y dos personajes que ocuparon la magistratura suprema en varias ocasiones. Se trata de Abū l-Qāsim Muḥammad b. Aḥmad b. Muḥ ammad al-Ḥusaynī l-Sabtī[16] y de Abū Barakāt Muḥammad b.

[16] Cadí supremo de Granada bajo Yūsuf I (733-755/1333-1354) y el primer reinado de Muḥammad V (755-760/1354-1359); véase R. Arié, *L'Espagne Musulmane au temps des Naṣrides (1232-1492)*, réimpression (Paris,

Muḥammad b. Ibrāhīm al-Sulamī l-Balʿabaʿī,[17] que se hallaba de visita en aquellos días.

CONCLUSIONES

De todo lo expuesto destacan varios aspectos que merecen ser considerados. Unos se refieren a la práctica y a las instituciones jurídicas y otros a la mentalidad y actitud de Ibn Baṭṭūṭa ante las mismas.

Entre los aspectos puramente jurídicos e institucionales del relato, referidos a los países del Mediterráneo, hay que señalar los siguientes:

Convivencia de las doctrinas jurídicas: en el tiempo del relato de Ibn Baṭṭūṭa las cuatro doctrinas jurídicas ortodoxas convivían en armonía en Egipto y Siria, en especial la *mālikī* y la *shāfiʿī*, si bien ésta última conservaba la supremacía,[18] mientra que en al-Andalus y el Magreb el madhab de Malik era dominante y oficial, como lo era la escuela *ḥanafī* en Anatolia.

1990), pp. 279-280; I. Calero Secall, "Cadíes supremos de la Granada Naṣri", en *Actas del XII Congreso de la U.E.A.I.* (Málaga, 1986), p. 146.

[17] Se trata de Abū l-Barakāt Muḥammad b. al Ḥājj al-Balafīqī, también cadí supremo de Granada bajo Yūsuf I, primer reinado de Muḥammad V y Muḥ ammad VI (761-763/1360-1362); véase C. de la Puente, "La familia de Abū Is ḥāq de Velefique", en *Estudios Onomásticos-Biográficos de al-Andalus (Familias andalusíes V)*, eds. M. Marín y J. Zanón (Madrid, 1992), pp. 333-343, ofrece una extensa y detallada biografía; Arié, *L'Espagne*, pp. 279, 281; Calero Secall, pp. 146-147.

[18] Bajo los *ayyūbíes* y los mamelucos la doctrina *mālikī* recuperó importancia e imfluencia en Oriente debido, entre otras causas, a la emigración de andalusíes y norteafricanos. Véase A. Bekir, *Histoire de l'école malikite en oriente jusqu'à la fin du Moyen Âge* (Paris, s. d.), pp. 144 y ss., 168-175.

Instituciones jurídicas y religiosas: la *Riḥla* ofrece información sobre distintos cargos relacionados con el Derecho y la administración de la justicia, así como sobre otros dedicados al ritual religioso y a la enseñanza.

a) Cadíes: Ibn Baṭṭūṭa distingue varios tipos de cadíes según las competencias asignadas. Así encontramos en su relato la figura del simple cadí de una población y la del cadí supremo - el juez de jueces *(qāḍī al-quḍāt)*[19] en Oriente y juez de la comunidad (*qāḍī l-jamāʿa*)[20] en el Norte de Africa y al-Andalus, así como la del sustituto (*nāʾib*) de ambos. La *Riḥla* confirma las diferencias que la magistratura suprema tenía en una y otra latitud. En las ciudades orientales más importantes había un cadí supremo de cada una de las cuatro doctrinas ortodoxas (El Cairo, Alepo y Damasco) entre cuyas competencias estaba la de designar, inspeccionar o destituir a los cadíes de poblaciones menores. El en Magreb, por el contrario, existía un único cadí supremo (Túnez y Granada), en principio de igual categoría que los cadíes de provincias, que residía en la capital del país y que actuaba como consejero del soberano.

En dos ocasiones menciona cadíes con una competencia específica, como el cadí de matrimonios (*qāḍī al-ankiḥa*)[21] de Túnez y los que actuaban junto a los notarios de Damasco. También

[19] Sobre el *qāḍī l-quḍāt*, véase Tyan, pp. 128-133; *Encyclopédie de l'Islam*, op. cit., 4:390-391 (E. Tyan, s. v. "*Kāḍī*"); Bekir, pp. 177-178.

[20] Sobre el *qāḍī l-jamāʿa*, véase Tyan, pp. 91, 133, 523; *Encyclopédie de l'Islam*, op. cit., 4:390-391; R. Arié, "España Musulmana (siglos VIII-XV)", en *Historia de España*, dirigida por M. Tuñón de Lara, 10 vols. (Barcelona, 1982), 3:90-92; Bekir, pp. 177-178.

[21] Se trata más bien de un delegado del cadí para desempeñar las funciones de éste en materia de matrimonios, véase Tyan, pp. 111, 560-561.

aparece la figura del *qāḍī l-ḥajj,*[22] el juez de la caravana de peregrinos a los Santos Lugares del Islam, cargo para el que fue elegido el propio Ibn Baṭṭūṭa.

En cuanto al nombramiento de los cadíes, se aprecia que no sólo se producía por concurrir en la persona propuesta una serie de cualidades idóneas para el cargo (piedad, conducta intachable), se sino que también se accedía al cargo mediante el pago de una suma de dinero, como en el caso de Ibn Miskīn.

b) Alfaquíes: numerosos personajes citados en la *Riḥla* eran alfaquíes y, como personas de amplios conocimientos del fiqh, muchos de ellos desempeñaron cargos jurídicos y religiosos, como el de *imām*, cadí, muftí o notario.

c) Muftíes: entre las escasas referencias a muftíes, destaca la noticia sobre el lugar y modo de emitir fatwas del muftí de Túnez.

d) Notarios: Ibn Baṭṭūṭa utiliza los términos *ʿudūl* y *shuhūd* para designar a los notarios.[23] La única información se refiere a los notarios de Damasco, quienes, pertenecientes a las distintas doctrinas jurídicas, compartían su sede con los cadíes de matrimonios.

e) *Imāmes:* la *Riḥla* ofrece una detallada relación de los *imāmes* de los cuatro ritos ortodoxos de la Gran Mezquita de Damasco, así como sus actividades rituales y jurídicas.

[22] No se conocen bien la competencias del cadí de las caravanas, véase Bekir, pp. 179-180.

[23] Estos términos eran usuales en Oriente. Sobre la figura del notario, véase *Encyclopédie de l'Islam*, op. cit., 7:262 (W. Heffening, "*Shāhid*"); E. Levi-Provençal, "España musulmana", en *Historia de España*, dirigida por R. Menéndez Pidal (Madrid, 2ª edicion) 5: 75; Arié, "España musulmana", pp. 97-99 y *L'Espagne*, pp. 287-289; P. Cano Avila, "El notario musulmán andalusí", en *Actas del II Coloquio Hispano-Marroquí de Ciencias Históricas* (Granada, 1992), pp. 89-106.

f) Profesores: las *madrasa*s contaban con profesores cuya misión era formar en la religión y el derecho a sus alumnos y, en algunos casos, eran la sede del cadí supremo de la doctrina jurídica a la que pertenecía la escuela. En Damasco las *madrasas shāfiʿes* eran las más numerosas, por el contrario, los mālikıes sólo contaban con tres de ellas.

Funcionamiento y práctica de las instituciones judiciales: Ibn Baṭṭūṭa relata el funcionamiento de los tribunales referido a casos concretos y a personajes concretos. Así tenemos datos sobre: a) sentencias (pena de muerte en Alepo en 748/1348, por blasfemia; prisión y azotes para el alfaquí que contradijo en público a Ibn Taymiyya; prisión de Ibn Taymiyya por sus manifestaciones; 200 azotes y paseo vejatorio a lomos de un asno, por llamar mentiroso a un cadí supremo shāfiʿī de Damasco); b) procedimiento (actuación de los testigos ocultos en Latakía; juramentos y alegatos en la Gran Mezquita de Damasco); c) competencias (administración de legados píos; reclamaciones e injusticias que el propio soberano, al-Malik al-Nāṣir, presidía en El Cairo).

Respecto a la práctica ritual ofrece una detalladísima información sobre la Gran Mezquita de Damasco, con la actuación de los imāmes de los cuatro ritos, y sobre sus madrasas, que solían ser la sede del correspondiente cadí supremo.

En cuanto a la visión personal de Ibn Baṭṭūṭa, tambien es importante destacar algunos puntos.

El viajero de Tánger visitó varios países del Mediterráneo, algunos de ellos con una sóla doctrina jurídica implantada oficialmente, como el Magreb (*madhhab mālikī*) y Anatolia (*madhhab ḥanafī*) y otros, como Egipto y Siria, en los que convivían en armonía las cuatro principales doctrinas ortodoxas, si bien los šāfiʿíes tenían una clara supremacía.

Ante esta diversidad de opciones jurídicas, Ibn Baṭṭūṭa, pese a ser alfaquí *mālikī*, se muestra ecuánime e imparcial, llegando a reconocer méritos a personas de otras doctrina y a censurar conductas dudosas y corruptas de los representantes *mālikíes*. Es más, compartió ceremonias de distinto ritual, como en el caso de la observación de la luna de *Ramaḍān*, en compañía del cadí de Ibyār, en Egipto.

Su relación con todos los personajes citados es de gran cordialidad. Siempre fue bien recibido y agasajado como huesped de honor por cadíes, alfaquíes, muftíes, etc. y, hasta en situaciones de enfermedad y falta de medios para proseguir su viaje, contó con la generosa ayuda de algunos de ellos.

Por último cabe señalar que Ibn Baṭṭūṭa destaca siempre el origen de los muchos magribíes que encontró en Oriente,[24] todos de la doctrina *mālikī*, bien mencionando el lugar exacto de su procedencia e incluso la de su padre, bien por medio de la *nisba (al-malaqī, al-sharīshī*, etc). El viajero tangerino muestra su satisfacción al comprobar el prestigio del que gozaban sus paisanos, por ello, con lógica satisfacción y orgullo manifiesta en su relato: "Los damascenos tienen una buena opinión de los magrebíes y les confían sus fortunas, familias e hijos" (p. 122).

[24] Sobre la presencia de *mālikíes* del Magreb en Oriente, véase L. Pouzet, "Maghebins à Damas au VIIe/XIIIe siècle", *Bulletin d'Etudes Orientales*, 28 (1976), 177-193; Bekir, chapitre IX, p. 168 y s.s.

Textual Cohesion of the Aljamiado *Hadith de Yuçuf*

Esther M. Martínez
The William Paterson College of New Jersey

The fifteenth-century[1] Aljamiado *Hadith de Yuçuf*[2] is a difficult text. The difficulty is in part lexical, orthographical and syntactical, and in part due to the necessarily inexact use of Arabic script to transcribe

[1] Ezequiel González dates it at the beginning of the fourteenth century; Menéndez Pelayo and Díez Borque in the mid-fourteenth century; Menéndez Pidal at the end of the fourteenth or the beginning of the fifteenth century; Johnson, Deyermond, Harvey, Saroïhandy and Nykyl concur with the fifteenth-century designation. See Alan D. Deyermond, *Historia de la literatura española, I: La Edad Media* (Barcelona, 1987); José María Díez Borque, coord., *Historia de las literaturas hispánicas no castellanas* (Madrid, 1980); Ezequiel González Mas, *Historia de la literatura española: época medieval (siglos X-XV)* (San Juan, Puerto Rico, 1968); L. Patrick Harvey, "Lengua y estilo en la literatura aljamiado-morisca", *Nueva Revista de Filología España* 30.2 (1981), 420-40; Marcelino Menéndez Pelayo, *Orígenes de la novela* (Madrid, 1961); Ramón Menéndez Pidal, *Poema de Yúçuf. Materiales para su estudio* (Granada, 1952); A. R. Nykl, "A compendium of Aljamiado literature", *Revue Hispanique* 77 (1929), 409-611; J. Saroïhandy, "Remarques sur le poème de Yúçef", *Bulletin Hispanique* VI (1904), 182-194.

[2] Or the *Poema de Yuçuf*. The text will be referred to as the *Poema* in the following pages. All quotations are from William Weisiger Johnson, *The Poema de José: A Transcription and Comparison of the Extant Manuscripts* (Mississippi, 1974).

what is for the most part Aragonese with Arabic imports. Another difficulty is that the poem survives in only two incomplete manuscripts, with significant sections of the poem to be found in only one or the other of the two. These questions, and others (such as provenance and dating), have been addressed by a distinguished succession of critics, with varying degrees of attention to detail, since the *Poema* was first published by Morf in 1883 and again in 1919 by Miguel Artigas.

But although the text has been the subject of a number of philological and linguistic studies, its narrative structure has not yet received much attention. This neglect is not surprising, since, as a number of critics have noted, the *Poema* is awkward and confused, lacking the style of other Joseph accounts.[3]

The biblical and Qur'ānic Joseph stories, on the other hand, because of their sacred character, have been for centuries the object of extensive and intensive analysis by Talmudic (especially Aggadah and Midrashic)[4] and by Qur'ānic[5] commentators. Such analysis and commentary continues vigorously in the present, and while these studies are frequently linguistic, philological, and exegetical, some attention is, on occasion, paid to narrative structure as well.

To some extent, the interest in structure, particularly in the Hebrew account, stems from the probable confluence of three major Joseph texts (J, E, and G) woven into one continuous narrative by a compiler. Inconsistencies not resolved by the compiler led exegetes to

[3] Such as the Judeo-Spanish *Coplas de Yoçef.*

[4] One of the most famous in Spain was the *Yalqut Shim'iní* (*Selección* de Rabí Simeón ha Darchán), twelfth century.

[5] The most renowned of the *tafsīrs* or commentaries on the Qur'ān were written by Bayḍāwī (*Anwār al-Tanzīl*), Zamakhsharī (*Kashshāf*) and al-Ṭabarī (*Tafsīr*). Bayḍāwī is the most popular and very thorough, commenting on almost every line.

attempt to resolve coherence anomalies and to either defend or deny the existence of more than one narrative thread. Qur'ānic commentators dealt with a less extensive narrative, but were concerned as well by exegetical questions and with filling in whatever gaps of detail and plot were left by the sacred text. Both cultures interpreted the principal themes of the Joseph story in such a way as to incorporate it into their own sacred history as a people and a faith.

In verse[6] 3 of Sūra XII, Muḥammad calls the Joseph account "the most beautiful of stories",[7] and Muslim preachers were fond of it, using it extensively in sermons to extol such virtues as wisdom, complete faith in God, loyalty to one's family/people, generosity, patience and trust in God in the face of adversity, the ability to be true to oneself, loyalty to legitimate authority, good administration of a public trust, and, of course, purity, including physical chastity. These two intentions, to explain and fill in the sacred text, and to use the expanded story in preaching the word to the people, led, in both cultures, to the addition, over the centuries, of legendary material.

Spain produced two Joseph poems, one, the *Coplas de Yoçef*, in Judeo-Spanish, based on a blending of Genesis and traditions, and another, the *Hadith de Yuçuf*, in Aljamiado, based on the Qur'ān's Joseph account, also with a good many added legendary and traditional elements.[8] In both communities the apocryphal stories and

[6] The Qur'ān is composed of 114 sūras. Each sūra is divided into "'āyāt" or sections, and each "'āya" contains one or more readings or "qirā'at".

[7] Bayḍāwī, in his "tafsīr" *Anwār al-Tanzīl*, explains that it is the "best kind of thing related" because it includes marvels, aphorisms, signs and instructive examples. See ʿAbd Allāh b. ʿUmar al-Bayḍāwī, *Baidawi's Commentary on Surah 12 of the 'Qur'ān'*, ed. A. F. L. Beeston (Oxford, 1963).

[8] This legendary material, like its Jewish counterpart, must be considered part of the dialogue of the sacred. It sought to fill in the sacred text where details

scenes, some very brief, some more extensive, served to capture the attention of the audience, and better dispose them to accept the moral lesson.[9] Many of these stories conflict with each other, giving us several versions of the same detail, incident, or episode. Moreover, some versions are probable, but others may appear improbable, or even fantastic by present standards. And yet, all were equally accepted as "tradition". This is a plurivalent critical stance not easily acceptable to modern readers, who may be looking not only for a good story, but for a probable, believable, and even historically verifiable account. We ask of a story that it at least not stretch our credulity. We forget that both the Bible and Qur'ān, and the traditional exegetical and legendary material to which they gave birth, have historical, prophetic, symbolic and even metaphysical connections, interpretations and uses which make simple verisimilitude of secondary importance. The more numerous the variations, the richer are the possibilities for interpretation. What may appear to be fanciful inventions and accretions to a serious biblical or Qur'ānic narrative, are actually of great interpretative worth. The fact that they are often very entertaining as well is added value.

If we put aside our prejudices as to historical truth or scientific probability, does the Aljamiado *Hadith de Yuçef* begin to look better purely as narrative? It cannot really be said so. Some of its disconnected character may be attributed to the fact that the poem comes to us in two incomplete fragments, MS. A, of the Academia de la Historia, and MS. B, of the Biblioteca Nacional. The title,

were scant or altogether missing, to enliven a pivotal scene, or to add a scene which would provide the listener with a sense of completion or balance.

[9] Even in the schools where serious Talmudic or Qur'ānic studies were conducted, it was standard practice to lace serious study of the Law with amusing anecdotes and legendary stories, so that the heavier material could be made more palatable.

salutation, invocation, and first ten stanzas appear only in MS. A, which ends with stanza 95. MS. B begins with stanza 10 and ends with 312.[10] It is cut off at the end, so that we do not know how much longer the original might have been.

A brief introduction gives us Joseph's provenance and condition; the narrative portion begins with the dream of the sun, moon and eleven stars which do homage to Joseph's star.[11] The general narrative outline of the story follows that of Sūra XII, verses 4 through to 101.[12]

As the outline of the *Poema* shows (see Figure One), the principal elements of the Qur'ānic Joseph story are all there: Joseph, the favoured son, reveals a prophetic dream which arouses the envy of his brothers. The latter sell him into slavery. Joseph is purchased by a powerful official who treats him well and entrusts him with the administration of his household. The official's wife attempts to seduce Joseph, and when she fails, causes him to be imprisoned. Joseph interprets the dreams of two of his fellow detainees, and later procures his release by interpreting Pharaoh's dream. Pharaoh appoints Joseph administrator of the national effort to combat the coming famine. The new "ᶜAzīz" acquits himself admirably. Joseph tests his brothers when they apply to Egypt for provisions. This time

[10] I am using Johnson's 1974 edition. MS. A is missing a folio after strophe 82 (also incomplete), resumes with the second half of 92, and ends with strophe 95. There is no stanza in A which corresponds to B33. A65, 73, and 92 are incomplete.

The first nine quatrains of MS. B are missing: the text begins with stanza B10. The stanzas corresponding to Johnson's A19, A23 are also missing.

[11] The dream of the sheaves, which appears in Genesis but not in the Qur'ān, is not mentioned in our poem.

[12] Sūra XII has 111 verses: the narrative proper begins with verse 4 and ends with verse 101. The first three verses are introductory and the last 10 are interpretative.

the brothers pass the test of fraternal loyalty and are forgiven. The *Poema* recounts Joseph's plan to reunite the family in Egypt but is cut short at the next encounter of Jacob and his returning sons.

However, even at this level there are a few minor variations in plot: Pharaoh, referred to as "el rrey", buys Joseph directly and eight brothers rather than eleven return to Canaan (Jerusalem in the *Poema*) to bring Jacob to Egypt. At the lower levels of plot structure, there are a good number of departures from the Qur'ānic text; so many, in fact, that of the 312 extant strophes, only about a quarter of the narrative material comes from the Qur'ān's 98 narrative verses. The departures are of five kinds:

1. material in the Qur'ān is omitted.
2. material in the Qur'ān is used, but altered or expanded with legendary material.
3. scenes or elements from the Qur'ān or traditional material are used but at a different point in the narrative.
4. entire episodes and scenes from legendary material are added to the narrative plot.
5. original material is introduced.

1. MATERIAL IN THE QUR'ĀN IS OMITTED.

From the first category, we have the omission of Jacob's warning to his young son not to tell his brothers of the prophetic dream. The scene is made unnecessary because the telling of the dream to Jacob and then to the brothers is conflated in the *Poema* into one scene in which he tells everyone the dream at once. The text explains that he does this because: "Como yera Yuuçuf ninno de poqos annos, /

Envisandolo el padre, non se cubrio de los ermanos" (A7ab).[13] The youth of the boy and his innocence is soon exploited to the hilt in the scenes recounting his betrayal and journey to Egypt.

Jacob's prophetic explanation to Joseph of what is to follow his dream, and the reason for it, is also eliminated:

[13] The *Poema* uses the gerund, "envisandolo" ("warning/admonishing him"); the line could be translated variously as "when his father warned him" or "having been warned by his father, he [nevertheless] did not protect himself / dissemble / hide himself [by hiding the information] from the brothers".

The *Poema* frequently explains motivation which the leaner Sūra does not make explicit. The Sūra does provide Jacob's reason for warning Joseph not to tell his brothers: "Relate not thy vision / To thy brothers, lest they / Concoct a plot against thee" (v. 5). All quotations from the Qur'ān are taken from *The Holy Qur'ān,* Text, Translation and Commentary by Abdullah Yusuf Ali, 4th ed. (Washington, D.C., 1946). But the Qur'ān does not narrate or even allude to a scene in which Joseph tells anyone besides his father of his dream. Verses 8-10 move directly into the brothers' conspiracy. And the brothers make no reference to the dream, but speak only of Joseph's status as favoured son.

Our Aljamiado text does not recount the scene in which Jacob warns Joseph against telling the dream to his jealous brothers, but by mentioning the warning together with the statement that Joseph did indeed reveal the dreams to his brothers, the poet provides a motivational link explicitly missing in the source text. There is then both an ellipsis (of the warning), and an insertion (a mention of the retelling of the dream).

The Genesis account has Joseph bring a report, or gossip, to his father about his brothers Dan, Naphtali, Gad and Ashar (sons of Bilhah and Zilpah). The hate of his brothers originally stems from Joseph's behaviour and from jealousy caused by the gift of the ornamented coat (37.3), and is reinforced when Joseph tells his brothers and father together of the first dream (37.9), without first going to Jacob. After he tells the second dream, the text observes, "His brothers envied him, while his father kept the matter in mind" (37.11). The father therefore has no opportunity privately to advise discretion to the son, as he does in the Qur'ān. The text says only, "but his father kept the whole thing in mind". All quotations from *The Schocken Bible: Volume I: The Five Books of Moses*, Translation, Introductions, Commentary, and Notes by Everett Fox, (New York, 1995). The warning referred to in the *Poema* is therefore not of biblical origin.

Thus will thy Lord
choose thee and teach thee
the interpretation of stories (and events)
and perfect his favour
to thee and to the posterity
of Jacob - even as he
perfected it to thy fathers
Abraham and Isaac aforetime!
For God is full of knowledge
and wisdom. (XII.6)

A second example: in the Aljamiado, Jacob does not mention fear of wolves (XII.13) when he is hesitating to send Joseph with his brothers, thus eliminating the pledge of the brothers to guard Joseph from wolves (XII.14).

Later on in the story, the ᶜAzīz's wife does not, as she does in the Qur'ān (vv. 26-28), use Joseph's torn coat as evidence of his attempted rape. Instead, the *Poema* substitutes a description of Zulaykhā's physical appearance, faked in order to deceive her husband. In one of several examples of narrative discontinuity, the episode of Zulaykhā's accusation is not concluded: it ends abruptly with stanza 88, in which Joseph protests his innocence. His master takes no action, thus dropping verses 26 through to 30 of the Qur'ānic version.

2. MATERIAL IN THE QUR'ĀN IS USED, BUT ALTERED OR EXPANDED WITH LEGENDARY MATERIAL.

A minor example of the second category is the interpretation of the baker's dream. When Joseph interprets the dream unfavourably, the baker pretends that he had merely made it up, in order to test Joseph. Joseph replies that it will come true nonetheless, since Allāh had sent that story to the baker. The pretended invention addresses some legendary material in which the wine steward and baker recount a fabricated dream in order to test Joseph before they tell him their real dreams. The *Poema* picks up the tradition, but folds the two accounts into one. Whether the conflation is accidental or intentional, it does serve to remind the reader of one of the principal themes of the Joseph story: that nothing takes place without the express will of God. It also reinforces Joseph's role as the interpreter of dreams, God's primary gift to him. When a conflation of this sort is successfully interpreted in the text, coherence is enhanced rather than adversely affected.

3. SCENES OR ELEMENTS IN THE "QUR'ĀN" ARE USED BUT AT A DIFFERENT POINT IN THE NARRATIVE.

An instance in which a plot element is used, but at a different juncture, is the scene in which Jacob's sons respond: "Padre, volved en vuesa cordura" (B312a), when, in stanza 311, he orders them to return to "the king" with a second letter and to bring back both Benjamin and Joseph. The warning of those around him that he is losing his mind appears in verse 94 of the Sūra, when Jacob detects the scent of Joseph's coat from a great distance.[14] The warning makes sense in this context because Jacob has not yet had an opportunity to talk with his returning sons. But in the *Poema*, the motif of the miraculous robe of Gabriel is omitted and Jacob and his sons are already speaking. The admonition to the grieving father is reallocated

[14] This detail comes from an apocryphal account of the origin of the coat not found in Genesis, but in Jewish legendary material. Joseph's coat had been a gift of the angel Gabriel to Abraham; it carried the scent of Paradise. See Louis Ginzberg, *The Legends of the Jews*, 7 vols. (Philadelphia, 5728/1967).

to the generally confusing scene of the reunion of Jacob and his eight sons.

4. ENTIRE EPISODES AND SCENES FROM LEGENDARY MATERIAL ARE ADDED TO THE NARRATIVE PLOT.

The fourth and most common kind of plot change in the *Poema* is the addition of traditional material, sometimes in expanded, sometimes in abbreviated form. Most of the traditional material serves to heighten pathos or intensify suspense; some offers explanations for actions or events; some, particularly those scenes which describe rich apparel, serve to underline improved status or the generosity of either the Pharaoh or Joseph and are much amplified by our author.

Sometimes, details from traditional material are provided to fill out a scene taken from the Qur'ān, for example the image of blood running on the hands and grapefruits of the women at the Zulaykhā's banquet (AB93).[15] The scenes of Joseph's separation from his brothers, of his prayer at Rachel's tomb, of his beating at the hands of the merchant's slave, and of the sand storm raised by Allāh in retribution, are all traditional and are milked for all the pathetic effect possible.

Another two examples of extended traditional material are the detailed explanation of Joseph's wise administrative policies, and his appointment of two agents to monitor the sale of grain, with

[15] A93 actually says "senos" (breasts) instead of MS. B's "manos" (hands), which Johnson assumes must be an error for "manos". This seems likely, since the difference between initial "sīn" and "mīm" in Arabic is only a small loop at the beginning of the letter. "Sīn" is normally also longer, but Arabic script is quite elastic in the horizontal. Of course, there is also the possibility, not verifiable, that the scribe preferred the more erotic "senos".

instructions that all foreign buyers be screened so that his family will be brought to him.

An example of a briefer added element is the scene in which Joseph's steward stops the search into the brothers' sacks just before looking into the last one, which is Benjamin's: he moves the search to "the castle" (B258), thus prolonging the suspense even further.

When material from tradition is added without regard to coherence, the results can be extremely confusing. The end of the manuscript is a vivid example: stanza 306 ends with Joseph sending his brothers off to bring Jacob and his family to Egypt. Instead of hearing the good news, as in the Qur'ān, Jacob immediately berates the brothers for leaving Simeon, Judas and Benjamin behind. The brothers, instead of explaining that everything is fine, proclaim Benjamin's guilt. (Benjamin has already been cleared and the brothers have repented their family disloyalty). Jacob wants to send the eight sons, carrying a letter addressed to the Pharaoh, in search of Benjamin and Joseph. In the final stanzas, Jacob's sons tell him to "get a grip",[16] because his two youngest are dead. Jacob replies that he knows what they do not. Each one of the elements in the last three stanzas belongs to the Joseph narrative, but all of them are misplaced. It is difficult to see how the manuscript could have unravelled this chaos satisfactorily, or to guess how long the attempt might have taken.

Of course, not all material absent from the Qur'ān comes exclusively from commentaries or popular legend: Muslim commentators referred to Genesis and Jewish studies of the Talmud as well, and several elements not found in Sūra XII, but which do appear in Genesis, appear in our poem. For example, the Qur'ān is entirely silent on Joseph's administration of the food supply; Genesis,

[16] "Y dixeronle: 'Padre, volved en vuesa cordura'" (B312a). ["And they said to him: 'Father, return to your senses (sanity)'"].

while very brief, does at least mention it (41:46-49). Again, in the Qur'ān Joseph does not take a hostage on his brothers' first visit, but in Genesis 42:24, he takes Simeon. The *Poema* explains the choice with legendary material that credits Simeon with cutting Joseph's rope at the well.[17] In stanza A33, we had been told also that the rope was cut when Joseph was only half-way down, the intention supposedly having been to inflict injury in the fall.[18]

5. ORIGINAL MATERIAL IS INTRODUCED.

Lastly, some of the material, although a very small amount, may be either original to our author or simply cultural/linguistic borrowings. Some examples are: the frequent fainting spells of Benjamin and Jacob; Jacob's prayer for Joseph's safety in A23, with its felicitous recalling of the beasts and cold of the well; and the added detail that the brothers re-entered the city in the heat of the day (B222).[19] There is also the only comic incident in the *Poema*: Joseph is discovered in the well when the lowered bucket lands on his head.

[17] Traditions differ: in Josephus's account, it is Reuben who lets Joseph down the well, and he does so gently.

[18] Jewish tradition names Simeon as the most virulent of Joseph's enemies, the one who argues for killing Joseph. Bayḍāwī names either Reuben or Judah as the brother who threw Joseph into the well. Bayḍāwī also reports the details of Joseph's beating at the hands of his brothers, which survives in our poem only in his being dragged to the well. Also mentioned by Bayḍāwī are the water and the rocks, and the fact that the rope is released when Joseph is only half-way down (p. 8).

[19] The moralising of stanza B110 may be of the author's invention, as Johnson conjectures (p. 113), but is more likely to have come from a commentary, or the author's recollection of one, or from the use of a preacher of such a source, since the false dream was probably a common traditional scene in the Joseph corpus.

These touches may be original, while the use of such terms as "rey", "castillo" (258), "vasallo" (258), "emperador" (308), and "traiçion"/ "traydores" (61) reflect current usage in society at large. So does the use of "pecado" (e.g., B83) for Satan,[20] and the repeated use of words and set expressions reminiscent of epic formulae - phrases such as "Q(ue)brantastes vuest(a)ras fe y vuest(o)ros amenajes / Perdistesme a mi fijjo, como desleales" (B212).[21]

On occasion, a detail is added to introduce symmetry: for instance, Zulaykhā tries to drag Joseph into her bedchamber by the skirt of his tunic (AB80), as well as trying to detain him later by pulling at it from behind (B84).

The successful integration of so many sources and traditions into a tightly structured, coherent text would have been difficult, requiring great skill. But either our poet was unequal to the task or subsequent tampering with the original created unresolved incoherencies. Parallel interpretations of an episode are offered to the reader side by side, or, even more confusing, the episode is retold, the second time differently, after the narrative has progressed beyond that episode. The poet does this most often when seeking pathetic affect, but makes no attempt to reconcile the contradictions.[22] An example of this occurs very early on in the poem, when Joseph has been thrown

[20] The Qur'ān uses "shayṭān".

[21] "You broke your faith (word) and your oaths / You lost my son, like traitors (disloyal ones)".

[22] Contradictory accounts are acceptable in Talmudic studies, in Midrashim, and in their Muslim counterparts, since they are not continuous narrative accounts but collections of lore, observations and explanations. Treatments of the Joseph story by such commentators as Josephus and Philo, while also exegetical in nature, are more in the mode of integrated narratives, and both authors are careful to explain any inconsistencies in the material. See Flavius Josephus, *The Life and Works of Flavius Josephus*, trans. William Whiston (New York, 1977); Philo, *The Works of Philo*, trans. C. D. Yonge (Peabody, Mass., 1993).

into the well (A21), Jacob has been told the story of the wolf, the wolf has spoken in her defence, and Jacob has resigned himself to the will of Allāh. At this point Joseph is again taken to the well, this time dragged along, and the details of the rope and the rocks in the well are added (33-35).

Sometimes the inconsistencies are amusing: the Joseph of tender years who betrays his vision to his brothers and who is carried into the desert on their shoulders suddenly sports a beard when he is taken from the well by the merchant's slave only a few hours later.[23]

Another glaring example is the episode in which Joseph is sold at the Egyptian slave market. Stanzas 60-64 describe the scene, which ends when the "king" buys Joseph for his weight in pearls and gives him into the safe-keeping of his wife Zulaykhā. The next stanza has the auctioneer again offering Joseph for sale, but this time Joseph reveals his true identity as a prophet, a true believer in the creator, and a man of noble lineage. The episode is introduced, apparently, to give the merchant who put him on the block the opportunity to redeem himself a second time[24] by refusing all profit from the sale.

[23] "Pusieron ye esfuerço, y salio la bella barba" (B36d). ("They put some effort into it / and [he of] the comely beard came out"). Bayḍāwī, while commenting on verses 5 and 15 of the Sūra, reports two different traditions on the age of Joseph when he is sold into slavery: 12 and 17. Our *Hadith* recovers both traditions without reconciling them.

Of course, "la bella barba" is a stock epithet, and its use could be purely referential, a substitution for the name Joseph, "he who [later] had a beautiful beard". But the reference nevertheless does evoke the image of a bearded man at an inappropriate moment in the narrative. It betrays the two conflicting traditions as to Joseph's age at the time of the abduction.

[24] He had repented already in the desert, when Joseph's prayer stopped the sandstorm. According to the *Poema*, only the merchant's contract with the brothers had prevented him from freeing Joseph altogether. Logically, the merchant could have released Joseph once they had crossed the border. Although such an option was not available within the Joseph story, the narrator does not explain why the merchant, so well-disposed towards Joseph, had not freed him.

And there are instances when the addition of a detail alters a theme of the source: upon his betrayal Jacob curses his sons, a posture which is out of character for the Jacob whose response in the Qur'ān was: "(For me) patience is most fitting against that which ye assert. It is God (alone) whose help can be sought" (v. 18). Our author seems more interested in Jacob the suffering father, than in Jacob the patriarch and keeper of the covenant.

The *Poema* does have some happy instances of coherence at smaller propositional levels from time to time: Jacob's prayer asking Allāh to protect Joseph from wild beasts and the cold reminds the reader of the actual conditions being suffered by Joseph in the well, as well as anticipating the apocryphal wolf scene. Also, the poet successfully integrates the letter theme into the story, in the beginning, middle and end of the *Poema*: the contract and bill of sale, in the form of a letter (AB40), reappears (B298) at the climactic scene of reconciliation, soon after the letter from Jacob pleading for the mercy and favour of the king is introduced. The letter motif is used once more (B311), although less fortuitously, at the very end of the extant text.

But sometimes, the explanation or detail seems rather limited in view of the wide range of possibilities. There are several explanations available as to why Jacob ordered his sons to enter the city by different gates, some of which were useful in highlighting Jacob's wisdom. Our text adopts none of them, but says simply "Porque seria mejor, porque ansi lo e p(o)rovado" (B221d) ("Because it would be better / because I have experienced it to be so").

The *Hadith de Yuçuf* is an entertaining narrative, with many engaging moments, but it fails to exploit well the available wealth of traditional and sacred resources. In weaving together the "ḥadīth" at its disposal, it sometimes manages a smooth and coherent propositional order, and at times fails to integrate opposing elements in any coherent manner. These limitations may have been the result of the limited education of the author, the lack of sophistication of the poem's audience, the marginal and isolated status of the mudejar community in fifteenth-century northern Aragon,[25] or a combination of all three. The reworking of the available manuscripts by scribes, the extent of which is difficult to assess, probably affected coherence as well. The *Poema* gathers and blends "ḥadīth" to form its narrative, at times succeeding in forming a coherent synthesis, and at times falling short.[26]

[25] See Mercedes Sánchez-Alvarez, "La lengua de los manuscritos aljamiado-moriscos como testimonio de la doble marginación de una minoría islámica", *Nueva Revista de Filología Hispánica* 30.1 (1981), 441-452; and Anwar G. Chejne, *Muslim Spain: Its History and Culture* (Minneapolis, 1974), pp. 101-105 and 381-383.

[26] As did Jewish and Muslim commentators, with the difference that what is acceptable in a verse-by-verse explanation, with appropriate transitional phrases such as "Others say that ...", "It is said ...", does not work well in this narrative poem.

Figure One

PLOT OUTLINE

Stanza		
1-2	I	Title, Invocation, Salutation
3-7	II	Joseph's Dream
		Background
		Joseph's dream
		Joseph reveals his dream
8-72	III	Joseph Sold into Slavery
		The brothers plot
		Joseph's brothers turn on him, 1
		Jacob's reaction
		Joseph's brothers turn on him, 2
		Joseph is sold
		Joseph takes leave of his brothers
		Joseph visits Rachel's tomb
		The sand storm
		Joseph is sold in Egypt, 1
		Joseph is sold in Egypt, 2
73-102	IV	The Seduction of Joseph
		The first attempt
		The second attempt
		Zulaykhā's banquet
		Zulaykhā's accusation
		The king imprisons Joseph

102-173	V	The Interpretation of Dreams
		The dream of the wine steward
		The dream of the baker
		The dream of the king
		Joseph is elevated to kingship and stewardship
		Joseph's administrative plans
174-204	VI	The First Visit of Joseph's 11 Brothers to Egypt
		Joseph tests his brothers with the measure, first divination
		Joseph accuses his brothers of being spies
		Joseph lays down conditions for future sales
		Joseph takes his brother Simeon as hostage
		Joseph has the purchase price returned to his brothers surreptitiously.
205-221	VII	The 10 Brothers Return to "Jerusalem"
		The accusation of Jacob
		The brothers find the money in their bags
		Jacob relents and agrees to send Benjamin to Egypt
		The letter and the oath

222-307	VIII	Benjamin and the 10 Brothers Return to Egypt: the Second Trip The welcome; the banquet Joseph reveals himself to Benjamin and plots with Benjamin to test their brothers Joseph tests his brothers with the measure, second divination Joseph plants the "magic" measure in Benjamin's sack Judas challenges Joseph in defence of Benjamin Joseph threatens to cut off the hands of the brothers Judas expresses repentance Joseph forgives his brothers Joseph sends his shirt to Jacob
308-312	IX	8 Brothers Return to "Jerusalem" Jacob's accusations and lament The brothers accuse Benjamin Jacob orders his sons to go back to Egypt and find his two sons, Joseph and Benjamin

...

Incomplete

Translation as seen by al-Jāḥiẓ and Ḥunayn ibn Isḥāq: Observer versus Practitioner

Myriam Salama Carr
University of Salford

The important role which translation played in the transmission of Greek philosophy and science, initially to the Arabo-Muslim world, and from there to medieval Europe at a later stage, is well known and researched. However translations which were performed into Arabic, from the second/eighth century onwards, either directly from Greek or via Syriac, did more than merely relay information and concepts. In the medieval tradition translation was associated with interpretation and exegesis of the source texts, and the medieval Arabic translations, it may be said, added to the Greek legacy. But this article is concerned not so much with the input of Arabic translations to what we refer to as the Greek corpus, nor with the integration of translations into the Arabic system of thought, but rather with the debate which was precipitated at that time by the practice of translation into Arabic, and with the comments which were made on this activity both by observers, and by the translators themselves.

Much of the current research in the field of translation studies focuses on historical aspects, and the textual analysis of previous translations, together with the study of early writings on the practice of translation, furnish a valuable historical framework. It goes without saying that certain periods and regional entities have been researched more comprehensively than others. In my view, the early translations into Arabic, together with the comments which were made on and about them, bear further investigation. Manuscripts of these translations are particularly informative as frequently they include numerous annotations and marginal comments, both by the translators themselves and also by later editors and revisers. These notes include references to specific translation problems, and give reasoned explanations for the strategies which were employed. One interesting example is that of a seventh-/thirteenth-century copy of an Arabic translation of Dioscorides' (fl. first or second century AD) seminal work of pharmacology, *Materia Medica*[1] *(Fī Hayūlā ᶜIlāj al-Ṭibb).* The first Arabic translation, which had been undertaken by Iṣṭifān ibn Bāsil (fl. third/ninth century),[2] included Greek terms, left as they were in the original as either there was no (or at any rate, the translator was unaware of any) equivalent in Arabic. The manuscript also includes later amendments which were made by Ḥunayn ibn Isḥāq (d. 260/873), who suggested Arabic terms as alternatives for the Greek terms which Iṣṭifān had simply reproduced in his Arabic translation. Another example of the progressive arabicisation of Greek input can be found in the replacement of the transliterated term

[1] Dioscorides, *Materia Medica*, Arabic manuscript *Fī Hayūlā ᶜIlāj al-Ṭibb*, Paris, Bibliothèque Nationale, MS ar. 2849.

[2] A member of the team of translators who were working with Ḥunayn ibn Isḥāq, along with Hubaysh and Mūsā b. Abī Khālid, among others, as reported by the historiographers Ibn Juljul, al-Qifṭī, and Ibṇ Abī Uṣaybiᶜa.

qāṭīghūryās (categories) which was later replaced by the Arabic *maqūlāt.*[3]

The comments made on translation by ᶜAmr b. Baḥr al-Jāḥiẓ (d. 255/868), and by the aforementioned Ḥunayn ibn Isḥāq, serve to illustrate an early instance of translation debate. In this paper I refer principally to the *Kitāb al-Ḥayawān*[4] by al-Jāḥiẓ, and the *Risālat ilā ᶜAlī ibn Yaḥyā fī Dhikr mā Turjima min Kutub Jālīnūs bi-ᶜilmihi wa Baᶜḍ lam Yutarjam*[5] by Ḥunayn ibn Isḥāq. The scholars were near contemporaries, though as far as I am aware there is no evidence of any intercommunication between them.

We have, on the one hand, al-Jāḥiẓ, one of the early masters of Arabic prose, who was associated with the religious and philosophical Muᶜtazilite movement. He writes a damning account of translation and of the failings of translators in his *Kitāb al-Ḥayawān.* On the other hand we have Ḥunayn ibn Isḥāq, one of the most famous translators of Greek and Syriac into Arabic, who lists and discusses his translations of Galen's (d. c. 200 AD) works in the *Risāla,* a missive addressed to ᶜAlī ibn Yaḥyā, a friend who was a secretary to the caliph al-Mutawakkil (232-247/847-861). Both texts, the *Kitāb al-Ḥayawān* and the *Risāla,* include references to translation problems, but each author adopts a very different perspective.

Al-Jāḥiẓ stresses the difficulty of translating prose, whether it be scientific, philosophical or sacred and, in his view, demonstrates that poetry is untranslatable due to its formal features. His comments raise issues that have long been, and remain, central to the debate on translation. Issues such as linguistic interferences between the

[3] F. E. Peters, *Aristotle and the Arabs* (New York, 1968), p. 65.

[4] ᶜAmr b. Baḥr al-Jāḥiẓ, *Kitāb al-Ḥayawān,* 2 vols. (Cairo, 1955), 1:74-75.

[5] Ḥunayn ibn Iṣḥāq, "Risālat-ilā-ᶜAlī ibn Yaḥyā fī Dhikr mā turjima min Kutub Jālīnūs bi ᶜilmihi wa baᶜḍ lam yutarjam", in *Ueber die Syrischen und Arabischen Galen Uebersetzungen*, ed. G. Bergsträsser (Leipzig, 1925).

working languages of the translators,[6] and their lack of subject knowledge[7] are advanced to support the contention that translations can never do justice to the originals, and that translators do not share the discernment and wisdom of the source-text authors.[8] This challenge to the principle of translation is accompanied by references to what one could call practical occupational hazards - the possibility that the translator does not possess the required linguistic skills, nor the adequate subject expertise, and the danger that the original manuscripts, and their subsequent translations, are unreliable due to the vicissitudes of time and the errors that the copyists would have introduced.[9]

These problems, which are presented in relation to the translation of scientific texts, as in the fields of geometry, chemistry, and astronomy, are seen as crucial should the source text be of a religious nature, with the danger that a translation is tantamount to

[6] Al-Jāḥiẓ, 1:76.

> We know that when the translator speaks two languages, he does wrong to both, as each one influences the other, they borrow from and contradict each other. How can the translator know both languages with the competence that he would have with only one?

(my translation).

[7] idem, "The more difficult and arduous a science is and the fewer are those that know it, the more difficult translation is and the greater the risk that the translator will err" (my translation).

[8] ibid., 1:77. "You cannot find a translator who is as wise as these sages" (my translation).

[9] ibid., 1:79.

> Initially the scribe makes a defective copy, then the translator asks a scribe to copy his translation, and this will introduce other errors, then the reviser risks leaving in the errors such as they are, if he is not himself able to correct them

(my translation).

tampering with the word of God.[10] The timelessness of this concern is evident when one looks at modern discussions of biblical translation which emphasise the unicity of the divine message and the need to "make certain that he [the receptor] is very unlikely to misunderstand it".[11] It must be borne in mind, though, that there are differences here as regards the concept of an untranslatable sacred language, the Bible having always been a "translated" book.

Al-Jāḥiẓ's reservations on translation cannot be seen in isolation from his own position as a scholar, and to an extent they were possibly underpinned by concerns of a linguistic and theological nature. Therefore, his comments can only be interpreted in the context of the development of the Arabic language, in contact with other languages, and when it was increasingly used by non-native speakers, as in the case of the early translators into Arabic. Concerns of a more theological nature have also been suggested, for instance by Badawi, who refers to the possibility that al-Jāḥiẓ may have felt uneasy about the translation of the Qur'ān and the implications and ramifications this might have.[12] Al-Jāḥiẓ was particularly aware of the potential risks posed by a massive importation of Greek philosophy into the receptor culture - however the *Kitāb al-Ḥayawān* itself

[10] ibid., 1:76.

> What can one say then on works of religion and theology which speak for God the highest: what is applicable or not, in the true sense of conformity to the unity of God, the contents are attributable to God, whatever men say or not say? The translator must distinguish between general and specific meanings, together with the relationships which can transform the general verses into specific ones?

(my translation).

[11] E. A. Nida and C. Taber, *The Theory and Practice of Translation* (Leiden, 1968), p. 2.

[12] A. R. Badawi, *La transmission de la philosophie grecque au monde arabe*, Etudes de philosophie médiévale LVI (Paris, 1968).

includes numerous quotations which were attributed to Aristotle (d. 322 BC). Al-Jāḥiẓ's comments provide early evidence of the fact that the way translation is perceived is defined ideologically, and that translation could be seen to be subversive. It should also be pointed out that when he casts doubts on the competence of translators,[13] and questions whether these translators were ever equal to Aristotle or Plato (d. 347 BC), he is referring to the early translators into Arabic, whose work was subsequently to be revised by their successors, amongst whom Ḥunayn is included. When advancing practical objections to translation, al-Jāḥiẓ is, in fact, expressing fundamental reservations about the very nature of this activity.

Al-Jāḥiẓ's criticisms are echoed by the comments of Ibn Sīnā (d. 428/1037), when the latter complains of the opacity of some of the Aristotelian texts in their Arabic versions,[14] and a further example of the translation debate is reported by the essayist Abū Ḥayyān al-

[13] Al-Jāḥiẓ, 1:75.

> Among those who defend poetry, treating it with high regard and arguing in support of it, there are those who declare that the translator can never render what the philosopher says, including the proper meanings, the truths of his doctrine, the subtleties of his concisions, and the intricacies of his definitions. The translator can never do him [the philosopher] justice or express him with fidelity, being unable to fulfil the mandate that he was given. How can he [the translator] express this, and render the meaning faithfully, without possessing the knowledge of the author as regards the subject, the ways in which terms are employed, and the interpretation of their ramifications. Ibn Biṭrīq, Ibn Naʿīma, Abū Qurra, Ibn Fahr, Ibn Wahīlī, Ibn al-Muqaffaʿ, - may God have mercy on them - have they ever been equal to Aristotle? Or Khalid to Plato?

(my translation).

[14] See Al-Qifṭī, *TarīH al-Ḥukamā'*, ed. J. Lippert (Leipzig, 1903), p. 415.

Tawḥīdī (d. after 399/1008).[15] In a controversy with the Aristotelian thinker and translator Mattā ibn Yūnus (d. 328/940), the philologist Abū Saᶜīd al-Sīrāfī (d. 368/978) questioned the authenticity of ideas which had been transferred initially from Greek to Syriac, and only subsequently from Syriac to Arabic, with all the distortions that this transfer was deemed to entail, thus denying the validity of concept-transfer between languages. As pointed out by Rosenthal,[16] whereas translations into Syriac were intended for use by scholars, the audience was wider for Arabic versions. It should be emphasised that all of the above objections to translation are best interpreted with reference to the medieval tradition, wherein the source text could be extensively manipulated, to the extent that in some cases the text and the translators' comments were merged.

In the *Risāla* Ḥunayn demonstrates the pragmatic views of the practitioner for whom translation is a perfectible act, either through revision or, if necessary, complete rewriting. Taking into account his emphasis on variables such as the competence of the translator, and the level of expertise and knowledge of the target reader, it is impossible to overemphasise the relevance of his comments to the practice of translation. Nor did he overlook the problems of faulty manuscripts, travelling extensively in search of reliable sources, journeying in Iraq several times, and also visiting Syria, Egypt and Byzantium in search of accurate copies. Though the many difficulties that the translator could encounter were not neglected in his explanations as to why he regarded a particular translation to be unsatisfactory, these problems were never viewed as insurmountable. Indeed Ḥunayn fully acknowledged the weakness of some of the

[15] Abū Ḥayyān al-Tawḥīdī, *Al-Imtāʿ wa l-Muʾānasa* (Cairo, 1939), pp. 67-68.

[16] F. Rosenthal, *The Classical Heritage in Islam*, translated from the German by Emile and Jenny Marmostein (London, 1992), p. 9.

translations that he came across or was asked to revise, providing clear reasons as to why he considered them inadequate. Perhaps the translator was not proficient enough in the target language, he was not conversant in the subject matter, he had insufficient practice in translation, or he was working from a faulty or incomplete manuscript. Ḥunayn placed emphasis on the importance of practice and imitation, together with the amendment of faulty translations. Furthermore he regarded the establishment of a workable source copy as obtainable by means of careful compilation and editing of parallel manuscripts.

The seventh-/thirteenth-century historiographer Ibn Abī Uṣaybiᶜa (d. 668/1269) reports that when Ḥunayn complains of his detractors who caused his disgrace with al-Mutawwakil, he emphasises that he provided translations which were both linguistically correct and intelligible to the non-expert owing to the translator's painstaking work.[17] Whilst al-Jāḥiẓ spoke in absolute terms to warn against the dangers of translation, Ḥunayn introduced pragmatic parameters, stating, for instance, at the beginning of the *Risāla*[18] that the quality of a translation depends not only on the skills of the translator, but also on the reader. Ḥunayn also refers to his translation strategy, declaring that he strived for accuracy in his translations whilst attempting not to impair the style of the target text, introducing an equilibrium which has long since been at the heart of translation discourse.[19]

Although our interpretation of past translation practice is bound to be shaped by the way in which we conceptualise translation today, it is my view that the study of medieval translation can make a

[17] Ibn Abī Uṣaybiᶜa, *ᶜUyūn al-Anbā' fī Ṭabaqāt al-Aṭibbā'* (Cairo, 1882), p. 191.

[18] Ḥunayn ibn Isḥāq, p. 2.

[19] ibid., pp. 22-23, 30 and 1-3, 31.

significant contribution towards the identification of key issues which constantly recur in disparate guises, often being cloaked in different terminology, whenever translation is discussed. It is also my view that current discourse on translation, should it acknowledge the historical dimension of this activity, cannot evolve without reference to earlier debates. The work of the Baghdād translators, as epitomised by Ḥunayn's contributions, and the discussions which were inspired by translation, demonstrated eloquently by al-Jāḥiẓ, deserve a more prominent place in the history of translation practice and theory.

La Littérature Arabe Représentée dans les Bibliothèques de *Waqf* en Bulgarie au XIXe Siècle

Stoyanka Kenderova
Bibliothèque Nationale de Bulgarie
St Cyrille et St Méthode à Sofia

Pendant la période de la domination ottomane en Bulgarie, un nombre considérable de manuscrits et d'anciens livres imprimés arabographiques était conservé dans les bibliothèques de *waqf*[1] et dans les collections privées.[2] Une partie essentielle de ce fonds riche forme aujourd'hui la collection de manuscrits orientaux de la bibliothèque Nationale *St Cyrille et St Méthode* à Sofia.[3] Les titres

[1] M. Stajnova, *Osmanskite biblioteki v bŭlgarskite zemi XV-XIX vek. Studii* (Les bibliothèques ottomanes dans les terres bulgares XVe-XIXe siècles. Etudes) (Sofia, 1982).

[2] Les "inventaires après décès" dans les *sicill* (registre de *qāḍī*) des certaines villes bulgares nous donnent une information riche sur la quantité et le contenu des livres, possédés par les décédés. Très souvent on trouve également le prix de chaque volume. Pour l'instant cette information est hors de notre sujet.

[3] V. Jordanov, *Istoriia na Narodnata biblioteka v Sofiia. Po sluchai 50 godishninata i. 1879-1929* (Histoire de la bibliothèque publique à Sofia. A l'occasion de son 50ème anniversaire. 1879-1929) (Sofia, 1930); B. Nedkov, "Orientalistikata v Sofiiskata narodna biblioteka" (Les etudes orientales dans la

en arabe y représentent environ 81,5%. Ils concernent plus au moins en détail tous les aspects du développement de la culture arabe écrite.[4]

La présente étude se propose d'examiner la place de la littérature arabe[5] de la période classique dans les plus grandes bibliothèques de *waqf* qui fonctionnaient autrefois sur le territoire de la Bulgarie.

Tout d'abord, c'est la Bibliothèque de Şerif Halil Paşa (m. en 1165/1752), près de la mosquée *Tombul* dans la ville de Shumen (Bulgarie du Nord-Est). Cette personnalité est née au village de Madara, ou bien dans la ville de Shumen. Pendant sa carrière professionnelle, il occupait des postes élevés dans la capitale de l'empire et dans la province.[6] Şerif Halil Paşa s'intéressait aussi de la poésie; il a fait des traductions de l'arabe et de la langue persane en turc ottoman.

bibliothèque publique de Sofia), in *Godishnik na Bibliotechno-Bibliografskiia Institut za 1945-6* (Sofia, 1948), pp. 226-239; M. Mihaĭlova, "90 godini Orientalski sbirki v Narodnata biblioteka Kiril i Metodiĭ", (90 années de la création des collections orientales dans la Bibliothèque Nationale Cyrille et Méthode), dans *Annales de la Bibliothèque Nationale Cyrille et Méthode*, 12 (18) (Sofia, 1971), 351-357.

[4] S. Kenderova, "Bulgaria", dans *World Survey of Islamic Manuscripts*, ed. G. Roper, 3 vols. (London, 1992), 1:121-142.

[5] Sur la place de la littérature persane en Bulgarie voir S. Kenderova, "La Diffusion de la littérature persane en Bulgarie au XVIIIe et au XIXe siècles", dans *Festschrift in Honor of Iraj Afshar* (Tehran, sous presse); sur la collection des manuscrits persans voir J. Sayyar, *Opis na persiĭskite rŭkopisi v Narodnata biblioteka Kiril i Metodiĭ* (Catalogue des manuscrits persans dans la Bibliothèque Nationale Cyrille et Méthode) (Sofia, 1973).

[6] M. Süreyya, *Sicill-i osmani*, 4 vols. (Istanbul, 1308-1311/1894), 3:142; H. W. Duda, *Balkantürkische Studien*, Österrechische Akademie der Wissenschaften. Philosophisch-historische Klasse. Sitzungsberichte, 226, Bd. 1. Abhandlung (Wien, 1949), pp. 63-69; O. Keskioğlu, "Şumnulu Şerif Paşa Vakfiyesi", *Vakıflar Dergisi* 19 (Ankara, 1985), 25-30.

En 1157/1744, il a fondé sa bibliothèque en faisant don de livres à titre de *waqf*. Dans son *waqfnamah*, Şerif Halil Paşa a determiné les différents services dans la bibliothèque et le mode d'utilisation des livres.

Aujourd'hui la collection manuscrite de cette bibliothèque renferme environ 800 volumes, dont certains ne sont conservés que fragmentairement. Le nombre des livres imprimés arabographiques est d'environ 1500 volumes. Cette riche collection est en train d'être cataloguée. Comme le démontrent les notes conservées sur plusieurs codices, un certain nombre en a été donné par d'autres habitants de la ville et de la région dans le but d'être abrités dans la bibliothèque édifiée par Şerif Halil Paşa.

Une des plus riches bibliothèques dans les Balkans au cours du XIIIe/XIXe siècle se trouvait dans la ville de Samokov.[7] C'est la Bibliothèque de Mehmed Hüsrev Paşa (m. en 1263/1847), originaire de la même ville. Il était nommé à des postes administratifs importants dans l'empire. En même temps, son activité était étroitement liée au développement économique et culturel de Samokov.[8]

Une source précieuse sur le fonds de cette bibliothèque pendant une étape de son histoire, c'est le catalogue original (Sofia, Bibliothèque Nationale de Bulgarie, Département Oriental, MS OR 1121), créé pas plus tard du premier *şevval* 1250/31 janvier 1835. Ce catalogue contient les descriptions de 540 volumes de livres. Beaucoup plus tard, après la fondation de la collection orientale en 1880 (aujourd'hui le département oriental), la Bibliothèque Nationale de Bulgarie a reçu 2485 manuscrits et livres imprimés de la Bibliothèque de Samokov. Évidemment, pendant les années qui

[7] M. Stajnova, pp. 38-80.
[8] M. Süreyya, 2:275.

se sont écoulées, la Bibliothèque de Hüsrev Paşa a abrité les collections des autres plus petites bibliothèques de la ville.

Les livres dans ce catalogue sont presentés en 26 rubriques selon la hiérarchie des domaines du savoir, typiques pour le Moyen Âge dans le monde musulman.[9] Grace à cela, on est en état d'analyser les ouvrages qui représentent chaque thème.

Cette possibilité s'ouvre aussi pour la bibliothèque du célèbre Osman Pazvantoğlu (1171-1222/1758-1807) de la ville de Vidin (Bulgarie du Nord-Ouest, au bord du Danube).[10] Le catalogue de sa bibliothèque (BNB, *Sicill* S 52a) est créé le 23 *zi'l-hicce* 1252/31 mars 1837 (30 ans après la mort du fondateur).[11] Il présente 2211 ouvrages manuscrits en 2390 volumes et 74 livres imprimés. Les descriptions sont réparties en 22 rubriques thématiques.

[9] I. E. Erünsal, *Türk Kütüphaneleri Tarihi. II. Kuruluştan Tanzimat'a kadar Osmanlı Vakıf Kütüphaneleri* (Ankara, 1988), pp. 213-235; S. Kenderova, "Traditions du catalogage des livres dans les Bibliothèques de *waqf* en Bulgarie au XIXe siècle", dans *Tradition et innovation dans l'Orient ottoman et iranien. Journées franco-allemagnes d'études ottomanes et iraniennes* (Mulhouse, 1995).

[10] Osman Pazvantoğlu provient d'une famille riche, d'origine bosniaque. En 1208/1794 il prend la ville de Vidin et la fait un centre de résidence au sultan Selim III (1203-1222/1789-1807), sous prétexte d'opposition aux ses réformes. Après le débarquement de Bonaparte en Egypte en 1798, le pouvoir ottoman est obligé à rappeler ses troupes des Balkans. Le sultan se replie devant les rebelles et Pazvantoğlu est nommé officiellement *paşa* de Vidin. Voir V. Mutafchieva, *Kŭrdzhaliĭsko vreme* (Le Temps des *kurdzhali*) (Sofia, 1977); *Histoire de l'Empire Ottoman*, réd. R. Mantran (Fayard, 1989), p. 428; G. Castelan, *Histoire des Balkans XIVe-XXe siècle* (Fayard, 1991), pp. 214, 231.

[11] Pour la première fois une information sur ce catalogue a été présentée par S. Kenderova pendant la session scientifique à l'occasion de 250 années de la naissance de Sofroniĭ Vrachanski (1739-1813) qui a eu lieu en 1989 à Vratsa. Les communications de cette conférence ne sont pas encore publiées. Le catalogue lui-même est en train d'être édité.

D'après la tradition, en premier lieu dans les anciens catalogues des bibliothèques sont décrites les copies d'*al-Qur'ān* et des ouvrages du domaine des sciences coraniques. Actuellement, la collection arabe de la Bibliothèque Nationale de Bulgarie comprend 120 manuscrits d'*al-Qur'ān.*[12] Ils se trouvaient autrefois dans les bibliothèques publiques ou privées en Bulgarie; une partie même été créée dans certaines villes bulgares (voir plus bas). Il y en a parmi ces manuscrits des exemples de la présentation calligraphique et artistique musulmane. Un tel exemplaire c'est la plus ancienne copie d'*al-Qur'ān* dans notre collection, achevée le 25 *ramaḍān* 669/7 mai 1271 (BNB, MS OR 2708) par le *khaṭṭāṭ* Muḥammad b. ᶜAbd al-Raḥman.[13]

Le catalogue de Vidin renferme au total huit descriptions d'*al-Qur'ān.* Ce qui fait par aillers impression c'est que l'écriture de trois de ces copies, non identifiées parmi les manuscrits de la Bibliothèque Nationale, est déterminée comme *khaṭṭ-i ᶜajam* (écriture persane). Il est difficile de dire quel genre d'écriture, élaborée en Perse, avait en vue dans ces cas l'auteur du catalogue. On peut supposer qu'il s'agit de *nestaᶜlīq,* l'écriture dans laquelle à la fin du Xe/XVIe siècle il y avait déjà des tentatives de copier le Coran.[14]

Les commentaires d'*al-Qur'ān* constituaient une partie essentielle dans les bibliothèques musulmanes en Bulgarie. *Tafsīr*

[12] Sur les manuscrits coraniques voir ᶜA. Darwīsh, *Fihris al-Makhṭūṭāṭ al-ᶜArabiyya l-Maḥfūẓa fī Dār al-Kutub al-Shaᶜbiyya Kīrīl wa-Mītūdī fī Ṣūfiya ᶜĀṣimat al-Jumhūriyya l-Shaᶜbiyya l-Bulghāriyya. Al-juz' al-awwal: al-Qur'ān wa-ᶜulūmuhu; al-ḥadīth wa-ᶜulūmuhu* (Damas, 1969); G. Petkova-Bojanova, *Opis na arabskite rŭkopisi. Tom I. Koran* (Registre des manuscrits arabes. Vol. I. al-Qur'an) (Sofia, 1977).

[13] G. Petkova-Bojanova, no. 1.

[14] A. Schimmel, *Islamic Calligraphy* (Leiden, 1970), p. 9.

al-Qur'ān d'Abū l-Layth Naṣr b. Muḥammad al-Samarqandī (m. en 373/983) est l'ouvrage le plus ancien sur ce sujet.[15] Parmi les auteurs du Ve/XIe siècle est Aḥmad b. Muḥammad al-Thaᶜālibī (m. en 427/1035); une copie de son *al-Kashf wa-l-Bayān fī Tafsīr al-Qur'ān* se trouvait dans la Bibliothèque de Samokov. Le siècle suivant est représenté par *Maᶜālim al-Tanzīl* d'Abū Muḥammad al-Ḥusayn b. al-Farrā' al-Baghawī (m. en 510/1116 ou 516/1122) et par *al-Kashshāf ᶜan-Ḥaqā'iq al-Tanzīl* de Maḥmūd b. ᶜUmar al-Zamakhsharī (m. en 538/1144). La Bibliothèque de Samokov possédait aussi deux *ḥāshiya* sur *al-Kashshāf. Anwār al-Tanzīl wa-Asrār al-Ta'wīl* de Nāṣir al-Dīn ᶜAbd Allāh b. ᶜUmar al-Bayḍāwī (m. en 685/1286), largement connu et répandu dans le monde arabe, jouissait de la même autorité en Bulgarie. En 1252/1837, la Bibliothèque de Vidin possédait neuf volumes de cet ouvrage. Elle pouvait aussi offrir aux habitants de la ville aussi un *talkhīṣ*, 12 *ḥāshiya* et trois *taᶜlīq*, au total 22 volumes, faits sur *Tafsīr al-Qāḍī l-Bayḍāwī.*

Les ouvrages juridiques occupaient une place essentielle dans les trois bibliothèques. À Vidin, par exemple, leur nombre était de 518 volumes de manuscrits, c.-à-d. 21,67 % du fonds de la bibliothèque. D'après le niveau du catalogage de la collection de Shumen, on a raison de dire que ce genre de littérature y était le mieux représenté. Dans les catalogues mentionnés les titres juridiques étaient divisés en trois rubriques: *uṣūl al-fiqh* (principes essentiels du droit musulman), *fiqh* (droit musulman) et *farā'iḍ* (droit successoral).

L'ouvrage le plus ancien, répandu en Bulgarie, était *al-Mukhtaṣar*, créé par Abū l-Ḥusayn Aḥmad al-Qudūrī l-Baghdādī (m. en 428/1037). *Al-Hidāya fī Sharḥ Bidāyat al-Mubtadi'* d'ᶜAlī b. Abī

[15] ᶜA. Darwīsh, pp. 66-70.

Bakr al-Marghīnānī (m. en 593/1197) était parmi les titres, créés au cours du siècle suivant et bien connus aux lecteurs musulmans de la région. La Bibliothèque de Vidin possédait huit manuscrits de cet ouvrage, neuf commentaires (*sharḥ*) sur lui et encore trois *ḥāshiya*. Maḥmūd b. Ṣadr al-Sharīᶜa, un auteur du VIIe/XIIIe siècle, était populaire en Bulgarie par son ouvrage *Wiqāyat al-Riwāya fī Masā'il al-Hidāya*. Les bibliothèques possédaient aussi sa variante abrégée - *al-Niqāya Mukhtaṣar al-Wiqāya* d'ᶜUbayd Allāh b. Masᶜūd Ṣadr al-Sharīᶜa (m. en 747/1346). Parmi ses commentaires, Ṣadr al-Sharīᶜa était le plus répandu. À Vidin il y avait aussi deux traductions en langue turque ottomane.

Quatre copies de l'ouvrage fondamental dans le domaine d'*uṣūl al-fiqh* - *Manār al-Anwar* d'ᶜAbd Allāh b. Aḥmad Ḥāfiẓ al-Dīn al-Nasafī (m. en 710/1310), étaient à la disposition des habitants de Vidin. Dans la bibliothèque il y avait aussi sept *sharḥ* et deux *ḥāshiya* de ces commentaires. *Kanz al-Daqā'iq fī l-Furūᶜ*, un autre ouvrage juridique d'al-Nasafī, et ses commentaires remplissaient les rayons des bibliothèques en Bulgarie.

Parmi les titres du IXe/XVe siècle et bien connus en Bulgarie étaient *Ghurar al-Aḥkām* de Muḥammad b. Farāmurz Munlā Khusraw (m. en 885/1480) et son commentaire d'auteur - *Durar al-Ḥikām fī Sharḥ Ghurar al-Aḥkām*.

Le catalogue de la Bibliothèque de Vidin présente quatre manuscrits des *fatwā* du célèbre Qāḍīkhān (m. en 592/1196) et plusieurs copies de l'ouvrage connu dans le domaine du droit successoral - *al-Farā'iḍ al-Sirājiyya* de Sirāj al-Dīn Muḥammad b. Muḥammad al-Sajāwandī (m. à la fin du VIe/XIIe s.).

Comme il est notoire, les grammaires occupaient une place importante dans les bibliothèques publiques et privées; elles étaient copiées soigneusement et recherchées par les lecteurs. Les titres sur ce sujet constituaient 11% de toute la collection de la Bibliothèque de Vidin en 1252/1837. C'étaient surtout des copies des ouvrages créés aux VIIe-IXe/XIIIe-XVe siècles sous la forme de brefs cours sur la grammaire arabe, ses commentaires et des livres remaniés pour les besoins scolaires. Parmi eux les manuels laconiques d'Ibn Ḥājib (m. en 646/1249) étaient très répandus. *Al-Shāfiyya fī l-Taṣrīf* était bien connu à Samokov et à Vidin.[16] La Bibliothèque de Vidin possédait aussi dix commentaires, dont l'un en langue turque. Les bibliothèques renfermaient aussi des exemplaires de l'autre ouvrage d'Ibn al-Ḥājib - *al-Kāfiyya* et de ses commentaires, traitant des questions de la syntaxe. Par exemple, à Vidin leur nombre était de 44.

Un autre ouvrage tres répandu en Bulgarie était *al-Taṣrīf lil-ᶜIzzī* d'ᶜIzz al-Dīn Abū l-Maᶜālī l-Zanjānī qui a écrit en 655/1257. Les bibliothèques possédaient aussi ses commentaires et ses supercommentaires. Il y a lieu de citer aussi *Marāḥ al-Arwāḥ*, écrit par Ibn Masᶜūd (début du VIIIe/XIVe s.). La Bibliothèque de Vidin disposait aussi de 15 volumes de *sharḥ* sur *Marāḥ al-arwāḥ*.

L'ouvrage *al-Maqṣūd fī l-Taṣrīf*, attribué à Abū Ḥanīfa l-Nuᶜmān b. Thābit (m. en 150/767) était connu sous la forme de quelques *sharḥ*.

Parmi les auteurs du VIIe/XIIIe siècle populaires en Bulgarie et qui ont écrit dans le domaine de la syntaxe, était Nāṣir b. ᶜAbd al-Sayyid al-Muṭarrizī (m. en 610/1213). Les bibliothèques possédaient beaucoup de commentaires sur son ouvrage *al-Miṣbāḥ fī l-Naḥw* (à Vidin, par exemple, 40 volumes de différents titres), parmi lesquels le commentaire le plus répandu était *Kitāb Ḍaw' ᶜalā*

[16] Sur la collection des manuscrits grammaticaux voir ᶜA. Darwīsh, *Fihris al Makhṭūṭāt al-ᶜArabiyya l-Maḥfūẓa fī l-Maktaba l-Shaᶜbiyya bi Ṣūfiya fī Bulghāriyā. Al-juz' al-thānī: ᶜulūm al-lugha wa-l-waḍᶜ; al-ᶜulūm al-ṣarfiyya; al-ᶜulūm al-naḥwiyya; al-ᶜulūm al-balāghiyya; ᶜilm al-ᶜarūḍ wa-l-qawāfī; al-funūn al-adabiyya* (Damas, 1974).

l-Misbāḥ de Muḥammad b. Muḥammad al-Isfarā'inī (m. en 684/1285).

Le secteur historique occupait une place plus modeste dans les collections en Bulgarie. Quand même on peut citer des ouvrages qui reflètent les genres principaux de cette littérature. L'histoire générale est présentée par *al-Muntaẓam wa-Multaqat al-Muntaẓam fī Akhbār al-Mulūk wa-l-Umam* d'Abū l-Faraj ibn al-Jawzī (m. en 597/1200), conservé autrefois à Vidin.[17] Une idée sur l'histoire des dynasties nous donnent *Kitāb al-Yamīnī* de Muḥammad b. ᶜAbd al-Jabbār al-ᶜUtbī (m. en 427/1036 ou en 432/1040), la source la plus importante sur l'histoire des ghaznévides, conservée aussi à Vidin; *al-Jawhar al-Thamīn fī Siyar al-Khulafā' wa-l-Salāṭīn* de Ṣārim al-Dīn b. Aydamur al-ᶜAlā'ī ibn Duqmāq (m. en 809/1407), conservée autrefois à Samokov, et *Ta'rīkh al-Khulafā'* l'ouvrage historique, le plus connu, de Jalāl al-Dīn al-Suyūṭī (m. en 911/1505). Deux ouvrages d'Ibrāhīm al-Fazārī (m. en 729/1329) *Bāᶜith al-Nufūs ilā Ziyārat al-Quds al-Maḥrūs* et *Mukhtaṣar Kitāb Faḍā'il al-Sha'm wa-Dimashq*, concernent l'histoire des pays et des villes. A cet égard, on peut citer aussi *Muthīr al-Gharām wa-Khulāṣat al-Kalām fī Faḍl Ziyārat Sayyidunā l-Khalīl, ᶜalayhi l-salām* d'Isḥāq b. Ibrāhīm al-Tadmurī l-Khalīlī (m. en 833/1429), conservé à Samokov; la description historique et topographique du Caire et des autres localités en Egypte - *al-Mawāᶜiẓ wa-l-Iᶜtibār fī Dhikr al-Khiṭaṭ wa-l-Āthār*, créé par Taqī l-Dīn al-Maqrīzī (m. en 845/1442); l'histoire d'al-Madīna *Khulāṣat al-Wafā' bi-Akhbār Dār al-Muṣṭafā* de Nūr al-Dīn al-Samhūdī (m. en 911/1506) et d'autres.

A part ces titres bien connus, on peut mentionner aussi des ouvrages qui sont plus rares dans les bibliothèques des autres pays.

[17] Une partie des manuscrits historiques et géographiques a été decrite dans un autre catalogue. Voir Y. ᶜIzz-al-Dīn, *Makhṭūṭāt ᶜArabiyya fī Maktabat Ṣūfiya l-Waṭaniyya l-Bulghāriyya Kīril wa-Mītūdī* (Baghdad, 1968).

Kitāb al-Wizārāt - un manuscrit du VIIIe/XIVe siècle (BNB, OR 1692) - conservé à l'époque à Vidin,[18] donne beaucoup de détails sur l'histoire socio-économique du Proche Orient du Ve/XIe siècle.

La géographie est une rubrique plus rare dans les anciens catalogues des bibliothèques.[19] Quand même elle figure dans la liste des livres accompagnant le *waqfnamah* de Şerif Halil Paşa. Évidemment, on y a pris en considération l'ouvrage connu de Abū b. ᶜAbdallāh Muḥammad al-Sharīf al-Idrīsī (m. en 561/1165) *Nuzhat al-Mushtāq fī Ikhtirāq al-Āfāq.* Le manuscrit (BNB, OR 3168), achevé le 24 *shawwāl* 963/31 août 1556 par Muḥammad b. ᶜAlī l-Ajhurī l-Shāfiᶜī, est une des quatre copies complètes, conservées jusqu'à nos jours dans le monde.[20] Il possède toutes les 70 cartes, jointes au texte des sections, et aussi la carte ronde du monde, qui figure au début du livre. Une des particularités de cette copie c'est qu'une partie en est collationnée avec l'autographe.

Un problème important concernant la diffusion de la littérature musulmane en Bulgarie, se rapporte au lieu de provenance des copies. La majorité en sont créées hors des Balkans - dans le monde arabe, en Iran ou bien en Anatolie. Le manuscrit le plus ancien de la collection de la Bibliothèque Nationale (OR 801): une copie d'*al-Jāmiᶜ al-Ṣaḥīḥ* de Muḥammad b. Ismāᶜīl al-Bukhārī (m. en 256/870),

[18] Y. ᶜIzz-al-Dīn, pp. 69-70.

[19] I. E. Erünsal, pp. 231, 234.

[20] B. Nedkov, *Bulgariiâ i sŭsednite i zemi prez XII vek spored Geografiîata na al-Idrisi* (La Bulgarie et les terres voisines d'après la Géographie d'al-Idrisi) (Sofia, 1960); S. Kenderova et B. Beševliev, *Balkanskiîat poluostrov izobrazen v kartite na al-Idrisi. Paleografsko i istoriko-geografsko izsledvane.* Chast I (La Péninsule Balkanique représentée sur les cartes d'al-Idrisi. Etude paléographique et historique-géographique. Part I) (Sofia, 1990).

datée du 4 *dhū l-ḥijja* 407/4 mai 1017, provient peut être de la Péninsule Arabe.[21] Elle appartenait à la Bibliothèque de Samokov.

Les copies réalisées en Afrique du Nord, ou bien en Espagne, étaient assez rares dans les collections en Bulgarie. Un manuscrit qui mérite l'attention, c'est *al- Jāmi*ᶜ *al-Ṣaḥīḥ* de Muḥammad b. ᶜĪsā l-Tirmidhī (m. en 279/892), achevé le 13 *dhū l-qa*ᶜ*da* 587/2 decembre 1191 par Marwān b. Muḥammad b. ᶜAtīq al-Maᶜāfirī b. Yaḥyā l-Qurashī *thumma* l-Qurṭubī en ecriture *maghribī* (BNB, OR 1638).[22]

Parmi les manuscrits arabes, conservés jusqu'à nos jours, on trouve des exemplaires dont l'histoire est liée à l'activité des copistes locaux. La collection de la Bibliothèque Nationale posséde un Coran (OR 1335), achevé à Sofia vers la fin du Xe/XVIe siècle; deux autres, copiés au cours du XIIe/XVIIIe siècle - l'un à Silistra (OR 2938) (Nord-Est de Sofia) en 1153/1740 et l'autre à Pleven (OR 2531) (Nord-Est de Sofia) en 1197/1786, et encore un à Vidin (OR 962), daté de 1237/1821.[23] Une autre copie (OR 1425), achevée en 1278/1861 par Muṣṭafā l-Wahbī, un des écoliers (*min al-talāmīdh*) de Muḥammad Afandī b. al-Ḥājj Darwīsh Afandī de la ville de Pazardzhik (Sud-Est de Sofia), provient évidemment du même lieu.[24]

Al-Sayyid al-Ḥājj *Ḥāfiẓ al-Qur'ān* Muṣṭafā al-Fahmī Pirāwadī (la ville de Provadiîa), un des écoliers (*min talāmīdh*) de Muḥammad Nūrī Shumnawī (c.-à-d. de la ville de Shumen) complète la liste des copistes locaux, spécialisés dans la création de

[21] S. Kenderova, *Catalogue of Arabic Manuscripts in SS Cyril and Methodius National Library Sofia Bulgaria. Hadith Sciences*, éd., M. I. Waley (London, 1995), no. 29.

[22] idem, no. 64.

[23] G. Petkova-Bojanova, nos. 31, 63, 70 et 78.

[24] idem, no. 86.

manuscrits d'*al-Qur'ān*. On a découvert déjà quatre exemplaires du livre sacré, faits par sa main entre 1290/1874 et 1294/1877, et conservés dans la Bibliothèque de Shumen (Sh R 117, 600-602).

Actuellement, la collection de manuscrits des *ḥadīth* de la Bibliothèque Nationale compte 243 ouvrages (124 titres),[25] dont 17 volumes créés dans différentes villes bulgares - Samokov, Sofia, Kiustendil, Pazardzhik et Russe, surtout dans la première moitié du XIIe/XVIIIe siècle. Parmi les copistes, huit portent le nom de provenance (*nisba*) Ṣamāquwī, c.-à.-d. originaires de Samokov. Cette petite ville, située à 50 km au Sud-Ouest de Sofia, jouait évidemment le rôle d'un centre particulier de la littérature musulmane. Le copiste le plus productif y était Aḥmad b. Abī Bakr b. Muḥammad b. Riḍwān al-Kashfī l-Ṣamāquwī. Selon l'information puisée au catalogue mentionné de la Bibliothèque de Samokov, 71 manuscrits au total sont son œuvre. Ils traitent différents sujets droit musulman - 13, *taṣawwuf* - 10, *majmūʿāt* - neuf, *tafsīr* - cinq, *ʿilm al-kalām* - cinq et d'autres. C'est un nombre considérable qui témoigne de la grande activité d'al-Kashfī comme copiste. Il représente 12,26% de tous les manuscrits qui se trouvaient en ce moment dans la bibliothèque. Grace à nos recherches sur les copies des *ḥadīth* son écriture est déjà identifiée.[26]

Al-Kashfī n'était pas seulement un copiste. Dans le domaine des *ḥadīth*, par exemple, il est probablement l'auteur de six ouvrages, dont l'un *al-Majmūʿa l-Laṭīfa wa-l-Jarīda l-Munīfa* (BNB, MS OR 666).[27] C'est une collection qui contient des extraits de titres bien connus et concernant des sujets differents - *tafsīr*, *ḥadīth*, *fiqh*, géographie etc. Elle a été achevée le 1er *rajab* 1127/3 juillet

[25] S. Kenderova, *Catalogue*, p. x.
[26] idem, no. 202; voir aussi l'application.
[27] idem, no. 178.

1715 et par la suite al-Kashfī a composé encore deux collections. C'est un, évidemment, grand erudit qui connaissait aussi la langue arabe (son nom ne figure pas dans le catalogue de la bibliothèque parmi les titres en persan). On peut supposer qu'il avait enrichi ses connaissances dans le monde arabe. Cette information nous est procurée par une note (MS OR 1618, fols. 175v-176r) du célèbre Ibn al-Nābulusī l-Shā'mī l-Dimashqī (m. en 1143/1731). Elle nous fait savoir qu'au mois de *ramaḍān* 1120/novembre-decembre 1708, al-Kashfī a visité al-Nābulusī dans sa maison à Damas ou ils ont discuté sur l'importance des *ḥadīth*.[28]

Un autre copiste originaire de Samokov est Ḥasan Afandī. Selon le catalogue mentionné, il a realisé 17 copies sur différents thèmes.

Dans la présente étude, on a abordé quelques sujets du développement de la littérature arabe jusqu'à la fin du IXe/XVe siècle. On a essayé de montrer le degré de diffusion du livre manuscrit arabe dans les collections des trois grandes bibliothèques de *waqf* en Bulgarie. Les recherches à venir fourniraient certains détails sur le fonds des autres bibliothèques qui fonctionnaient à Sofia, à Kîustendil, à Veliko Tŭrnovo et dans autres villes.

Notre exposé se fonde sur la collection manuscrite de la Bibliothèque Nationale de Bulgarie, formée avant tout par l'héritage des anciennes bibliothèques de *waqf*. On s'est référé aussi aux informations des deux catalogues originaux et inédits: l'un de la Bibliothèque de Samokov et l'autre de la Bibliothèque du célèbre Osman Pazvantoğlu de Vidin. Une attention particulière a été accordée à la collection manuscrite de la Bibliothèque de Şerif Halil Paşa à Shumen qui est en train d'être cataloguée. Tout cela nous permet de faire les conclusions suivantes.

[28] idem, no. 140.

Les bibliothèques de *waqf* qui fonctionnaient en Bulgarie au cours du XIIIe/XIXe siècle étaient parmi les plus riches dépôts de livres musulmans dans les Balkans. Elles étaient le résultat de l'activité de bienfaisance de personnalités du pays qui jouaient aussi un rôle important dans la vie politique, administrative, économique et culturelle non seulement dans leurs villes natales mais aussi dans le cadre de l'Empire Ottoman.

La plupart du fonds de ces bibliothèques - à peu près 80-85% - est formée de manuscrits et d'anciens livres imprimés en arabe. Il est évident que ce sont des ouvrages fondamentaux, créés pendant la période classique de l'histoire de la culture arabe, qui jouissaient d'un grand prestige dans le monde musulman. En même temps y étaient conservés des livres, considérés comme rares pour les fonds des bibliothèques contemporaines.

Une partie des copies, répandues à l'époque en Bulgarie, étaient réalisées dans le monde arabe, en Iran ou bien en Turquie; une autre, moins nombreuse, dans certaines villes bulgares et par des copistes locaux qui connaissaient évidemment la langue arabe. De ces villes, Samokov s'est formée comme un centre du savoir musulman. Parmi les auteurs et les copistes musulmans les plus productifs est al-Kashfī Afandī al-Ṣamāquwī, qui a vecu à la fin du XIe/XVIIe - le premier quart du XIIe/XVIIIe siècle.

Le thème de la propagation de la littérature musulmane dans les Balkans concerne aussi l'utilisation des livres dans ces bibliothèques et le groupe social des emprunteurs. Une autre question ce sont les possésseurs et les donateurs de livres[29] et leur

[29] Voir S. Kenderova, "A propos les donateurs des livres à la Bibliothèque d'Osman Pazvantoğlu", dans *Sociétés et cultures musulmanes d'hier et d'aujhourd'hui. Actes de la IXe réunion des chercheurs sur le monde arabe et musulman*, éd. M. Anastassiadou (Paris, 1996), pp. 182-185.

place dans les societés urbaines balkaniques. Tous ces problèmes sont l'objet de recherches futures.

- General Index -